DISCOVERY PROGRAMME REPORTS

DISCOVERY PROGRAMME REPORTS: 6

Royal Irish Academy/
Discovery Programme
Dublin 2002

THE DISCOVERY
PROGRAMME

AR THÓIR NA SEAN

First published in 2002 for the Discovery Programme
by the Royal Irish Academy,
19 Dawson Street, Dublin 2.
Copyright © Royal Irish Academy 2002.

All rights reserved. No part of this book may be reprinted or reproduced or utilised in any electronic, mechanical or other means, now known or hereafter invented, including photocopying and recording, or otherwise without either the prior written consent of the publishers or a licence permitting restricted copying in Ireland issued by the Irish Copyright Licensing Agency Ltd, The Writers' Centre,
19 Parnell Square, Dublin 1.

ISBN 1 874045 95 X

British Library Cataloguing-in-Publication Data.
A catalogue record for this book is available from the British Library.

Typeset in Ireland by Wordwell Ltd
Origination by Wordwell Ltd

Printed by W & G Baird

Cover: View of Ráith na Ríg, Tara, Co. Meath during excavation (C. Brogan, *Dúchas*).

The Discovery Programme gratefully acknowledges the financial support of the Heritage Council

CONTENTS

Preface		vii
Réamhrá		ix
Acknowledgements		xi
List of figures		xii
List of plates		xiv

1. GEOMAGNETIC SURVEY ON THE HILL OF TARA, CO. MEATH, 1998–9	Joe Fenwick and Conor Newman	1
2. EXCAVATIONS AT RÁITH NA RÍG, TARA, CO. MEATH, 1997	Helen Roche	19
Appendix 1: High-temperature workshop residues from Tara: iron, bronze and glass	Peter Crew and Thilo Rehren	83
Appendix 2: The animal bones from Tara	Finbar McCormick	103
Appendix 3: Observations on the occurrence of dog and horse bones at Tara	Edel Bhreathnach	117
Appendix 4: Human remains from Tara, Co. Meath	Barra Ó Donnabháin	123
Appendix 5: Plant remains from Tara, Co. Meath	Brenda Collins	126
Appendix 6: Micromorphological and bulk sample analyses of site contexts, Ráith na Ríg	Clare Ellis	127

PREFACE

At the outset of its work the Discovery Programme decided that, wherever possible, it would adopt an interdisciplinary approach to its research projects, applying the skills of a wide range of specialists. Since the inception of this work in 1992 the Discovery Programme has developed a number of research projects relating to the Hill of Tara. Initially two projects were established: the Tara Literary and Historical Project, to examine the corpus of documentary evidence relating to the site, and the Tara Survey, which set out to produce a detailed archaeological survey of the monuments on the hilltop.

The principal result of the Literary and Historical Project to date has been the publication in 1995 of Dr Edel Bhreathnach's *Tara: a select bibliography*, which consisted of an annotated and select listing of the published material relating to Tara, divided between primary and secondary sources and subdivided into a series of categories. This bibliography attempted to address the interests of various types of readers, be they linguistic, literary, historical or archaeological specialists, expert or amateur.

In 1997 Conor Newman's *Tara: an archaeological survey* was published. This consisted of a report on the detailed topographical, aerial, geophysical, geochemical and paper survey of the various features at Tara, which was the most intensive non-invasive survey ever carried out on an archaeological site in Ireland. The publication of this volume marked an enormously important step in our understanding of the evolution of the complex of monuments known collectively as 'Tara'.

Both before and since these two seminal monographs, Discovery Programme staff have also published a range of other papers relating to Tara (see detailed references in the articles in this volume), and in 1995 an illustrated guide-booklet to the site, jointly written by Edel Bhreathnach and Conor Newman, was published by the Stationery Office. Two other major monographs, aspects of the Literary and Historical Project, are close to completion and publication: *Tara: 400–800* by Edel Bhreathnach and *Tara and the Ark of the Covenant* by Mairéad Carew. The Programme plans also to develop an exhibition and educational pack for schools based on its explorations of Tara.

In 1997, the same year in which Conor Newman's survey was published, the Discovery Programme began a new phase of its research at Tara with archaeological excavations at Ráith na Ríg under the direction of Helen Roche. These excavations proved to be of great significance and the final report is published below.

In April 1998, in association with a Discovery Programme one-day public conference on the subject of Tara held at Dublin Castle, a separate workshop was organised for archaeologists and historians with a particular research interest in the site. This workshop set out to explore possible new research directions in relation to Tara for the Discovery Programme to become involved with. There was unanimous agreement that the Discovery Programme should continue its work on Tara, although there were varying views about what that work might entail. Such an important site, with a long history, steeped in legend and regarded as an icon of sorts, requires the most careful and responsible approach; there is no need for haste. Tara, however, does offer scope for important developments in our understanding of the past.

There was general approval at the 1998 workshop for additional geophysical survey of the hilltop, particularly in the light of the successful and pioneering survey published in 1997. With this in mind, in late 1998 the Discovery Programme commissioned the Centre for Archaeological Survey at the National University of Ireland, Galway, to undertake a further phase of geophysical surveying at Tara. The short seasons of work carried out there, in November 1998 and May 1999, proved to be spectacularly successful, and a full report of the results of that work is published below.

Following on from the workshop mentioned

above, early in 1999 the Directorate of the Discovery Programme established a Tara Strategy Committee with a view to formulating a document that would outline a plan for further work at Tara. That document was completed in 2000 and is now being reviewed by the newly appointed Directorate that came into being in January 2001.

As has been demonstrated above, throughout its own short existence the Discovery Programme has had a continuing interest in investigating all that relates to the history and prehistory of 'Tara of the Kings'. The publication of this special Tara issue of *Discovery Programme Reports* is another step in the development of that research programme.

Michael Ryan
Chairman

Discovery Programme Directorate
Prof. Michael Ryan (Chairman)
Prof. Terence Barry
Ms Rose Cleary
Prof. John Coles
Ms Margaret Gowen
Mr Raghnall Ó Floinn
Prof. Barry Raftery
Mr Michael Starrett
Prof. John Waddell

Directorate 1996–2001
Prof. George Eogan (Chairman)
Prof. Terence Barry
Mr John Bradley
Prof. Séamas Caulfield
Prof. Gabriel Cooney
Ms Claire Foley
Mr Noel Lynch
Dr William O'Brien
Mr Paul Walsh

RÉAMHRÁ

Agus iad ag cur tús lena gcuid oibre bheartaigh an Discovery Programme go nglacfadh siad cur chuige idirdhisciplíneach, nuair ab fhéidir, lena dtionscadail taighde, ag feidhmiú scileanna réimse leathan speisialtóirí. Ó cuireadh tús leis an obair seo i 1992 d'fhorbair an Discovery Programme roinnt tionscadal taighde a bhaineann le Teamhair. Bunaíodh dhá thionscadal ar dtús: Tionscadal Litríochta agus Staire, chun iniúchadh a dhéanamh ar an bhfianaise cáipéisíochta a bhaineann leis an suíomh, agus Suirbhé Teamhrach a rinne iarracht mionsuirbhé seandálaíochta a dhéanamh ar na séadchomharthaí ar bharr an chnoic.

Ba é príomhthoradh an Tionscadail Litríochta agus Staire go dtí seo foilsiú leabhar an Dr Edel Bhreathnach *Tara: a select bibliography* i 1995, leabhar ina raibh liostáil roghnach le nótaí den ábhar foilsithe a bhaineann le Teamhair, roinnte idir príomhfhoinsí agus foinsí tánaisteacha agus foroinnte i sraith catagóirí. Rinne an leabharliosta sin iarracht aghaidh a thabhairt ar spéiseanna chineálacha éagsúla léitheoirí, bídis ina léitheoirí teangeolaíochta, litríochta, staire nó seandálaíochta, saineolaithe nó amaitéaraigh.

I 1997 foilsíodh *Tara: an archaeological survey* le Conor Newman. Is é atá ann ná tuairisc ar an mionsuirbhé topagrafach, aeir, geofisiciúil, geoceimiceach agus páipéir de na gnéithe éagsúla i dTeamhair, agus bhí sé ar an suirbhé ba dhéine a rinneadh agus ba lú a chuir isteach ar shuíomh seandálaíochta in Éirinn. Bhí foilsiú an imleabhair sin mar chéim fhíorthábhachtach inár dtuiscint ar éabhlóid na séadchomharthaí casta ar a dtugtar Teamhair.

Roimh an dá mhonagraf thábhachtacha agus úrnua sin agus ina ndiaidh, d'fhoilsigh foireann an Discovery Programme réimse páipéar eile a bhain le Teamhair (féach miontagairtí sna hailt san imleabhar seo), agus i 1995 d'fhoilsigh Oifig an tSoláthair treoirleabhar le léaráidí faoin suíomh scríofa ag Edel Bhreathnach agus Conor Newman. Tá dhá mhonagraf mhóra eile, gnéithe den Tionscadal Litríochta agus Staire, nach mór tugtha chun críche agus foilseofar sa bhliain amach romhainn iad: *Tara: 400–800* le Edel Bhreathnach agus *Tara and the Ark of the Covenant* le Mairéad Carew. Tá sé i gceist againn freisin taispeántas agus pacáiste eolais do scoileanna a ullmhú bunaithe ar an taiscéalaíocht ag Teamhair.

I 1997, an bhliain chéanna inar foilsíodh suirbhé Conor Newman, thosaigh an Discovery Programme ar chéim nua dá gcuid taighde ag Teamhair nuair a cuireadh tús le tochailtí seandálaíochta ag Ráth na Rí faoi stiúr Helen Roche. Bhain an-tábhacht leis na tochailtí sin agus tá an tuarascáil dheireanach foilsithe thíos.

I mí Aibreáin 1998, i gcomhar le comhdháil aonlae de chuid an Discovery Programme faoi Theamhair a tionóladh i gCaisleán Átha Cliath, eagraíodh ceardlann ar leithligh do sheandálaithe agus do staraithe a bhfuil spéis taighde ar leith acu sa suíomh. Rinne an cheardlann sin iarracht iniúchadh a dhéanamh ar threonna nua taighde a bhaineann le Teamhair ar féidir leis an Discovery Programme a bheith rannpháirteach iontu. Aontaíodh d'aonghuth ag an gceardlann go leanfadh an Discovery Programme ar aghaidh lena gcuid oibre ag Teamhair, cé go raibh tuairimí éagsúla ann faoi chineál na hoibre sin. Teastaíonn cur chuige cúramach foighneach maidir le láithreán a bhfuil a oiread sin tábhachtacha ag baint leis. Láithreán is ea é a bhfuil stair fhada ag gabháil leis, láithreán a dtráchtar air go mion minic sna finscéalta agus a mheasann daoine gurb íocón atá ann. Níl feidhm ar bith le deifir, ach tá deiseanna tábhachtacha ag baint le Teamhair a chabhróidh linn ár stair a thuiscint.

Aontaíodh go ginearálta, áfach, le suirbhé geofisiciúil ar bharr an chnoic, go háirithe i bhfianaise an tsuirbhé cheannródaíoch rathúil a foilsíodh i 1997. Agus an méid sin á ghlacadh san áireamh acu, rinne an Discovery Programme coimisiniú, déanach sa bhliain 1998, ar an Ionad do Shuirbhé Seandálaíochta in Ollscoil na hÉireann, Gaillimh chun tabhairt faoi chéim bhreise de shuirbhéireacht geofisiciúil ag Teamhair. D'éirigh go hiontach go deo leis na séasúir ghearra oibre a rinneadh ann, i mí Dheireadh

Fómhair 1998 agus i mí Bhealtaine 1999, agus tá tuairisc iomlán na hoibre sin foilsithe thíos.

Ag leanacht ar aghaidh ón gceardlann a luadh thuas, bhunaigh Stiúrthóireacht an Discovery Programme Coiste Straitéise Teamhrach go luath sa bhliain 1999 chun cáipéis a chur le chéile a dhéanadh imlíniú ar phlean d'obair bhreise ag Teamhair. Críochnaíodh an cháipéis sin sa bhliain 2000 agus tá sí á hathbhreithniú faoi láthair ag an Stiúrthóireacht nuacheaptha ar tháinig ann di le linn Eanáir 2001.

Mar a léiríodh thuas, le linn an achair ghearr arbh ann dóibh, bhí leas leanúnach ag an Discovery Programme in imscrúdú a dhéanamh ar gach a bhaineann le stair agus le réamhstair Teamhair na Rí. Is céim é foilsiú an eagráin speisialta Teamhrach seo de *Discovery Programme Reports* in éabhlóid an chláir thaighde sin.

Michael Ryan
Cathaoirleach

ACKNOWLEDGEMENTS

The Discovery Programme is extremely grateful for the continuing financial support of the Heritage Council. We would like to record our gratitude also for the support, assistance and co-operation of *Dúchas*, and various other sections of the Department of Arts, Heritage, Gaeltacht and the Islands. The advice of many archaeologists and other specialists is also much appreciated.

LIST OF FIGURES

Geomagnetic survey on the Hill of Tara, Co. Meath

1 Symbol plot of magnetic susceptibility. Volume-specific measurement of each sample point is represented by a circle whose diameter is directly proportional to the numeric value.
2 Grey-scale image of the 1998–9 fluxgate gradiometry survey, dominated by the remarkably clear signature of the ditched pit circle (31:33:71).
3 Interpretational line map of some of the most clearly defined archaeomagnetic anomalies.
4 Upper: Detail of the western sector of the ditched pit circle (31:33:71).
Lower: Three-dimensional representation of the gradiometry data values for the same area. Magnetic polarity has been inverted so that positive anomalies appear as troughs and negative anomalies as peaks.
5 Upper: Details of the three conjoined positive magnetic rings (31:33:72–4) lying to the west of Ráith na Senad.
Lower: Three-dimensional representation of the gradiometry data values for the same area with magnetic polarity reversed.
6 Fluxgate gradiometry data expressed as a three-dimensional model in perspective, looking from the south-west.

Excavations at Ráith na Ríg, Tara

1 Hill-shaded model of the Hill of Tara, viewed from the south (based on the Tara archaeological survey).
2 Cutting 23 (A–A), west-facing section through the bank and ditch of Ráith na Ríg and palisade trench, as recorded by Ó Ríordáin, 1952–3. (Archaeology Department, UCD)
3 Cutting 1 (B–B), west-facing section through the bank and ditch of Ráith na Ríg and palisade trench, as recorded in 1997.
4 Cutting 24 (G–G), 1955: east-facing section through the bank and ditch of Ráith na Ríg and palisade trench, as recorded by Seán P. Ó Ríordáin and Ruaidhrí de Valéra, 1955, 1956 and 1959 (U. Mattenberger, Archaeology Department, UCD).
5 Hill-shaded model showing area of 1997 excavation (based on the Tara archaeological survey).
6 Ground-plan of 1997 excavation.
7 Reference location for section drawings.
8 Cutting 1 (D–D): east-facing section through the bank of Ráith na Ríg.
9 Cutting 1: ground-plan of features associated with industrial activity beneath the bank of Ráith na Ríg.
10 Cutting 1. Top: section through metalworking hearth (F38) from north.
Bottom: section through metalworking hearth (F38) from south.
11 Cutting 1 (C–C): east-facing section through the bank and ditch of Ráith na Ríg and palisade trench.
12 Cutting 1 (E–E): west-facing section through the ditch of Ráith na Ríg and palisade trench.
13 Cutting 1 (F–F): east-facing section through the ditch of Ráith na Ríg (stepped amalgamation) and palisade trench.
14 Cutting 1: burial of child F105, 0.96m above the base of the ditch fill.
15 Cutting 1: animal bone scatter on surface of F12, 1.97m above the base of the ditch fill.
16 Cutting 2 (I–I): east-facing section through the bank and ditch of Ráith na Ríg and palisade trench.
17 Cutting 2 (H–H): west-facing section through the bank and ditch of Ráith na Ríg and palisade trench.
18 Cutting 2 (K–K): east-facing section through the ditch of Ráith na Ríg.
19 Cutting 2 (J–J): west-facing section through the ditch of Ráith na Ríg (stepped amalgamation).
20 Cutting 2: animal bone scatter on surface of F56a, 1.25m above the base of the ditch fill.
21 Palisade trench, ground-plan and long section (running east–west).

22 Sections (north–south) through palisade trench.
23 Cutting 1: ground-plan of features associated with later activity (Phase 4) beneath the bank of Ráith na Ríg.
24 Iron, bronze and ceramic artefacts from pre-bank layer, bank and ditch fill.
25 Socketed iron axehead from pre-bank industrial layer.
26 Iron, bronze, glass and ceramic objects from ditch fill, palisade trench and humus.
27 Neolithic artefacts from disturbed contexts.

Appendix 1: High-temperature workshop residues from Tara
1 Slag types, by weight range, by number.
2 Slag types, by weight range, by weight.
3 Vitrified lining with fine sandy fabric.
4 Vitrified lining with coarse stone-grogged fabric.
5 Low-density fluxed lining slags (FLS type).
6 Low-density fluxed lining slags (FLS type), small fractured pieces from the SS64 sample.
7 Smithing hearth slag cakes, upper surfaces.
8 Double smithing hearth cake: side view of fractured surface showing dense internal structure.
9 Double smithing hearth cake.
10 Smithing hearth cake with heavy corrosion products.
11 Crucible rim sherds, internal faces.
12 Section of crucible sherd from F34:05.
13 Thin section through crucible sherd from F34:05.
14 Thin section through crucible fragment from F34:09.
15 Reflected-light image of a high-tin phase in a crucible fragment from F34:09.
16 Reflected-light image of highly oxidised bronze prill on crucible fragment from F30:35.
17 Internal reflection image of the mixed oxide seam around the oxidised bronze prill from F30:35.
18 Mould sherds, larger examples showing traces of surface shaping.
19 Thin section through mould fragment from F34:03.
20 Outer face of fragment of red opaque bangle from F63:1.
21 Detail of inner face of red opaque bangle from F62:1 with the lead droplet.
22 Side view of fragment of purple bangle from F102:1.
23 Inside face of purple bangle from F102:1, showing iron oxide scale.
24 Detail of inner face of purple bangle from F102:1, showing iron oxide scale.
25 Fragment of transparent blue glass from F31:58.

Appendix 6: Micromorphological and bulk sample analyses of site contexts, Ráith na Ríg
1 Cutting 1. Bank of Ráith na Ríg, west-facing section.
2 Cutting 1. Bank of Ráith na Ríg, east-facing section.
3 Cutting 2. Bank of Ráith na Ríg, west-facing section.

LIST OF PLATES

Geomagnetic survey on the Hill of Tara, Co. Meath

1 Aerial photograph of Tara from the south-east. A combination of raking sunlight and frost reveals the ditched pit circle as an arcuate, low-relief depression to the west of Ráith na Senad (photo courtesy of Jacqueline O'Brien).

Excavations at Ráith na Ríg, Tara

1 Cutting 23. Ó Ríordáin's excavation across Ráith na Ríg, 1953 (Archaeology Department, UCD).
2 Cutting 24. Portion of palisade trench excavated by Ó Ríordáin, 1955 (Archaeology Department, UCD).
3 View of site during excavation, from north-east (C. Brogan, *Dúchas*).
4 Cutting 1 and Extension 1 from north, showing pre-bank, charcoal-rich industrial level (F31) and associated features. Cultivation trenches representing later activity (F79, F80) are in the foreground (H. Roche).
5 Cutting 1: Extension 1. East-facing section through bank of Ráith na Ríg and underlying industrial layer F31 (H. Roche).
6 Cutting 1: Extension 1. East-facing section through bank showing its northern extent and the underlying surviving limits of the charcoal-rich layer F31 (H. Roche).
7 Cutting 1: Extension 1. View of pre-bank industrial level from south-east, showing metalworking hearth F38 and associated features (H. Roche).
8 Cutting 1: Extension 1. Metalworking hearth (F38) beneath bank of Ráith na Ríg from north, showing accumulated burnt debris within hearth (H. Roche).
9 Cutting 1: Extension 1. Metalworking hearth (F38) beneath bank of Ráith na Ríg from east (H. Roche).
10 Cutting 1 (B–B), west-facing section through ditch of Ráith na Ríg (C. Brogan, *Dúchas*).
11 Cutting 1: Extension 1. Burial of child (F105) within ditch of Ráith na Ríg (H. Roche).
12 Cutting 1: Extension 1. Animal bone scatter on surface of Iron Age stony fill (F12) within ditch of Ráith na Ríg (H. Roche).
13 Cutting 2 (K–K), east-facing section through ditch of Ráith na Ríg (C. Brogan, *Dúchas*).
14 Cutting 2: Extension 3. Animal bone scatter on surface of Iron Age stony fill (F56a) within ditch of Ráith na Ríg (H. Roche).
15 View of excavated portion of palisade trench, from west (C. Brogan, *Dúchas*).
16 View of excavated portion of palisade trench, from east (C. Brogan, *Dúchas*).
17 Cutting 2. View of palisade trench from east, showing secondary cut at western limit of excavation and the shallow trench (F67) immediately to the north (H. Roche).
18 Cutting 1. West-facing profile of palisade trench, as exposed by Ó Ríordáin.
19 Finely executed bronze nail from pre-bank industrial layer 31:5 (D. Jennings, University College Dublin).
20 Socketed iron axehead from pre-bank industrial layer 31:20 (D. Jennings, University College Dublin).
21 Portion of a bronze spearbutt from upper level of Cutting 1 ditch fill 2:14 (D. Jennings, University College Dublin).
22 Portion of violet-coloured glass bangle from lower level of Cutting 1 ditch fill 102:1 (D. Jennings, University College Dublin).
23 Portion of opaque red glass bangle from fill of palisade trench 62:1 (D. Jennings, University College Dublin).
24 Portion of a bronze fibula from Cutting 2 ditch fill 55:1 (D. Jennings, University College Dublin).
25 Portion of a clay mould from upper fill of metalworking hearth 34:13 (D. Jennings, University College Dublin).

Appendix 2: The animal bones from Tara
1 Horse radius 9 (F108). Chop-marks on medial face of proximal metaphysis.
2 Horse radius showing roast-marks on the shaft.
3 Dog pelvis (F20). Cut-marks on medial aspect of acetabulum below pubis.

Appendix 6: Micromorphological and bulk sample analyses of site contexts, Ráith na Ríg
1 Sample 7, context 206, microlaminated dusty clay coatings. Magnification x 32.
2 Sample 7, context 206, clay coatings within a degraded chert fragment. Magnification x 32.
3 Sample 3, context F33, organic layer. Magnification x 25.
4 Sample 12, context F31, charcoal-rich veriform. Magnification x 12.5.
5 Sample 11, context F31, burnt bone and charcoal fragments. Magnification x 25.
6 Sample 2, context F30, *in situ* rootlet. Magnification x 16.
7 Sample 11, context F30, charcoal- and silt-rich veriform. Magnification x 16.
8 Sample 11, context F33, burnt matrix and organic material. Magnification x 32.
9 Sample 12, context F31, charcoal and general 'midden' material. Magnification x 32.
10 Sample 2, context F33, burnt bone. Magnification x 12.5.
11 Sample 10, context F30, buried organic layer. Magnification x 16.

1. GEOMAGNETIC SURVEY ON THE HILL OF TARA, CO. MEATH, 1998–9

Joe Fenwick and Conor Newman

Pl. 1—Aerial photograph of Tara from the south-east. A combination of raking sunlight and frost reveals the ditched pit circle as an arcuate, low-relief depression to the west of Ráith na Senad (photo courtesy of Jacqueline O'Brien).

Introduction

Further geomagnetic survey of the Hill of Tara was carried out by the Centre for Archaeological Survey, NUI, Galway, in collaboration with the Discovery Programme. The surveys were implemented in two stages in November 1998 and May 1999 and comprised reconnaissance magnetic susceptibility survey and high-resolution magnetic gradiometry. The survey utilised a 'common archaeological grid system' of 10m squares (panels) aligned to and synchronised with 10m multiples of the National Grid. Both techniques were initially applied over a rectangular panel (200m north–south by 100m east–west) immediately to the west and north-west of Ráith na Senad, where, along with a host of interesting features, the western half of a large and obviously important new oval enclosure was revealed. Passing a few metres to the south of the Tech Midchúarta and curving around to the south of Duma na nGiall, it was instantly apparent that this monument was large enough to enclose the whole churchyard at Tara. The gradiometry survey was therefore further extended to the south and east in order to fully map it and some of the surrounding ground, including a significant portion of the northern half of Ráith na

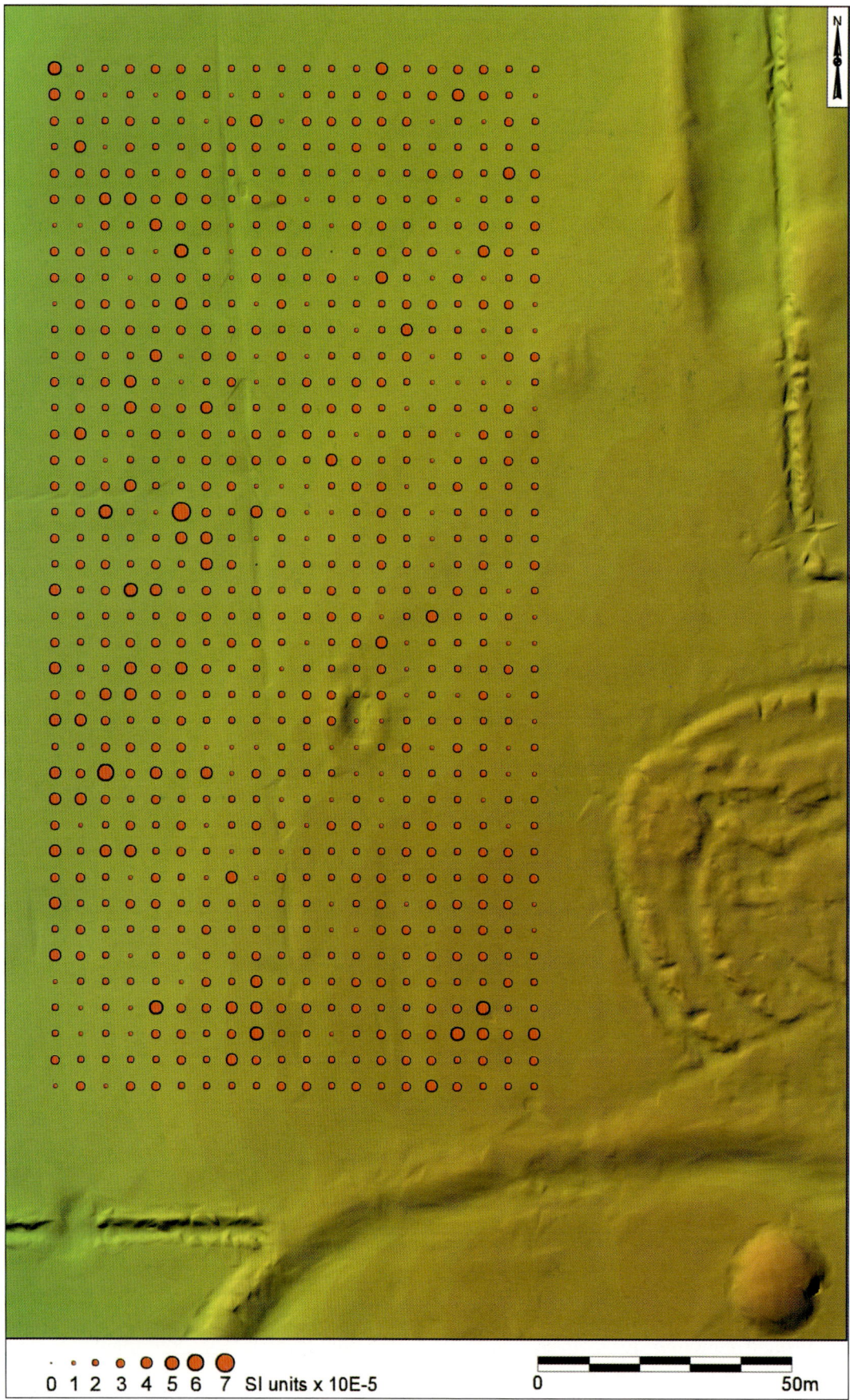

Fig. 1—Symbol plot of magnetic susceptibility. Volume-specific measurement of each sample point is represented by a circle whose diameter is directly proportional to the numeric value.

Ríg. Most of the area covered had not previously been subjected to geophysical survey and the purpose of this paper is to report on the results of this survey, to present preliminary comparative analyses and to comment on the implications of this work for our understanding of Tara.

Magnetic susceptibility

A reconnaissance magnetic susceptibility survey was undertaken using a Bartington MS2 and MS2D field loop. Measurements were taken at 5m intervals along north–south parallel transects set 5m apart within a 195m by 95m area to the west and north-west of Ráith na Senad. The resulting image is therefore generated from a total of 800 readings of magnetic susceptibility.

This survey was undertaken to detect general magnetic trends across the hillside in order to identify areas of anthropogenically enhanced susceptibility which could then be targeted for higher-resolution fluxgate gradiometry survey. Higher susceptibility values due to anthropogenic factors are largely a result of activities which involved intensive burning, for example a hearth, kiln or furnace (Clark 1990, 100–1). Such features and activities can usually be detected as areas of relatively high susceptibility values contrasting with those of the natural background levels. Surprisingly, and despite considerable past activity, clearly evidenced by the wealth of archaeological monuments on the hill, the image displays no significant contrasts or specific areas of enhanced values of magnetic susceptibility (Fig. 1).

Fluxgate gradiometry survey

The magnetometer survey was undertaken using a Geoscan FM36 fluxgate gradiometer. Readings were taken at 0.5m intervals, south to north, along parallel transects set 0.5m apart. This amounts to a total of 400 readings per 10m by 10m panel. The survey is therefore at twice the resolution of previous magnetometer surveys conducted on the hill during the course of the original Tara Survey (undertaken by GeoQuest Ltd between 1992 and 1995). The combined survey consists of a total of 474 panels, amounting to nearly 190,000 individual measurements of magnetic gradient, and covers an irregular area of over 4.5ha with maximum dimensions of 320m north–south by 280m east–west (Fig. 2).

These data have undergone a number of simple processing procedures. Survey panels have undergone de-drifting and edge-matching procedures to provide as close to a seamless join as possible between adjacent panels. The data range has been de-spiked to remove excessively high and low magnetic anomalies which are likely, for the most part, to be caused by ferrous litter. In addition, it has been clipped to the statistical bulk of the data set in order to isolate or enhance some of the weaker magnetic anomalies of archaeological significance. No filters have been applied and therefore the resulting image is essentially that of the raw survey data which have undergone only editorial manipulation. The resulting image is one of extraordinary clarity and displays a wealth of subsurface magnetic anomalies, many of which are clearly of archaeological significance.

Archaeological interpretation

Much of the hilltop was subjected to extensive ridge-and-furrow cultivation in the past. The evidence of this can be traced as low-relief undulations on the surface of the fields today. It is likely, therefore, that many of the archaeological features lying close to the surface (perhaps up to 0.5cm deep) will have been substantially destroyed or completely erased. Similarly, features set deeper in the subsoil will have been truncated to the depth of the ploughzone horizon but may remain relatively undisturbed in the underlying subsoil layers. Volume-specific measurement of magnetic susceptibility employing a field loop, though probing only to a depth of about 0.2m, was deemed appropriate in this context as it can, nonetheless, detect thin lenses or spreads of magnetically enhanced material even if disturbed from their original context.

Though at first glance the magnetic susceptibility image may appear rather disappointing, the distinct lack of anomalous zones does seem to suggest that this part of the hill did not see any significant domestic, industrial or ritual activity involving intensive burning (Fig. 1).

The pattern of ridge-and-furrow cultivation is also evident in the gradiometry image as faint, alternating parallel bands of positive and negative magnetic gradient (Fig. 2). The survey confirms the surface indications that the hilltop was formerly subdivided into a number of individual, roughly rectangular, plots or fields (Newman and Fenwick 1997, 35–8, figs 12 and 13). These and some of the more recent disturbance in the geophysical image will be identified before discussing other features of potential archaeological significance.

Fig. 2—Grey-scale image of the 1998–9 fluxgate gradiometry survey, dominated by the remarkably clear signature of the ditched pit circle (31:33:71).

The area to the west and north-west of Ráith na Senad is divided into three distinct plots on either side of a disused field boundary. This boundary is visible as a broad, linear, low-relief depression running north–south on the ground surface, and is also displayed as a broad negative lineation in the gradiometry image. The cultivation ridges run parallel on either side of the dividing boundary, with the exception of a third field or plot in the north-west corner of the image, where the ridge-and-furrow cultivation pattern runs at right angles, east–west, to the principal boundary.

The cultivation pattern to the north of Ráith na Senad and east of the disused field boundary running along the eastern bank of the Tech Midchúarta is evident as a low-relief surface feature and also appears as a faint banding of alternating negative and positive magnetic lineations oriented east–west. Interestingly, there are also faint traces in the gradiometry image of a cultivation pattern running at right angles to this which possibly reflects an earlier episode of cultivation within the same plot but whose subsurface presence was not completely erased by the penultimate ridge-and-furrow pattern. The pattern within the small triangular field between the carpark and the path leading to the churchyard (i.e. north-east of the churchyard), though having no readily apparent surface expression, appears to be oriented north–south in the gradiometry image. The ridge-and-furrow cultivation pattern in the long rectangular field to the east of the churchyard and Ráith na Ríg extends downhill, west to east, towards the modern road. Within this field are also a number of disused field boundaries (running east–west) which, like the fossil cultivation pattern, run perpendicular to the road.

The ridge-and-furrow pattern to the south of Ráith na Senad and within the northern sector of Ráith na Ríg is subdivided into two distinct areas. One lies to the east of Duma na nGiall and here the ridge-and-furrow cultivation runs north–south, parallel to the field boundary which adjoins Ráith na Ríg. Though this pattern is more distinctive within Ráith na Ríg, it appears to continue over the ramparts to fill the triangular area up to the churchyard wall. The second system lies to the west of Duma na nGiall and has an east–west orientation within Ráith na Ríg. In this instance, however, it stops short of the rampart. It is clear from the gradiometry image that a number of magnetic anomalies must lie below, and therefore pre-date, this cultivation horizon as none display obvious surface evidence or interference with the ridge-and-furrow overprint.

The most clearly defined of these anomalies is a large oval enclosure that dominates the centre of the image (Figs 2 and 3). This feature is expressed as a broad negative–positive–negative magnetic band (typically from −4 to +4 nT/0.5m), about 5m in width, to either side of which is a series of regularly spaced, roughly circular, discrete positive magnetic anomalies (Fig. 4). These anomalies, 1.5–2m in diameter, are spaced approximately 4m apart, centre to centre, around the entire circumference of the ring and roughly 8m apart across the dividing lineation. The enclosure is on a monumental scale. With maximum dimensions of 210m north–south by 175m east–west, and enclosing an area of some 3ha, it extends from the southern end of the Tech Midchúarta southwards to encompass Ráith na Senad, most of St Patrick's churchyard and Duma na nGiall within its circuit. Physical obstructions, such as graves, headstones, railings and the overburden of accumulated material, render the interior of the churchyard unsuitable for surveying.

The negative–positive–negative lineation can be traced as a broad low-relief depression to the west and north of Ráith na Senad (Pl. 1). It is likely, therefore, that this anomaly represents a fosse whose fill is composed of a significant volume of magnetically enhanced sediments. In addition to burnt material, topsoil in general is inherently more magnetically susceptible than the underlying B horizon. The presence of decaying organic matter may also have a bearing, though perhaps to a lesser degree, on the magnetic quality of soil sediments in the fosse. It is likely, however, because of the extraordinary clarity of the magnetic signature of this feature, that the fosse contains significant quantities of burnt material. In addition, there is the distinct possibility that, like the substantial fosses defining Ráith na Senad or Ráith na Ríg, it may be rock-cut. On the summit of the hill the upper surface of the bedrock occurs, on average, about 1m below the present ground surface (Cummins 1997, 256). By contrast, the underlying Lower Carboniferous limestone has little or no inherent magnetic presence, and therefore the proportionately greater volume of magnetically enhanced material within a rock-cut fosse will register particularly clearly. The discrete equi-spaced magnetic anomalies, up to 300 in total, on either side of the fosse may represent pits or possibly post-pits for large upright timbers. A similar explanation may be advanced for their particularly clear geomagnetic expression. Between them, therefore, these two sets of anomalies can be interpreted as a large fosse on either side of which are regularly spaced pits, and this is provisionally described hereafter as a ditched pit circle

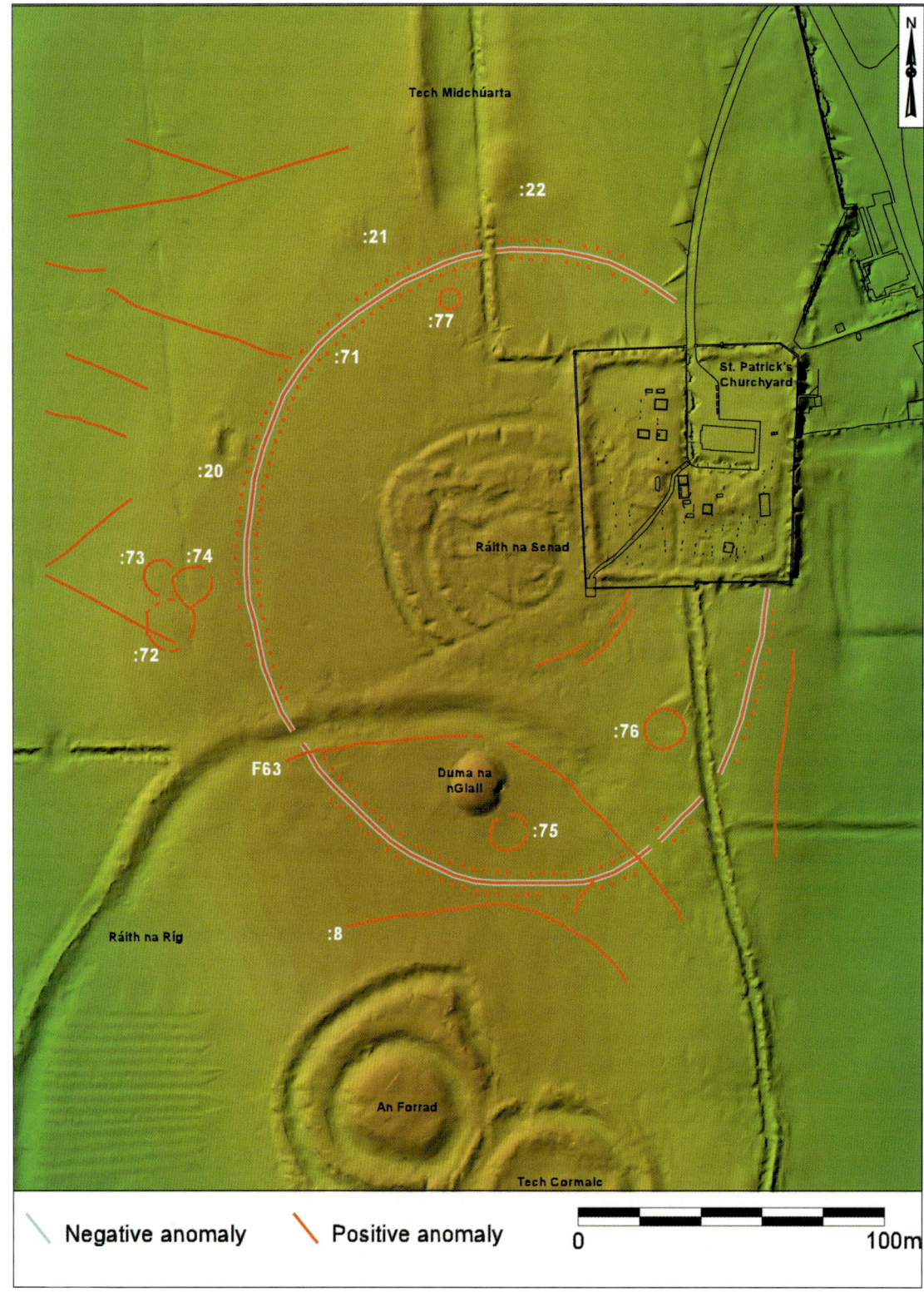

Fig. 3—Interpretational line map of some of the most clearly defined archaeomagnetic anomalies.

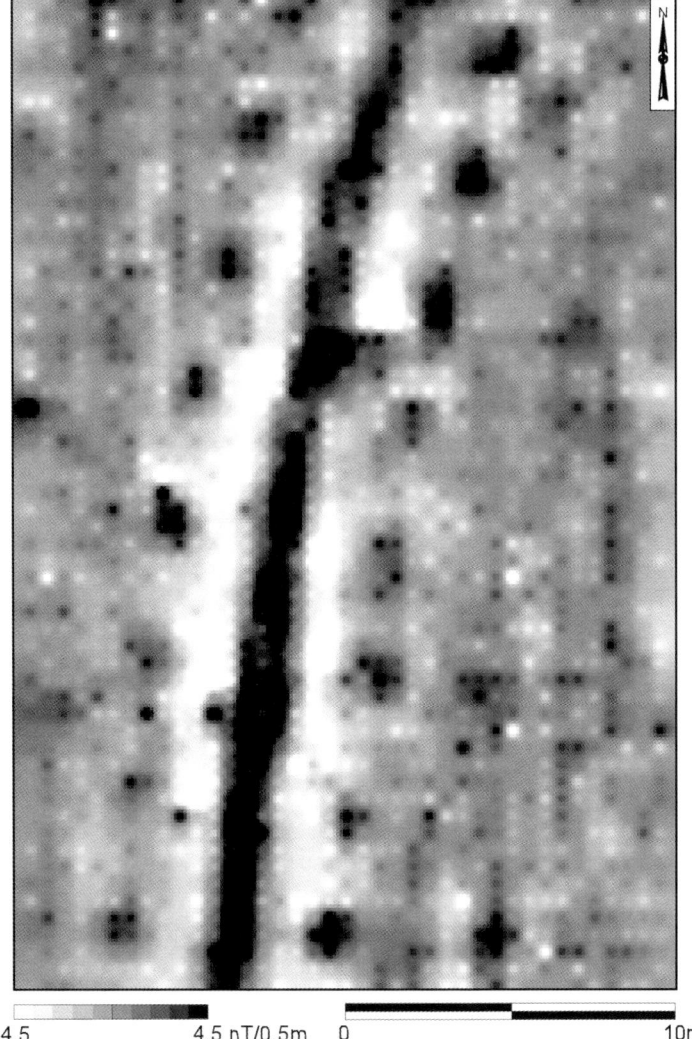
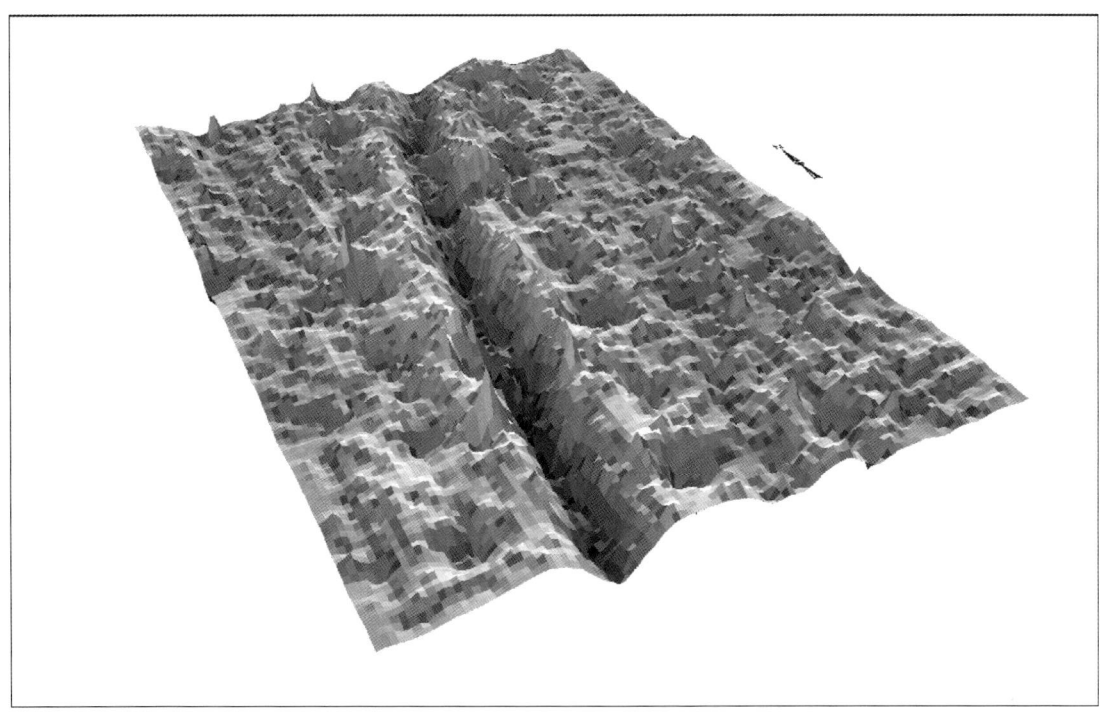

Fig. 4—Upper: *Detail of the western sector of the ditched pit circle (31:33:71).*
Lower: *Three-dimensional representation of the gradiometry data values for the same area. Magnetic polarity has been inverted so that positive anomalies appear as troughs and negative anomalies as peaks.*

(31:33:71). Interestingly, there is no obvious evidence of an entrance or formal approach to this monument. It may, unfortunately, be the case that this lies somewhere within the unsurveyed area in the churchyard.

In addition to the large enclosure, a number of smaller, less dramatic—though no less important—circular, arcuate and linear positive magnetic anomalies can be distinguished in the image. Many are just discernible above the threshold of background noise and are particularly difficult to distinguish without the benefit of viewing them on a computer screen. Only the more obvious features will be discussed here, though it is evident, on more detailed inspection, that there may be many other features of potential archaeological significance in the gradiometry data.

A number of strong magnetic anomalies within the interior of the enclosure are due to modern features and can therefore be ignored. These features have been edited out of the data set as the strength of their signal would tend to overwhelm or mask some of the more subtle magnetic features of archaeological significance. The memorial cross surrounded by railings, commemorating the 1798 rebellion, in the south-western corner of the enclosure exhibits a considerable magnetic presence and has been removed from the data set. The magnetic signatures of the steel supports for the signs marking Ráith na Ríg and Duma na nGiall, both lying immediately to the north of Duma na nGiall, have also been deleted from the image, as has that of the *Fógra* pillar to its north-west. In addition, Duma na nGiall itself and areas to its east and north were not surveyed as the gate, the steel reinforcements and the wire mesh used to consolidate the reconstituted mound all contribute spurious strong magnetic signals. The majority of the remaining features visible in the image are, however, of potential archaeological significance.

A number of these features occur within the ditched pit circle. However, only peripheral parts of Ráith na Senad were subjected to geophysical survey as this monument has been extensively excavated in the past (Ó Ríordáin 1961). It was traversed by a wall, now removed, running south-west/north-east, marking the Castletown Tara/Castleboy townland boundary. The position of this wall can be traced in the gradiometry image as a broad, rather noisy band of randomly dispersed dipolar anomalies. This pattern is likely to reflect a concentration of ferromagnetic objects—perhaps the buried remains of corroded wire. That part of the monument lying to the north of the townland boundary (in Castletown Tara) remains as an extant earthwork, whereas to the south (Castleboy) it has been all but erased. The outer ramparts in this south-eastern quadrant can still, however, be discerned as a low-relief earthwork. The gradiometry survey of this part of the monument reveals two of the outermost concentric fosses as faint, broad, positive magnetic bands separated by a narrow, more distinct lineation, perhaps representing the subsurface remains of a substantial slot trench or palisade which may have functioned as a bank revetment.

The area immediately north of Ráith na Senad displays a significant concentration of magnetic disturbance, principally strong dipolar anomalies. If these are of archaeological significance, they may indicate that this area saw intense burning, possibly associated with metalworking, or a significant concentration of ferrous objects. These features may equally, of course, be due to a concentration of ferrous litter of relatively modern date which may be of no archaeological consequence. It is interesting to note, however, that there are also significant anomalous magnetic sources, many of which display large discrete dipolar signatures, around the periphery of the churchyard, and particularly along its northern boundary and the field boundary extending from it to the west. It is recorded that during the Battle of Tara in 1798 the rebel forces were entrenched in some of the field boundaries and archaeological earthworks on the hill (Steen 1991). Some of them retreated to the churchyard, where they came under sustained fire from Crown forces. There is the distinct possibility, therefore, that some of the anomalous sources around the churchyard and field boundary may be the remnants of grapeshot or cannon balls fired at the rebel forces during the course of the confrontation.

At the southern part of the image the rampart of Ráith na Ríg is clearly defined. Interestingly, the external bank appears to be effectively transparent to magnetic gradiometry survey, but the internal fosse is expressed as a broad negative–positive–negative magnetic band. Parallel to this is a narrow, unbroken, sharply delimited, positive magnetic line representing the palisade trench (feature 62 in Roche, this volume; hereafter F62) identified by Ó Ríordáin during excavations in the late 1950s. Curiously, there is a very localised area of intense magnetic disturbance to the north-east of Duma na nGiall. This area, composed of a concentration of magnetic dipoles, correlates with the area of metalworking identified in recent excavations below the bank of Ráith na Ríg (Roche 1999). Though the majority of point-source magnetic anomalies may represent metalworking detritus, a number of the larger discrete anomalies may possibly correspond to the location of individual furnaces.

Immediately to the south of the ditched pit circle is a slender positive magnetic arcuate lineation, running roughly east–west, which continues beyond the limits of the present survey and possibly encircles the conjoined monuments of the Forrad and Tech Cormaic. Interestingly, this feature appears to reflect the curvature of the rampart of Ráith na Ríg, and its scale and the nature of the magnetic signature are remarkably similar to those of palisade trench F62. This feature, therefore, may also represent the remains of a palisade trench. There are other amorphous areas of magnetic disturbance, several faint linear features and a number of strong dipolar anomalies within Ráith na Ríg, but none provides an easily recognisable or coherent pattern. Certainly, the gradiometry image of parts of the interior of Ráith na Ríg seems to exhibit evidence of activity, but it would appear that many of these areas have been considerably disturbed by later cultivation.

A number of more easily identifiable archaeological features, appearing as annular anomalies, occurs within the confines of the ditched pit enclosure (31:33:71). A circular, positive magnetic anomaly (31:33:75), defined as a broad annulus 2–3m wide and approximately 13m in diameter, occurs adjacent to the south-eastern quadrant of Duma na nGiall. This is a ring-ditch, the north-western quadrant of which was investigated during the excavation of the passage tomb (Muiris O'Sullivan, pers. comm.). A more clearly defined slender annulus (31:33:76), composed of an unbroken ring 1m wide and roughly 14m in diameter, occurs in the south-eastern quadrant of the ditched pit enclosure. A more ephemeral example (31:33:77), approximately 7m in diameter, occurs in the extreme north of the enclosure and appears to be aligned with the southern end of the Tech Midchúarta.

In the north-west of the image, and outside the ditched pit circle, is a series of additional annular anomalies. The most clearly defined are three conjoined circles (31:33:72, 31:33:73 and 31:33:74) to the west which appear as broad magnetic bands, roughly 2m wide, with approximate diameters of 18m, 12m and 14m respectively (Fig. 5). These features appear to have been significantly disturbed by the ridge-and-furrow cultivation. The deeper furrows have, in places, cut through the circular anomalies, giving them the appearance of being composed of a series of contiguous arcs. Other, more ephemeral circular anomalies apparent in the image may have been truncated almost to the point of total obliteration.

In addition to the predominantly north–south, corduroy patterning of the plough furrows, a number of lineations, some quite faint, are evidenced. With the exception of a prominent north–south lineation (Figs 2 and 3) lying slightly to the west of the mid-line, which is the remains of an early field boundary (Newman 1997, fig. 12), the remaining lineations cross the surveyed area in a general east–west direction. These clearly pre-date the surviving ridge-and-furrow pattern because they have no surface expression. Eight (or possibly nine) are orientated north-west/south-east and, at the south end of the surveyed area, are arguably quite regularly spaced. The remaining two are orientated in the opposite direction, roughly east-north-east/west-south-west, but they are not quite parallel with one another. There is a fairly strong likelihood that these are agricultural features, particularly the group orientated north-west/south-east. It would be premature, however, to write off all of these features as the remains of relatively recent agriculture.

It should be noted that magnetic gradiometry will detect only those archaeological features whose magnetic signature is sufficiently distinct for them to be recorded above the natural background noise. A clear reminder of this is the apparent transparency of mounds 31:33:20 and 31:33:21. These monuments, though extant as topographical features, remain effectively invisible to geomagnetic methods, though not to resistivity, as demonstrated previously (Newman 1997, 14–16).

Discussion

Annular features

This latest geophysical survey has revealed a host of interesting new features. The arcuate and annular anomalies (31:33:72–7) can, as before, be provisionally described as ring-ditches and therefore may be of Bronze Age date, though this form may have a very long chronology (see Newman 1997, 160–70). In general, they may be considered as funerary monuments, though even this is open to question in many cases. Overlapping of adjacent specimens is a recurring feature of such monuments, as seen, for example, elsewhere at Tara (e.g. 31:33:41–2) and most recently at Elton, Co. Limerick, and possibly also at Chancellorsland (Doody 1999). It seems highly unlikely that this is coincidental, a function of their having so slight a physical presence that the exact whereabouts of earlier ones have simply been

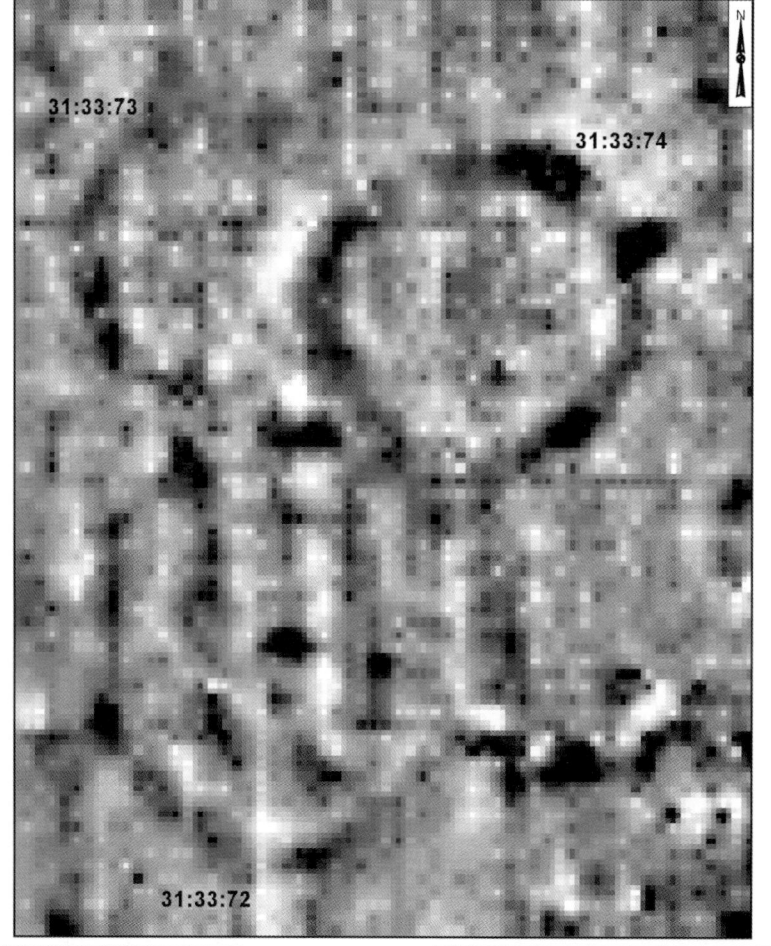

Fig. 5—Upper: *Details of the three conjoined positive magnetic rings (31:33: 72–4) lying to the west of Ráith na Senad.*
Lower: *Three-dimensional representation of the gradiometry data values for the same area with magnetic polarity reversed.*

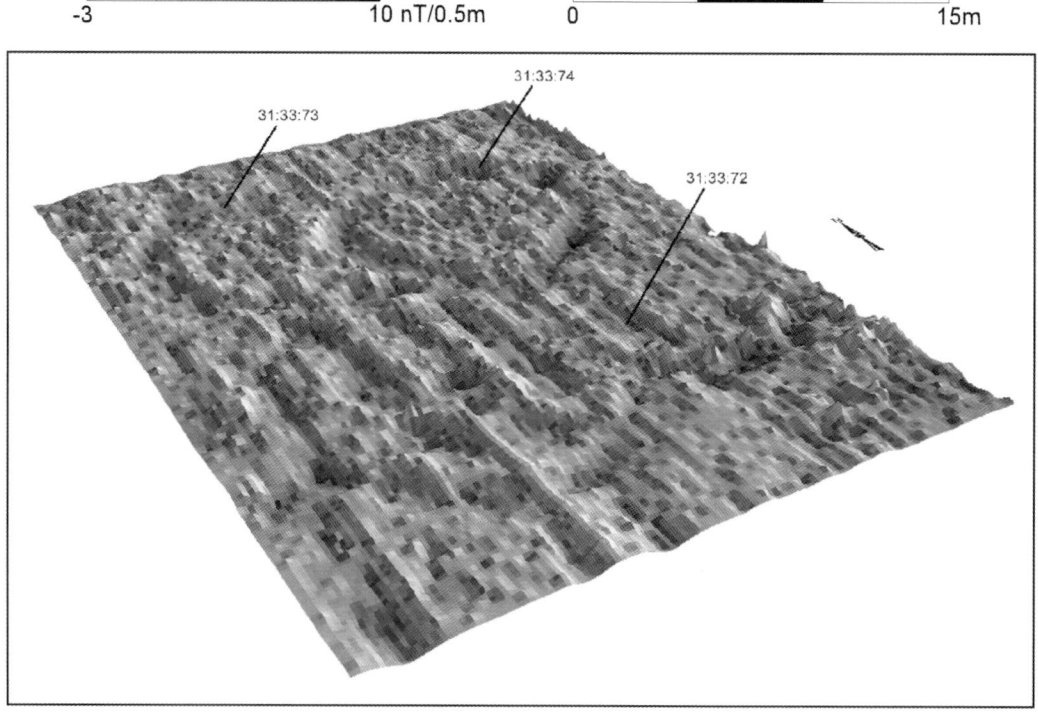

overlooked or forgotten. Rather, it suggests close affiliation, perhaps of a familial nature, among such groups and is therefore worthy of further consideration.

A reasonable case can be made for suggesting that these and the previously recorded barrow and ring-ditch monuments in this area (namely 31:33:6, 31:33:20–2 and 31:33:72–4) encircle the newly identified hengiform enclosure and, in so far as their positioning is concerned, that they have taken their cue from this earthwork (Figs 2 and 3). Moreover, the occurrence of at least three annuli (31:33:75–7) around the internal perimeter of the ditched pit enclosure may indicate another such ring of burial monuments. Further discoveries, of course, may disprove this, but in the meantime it is a worthwhile hypothesis in that it adheres to the notion that the position of monuments, particularly in so dense a concentration as on the Hill of Tara, can be determined by the location of significant earlier monuments. It would also suggest that they are later than the ditched pit circle, which might be suspected anyway on the grounds of comparative chronologies.

It is finally worth noting that this present survey 'ground-truths', albeit a posteriori, an annular positive magnetic anomaly, for, as we have seen, the magnetometry survey also covered a ring-ditch (33:31:75) to the south-east of Duma na nGiall, one quadrant of which was previously excavated by de Valera. Full publication of this excavation will doubtless allow for more detailed concordance of geophysical and excavated evidence than is presently possible, but in the interim the results should inspire confidence in the ability of geophysics to record genuine archaeological features in a meaningful and accurate way.

Ditched pit circle (31:33:71)

The image is, of course, dominated by the very large and impressive new enclosure 31:33:71, the geophysical presentation of which suggests, as we have already seen, two rows of regularly spaced pits on either side of a fosse (Fig. 6). While it is not yet known whether or not the pits and the fosse originally supported upright timbers, the exceptional clarity of the signature invites comparison with the growing corpus of palisaded enclosures and pit and timber circles from Ireland and Britain. Studied most recently by Alex Gibson (1994; 1996; 1998), these monuments frequently occur in ceremonial complexes and present very similar architectural motifs, factors that incline many commentators to the view that they are possibly just variations on a theme, one driven by religious conventions.

Mindful of the fact that in the present state of knowledge the monuments themselves cannot sustain too rigid a classification, Gibson applies a general distinction between timber circles and palisaded enclosures on the basis of shape and, implicitly, size. At one extreme is Hindwell II, Radnorshire, an enormous oval-shaped palisaded monument enclosing a massive 34ha (Gibson 1996; 1998; Gibson *et al.* 1999). Although somewhat dwarfing them, Hindwell II is classified along with enclosures such as those at Mount Pleasant, Dorset (Wainwright 1989), and West Kennet, Wiltshire (Whittle 1991). The size and irregular elliptical plan of these monuments suggest that they are, first and foremost, enclosures: their primary job is to demarcate, on a grand scale, sacred and/or secular spaces. Though evidently of quite singular dimensions, the effectiveness of such boundaries probably depended more on social dictates and religious mores than on physical impedance, especially where they defined religious space. This is borne out by the fact that some of these enclosures, e.g. Forteviot (Harding and Lee 1987) and Walton (Gibson 1995), are defined by most unpalisade-like, widely separated posts. At the other end of the typological spectrum are the sometimes diminutive timber circles, such as the 7m-diameter timber circle at Hungerford and the 8m-diameter circle on Conygar Hill (Gibson 1994, fig. 33). Most timber circles are indeed circular, and oval and elliptical shapes are quite rare. It is highly probable, therefore, that the prescribed or ideal shape was circular (see Gibson 1994, 192). Consequently, shape is, for Gibson, an important criterion in distinguishing between timber circles and palisaded enclosures. Being far more open-plan, timber circles are not as manifestly delimiting as palisaded enclosures, though evidently one of their primary functions was to demarcate sacred spaces. Insofar as most timber circles consist of fairly widely spaced, free-standing posts, they describe spaces that are delimited on a conceptual level.

Sites occupying the middle size ranges (i.e. the smaller of Gibson's palisaded enclosures) challenge such loose divisions: large, elliptical monuments, such as at Ballynahatty (BNH5 in Hartwell 1998) and now Tara 31:33:71, could, with some justification, be classified either way. Indeed, it is examples such as these that argue against imposing too rigid a classification. The frequency with which these middle-range enclosures are associated with religious monuments and ritual complexes means, in all probability, that they too have a significant religious dimension and are unlikely to be radically different from timber circles. That said, sites such as

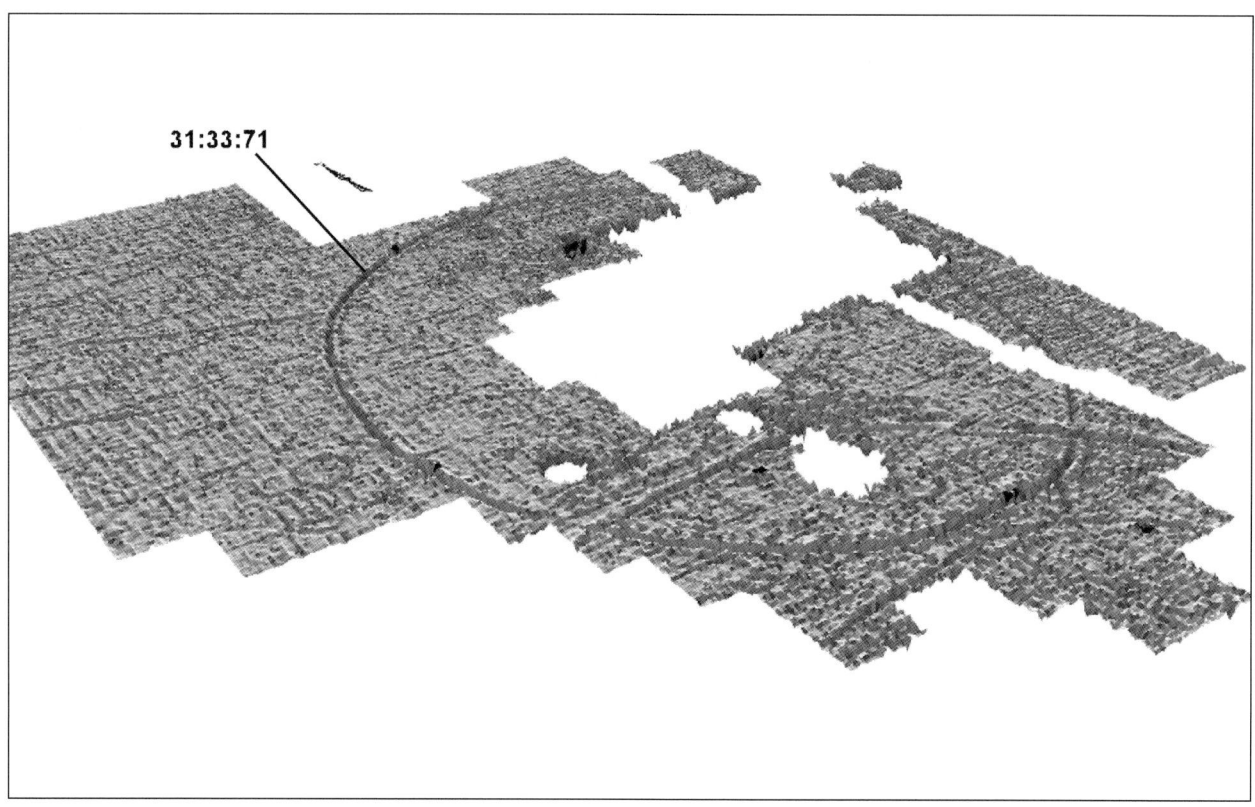

Fig. 6—Fluxgate gradiometry data expressed as a three-dimensional model in perspective, looking from the south-west.

Ballynahatty, where both forms are combined, suggest specificity of function and hierarchy—equivalent, perhaps, to the progression in sanctity of medieval ecclesiastical enclosures from *sanctus* to *sanctissimus* (Doherty 1985; although see also Swift 2000).

Gibson (1998) arranges the palisaded enclosures of Neolithic Britain and Ireland into three groups on the basis of different constructional procedures evidenced by the relative proximity of the perimeter post-holes to one another. His first group is characterised by distinct and quite widely spaced post-holes, whereas the second and third types have closely spaced post-holes and continuous bedding trenches respectively. From this last group can be distinguished what Gibson refers to as 'fenced sites'. Dating from the earlier Neolithic period, the latter are defined by continuous trenches of relatively modest proportions, probably capable of supporting posts no taller than about 3m in height, which contrast sharply with the monumental scale of the remaining palisaded enclosures. 'Fenced sites' aside, radiocarbon dates from the remaining three types suggest a general progression from enclosures with widely spaced post-holes, through specimens with overlapping post-holes, to those defined by trenches supporting contiguous palisades. It is also worth considering that each of the three types would have exhibited significantly different superstructures.

The widely spaced post-holes of Gibson's first group may, in many cases, have originally presented as ellipses or circles of free-standing posts, whereas the superstructure of sites with continuous bedding trenches would have been more palisade- or stockade-like, comprising an unbroken barrier that physically limited access and visibility into the interior (though Gibson's suggestion that the free-standing posts may have supported horizontal plank shuttering introduces the possibility that these too would have presented a similar barrier).

Allowing for the fact that full ground-plans are available for only a small number of sites, if any pattern is emerging it is that the largest palisaded enclosures, such as those at Hindwell II, Walton and Forteviot (Gibson 1998, fig. 6.5), tend to have a single row of posts or palisade, whereas the smaller ones, such as those at Ballynahatty, Dunragit (*ibid.*; Hartwell 1998) and now Tara 31:33:71, are more often defined by twin rows. A case can be made, therefore, for considering a more explicit distinction between the latter and the larger, single-palisade sites. Indeed, the theme of twinning or pairing posts recurs throughout this group and the timber circles (Gibson (1994) even distinguishes a double-post class of timber circles) and appears to operate in a number of different ways. For instance, in the case of Ballynahatty, Co. Antrim

(Hartwell 1998), the double-ringed 'sanctum' (BNH6) of phase 2 was within a large oval enclosure, similarly defined by a double row of radially paired posts (BNH5). At Newgrange, Sweetman (1985) uncovered six concentric rows of post-holes and pits arranged into two distinct groups, comprising four outer circuits (nos 1–4) separated by a little over 2m from two remaining inner circuits (nos 5 and 6). Although total consistency appears to be lacking, Sweetman has suggested that circuits 1 and 3 originally held posts, while circuits 2 and 4 and 5 and 6 may not have been intended for such a purpose and were, instead, originally burial pits.

The morphology and size of the new enclosure at Tara, as indicated by the geophysics, strongly suggest that it is most closely related to those at Newgrange and Ballynahatty, a connection that would in turn imply a later Neolithic/early Bronze Age date (Hartwell seems disinclined to lend much credence to the early date, 3018–2788 cal. BC, returned for BNH5). That parallels such as these are more than just morphological is attested by the fact that both the Newgrange and Tara specimens enclose undifferentiated passage tombs (the association is repeated at Ballynahatty) and by associated Grooved Ware and Beaker assemblages at some of the excavated sites.

Extending well into the Iron Age, however, timber circles in Ireland appear to have a considerably more protracted existence than in Britain, and this raises the possibility that Tara 31:33:71 could date from the later prehistoric period. Timber circles of Iron Age date, such as the 'Forty Metre Structure' at Navan Fort and the 'Mauve Phase' structures at Knockaulin (Wailes 1990), can be quite elaborate. The known examples describe very regular but quite modest circles, the largest one being at Navan Fort. A comparable motif has been identified in the gradiometry survey on the summit of Rathcroghan mound, Co. Roscommon (Fenwick et al. 1999). In this instance there is a 32m-diameter pit circle comprising large, radially paired pits/post-holes. Of further possible relevance is the fact that Rathcroghan mound itself is surrounded by a very large ditched enclosure over 370m in diameter. Lastly, a comparable structure has been postulated by Cooney and Grogan (1991, 36) in the case of Ráith na Senad. In his recent review of the dating evidence Gibson (1995) has also highlighted the existence in Ireland and Britain of a number of timber circles and palisaded enclosures of middle and later Bronze Age date. At Haughey's Fort, Co. Armagh, for example, a triple arc of posts consisting of two outer rows of stake-holes and an inner row of larger post-holes was uncovered (Mallory et al. 1996). Though parallel to one another in plan, and therefore arguably contemporary, radiocarbon dating places the stake-holes at between 2450 and 1550 BC, while the post-holes date from 1250–900 BC. Taken at face value, this feature is also comparable to Tara 31:33:71.

Comparisons such as these emphasise the post and/or pit aspect of Tara 31:33:71. The earthwork component, however, is clearly of great significance in its own right and, in so far as it gives this monument its lasting physical presence, continued to be important for some considerable time after the putative posts had been removed or rotted. Fortunately, traces of the fosse survive topographically (Pl. 1) and were captured in the recent detailed survey, although they were not recognised for what they were. At the surface it measures about 4–5m wide, which is slightly narrower than the excavated fosse of Ráith na Ríg, though obviously its depth is still unknown. It is the existence of the fosse that suggests comparison with the broader family of henges or hengiform monuments. However, far from being mutually incompatible, as is obvious from some of the foregoing examples, a recurring association exists between henges and embanked enclosures and timber circles, one which in Ireland endures into the early centuries AD, as demonstrated at Raffin Fort, Co. Meath (Newman 1993). Irish Iron Age timber circles, however, tend to be relatively small and to adhere closely to a true circle in plan, and this may be an important distinguishing characteristic. Moreover, in the case of earlier prehistoric circles (at least) timber and stone verticals appear to have been effectively interchangeable, though one medium was obviously more durable than the other, with the result that the range of relevant comparanda can be legitimately widened to include variations such as embanked stone circles, circle henges (sic: Condit and Simpson 1998) and select monuments less amenable to conventional classification such as Lugg, Co. Dublin (Kilbride-Jones 1950), and Phase 3(i) at Navan Fort, Co. Armagh (Lynn 1997, 14–16). Current analysis of this broad family of henges (e.g. Clare 1986) emphasises variability of form, allowing for numerous combinations of any or all of the three constituent architectural motifs (fosse, bank and posts, standing stones and pits) and thus would comfortably accommodate Tara 31:33:71.

Nevertheless, the majority of such sites have banks, however slight (e.g. Reanascreena South, Co. Cork; Fahy 1962). There is, so far, no evidence that the ditched pit circle at Tara had a bank, either hard by the fosse (which would have a direct bearing on the relationship of the pits to the fosse) or at some remove from it, and in this respect the monument finds an interesting, if comparatively late, companion in Phase 3(i) at Navan Fort. Here Waterman uncovered a penannular ditch (46m in diameter, 4.3–5.5m wide and 1.1–1.2m deep) inside which was a more or less concentric circle of large, regularly spaced pits (ranging from 3.5m to 1.8m in width and around 4m apart) which are believed to have once held upright posts, some or all of which were deliberately removed before they decayed. Analysis of associated Coarseware and two radiocarbon dates from the primary silt of the ditch suggest that this element may date from between the ninth and fourth centuries BC, but the contemporaneity of the pits, which is argued on the basis of their being concentric with the ditch and on the presence of Coarseware pottery in the pit fills, is not certain. Radiocarbon dates from two of the pits are at variance with each other by a number of centuries (from the mid-seventeenth century BC to around the birth of Christ) but at maximum range allow for overlap with the dates returned for the ditch between the ninth and eighth centuries BC (Lynn 1997, 189ff). This latter appears to be the preferred dating of the editorial team. The question of the possible function of this monument has not been satisfactorily resolved, but in the absence of evidence to the contrary, and considering the later history of the site, a religious purpose is distinctly possible. An earlier though similar configuration is evidenced at Stonehenge (Phase 1), comprising a penannular ditch with internal bank and 56 so-called 'Aubrey Holes' (possibly slightly later than the earthwork) (Cleal et al. 1995).

In summary, therefore, the weight of evidence suggests that Tara 31:33:71 is a form of henge monument (applying the word henge in its broadest definition) and that it is prehistoric. In terms of its size and shape it fits in best with earlier prehistoric monuments, but the possibility of a date as late as the early centuries BC cannot be ruled out, particularly in an Irish context.

Configuration and juxtaposition of the ditched pit enclosure (31:33:71)

The monument, as revealed, is situated slightly to the east of the spine of the hill, which runs north–south. This may partly explain its elongation along this axis. It encloses Ráith na Senad and Duma na nGiall, intersects with Ráith na Ríg and passes close by the south end of Tech Midchúarta—relationships which, in their own right, raise interesting possibilities. In considering these, it is important to bear in mind that the outline of the ditched pit circle is likely to have been readily visible for some time (the fosse still survives today as a low-relief, arcuate depression to the west of Ráith na Senad) and must have been acknowledged by the builders of some later monuments. It is strongly suspected that the positioning of monuments generally is not a random act, and it is highly significant that in this case Ráith na Senad is centrally located within the newly identified monument, even though they may be separated in time.

The possibility that 31:33:71 is quite early in the monument sequence at Tara may be reflected in the fact that, according to the geophysical image, it does not appear to have cut or truncated any monuments (though the strength of its 'signature' might effectively obliterate or mask lesser features). It is quite possible that its incorporation of Duma na nGiall is deliberate, and therefore that the ditched pit circle post-dates the passage tomb. Supporting this suggestion is the fact that the pit circle at Newgrange, which compares quite well with the Tara specimen, also encloses an undifferentiated passage tomb and so it is possible that this type of couplet is a recurring motif.

Enclosure 31:33:71 is positioned very close to the southern end of Tech Midchúarta, appearing to pass fractionally to the south of the remains of a possible low, ploughed-out, terminal bank identified previously (Newman 1997, 104). This means that any attempt to ascertain the relationship between the two monuments by excavation at this point is unlikely to resolve this issue (particularly given that the terminal bank is ploughed over and would be difficult to identify through excavation in any case). The enclosure does not appear to be gapped or altered in any way at this point. In other words, neither monument appears to 'acknowledge' the presence of the other and as a result it is not possible to suggest a relative chronology. Moreover, the classification and dating of Tech Midchúarta is quite problematical, though it has been suggested that it might be a cursus monument (Condit 1995; Newman 1997, 150–2). In very broad terms cursus monuments are generally (though by no means always) dated earlier than pit or timber circles and henges, and if Tara follows this trend it can be postulated that 31:33:71 might be later than Tech Midchúarta.

A clear *terminus post quem* is indicated, however, by the fact that the ditched pit circle is truncated by the internal fosse of Ráith na Ríg, which has recently been dated to within the last few centuries BC (Roche 1999; this volume), and this could be quite easily tested with excavation at the junction of the two monuments. One possibility is that the construction of the later monument implies that the ditched pit circle had become obsolete by the Iron Age and was simply ignored. However, in as much as Ráith na Ríg intersects with it, this conforms to an established pattern of the incorporation of earlier monuments into the fabric of later ones, often producing a figure-of-eight shape. Since this is an important recurring motif at Tara, and indeed at all of the so-called 'royal' sites, it was possibly an intentional consequence of the positioning of Ráith na Ríg. Moreover, looking at the respective ground-plans of the two monuments, it is tempting to conclude that what they have in common is an explicit desire to incorporate Duma na nGiall, which was obviously of considerable importance well into the medieval period. It has been noted that the rampart of Ráith na Ríg bulges outwards slightly in order to proclaim the deliberate incorporation of Duma na nGiall within its circuit (Newman 1997, 68). A similar case might be advanced on behalf of the ditched pit circle. In this respect, it is noteworthy that the builders of the enclosure deliberately chose an area whose eastern sector slopes significantly in preference to the relatively flat, level ground on the summit of the ridge little more than 50m to its west.

The potential significance of the fact that 31:33:71 encloses both Ráith na Senad and the church grounds cannot be overstated, not least because it raises intriguing questions about factors that might have determined the location of both and about the compound importance of Ráith na Senad, which is the last of at least four distinct phases of activity on this spot. The 'central' point of 31:33:71 corresponds with the central area of Ráith na Senad but it is unlikely to be contemporary with the latest phase of the latter (the multivallate earthwork) on account of the chronological conflict that arises between the date of the Romano-British material associated with the latest phase of Ráith na Senad and the somewhat earlier date for Ráith na Ríg, which, as we have seen, appears to cut 31:33:71. Furthermore, it has also been suggested, on topographical grounds, that Ráith na Senad is later than Ráith na Ríg (Newman 1997, 230).

Three pre-earthwork phases were identified during the excavations of Ráith na Senad in the 1950s. The third or penultimate phase in the developmental sequence saw the site being used as a flat cemetery. O'Brien (1990, 38) suggests that the mixed burials date from the first/second century AD, placing them somewhat later than Ráith na Ríg and therefore also later than the ditched pit circle. The second phase of Ráith na Senad is evidenced by the construction of palisaded circles comparable in some measure with those at Navan Fort and Knockaulin (Cooney and Grogan 1991), though how much earlier than the Phase 3 cemetery is unknown. The dating of the Knockaulin and Navan specimens suggests, *inter alia*, general contemporaneity between this phase of Ráith na Senad and the construction of Ráith na Ríg, though precise details have yet to be ascertained. Of interest in this context is Cooney and Grogan's suggestion of the existence of a double-post timber circle within one of the enclosures. Dating aside, the configuration of this proposed circle and the ditched pit circle would be very reminiscent of the Ballynahatty structures, and a connection cannot be ruled out at this early stage.

The first phase of Ráith na Senad comprises a small ring-ditch, co-extensive with the central area of the earthwork. Though the majority of such earthworks date from the earlier and later Bronze Age, comparative analysis suggests that the form was in use from the Neolithic to the later Iron Age/early historic period transition, and this at least introduces the possibility of a connection with 31:33:71.

Enclosure 31:33:08
Previous geophysical survey in the interior of Ráith na Ríg revealed the existence of two (possibly three) narrow, arcuate lineations which, it was tentatively suggested, might all belong to a palisaded enclosure (31:33:08). These occurred to the east of Tech Cormaic and to the north-west of the Forrad respectively, so that the postulated enclosure was seen to encircle these two monuments, though it was not considered to have been connected with them (Newman 1997, 75–85). In the north-western quadrant a second such lineation, outside the first, was also recorded, suggesting the possibility that there had been two concentric rings. The anomalies, however, are very faint in this area, cautioning against too assertive an identification. In contrast, to the east of Tech Cormaic the anomalies are very strong, presenting a distinct signature.

It was speculated at the time that this putative enclosure might be one and the same as that reported (but not illustrated) by de Paor (1957) and Longworth (1960) to have been found in the old ground surface beneath Duma na nGiall. This can now be disregarded because, according to a plan of pre-tomb features used by Muiris O'Sullivan to illustrate a lecture on the excavations presented at the Dublin Castle conference on Tara in April 1998, the small enclosure referred to by de Paor extended to the west of the passage tomb. This now places a further question mark over the existence of the proposed outer ring as this is the one that we speculated projected beneath the tomb. The current geophysical survey has, however, confirmed the westward continuation of the distinct anomaly first recorded to the west of Tech Cormaic, thus preserving the possibility that at least the inner enclosure exists. In fact, this now seems most probable, and therefore we recommend retaining the original number (31:33:08) to describe this feature.

In terms of their respective geophysical signatures, 31:33:08 compares well with the palisade trench that runs around the internal perimeter of Ráith na Ríg (F62, after Roche, this volume). Excavation reveals the latter to be as much as 90cm wide and 1.19m deep (Roche 1999, 27), and this is a useful indication of the possible dimensions of 31:33:08. The comparisons do not end there, however, for both features follow the same ground-plan (albeit on different scales) and, in particular, both have a distinctive angle, or elbow, in the north-eastern quadrant. It can be argued that the 'elbow' in F62 derives from an equivalent angle in the ground-plan of Ráith na Ríg, which it follows so faithfully. However, no such pre-emption can be argued in the case of 31:33:08, unless it is postulated that it too takes its cue from Ráith na Ríg or, as seems more likely under the circumstances, from F62.

This, of course, has implications for the dating, and therefore the role, of both trenches because it introduces the possibility that they are contemporary with one another. The case has previously been made for suggesting that F62 dates from substantially later than the construction of Ráith na Ríg and that its role was to convert a hengiform enclosure into an ostensibly defensible one. In terms of these speculations, therefore, much now hinges on the relationship between the innermost trench (33:31:08) and the Forrad and Tech Cormaic. On present evidence, all that can be said is that, as projected, 31:33:08 appears to skirt very close to the eastern side of Tech Cormaic, though whether it is overlain slightly by the outer bank is unknown. This will be ascertained in due course through further geophysical prospection. If, however, 31:33:08 does indeed encircle Tech Cormaic, then it can be argued that it appears very late in the history of the complex and opens up a debate, touched on earlier, concerning the hierarchies of concentric enclosures such as those documented in the case of early medieval monasteries but now a recurring feature of prehistoric religious and secular monuments.

Acknowledgements

We gratefully acknowledge Sinead Armstrong, Louise Finegan, Owen Keiron and Linda Shine for their assistance in the field. Thanks are also due to Joan and Desmond Maguire. We are indebted to Barry Masterson of the Discovery Programme, whose time and expertise in the production of the publication figures are greatly appreciated. The plate was generously made available for this publication by Jacqueline O'Brien and was first published in her *Ancient Ireland: from prehistory to the Middle Ages*, co-authored by Peter Harbison (Widenfeld and Nicolson, 1996).

References

Clare, T. 1986 Towards a re-appraisal of henge monuments. *Proceedings of the Prehistoric Society* **52**, 281–316.

Clark, A. 1990 *Seeing beneath the soil*. London.

Cleal, R., Walker, K. and Montague, R. 1995 *Stonehenge in its landscape: twentieth century excavation*. London.

Condit, T. 1995 Avenues for research. *Archaeology Ireland* **34**, 16–18.

Condit, T. and Simpson, D. 1998 Irish hengiform enclosures and related monuments: a review. In A. Gibson and D. Simpson (eds), *Prehistoric ritual and religion: essays in honour of Aubrey Burl*, 45–61. Stroud.

Cooney, G. and Grogan, E. 1991 An archaeological solution to the 'Irish' problem? *Emania* 9, 33–43.

Cummins, T. 1997 Description of soil profiles at the Hill of Tara. In C. Newman, *Tara: an archaeological survey*, 253–9. Dublin.

de Paor, M. 1957 Notes on excavations in Eire, England, Northern Ireland, Scotland and Wales, during 1956. Mound of the Hostages, Tara, Co. Meath. *Proceedings of the Prehistoric Society* **23**, 220–1.

Doherty, C. 1985 The monastic town in early medieval Ireland. In H.B. Clarke and A. Simms (eds), *The comparative history of urban origins in non-Roman Europe*, 45–75. British Archaeological Reports 255. Oxford.

Doody, M. 1999 The Ballyhoura Hills Project. *Discovery Programme Reports* **5**, 97–100.

Fahy, E.M. 1962 A recumbent-stone circle at Reanascreena South, Co. Cork. *Journal of the Cork Historical and Archaeological Society* **67**, 59–69.

Fenwick, J., Brennan, Y., Barton, K. and Waddell, J. 1999 The magnetic presence of Queen Medb:

magnetic gradiometry at Rathcroghan, Co. Roscommon. *Archaeology Ireland* **47**, 8–11.

Gibson, A. 1994 Excavations at Sarn-y-bryn-caled cursus complex, Welshpool, Powys, and the timber circles of Great Britain and Ireland. *Proceedings of the Prehistoric Society* **60**, 143–224.

Gibson, A. 1995 The dating of timber circles: new thoughts in the light of recent Irish and British discoveries. In J. Waddell and E. Shee Twohig (eds), *Ireland in the Bronze Age*, 87–9. Dublin.

Gibson, A. 1996 A Neolithic enclosure at Hindwell, Radnorshire, Powys. *Oxford Journal of Archaeology* **15** (3), 341–8.

Gibson, A. 1998 Hindwell and the Neolithic palisaded sites of Britain and Ireland. In A. Gibson and D. Simpson (eds), *Prehistoric ritual and religion: essays in honour of Aubrey Burl*, 68–79. Stroud.

Gibson, A., Becker, H., Grogan, E., Jones, N. and Masterson, B. 1999 The Walton Basin, Wales: survey exploration and preservation of the archaeological heritage (SEPAH). *Archaeology Ireland* **47**, 21–3.

Harding, A.F. and Lee, G.E. 1987 *Henge monuments and related sites of Great Britain*. British Archaeological Reports 175. Oxford.

Hartwell, B. 1998 The Ballynahatty complex. In A. Gibson and D. Simpson (eds), *Prehistoric ritual and religion: essays in honour of Aubrey Burl*, 32–44. Stroud.

Kilbride-Jones, H. 1950 The excavation of a composite early Iron Age monument with 'henge' features at Lugg, Co. Dublin. *Proceedings of the Royal Irish Academy* **53C**, 311–32.

Longworth, I. 1960 Notes on excavations, 1959 (Eire): Mound of the Hostages, Tara, Co. Meath [based on information provided by M.J. O'Kelly]. *Proceedings of the Prehistoric Society* **26**, 341–2.

Lynn, C.J. (ed.) 1997 *Excavations at Navan Fort 1961–71 by D.M. Waterman*. Northern Ireland Archaeological Monographs No. 3. Belfast.

Mallory, J., Moore, D.G. and Canning, L.J. 1996 Excavations at Haughey's Fort 1991 and 1995. *Emania* **14**, 5–20.

Newman, C. 1993 'Sleeping in Elysium'. *Archaeology Ireland* **7** (3), 20–3.

Newman, C. 1997 *Tara: an archaeological survey*. Discovery Programme Monographs 2. Dublin.

Newman, C. and Fenwick, J. 1997 History of the landscape at Tara. In C. Newman, *Tara: an archaeological survey*, 31–43. Dublin.

O'Brien, E. 1990 Iron Age burial practices in Leinster: continuity and change. *Emania* **7**, 37–42.

Ó Ríordáin, S.P. 1961 *Tara: the monuments on the hill*. Dundalk.

Roche, H. 1999 Late Iron Age activity at Tara, Co. Meath. *Ríocht na Midhe* **10**, 18–30.

Steen, L.J. 1991 *The Battle of the Hill of Tara 26th May 1798*. Trim.

Sweetman, D. 1985 A Late Neolithic/Early Bronze Age pit circle at Newgrange, Co. Meath. *Proceedings of the Royal Irish Academy* **85C**, 196–221.

Swift, C. 2000 Forts and fields: a study of 'monastic towns' in seventh and eighth century Ireland. *Journal of Irish Archaeology* **9**, 105–26.

Wailes, B. 1990 Dún Ailinne: a summary report. *Emania* **7**, 10–21.

Wainwright, G.J. 1989 *The henge monuments*. London.

Whittle, A.W.R. 1991 A Late Neolithic complex at West Kennet, Wiltshire. *Antiquity* **65**, 256–62.

2. EXCAVATIONS AT RÁITH NA RÍG, TARA, CO. MEATH, 1997

Helen Roche

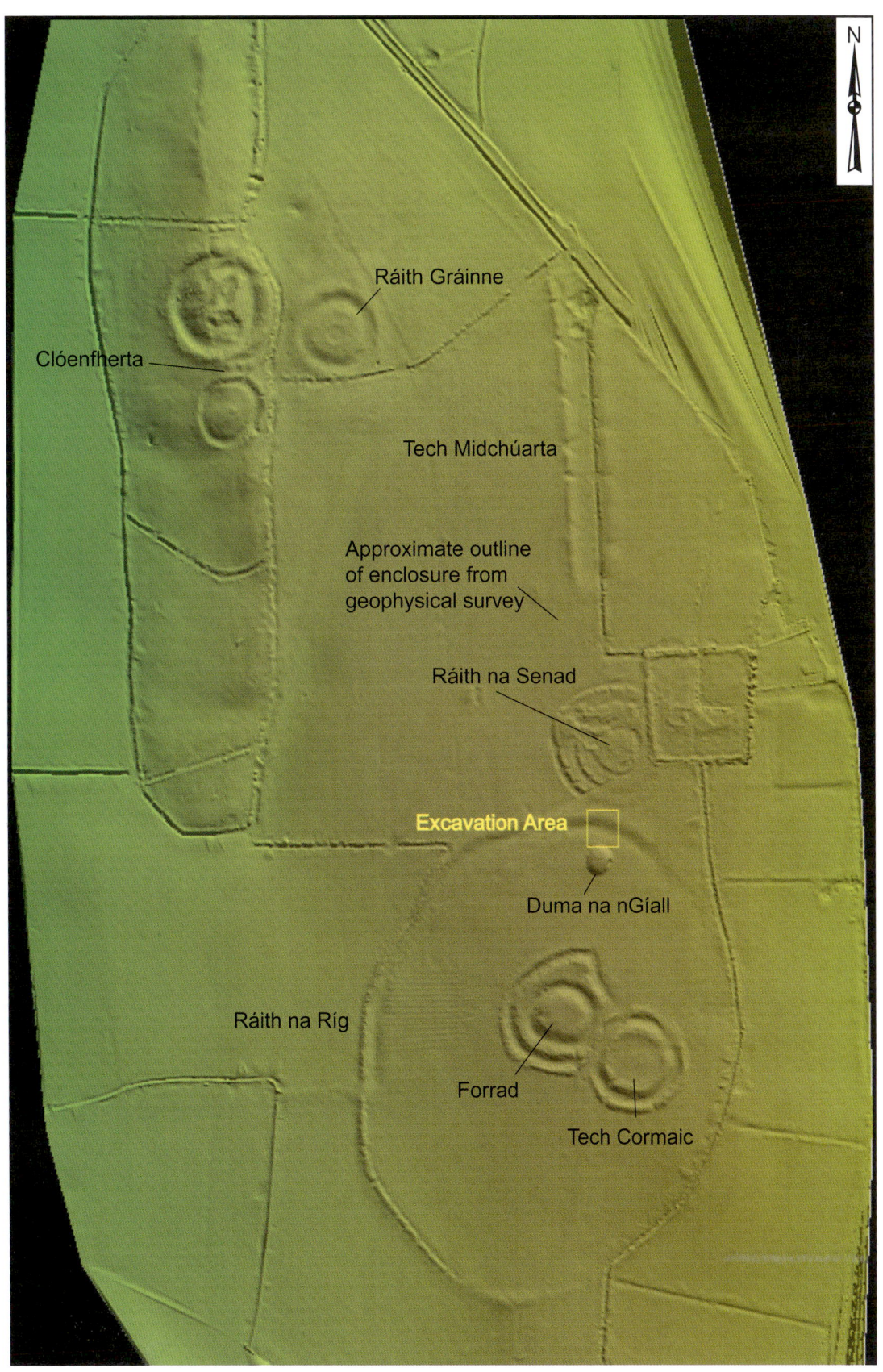

Fig. 1—Hill-shaded model of the Hill of Tara (based on the Tara archaeological survey).

Introduction

Tara, encapsulating the elements of power, prestige, kingship and mythology, has captivated the imagination of people for centuries. The earliest recorded survey of the monuments on the hill is found in the *Dindshenchas* ('History of places'), the earliest version of which is in the Book of Leinster, dating from about AD 1160 (Newman 1992, 70; Bhreathnach 1995, 27). This comprehensive study consists of a collection of Middle Irish legends, compiled in the form of prose and poetry, that claim to explain the origin and background of the names of the monuments at Tara. Further surveys were undertaken during the nineteenth century. In the 1830s a cartographic survey was carried out by the Ordnance Survey in conjunction with John O'Donovan, who researched some of the placenames. This was followed by the first archaeological survey of Tara, by George Petrie, the results of which were published in 1839. This survey was a landmark in the development of Irish archaeology and is still regarded as a valuable source of information concerning Tara. The work included an in-depth analysis of the principal documentary sources relating to Tara, detailed descriptions and scale drawings of all surviving monuments on the hill, and the production of an idealised map of Tara in which he included monuments which were no longer visible but whose general location he calculated from his reading of *Dindshenchas*. Some years later a shorter survey, based mainly on Petrie's work, was compiled by the Rev. Denis Murphy and Thomas J. Westropp (1894). In the early 1900s further survey was carried out by R.A.S. Macalister (1919; 1931; 1938-56).

Throughout the centuries Tara has generated an aura of uniqueness, symbolic of Irish identity and, above all, as a place that is regarded as sacred and special. Because of this reputation Tara was subjected to the deplorable depredations carried out by the British Israelites between 1899 and 1903, with their partial destruction of Ráith na Senad (Newman 1997, 94–5; Carew, forthcoming). It was thus with great sensitivity and political diplomacy that Professor Seán P. Ó Ríordáin began excavations on the Hill of Tara in 1952. This project began with excavations at Ráith na Senad between 1952 and 1953, followed by Duma na nGíall between 1955 and 1956. The plan of campaign was sadly cut short by Professor Ó Ríordáin's untimely death in 1957. Professor Ruaidhrí de Valéra completed the excavations at Duma na nGíall in 1959.

As a result of this work, and in combination with more recent research and fieldwork, a considerable body of knowledge concerning the site has now been amassed (Ó Ríordáin 1955; Swan 1978; Raftery 1994, 65–70; Bhreathnach 1995; Fenwick 1997). In addition, detailed survey using the most modern methods and equipment has been carried out by the Discovery Programme under the direction of Conor Newman, which has increased significantly the number of recognised sites on the hill and established a foundation for all subsequent archaeological work at Tara (Newman 1997).

EXCAVATIONS CARRIED OUT DURING THE 1950s

As a result of the excavations carried out by Ó Ríordáin and de Valéra details concerning some of the monuments on the hilltop are now better understood. Although largely unpublished,[1] the surviving archives are available for study. Ráith na Senad, a complex series of earthworks, produced a wealth of information about activity dating from as far back as the Bronze Age and extending up to the late Iron Age (Cooney and Grogan 1994, 187–93; Waddell 1998, 330). The excavations carried out at Duma na nGíall not only confirmed that it was a passage tomb but also that it was reused for burial during the early and middle Bronze Age (Ó Ríordáin 1955). However, it is not specifically the details of these monuments that concern us in this report, but rather the excavation of two cuttings (Nos 23 and 24) across Ráith na Ríg, a large, roughly oval enclosure measuring 318m north–south by 264m east–west, which encompasses an area of about 5ha (55,000m^2) on the summit of the hill. This work was carried out by Ó Ríordáin between 1952 and 1955.

Excavation of Ráith na Ríg, 1952–5 (Fig. 2; Pl. 1)

In August 1952 the excavation of Cutting 23 was carried out 'to reveal whatever was left of the two outer banks of Ráith na Senad, and also to ascertain the relation (if any) between the outer ditch and bank of the Rath and the bank of Ráith na Ríg' (Ó Ríordáin 1953, site notebook). Cutting 23 consisted of a 2m-wide extension of the main north–south cutting across Ráith na Senad. A detailed ground-plan of this excavation was not located; only a west-facing section drawing survives (Fig. 2). Part of the excavation of Cutting 24 was carried out at the same time, extending from Ráith na Senad as far as the crest of the bank of Ráith na Ríg. This cutting was not

Pl. 1—Cutting 23. Ó Ríordáin's excavation across Ráith na Ríg, 1953 (Archaeology Department, UCD).

completed until 1955 (Fig. 4), when, as part of the Duma na nGíall campaign, a cutting was excavated running from Duma na nGíall to connect with the original 1953 cutting. As recorded by Ó Ríordáin, it was 'almost in line with Cutting 24 of 1953'. Apart from general notes, the only documentation to survive from the 1950s excavation of Cutting 24 is a drawing of the east-facing section and a ground-plan of the palisade trench.

These excavations revealed that Ráith na Ríg consisted of a bank with an internal ditch, V-shaped in profile. In addition, a palisade trench was located 2m from the inner edge of the ditch. The following descriptions and interpretations are from Ó Ríordáin's 1953 and 1955 site notebooks and from two section drawings recording the bank, ditch and palisade trench. The section drawing of Cutting 23 was recorded over two seasons on two separate sheets, with the junction between the drawings being the 'south peg' that was positioned on the surface of the bank. Ó Ríordáin distinguishes the layers by the use of coloured pencils. As the numbers visible on the section are a recent addition they will not be used in this report. Throughout the text the find numbers will be included with the appropriate layers, while descriptions will be found after the stratigraphic details.

Cutting 23: west-facing section

The bank (Figs 2 and 7 A–A)

This cutting as recorded by Ó Ríordáin shows the surviving bank measuring 10m in width and 0.8m in height, and apparently consisting mainly of redeposited boulder clay, presumably derived from the upper levels of the internal ditch. The first layer above bedrock was described as a *dark greyish layer*, above which was a thin layer referred to as a *humus-like layer*.

Pl. 2—Cutting 24. Portion of palisade trench excavated by Ó Ríordáin, 1955 (Archaeology Department, UCD).

This in turn was sealed by a *light brown/bright yellow layer*. Above this, and extending across most of the area of the bank for a distance of 5.4m from north to south, was another thin layer, described by Ó Ríordáin as a *black charcoal layer* and *black habitation stratum under bank of Ráith na Ríg*. A layer directly above this charcoal lens, described as *light brown,* was present on the southern face of the bank, while a fairly thick layer of *dark stony, shaly upcast* formed the upper portion of the northern face. A quantity of iron slag amounting to 5.44kg was found within this layer. It directly overlay the charcoal and also the southern light brown layer. A humus layer seals the bank. Ó Ríordáin recorded that the black charcoal-rich layer, which he considered to pre-date the construction of the bank, contained evidence for metalworking activity in the form of a crucible fragment, iron slag, iron staples, nails and bronze fragments, as well as a flint flake. Animal bones were also found within the layer. The only features that he recorded were two post-holes with shallow gullies running from them. These gullies had been truncated by the 0.4m trench that he had excavated along the eastern face of the cutting. Ó Ríordáin's notes reveal that they were cut from the black layer and that their fill was consistent with that of the black layer. He also recorded that iron slag and charcoal were found within the fill of the small trenches. Another similar post-hole is visible in Ó Ríordáin's eastern section face, as well as a small stake-hole.

Finds from the black charcoal-rich layer beneath the bank (too poorly preserved to justify illustration)

BRONZE

E615:225.[2] Flat strip found in two conjoining pieces. One side is flat in section, the other slightly

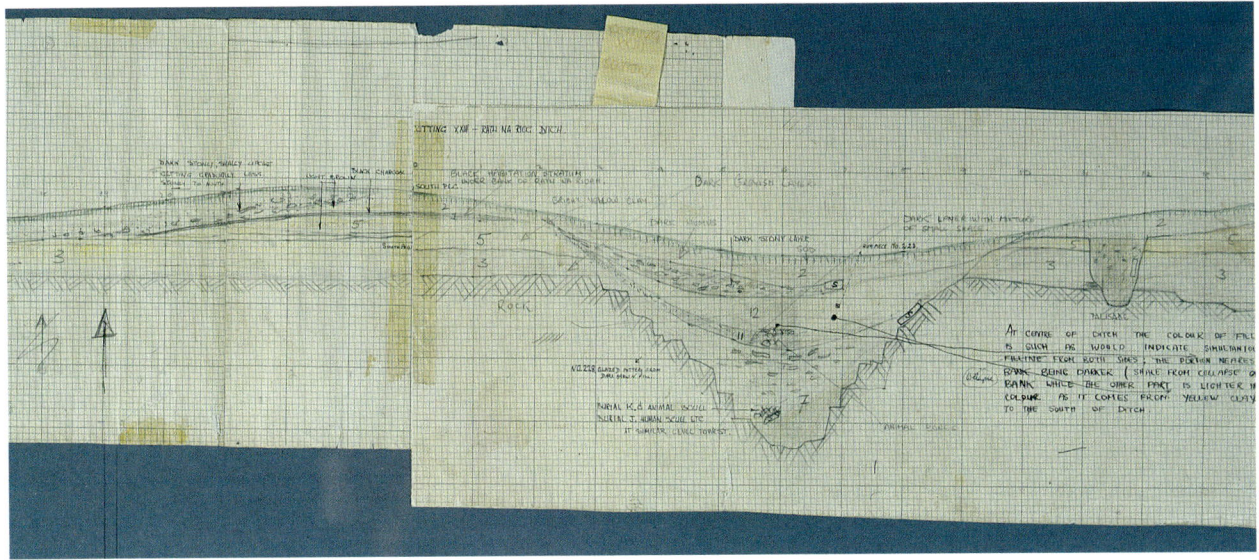

Fig. 2—Cutting 23 (A–A), west-facing section through the bank and ditch of Ráith na Ríg and palisade trench, as recorded by Seán P. Ó Ríordáin, 1952–3 (Archaeology Department, UCD).

convex; the latter end has a central V-shaped notch 2.9mm deep, with immediately beyond it a sunken rivet (D. 2mm).[3] The opposite end, which is poorly preserved, has what may be the vestige of another notch. 46mm by 7.4mm by 1.2mm.

IRON

E615:231a, b, c. No. 231a is a staple with rectangular cross-section. L. 97mm by 7mm by 8–5mm; tines 24mm by 9–5mm by 5–4mm. Nos 231a and c are two unidentifiable lumps of iron accreted with slag.

E615:232. Corroded tanged iron object, 47mm by 12mm by 10mm; tang 9mm by 7mm.

E615:246a, b. A staple or joiner's dog in two pieces with nails embedded. Staple 93mm by 11–9mm by 8mm; tine 24mm by 10mm by 6mm; nails L. 42mm and 26mm.

E615:252. Disintegrated iron object described in the find index as an iron nail. L. 54mm.

E615:253. Corroded iron strip, 68mm by 20mm–8mm by 4mm.

E615:254a, b. Two stems and fragments; 254a: 40mm by 10–5mm; 254b: 40mm by 6mm.

E615:226. Nail or tack, possibly Roman. L. 22mm. The square-sectioned stem is 3.5mm; the flat corroded head is 16mm by 11mm.

CRUCIBLE FRAGMENT

E615: S21. Fragment of crucible; fine-grained grey material with bronze accretions. L. 23mm.

FLINT

E615:24a. Flint flake.

The ditch (Figs 2 and 7 A–A)

The ditch reached an impressive depth of up to 3m and was 7m in maximum width. It had been cut through boulder clay into the underlying shale, and the rock-cut edges had been excavated in a series of narrow shelves or steps (Pl. 10). Ó Ríordáin's section drawing records seven distinct layers. The basal layer appears to consist of primary silting (not labelled), above which is a stony earth layer (not labelled). At the junction between the two layers human bones (labelled Burial K) and an animal skull (not identified) came from close to the outer (northern) edge of the ditch. Ó Ríordáin also records finding part of a human mandible and seven teeth (labelled Burial J) at the same level on the western side of the cutting. Both 'burials' most likely represent part of the same deposit. It is not clear whether the animal and human bones were associated or whether the human remains represent a formal or a casual deposit. Neither of these layers is labelled on the section drawing. At a level of 2.4m above the base of the ditch is a layer described as a *dark layer with a mixture of small shale*. This layer stretches right across the ditch fill and contained animal bone and a small quantity of iron slag. Above this is a substantial layer described as representing simultaneous collapse from both sides of the ditch. The northern side, containing more shale, came from the bank material, and the southern side was lighter in colour *as it comes from yellow clay to the south of the ditch*.

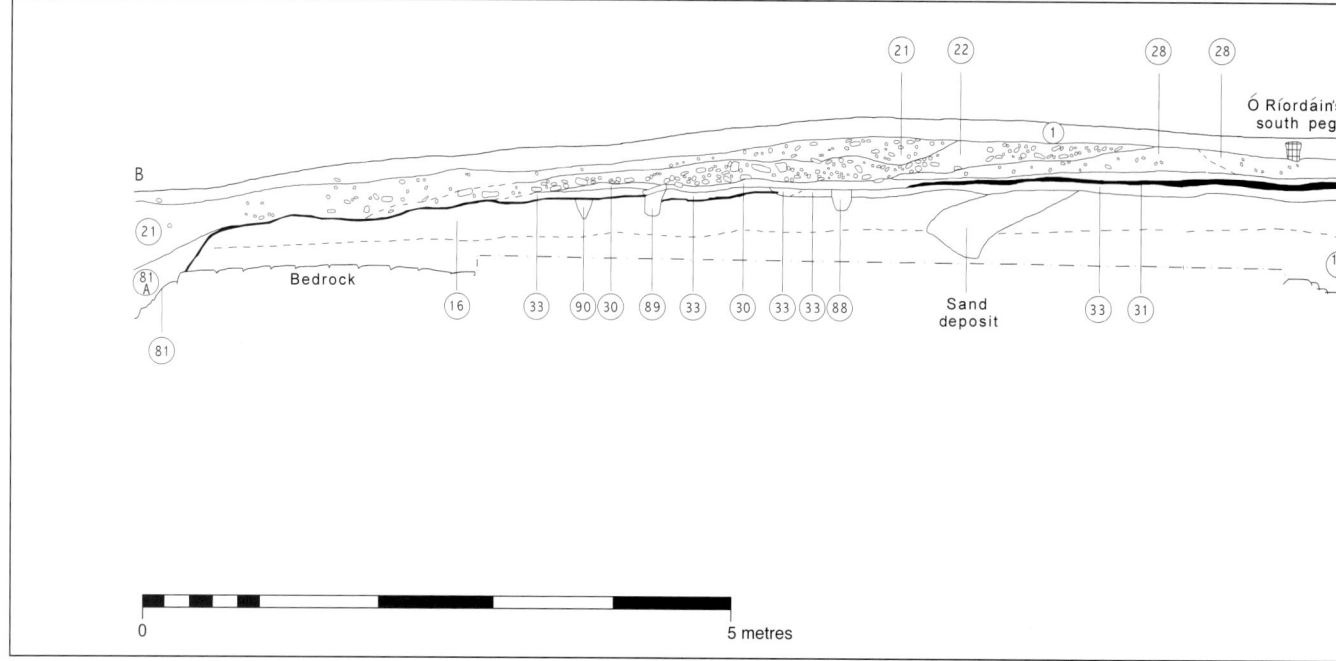

The only find recorded from this layer is an unglazed rim sherd. Above this, stretching from the northern side of the ditch and reaching about midway along it is a *dark stony layer*, within which a sherd of post-medieval pottery was found. The uppermost layers below sod are labelled as *dark humus*, which is recorded as containing about 0.4kg of iron slag.

Finds from the ditch

POTTERY

E615:222. Unglazed rim sherd with internal bevel.

E615:228. Post-medieval base-angle sherd with lower portion of applied handle. Brown glaze is present on the interior and exterior surfaces.

The palisade trench (Figs 2 and 7 A–A)

From the surviving section drawings it was known that the palisade trench was located about 2m south of the ditch of Ráith na Ríg, running east–west. It is 0.64m wide and 1.08m deep, the lower 0.22m being cut into the underlying shale bedrock. Ó Ríordáin recorded that the trench was identified with great difficulty, as the fill was only slightly darker than the material from which it had been dug. A scatter of stones was exposed on reaching the upper levels of the trench (one of which is still visible in the eastern section face); he interpreted these as representing packing stones that would have secured upright posts. He also records that between the stones a small number of burnt bone fragments and indeterminate pieces of iron were found; however, none of these survive. The stratigraphy recorded on the section drawing in this area is not labelled, but following the colour of the shading on the bank and ditch portion of the drawing, it can be said that below the sod was a layer of dark humus similar to the uppermost layer within the ditch fill of Cutting 23. Below this, and the level from which the palisade trench was cut, was a layer of bright yellow clay. Finally, a thick layer of dark greyish clay, similar to that below the bank, was present above bedrock.

Cutting 24: east-facing section

The bank (Figs 4 and 7 G–G)

This cutting was excavated and recorded in the same manner as Cutting 23; as with the first cutting, Ó Ríordáin excavated a 0.4m-wide trench along the eastern face of the bank and palisade area until he reached bedrock. Under the southern portion of the bank a large oval charcoal deposit was noted at a depth of 0.55m. This layer, which Ó Ríordáin suggests might represent the old ground surface, extends north–south for a distance of 4.5m. He recorded that the layer representing the 'old ground level' dips into a wide trench or pit whose fill was composed of soft, dark clay in which a large quantity of charcoal appeared. It also included fragments of iron slag and bloom, a possible crucible fragment, a number of animal bones and what may be wattle impressions. It is not clear from the notebooks whether the latter were wattle impressions on clay fragments or impressions on the sides of the pit. Unfortunately it was not possible to locate these objects. The only other feature recorded from the dark charcoal layer is a small pit. Below the

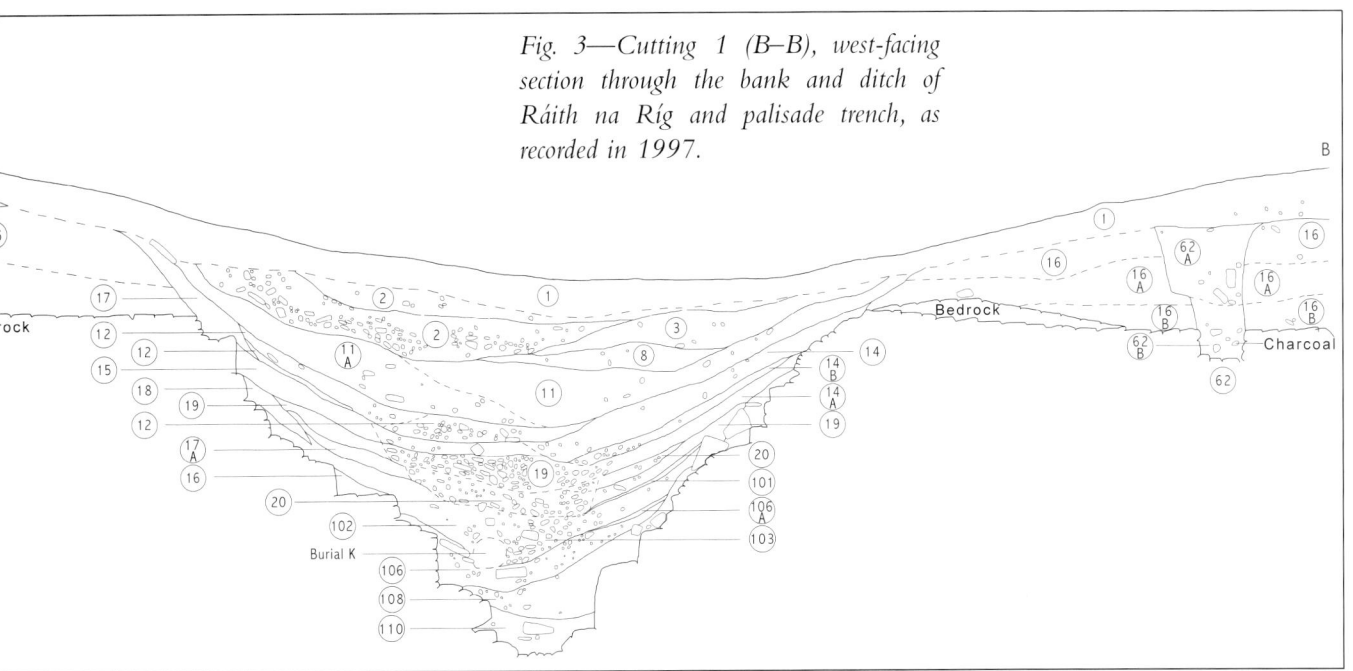

Fig. 3—Cutting 1 (B–B), west-facing section through the bank and ditch of Ráith na Ríg and palisade trench, as recorded in 1997.

dark layer Ó Ríordáin also noted a grey layer flecked with charcoal. Above the 'old ground level' was the bank of Ráith na Ríg, consisting of boulder clay below a level of shaly material.

The ditch (Figs 4 and 7 G–G)

Ó Ríordáin's section drawing records five distinct layers. The basal layer appeared to consist of primary silting. Within this layer, at a depth of 2.07m below sod, fragments of skull, described as possibly human, were found. Ó Ríordáin concluded that they were obviously thrown in as fragments and did not represent a formal burial. Above this was a dark fill containing lumps of shale and a large number of animal bones. The next layer consisted of a slightly curving deposit of decayed shale and dark soil 0.05m deep.

Above this was a band of dark humified brown soil that extended to a depth of 0.8m. Fragments of glazed pottery were apparently found within it. The uppermost layer, immediately under the sod, was a layer of shale slabs and stony dark clay, 0.4m in maximum depth, which Ó Ríordáin suggested was a recent deliberate fill.

The palisade trench (Figs 4 and 7 G–G; Pl. 2)

Ó Ríordáin recorded that at a depth of 0.3m below sod the line of the palisade trench appeared as a dark band with stones set on edge within it, running east–west. At approximately 0.45m below the sod post-holes within the trench became apparent. He recorded that the trench *was partly excavated at the eastern half and it was possible to distinguish post-holes and empty them*. Apparently, almost all contained packing stones, some bone and charcoal.

Discussion

The notes concerning the excavation of Ráith na Ríg are limited, with little interpretation presented by the excavator. It is clear, however, that Ó Ríordáin regarded the *black charcoal layer* that contained metalworking debris as a sealed deposit beneath the bank, thus pre-dating the construction of the large enclosure. There are no details concerning the interpretation of the relationship between the enclosure and the palisade trench. However, notes added to the field section indicate that Ó Ríordáin believed that the material thrown up from the palisade trench was deposited in the ditch at a high level, represented in the material on the southern side of the *dark layer with a mixture of small shale*, which was described as being lighter in colour than the material on the northern side. This would suggest that Ó Ríordáin considered the palisade trench to be a much later feature, post-dating a long period of bank collapse from the northern side of the ditch.

Little discussion was devoted to the finds uncovered during the excavation other than specifying that post-medieval sherds were found in the upper layer of the ditch in both cuttings. A discussion of the finds uncovered during the 1950s excavations will be included below with those from 1997.

Prior to the 1997 excavations, attempts were made to interpret the stratigraphy as recorded in the 1950s and to present a chronological sequence for Ráith na

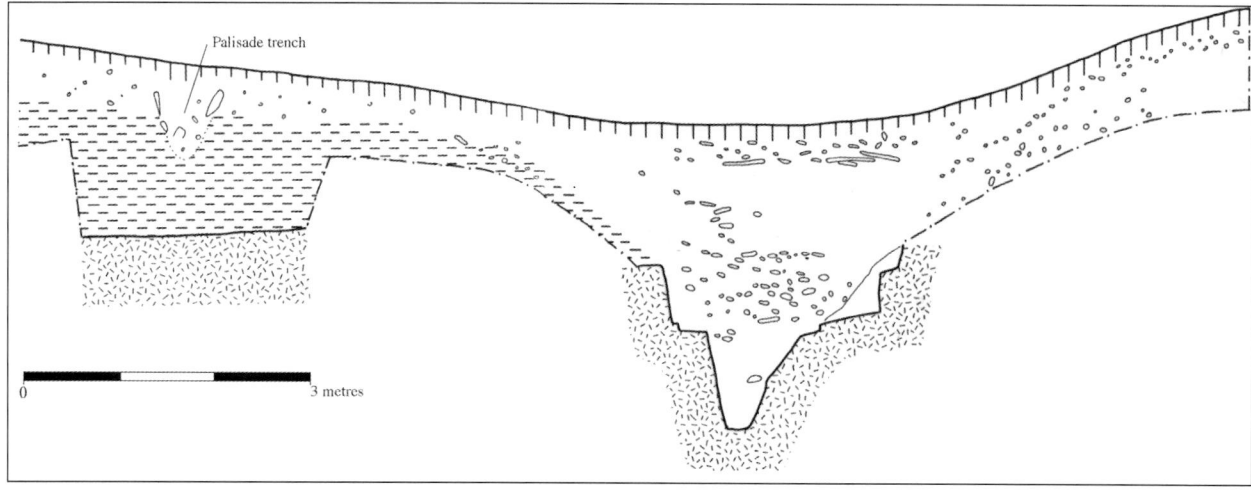

Fig. 4—Cutting 24 (G–G), 1955: east-facing section through the bank and ditch of Ráith na Ríg and palisade trench, as recorded by Seán P. Ó Ríordáin and Ruaidhrí de Valéra, 1955, 1956 and 1959 (U. Mattenberger, Archaeology Department, UCD).

Ríg and the palisade trench (Raftery 1994, 66; Newman 1997, 170–4). Accurate interpretations were hampered, of course, by lack of detailed information, but more importantly by confusing elements on the original section drawings. The main problem was that the natural, undisturbed boulder clay beneath the bank was interpreted as redeposited boulder clay. It should be pointed out that Ó Ríordáin clearly understood the true nature of the stratigraphy, but the vague labelling on the section drawing later led to misinterpretation. Another difficulty was that the west-facing section of Cutting 23 was recorded on two separate sheets over two seasons—the northern portion in 1952, the southern in 1953. The junction of the two drawings occurs at the 'south peg', which was positioned on the summit of the bank. Unfortunately the drawings were not matched accurately, thus understandably leading to misinterpretation. The reopening of the cutting in 1997 instantly clarified these anomalies, the interpretation of which will be presented below.

EXCAVATION OF RÁITH NA RÍG, 1997 (Figs 1, 3, 5 and 6; Pl. 3)

Thirty-eight years after the original campaign at Tara ended, the Discovery Programme resumed excavations. The objective of the excavations, which were carried out over a period of fifteen weeks from 18 August to 28 November 1997, was to reopen the old Cuttings 23 and 24[4] across the bank, ditch and palisade trench (Fig. 5). The main purpose was to excavate, record and sample the stratigraphy, using modern methods to answer specific questions. The aims outlined in the research design were: (1) to date the bank and ditch; (2) to retrieve environmental samples to provide background information on the flora, fauna and development of the site over time; (3) to provide information on the morphology and date of the palisade enclosure recorded on the interior of the ditch; (4) to investigate a potential deposit of metal slag from what then appeared to be within the make-up of the bank and from the ditch fill. During the 1950s excavations metal slag was found, but unfortunately these samples have not survived. It was anticipated that, if further examples were uncovered, their exact stratigraphic position would be recorded and that the metal content would be scientifically analysed. It was also hoped to establish the relationship between the bank and ditch of Ráith na Ríg and the palisade trench.

It was also initially proposed that a third cutting, on either the western or southern side of the enclosure, would be excavated to compare the stratigraphy with the evidence from the first two cuttings. Unfortunately, owing to the complexity and scale of Cuttings 1 and 2, time did not allow for this, and the excavation of a third cutting was postponed.

Pl. 3—View of site during excavation, from north-east (C. Brogan, Dúchas).

Cutting 1 (Fig. 6)

Prior to excavation, a survey was carried out by the survey department of the Discovery Programme to establish the exact location of Ó Ríordáin's original cuttings. After de-sodding of the area, it immediately became apparent that there was a problem concerning the southern limit of the cutting, which appeared to be unexcavated. However, when the position of Ó Ríordáin's 'south peg' (which was found in its original position) was reached, this puzzling situation was clarified. Instead of extending in a straight line from north to south, as recorded by Ó Ríordáin, the cutting in fact turned sharply to the west on reaching the 'south peg'. This presumably was decided by Ó Ríordáin in order to avoid a diagonal crossing of the ditch, which would have given a false impression of its scale.

When the backfill was removed from Ó Ríordáin's 2m-wide cutting, it was revealed that it had been excavated down to boulder clay, and no trace of his *black charcoal layer* survived (except in section). In addition, on reaching the undisturbed boulder clay, he excavated a narrow, 0.4m-wide trench flush with the west-facing section, down to the underlying shale bedrock. The only features still visible were two odd-shaped depressions in the boulder clay (Fig. 9). When the backfill was removed it was revealed that they were two post-holes with shallow trenches running from them (post-holes 1 and 2). These trenches had been truncated by the narrow trench that Ó Ríordáin had excavated along the eastern edge of the cutting. However, another such post-hole, as well as a small stake-hole, are visible in Ó Ríordáin's section face. Ó Ríordáin recorded these features in his notebook. He stated that they were cut from the black layer and that the fill was consistent with that from the black layer. He also noted that iron slag was found within the fill of both post-holes. They were quite substantial in size; post-hole 1 measured 0.28m by 0.25m by 0.34m deep, while post-hole 2 measured 0.23m by 0.25m by 0.44m deep. Post-hole 1 tapers from its mouth to a rounded base, while post-hole 2 tapers from its mouth to a pointed base. Both have a shallow but distinct trench extending north-eastwards. It is possible that a continuation of the trench from post-hole 2 is visible in the west-facing section. The third post-hole, visible in the section face, is 0.19m wide and 0.18m deep. It was also cut from the black layer. It was not possible, owing to the limited area excavated, to explain what

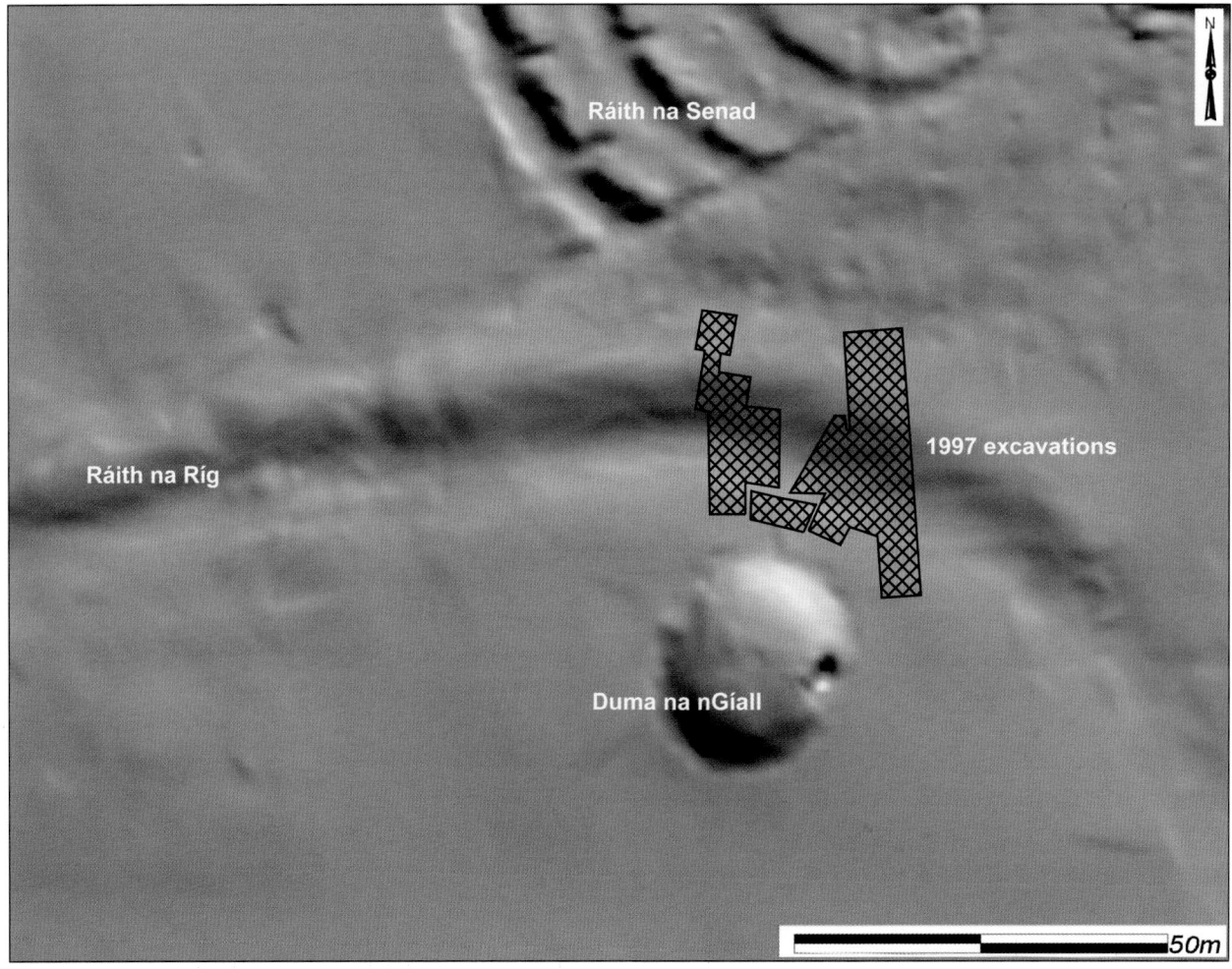

Fig. 5—Hill-shaded model showing area of 1997 excavation (based on the Tara archaeological survey).

they represent, but it is likely that they formed part of a structure. It was anticipated that the excavation of the extension through the bank would throw more light on their function.

Finds recovered from Cutting 2 backfill

From area of bank (not illustrated)

IRON

B:24.[5] Curved length of iron with a visible joining seam along the length of the object. Possibly part of a vessel handle. L. 54.5mm. D. 3.1mm.

B:25. Small, slightly curved object, 13.5mm by 14.9mm, T. 2.4mm.

B:56. A round-sectioned rod with a corroded expanded head, probably a nail. L. 52.4mm. D. 6.3mm.

B:57. Fragments of a flat object, probably a knife blade.

B:58. Horseshoe nail. L. 33mm. D. 14.4mm.

B:60a–b. 60a is a thin round-sectioned rod which appears to be hollow at one end, possibly a needle. L. 6.4mm. T. 4.2mm. 60b is part of a square-sectioned stem which tapers to a rounded point, probably part of a nail.

B:51. Irregular lump, 39mm by 21.3mm.

B:98. Irregular lump, 26.6mm by 21.8mm.

From area of ditch

LITHICS

B:97a, b. Chert.
B:15. Quartz.

POTTERY

B:66. Body sherd fragment, very hard micaceous fabric with a high grit content (≤ 1.8mm). Grits and mica visible on both surfaces. Exterior surface orange; grey core; interior surface orange. T. 6.9mm. Probably from an Early Neolithic carinated bowl. From same vessel as **49a:1–3**, **45:3**, **48:1** and **41:8**.

VITRIFIED CLAY FRAGMENTS
  B:4   B:34
  B:10–13   B:37
  B:18   B:49
  B:20–3   B:99
  B:30

IRON SLAG
  B:1–3   B:24   B:50
  B:5–9   B:27   B:52
  B:14–17   B:29   B:55
  B:19   B:31–6   B:57
  B:22   B:38–42

After Ó Ríordáin's cutting had been examined and recorded, a 2m by 10m extension was opened on the western side across the bank and ditch. The area through the bank will be referred to as Extension 1, and two small areas which were excavated to the south-west and to the east of the main cutting will be referred to as Extension 1A and Extension 1B; the new cutting through the ditch will be referred to as Extension 2 (Fig. 6). From the 1997 excavation four phases of activity were identified.

Phase 1. Industrial activity sealed by the bank of Ráith na Ríg: it consisted of a metalworking area with evidence for iron-, bronze- and possibly glass-working.

Phase 2. A grey sticky layer which possibly represented a period of inactivity, when an accumulation of natural material sealed the industrial activity, prior to the construction of the bank.

Phase 3. The construction of the bank and ditch of Ráith na Ríg and the palisade enclosure.

Phase 4. Modern agricultural activity in the form of linear trenches, which represented nineteenth-century cultivation ridges.

Phase 1: pre-bank industrial activity (Figs 8, 9 and 7 D–D; Pls 4–7)

This layer (F33), which seemed to represent an old sod level, was the earliest phase of activity in the excavated area. In section it was recognisable above the undisturbed boulder clay (F16) as fine, light brown silty clay, gritty and sticky in consistency, that averaged between 0.06m and 0.07m thick. It was found over most of the excavated area except at the northern end outside the area of the bank, where it was presumably removed by later cultivation (Fig. 8). The soil micromorphological analysis that was carried out on various soil horizons throughout the excavation revealed that F33, although primarily a boulder clay layer, showed evidence for biological activity in the form of ash, charcoal flecks and burnt bone inclusions. It is suggested that the ash content may represent 'ash manure', added to improve a poorly developed soil (see Appendix 6), though it might well be just the result of the intensive human activity that was carried out in the area at this time.

Several features were found cut into this layer, the most important being a metalworking hearth (F38). A black charcoal-rich spread (F31), 0.01–0.03m thick, sealed all the features and may represent the accumulated debris or rake-out from the large hearth (F38), or from another hearth that was not uncovered in the area of excavation. Soil micromorphological analysis suggests, because of inclusions of rounded, burnt bone fragments and organic matter, that the bulk of the deposit was derived from occupation debris (see Appendix 6). It was present over most of the excavated area, being especially dense in the immediate vicinity of the metalworking hearth (F38), where it was composed of pure charcoal. In places it was patchy and thin and, as in the case of F33, it did not survive outside the northern limits of the overlying bank. There were also patches of orange scorching around the hearth. Seventy-three lumps of slag were present within this layer, the majority found in the immediate vicinity of the hearth. Objects and fragments of bronze[6] and iron, including a complete axehead (**31**:20), as well as fragments of shattered blue glass, crucible and mould fragments and pieces of vitrified clay were found throughout this layer. Crew (this volume) identified a further nineteen iron fragments while examining the slag from this layer. A small number of bones, including those of cattle, horse and pig, were also found (see Appendix 2). Radiocarbon results of bone samples produced a date of 370–60 cal. BC (OxA-8824; 2170 ± 40 BP).

Features associated with Phase 1 level of activity

Metalworking hearth F38 (Figs 8–10; Pls 8 and 9)

This was centrally located along the west baulk of the cutting and only a portion was accessible in the 2m-wide cutting. Approximately half of it continued beneath the baulk. The portion excavated measured 1.1m north–south by 0.96m east–west. It had gently sloping sides and a maximum depth of 0.3m into subsoil. The base and sides were coated with a red clay lining (F84), up to 1.5cm thick. The fill consisted of distinctive layers of ash and charcoal representing intensive burning (Fig. 10). The basal layer (F37b) consisted of pure charcoal containing larger-than-

Pl. 4—Cutting 1 and Extension 1 from east, showing pre-bank, charcoal-rich industrial level (F31) and associated features. Cultivation trenches representing later activity (F79, F80) are to the right of the photograph (H. Roche).

Pl. 5—Cutting 1: Extension 1. East-facing section through bank of Ráith na Ríg and underlying industrial layer F31 (H. Roche).

Pl. 6—Cutting 1: Extension 1. East-facing section through bank showing its northern extent and the underlying surviving limits of the charcoal-rich layer F31 (H. Roche).

Pl. 7—Cutting 1: Extension 1. View of pre-bank industrial level from south-east, showing metalworking hearth F38 and associated features (H. Roche).

Pl. 8—Cutting 1: Extension 1. Metalworking hearth (F38) beneath bank of Ráith na Ríg from north, showing accumulated burnt debris within hearth (H. Roche).

Pl. 9 —Cutting 1: Extension 1. Metalworking hearth (F38) beneath bank of Ráith na Ríg from east (H. Roche).

Pl. 10—Cutting 1 (B–B), west-facing section through ditch of Ráith na Ríg (C. Brogan, Dúchas).

Pl. 11—Cutting 1: Extension 1. Burial of child (F105) within ditch of Ráith na Ríg (H. Roche).

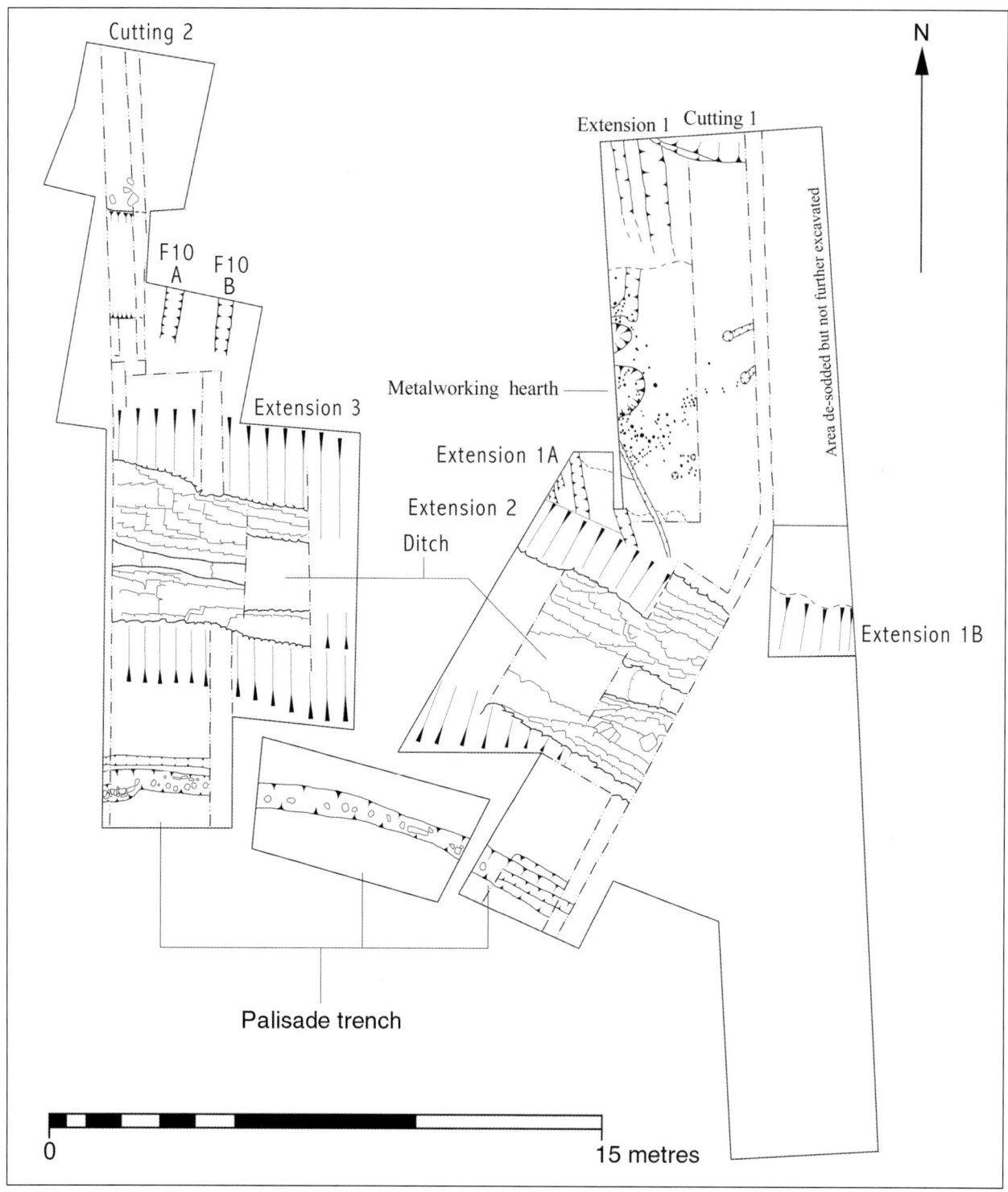

Fig. 6—Ground-plan of 1997 excavation.

average lumps. Above this was a layer of white ash with charcoal flecks (F37a), up to 0.04m thick. This was followed by another layer of pure charcoal (F37), up to 0.02cm thick. Above this was a deposit of creamy white charcoal-flecked ash (F36), 0.03cm thick, containing fragments of burnt bone, a block of burnt oak and a lump of granite that fell to pieces on removal. Samples from the oak produced a date of 200 cal. BC–16 cal. AD (UCD-9822; 2090 ± 60 BP). Towards the surface of the hearth was a dense charcoal layer with white ash inclusions (F34). This filled the centre of the hearth but also spilled out over the southern side. It measured 1.7m north–south by 0.69m east–west and was up to 0.02m thick. The

Pl. 12—Cutting 1: Extension 1. Animal bone scatter on surface of Iron Age stony fill (F12) within ditch of Ráith na Ríg (H. Roche).

uppermost layer consisted of a mixture of grey and white ash with charcoal flecks (F32). It measured 1.2m north–south by 0.7m east–west and was 0.01m thick. Finds associated with the hearth consist of bronze fragments, crucible and mould fragments, vitrified clay fragments and lumps of iron slag (see Appendix 1). Five fragments of blue glass were found in the immediate vicinity of the hearth. In addition, while examining the slag samples Crew (this volume) identified three further iron fragments.

Around the edge or rim of the hearth a number of stake-holes were present. They had an average diameter of 0.02–0.03m, and some were up to 0.2m deep. Others occurred in pairs, which may be evidence for supports for a clay superstructure surrounding the hearth (see Appendix 1).

Patches of red clay or scorching (F84a) were found around the north-eastern edge of the hearth, and a layer of mixed ash with red burnt clay inclusions (F35), measuring 1m by 0.5m in maximum dimensions, was located on the southern side of the hearth. Iron fragments, crucible, mould and vitrified clay fragments and slag were found within.

Further evidence for structures, perhaps shelters or screens, was provided by 190 stake-holes (F39) scattered throughout most of the excavated area, with the majority occurring immediately south of the hearth.

Four more substantial post-holes were found while excavating F31. The largest (F72) was located 1.1m to the east of the hearth. It measured 0.33m in diameter at the surface, 0.13m at the base, and was 0.3m deep. Three stratified layers of fill were observed. The basal fill (F72c) consisted of brown clay silt, very soft in consistency and containing decaying granite. F72b was a light brown stony clay, loose in consistency, 0.06m deep. The uppermost layer (F72a) consisted of yellow clay silt, which reached a maximum depth of 0.12m and contained a vitrified clay fragment. The black charcoal-rich layer (F31) surrounded and sloped into the sides of the post-hole. It would appear that F31 accumulated around the post and slipped into the sides when the post was in position.

Post-hole F71, in the south-east area of the cutting, measured 0.24m north–south by 0.21m east–west by 0.15m deep. The upper portion of the fill (F71a) consisted of grey-brown silt clay with charcoal flecks and some small stones. The lower 0.15m was similar but looser in consistency. It contained three lumps of iron slag.

Post-hole F76 was located in the southern area of the cutting. The fill consisted of brown/grey silt clay with charcoal flecks and some small stones, and also contained mica fragments from decayed granite. It measured 0.18m east–west by 0.16m north–south by 0.11m deep.

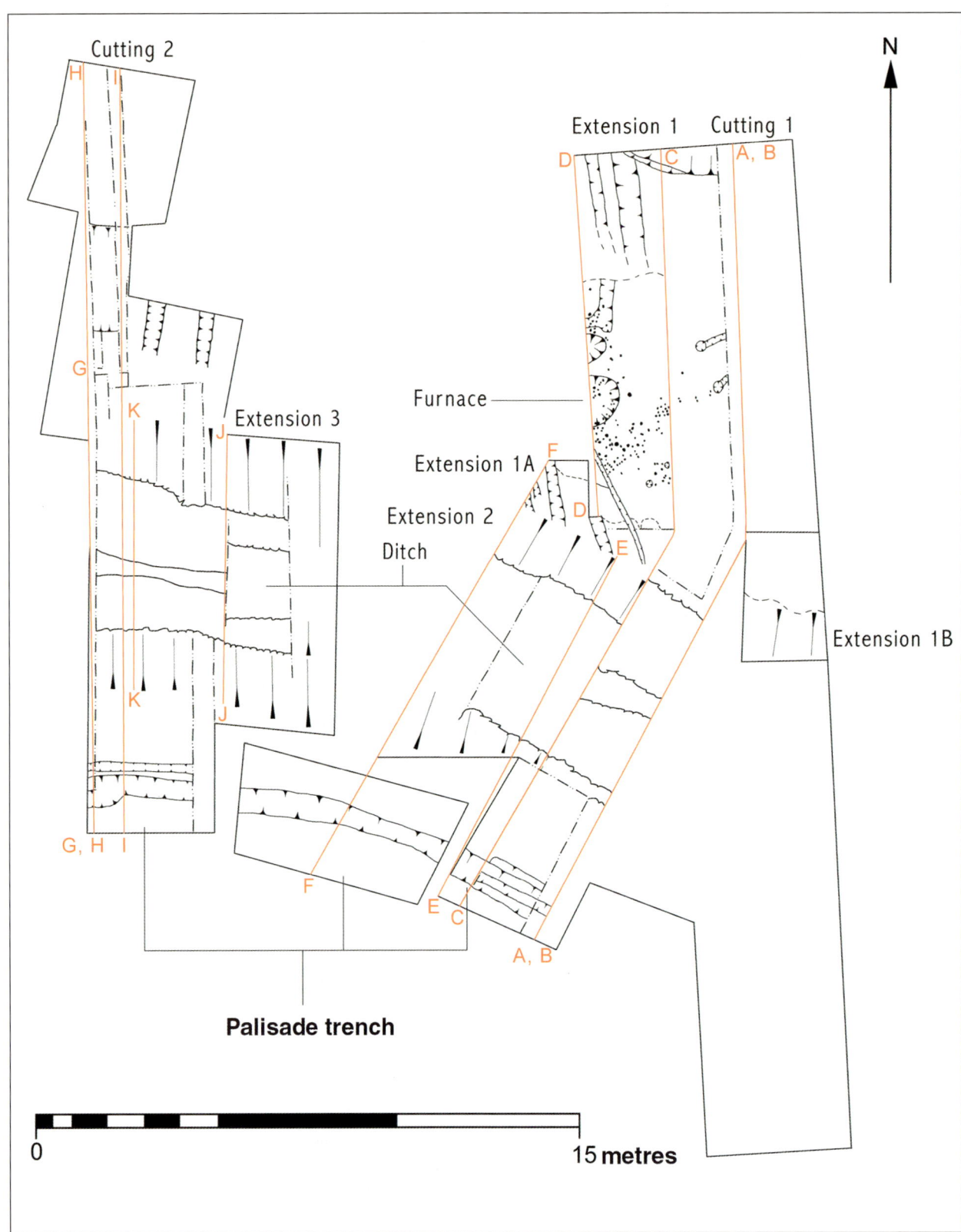

Fig. 7—Reference location for section drawings.

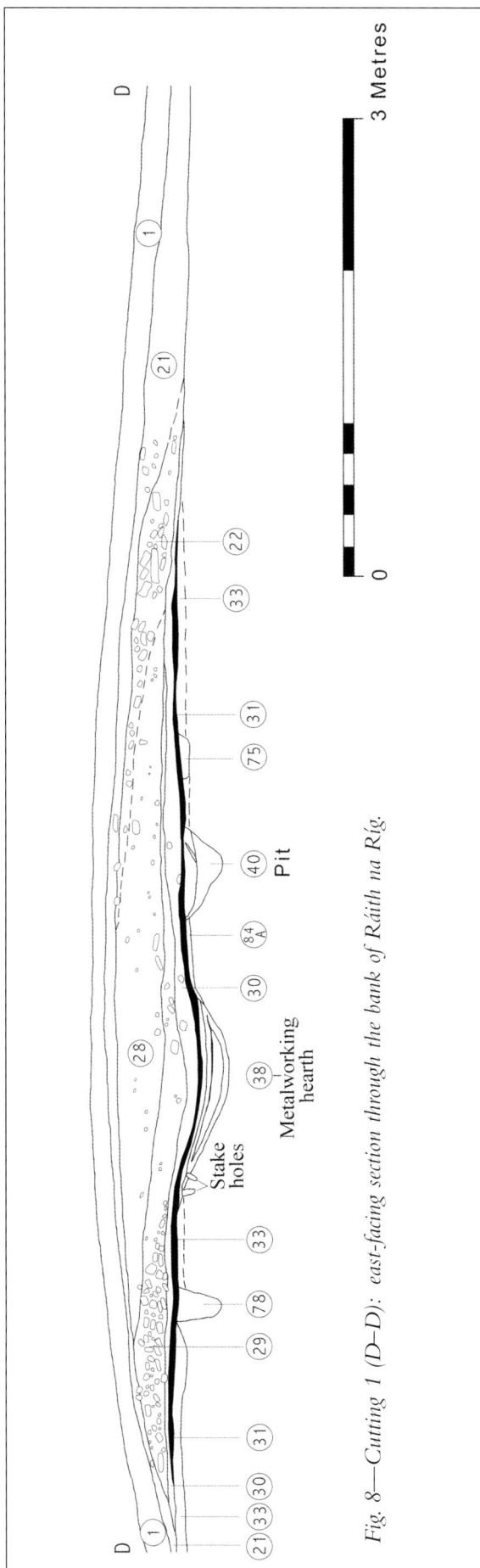

Fig. 8—Cutting 1 (D–D): east-facing section through the bank of Ráith na Ríg.

The smallest post-hole, F73, was located 0.14m to the east of the metalworking hearth. It was 0.12m in diameter and 0.18m deep. The fill consisted of soft, dark brown silt clay containing charcoal and mica flecks from decayed granite. A vitrified clay fragment and lumps of slag were found within the fill.

An oval pit (F40) was located 0.4m to the north of the metalworking hearth and ran into the western limit of the excavation. It measured 0.7m north–south by 0.5m east–west by 0.23m deep. Four stratified layers were observed within the pit. From base to surface these consisted of a light brown/yellow silt clay (F40d), 0.15m deep, which contained some charcoal flecks and iron fragments. Above this was a thin layer, 0.02–0.03m deep, of grey charcoal-flecked ash (F40c), followed by a charcoal layer less than 0.01cm deep (F40b). This was sealed by F40a, an ash and clay layer less than 0.01m deep.

A narrow, slot-type trench (F78) was found in the southern area of the cutting (Fig. 9). It was U-shaped in profile and measured 3.2m in length with an average width of 0.18m and depth of 0.3m. The fill consisted of a dark, charcoal-flecked clay/silt and included a few lumps of iron slag and an occasional fragment of animal bone. There was no evidence for posts or planking and it is possible that it represents a flue from the metalworking hearth. It ran into the west baulk and was truncated at its southern end by the ditch of Ráith na Ríg.

Approximately 1.3m north of the metalworking hearth a feature that may represent the corner of a rectangular structure was uncovered (F75). It consisted of a shallow, north–south trench that formed a right angle with another shallow trench running into the west baulk (Fig. 9). The north–south trench showed up as a linear spread of pure charcoal pieces, while the east–west trench was more of a grey, charcoal-flecked material. The north–south trench measured 1.3m in length, 0.3m in width and 0.06–0.08m in depth. The east–west trench was 0.5m long, 0.24m wide and 0.05–0.07cm deep. Two stratified layers of fill were observed within each. The upper portion of the fill consisted of charcoal-rich earth (F75a) containing iron fragments and a fragment of blue glass. The lower portion (F75b) consisted of an orange/brown charcoal-flecked earth. When the fill was removed, eight stake-holes were found at the base of the trench. It is difficult to say whether they are contemporary with the structure or represent later features contemporary with activity surrounding the metalworking hearth. The northern part of the trench appears to have been destroyed by later agricultural activity, the surviving portion having been protected

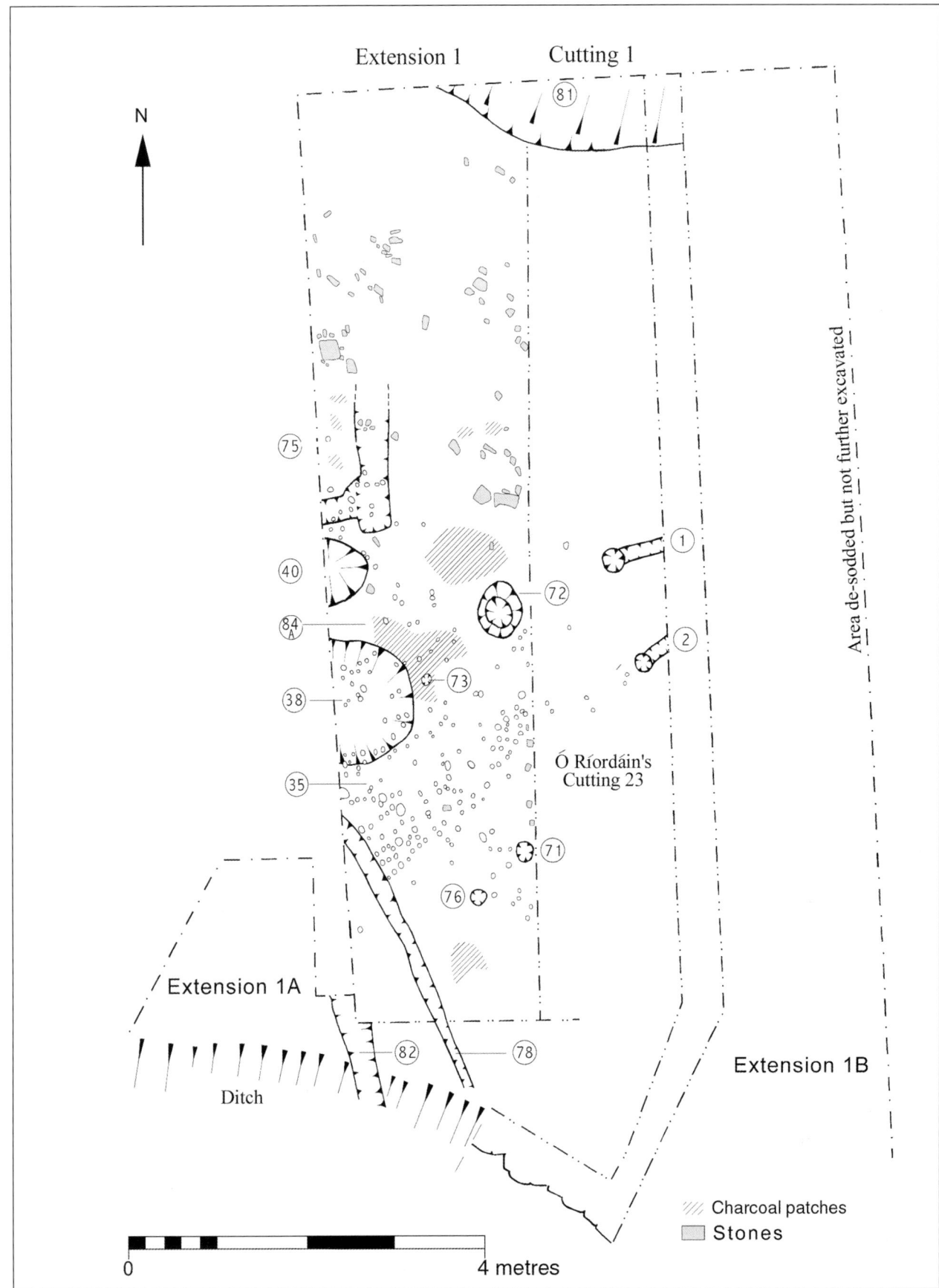

Fig. 9—Cutting 1: ground-plan of features associated with industrial activity beneath the bank of Ráith na Ríg.

by the overlying bank layers.

The only other feature recovered at this level was part of the outer ditch of the later monument, Ráith na Senad (F81). This was located at the northern limit of Cutting 1. It was only possible to excavate the upper fill as the excavated area, which was 2.4m long and 0.7m wide, just caught the southern edge of the ditch. The fill consisted of sterile, gritty clay and no finds were recovered.

Extensions 1A and 1B (Figs 6 and 9)

These two small areas were excavated in order to investigate the relationship between the black charcoal-rich layer (F31) and the ditch of Ráith na Ríg. The evidence for the charcoal-rich layer at the southern end of Extension 1 was patchy and it was not possible to ascertain whether it had originally extended out as far as the ditch of Ráith na Ríg or whether it had in fact been cut by the ditch. Excavation of Extension 1A revealed that the cultivation layer (F21) was directly on the subsoil and very little of the black survived; again it was not possible to establish conclusively the relationship between it and the ditch.

Apart from evidence for further modern cultivation trenches (F77, F85 and F86, which will be discussed later) the only archaeological feature found in this small area was a linear trench (F82). It ran in a north–south direction, continuing beneath the west baulk of Extension 1; the visible portion was 1.2m long, 0.2m wide and 0.14m deep. The fill consisted of dark brown clay/silt, loose in consistency and charcoal-flecked throughout. Iron slag and fragments of vitrified clay were found within the fill. The trench was truncated by the ditch of Ráith na Ríg and there is no evidence to suggest that it was not contemporary with Phase 1 activity beneath the bank.

The excavation of Extension 1B was more successful, even though the stratigraphy was again relatively shallow. However, the charcoal-rich layer (F31) survived up to a depth of 0.02m in this area and it was clear that the ditch of Ráith na Ríg had indeed cut through this layer.

Finds from pre-bank industrial activity (Figs 24, 25; Pls 19, 20, 25)

BRONZE

34:1. Rod fragment, square in section. L. 53.4mm. Max. T. 2.7mm.

34:2. Fragment of sheet bronze with part of a small circular perforation, 8.4mm by 7.7mm.

34:11. Small irregularly shaped lump of bronze.

31:1. Two fragments from a small circular perforated object, 6.4mm by 4.3mm.

31:4. Small solid oval droplet. D. 8.9mm. T. 5.8mm.

31:5. Finely executed nail with a finely tapering point; the head is hammered flat. L. 17.9mm. D. of head 1.8mm.

31:9. Rod fragment, square in section, tapering from a diameter of 2.5mm to 1.7mm. L. 34.9mm.

31:77. Two small corroded lumps of bronze.

31:23. Bronze flecks.

IRON

75a:1a, b, c. No. 75a:1a is a thin, round-sectioned length of iron. L. 40.5mm, D. head 4.4mm, D. stem 3.5mm. No. 75a:1b is a curved fragment, possibly part of a gouge. L. 19.6mm, T. 2.6mm. No. 75a:1c is a flattish oval fragment, 28.2mm by 13.7mm, T. 7.4mm.

35:2. Flat-headed nail with square-sectioned stem. L. 36.3mm. W. 13.7mm. T. 10.1mm.

35:6a, b. Two irregularly shaped lumps; the larger may be a nail. 35:6a — L. 31.7mm, T. 17.6mm. 35:6b — L. 22mm, T. 15.7mm.

31:2. A square-sectioned hollow rod with a slight expansion at one end. L. 62.8mm. Max. D. 6.5mm.

31:2a. Rectangular-sectioned, tapering length of iron. L. 27.4mm. T. 7.8mm.

31:8. Large curved object, possibly part of a bracket, 40.6mm by 32.9mm, T. 5.5mm.

31:11. Rectangular-sectioned rod. L. 23.4mm. T. 6mm.

31:12. Rectangular lump which tapers towards a rounded end; the other end is damaged. Rectangular in section. 20mm by 11.8mm, T. 9.2mm.

31:20. Unlooped, socketed axehead. The blade expands gently from the socket, forming a narrow waist below the socket. One side of the cutting edge is missing, but it appears to have been slightly curved. The mouth of the socket is rectangular in shape. L. 150mm. Average T. 6mm. W. of blade 52mm. External W. of socket 30mm by 22mm. Internal W. of socket 22mm by 12mm.

31:22. Large rectangular lump, 37.8mm by 21.9mm, T. 13.6mm.

31:24. Triangular object with the narrow end round in section. L. 35mm. Max. T. 15.7mm.

31:61. Curved fragment, 45.8mm by 42.1mm, T. 8.5mm.

31:70. Square-sectioned rod, with one pointed end. A possible awl. L. 35.9mm. Tapers from 6.1mm in diameter to 4.6mm.

31:71. Round-sectioned fragment which is hollow at one end. Possibly part of a socketed tool. L. 43.8mm. T. head 17.7mm. T. shank 9.7mm.

31:78. Small lump, 19.2mm by 12.6mm, T. 8mm.

31:79. Small circular hollow object, a possible pinhead, 4.3mm by 4.5mm.

31:80a-d. Four fragments; two are flat, with one showing the remains of a possible tang, which might indicate that the fragments represent a knife. It is possible that the two smaller pieces are not part of the same object.

31:100. Large irregular-shaped lump which appears to represent a flat-headed nail with a round-sectioned stem, embedded in corrosion.

GLASS

75a:2. Tiny flecks of cobalt blue glass.

31:21. Shattered, cobalt blue glass fragment, 6.1mm by 3mm.

31:57. Shattered, cobalt blue glass fragment, 8.2mm by 6.4mm.

31:58. Shattered, cobalt blue glass fragment, 11.8mm by 8.1mm.

31:59. Shattered, cobalt blue glass fragment, 4.1mm by 2.9mm.

31:60. Shattered, cobalt blue glass fragment, 8.7mm by 3mm.

31:94. Shattered, cobalt blue glass fragment, 3.5mm by 1.7mm.

CRUCIBLE FRAGMENTS

34:3a, b. Two rim fragments. They are thicker than the other examples and perhaps represent different objects. 34:3a — L. 20.4mm, W. at rim 29.6mm, T. at rim 13mm. 34:3b — L. 14.9mm, W. at rim 28.5mm, T. at rim 15.2mm.

34:4a, b. Two fragments; no. 34:4a is part of the rim. Vitrified matter is present on the exterior surfaces. No. 34:4a — L. 11.6mm, W. at rim 18.9mm, T. at rim 7.1mm. No. 34:4b — 28.1mm by 25.8mm, T. 8.7mm.

34:5a, b. Two fragments; no. 34:5a is part of a rim; both are vitrified on the exterior surface. No. 31:5a — L. 25.7mm, W. of rim 19.4mm, T. of rim 6.6mm. No. 34:5b — 24.3mm by 19mm, T. 9.6mm.

34:35. Fragment; vitreous matter on exterior, bronze residue visible on interior. L. 25.2mm. W. 25.9mm. T. 8.8mm.

34:6a–e. Five fragments; vitrified matter is present on the exterior surface of no. 34:10a. The largest fragment measures 26.1mm by 18.3mm in dimensions and 8.2mm thick.

34:12. Rim fragment. L. 23.4mm. W. at rim 17.5mm. T. of rim 7.6mm.

34:9. Rim fragment; vitrified matter present on both surfaces. L. 27.2mm. W. of rim 25.2mm. T. of rim 5.5mm.

35:1. Rim fragment; vitreous matter on interior. There is a splash of blue residue on the exterior surface. L. 18.3mm. W. of rim 5.9mm. T. of rim 6.7mm.

35:3a,b. Two rim fragments with vitrified matter on interior. No. 35:3a — L. 25.4mm, W. of rim 17.5mm, T. of rim 7.6mm. No. 35:3b — L. 19.7mm, W. of rim 20.3mm, T. of rim 7.7mm.

31:3. Fragment, 18.5mm by 15.1mm, T. 9.3mm.

31:10. Tiny fragment with bronze residue on interior, 4.9mm by 11.2mm, T. 6mm.

31:18b–f. Five fragments. Vitrified matter is present on both surfaces of the fragments. No. 31:18b — 25.4mm by 21mm, T. 8.2mm. No. 31:18c — 22.3mm by 13.1mm, T. 7.7mm. No. 31:18d — 16.7mm by 16.5mm, T. 11.9mm. No. 31:18e — 15.1mm by 12.2mm, T. 10mm. No. 31:18f — 20.1mm by 9.7mm, T. 9.9mm.

31:37. Fragment, 28.6mm by 21.8mm, T. 11mm.

31:37a. Rim fragment; vitrified matter on interior. L. 27mm. W. at rim 18.5mm. T. at rim 7.4mm.

MOULD FRAGMENTS

34:10. Five fragments and crumbs. The abraded fabric is compact, sandy and grit-free, ranging from grey to buff-orange in colour. The three largest examples show evidence for surface shaping but it is not possible to suggest the type of objects being cast.

34:13. Part of a mould with a curved exterior surface and rim. A subrectangular hollow with raised ridges at the edges is present on the interior surface. The fabric is hard and compact and contains visible grits. Vitrified matter is present on both surfaces, 28.9mm by 22mm, T. 16.8mm.

34:3. Thirty-nine fragments and crumbs. The abraded fabric is compact, sandy and grit-free, ranging from grey to orange in colour. The largest fragment measures 19mm in length. Some examples show evidence for surface shaping but it is not possible to suggest the type of objects being cast.

35:8. Eight featureless fragments and crumbs.

31:18a Part of a mould similar in form and fabric to 34:13, with a curved exterior surface and rim. A subrectangular hollow is present on the interior surface. Hard, compact fabric with some visible grits. Vitrified matter is present on both surfaces, 26.5mm by 27.9mm, T. 7.4mm.

VITRIFIED CLAY FRAGMENTS

34:9	73:8	31:33
34:14	31:6	31:34–5
34:16	31:14	31:40
35:4	31:17–19	31:75
72a:1	31:26–7	

IRON SLAG
34:7–8	39:51	31:7	31:62–9
34:13a	71b:1–2	31:15–16	31:72–4
34:15	72c:1	31:25	31:76
35:5	72c:2	31:28–32	31:81–93
35:7	73:1	31:36	31:97
36:1–4	74a:1	31:38–9	31:13
37b:2	82:1	31:41–56	

Phase 2: pre-bank grey sod layer F30 (Figs 8 and 7 D–D)

This layer sealed the Phase 1 activity and consisted of moist, medium-grey silty clay which contained some iron-pan. It extended from the southern area of the cutting for approximately 5.5m northwards. At the southern end it faded out approximately 1m short of the northern edge of the ditch of Ráith na Ríg. This appears to be a result of modern cultivation as there was about 0.25m of surface cover over the layer in this area. Along the northern end it faded out and became patchy where the bank of Ráith na Ríg ran out. Thus, as in the case of F33 and F31, it survived only where it was protected by the overlying bank material. This grey layer formed an even surface but varied considerably in depth, ranging from 0.1m to 0.01m. It was at its deepest where it sealed the area of the metalworking hearth (F38) and pit (F40). The surface of this layer was clean and smooth and also quite level, with no features cut into it. Cattle, horse and pig bones were impressed into the surface (see Appendix 2), and samples produced a date of 153–41 cal. BC (UB-4478; 2065 ± 16 BP). Fragments of bronze, iron, crucibles and vitrified clay were found near the base of the layer. A significant amount of charcoal flecking was present throughout the layer and there were twenty lumps of slag particularly concentrated towards the base of the deposit. However, most of this slag may well be from the surface of the underlying black charcoal-rich layer (F31). While examining the slag from this layer Crew (this volume) identified two further iron fragments.

It is uncertain whether this layer represented a natural accumulation or was deliberately spread over the industrial area before the bank was constructed. The results of the soil micromorphological analysis revealed that it was similar to F33, and the primary source for the deposit was glacial till or boulder clay. Biological activity had also resulted in the limited mixing of underlying F31 (black charcoal-rich layer) and F30, resulting in the upward movement of material. As well as containing charcoal and bone fragments, there was a relatively high proportion of organic matter. The observation of the *in situ* growth of rootlets was interpreted as suggestive of a vegetated surface, upon which the later bank material was dumped (see Appendix 6). However, since this layer was also visible in the section of the bank in Cutting 2, some 16m to the west, it is more likely to represent natural accumulation.

Finds from grey sod layer (Fig. 24)

BRONZE

30:1. Small, roughly circular solid bronze object, one end slightly pointed. D. 6.1mm. T. 4mm.

30:10. Small, circular, flattened solid object. D. 9.1mm. T. 5.6mm.

30:31. Fragment of sheet bronze, probably part of a mounting or binding on a wooden or leather object, 13.2mm by 7.2mm.

30:32. Small, roughly circular solid object. D. 7mm. T. 5.1mm.

IRON

30:2. Triangular object, possibly part of a small tanged chisel. L. 31.6mm. Max. T. 7.2mm.

30:3. A rectangular-sectioned rod. L. 43.1mm. Max. D. 6.9mm.

CRUCIBLE FRAGMENTS

30:13. Rim fragment, slightly vitrified on interior with bronze residue visible. L. 21.3mm. W. at rim 19.3mm. T. at rim 8.2mm.

30:29. Fragment, 28.1mm by 20.6mm, T. 6.9mm.

30:30. Rim fragment. Vitreous matter on rim interior, traces of bronze visible on interior. L. 33.5mm. W. at rim 21.2mm. T. at rim 7.2mm.

30:35. Rim fragment; vitreous matter on interior. L. 20.5mm. W. at rim 29mm. T. at rim 7.4mm.

VITRIFIED CLAY FRAGMENTS
30:11	30:21
30:15	30:27–8
30:17–19	30:33–4

IRON SLAG
30:4–9	30:20
30:12	30:22–6
30:14	30:36–40
30:16	

Discussion

Evidence from the pre-bank levels represents an important and complex chronological sequence. The number of features and finds associated with metalworking indicate intense activity. What is also of particular importance is that both ferrous and non-ferrous metalworking, and possibly also glass-working, were carried out at the Tara workshop. It was initially thought that the large hearth (F38) was a metalworking furnace (Roche 1999, 23–6), but scientific examination of the slag, and the presence of hammer scale, has confirmed that there is no evidence for smelting and that this large feature is more likely to represent a metalworking hearth which could have been used both for iron-smithing and for non-ferrous metalworking. As Crew and Rehren point out (see Appendix 1 for detailed analysis and discussion), 'the size distribution of the Tara slags is typical of small-scale secondary metalworking and the large number of low-density slag fragments seems to be a particular characteristic of non-ferrous metalworking'. Despite these observations, there is doubt concerning the exact function of the hearth, as it seems unnecessarily large to carry out the functions of a smithing hearth, and no comparative examples can be cited (see Appendix 1). Evidence for Iron Age metalworking activity from sealed contexts in Ireland is rare. A recent excavation at Ballydavis, Co. Laois (Keeley 1999, 29), uncovered the remains of eight furnaces that appear to be more or less contemporary with the Tara hearth. One of these measured 2.3m in diameter and it can be suggested that, like the Tara example, it is overly large for a furnace. An example of a small furnace was found at Rathgall, Co. Wicklow (Raftery 1994, 148). However, this has been dated to the second or third century AD, making it much later than the Tara example (Table 1, p. 57). The crucible and mould fragments at Tara present a rare example of stratified Iron Age bronzeworking in Ireland. The black charcoal-rich layer appeared to have accumulated during the life of the metalworking activity but also continued to accumulate when this activity, at least in the area excavated, had ceased. It is possible that the lower levels of the black layer represent rake-out from the large metalworking hearth, but the accumulation of the upper level that actually seals the hearth was the result of throw-out from burning activity from an area not yet excavated. However, as already mentioned, the black material is not solely the result of industrial activity. As well as a small number of animal bones found during the excavation, soil micromorphological analysis revealed tiny fragments of bone and organic matter within the layer, indicating that there was also a domestic element within this horizon.

Visually the overlying grey layer (F30) resembled an accumulated sod level, and this interpretation was strengthened by the results of soil analysis. The presence of *in situ* rootlets and the distinct boundary between the surface of F30 and the first layer of the overlying bank suggest an abrupt dumping of material on a grassy surface (see Appendix 6). Inclusions of bone, charcoal and finds within F30 show that activity was continuing nearby. It should be pointed out, however, that the finds were mainly found near the base of the layer and could well have been incorporated from the underlying black layer. It is clear that a period of inactivity occurred in this area, which continued long enough for a sod layer to develop. Unfortunately it is not possible to calculate exactly how long it would have taken for this to accumulate, but the dates obtained for this layer and that of the metalworking activity overlap and indicate that it developed over a relatively short period of time (Table 1, p. 57). A similar turfline sealed smithing deposits in the east gateway at Maiden Castle. Within this layer parts of three articulated skeletons of two cows and a sheep were found (Sharples 1991, 100). These deposits were interpreted by Hingley (1997, 12) as possibly associated with rituals connected with the final act of ironworking or as rather later in date.

The finds

The excavation of this limited area produced a small but informative sealed assemblage of finds that from the results of the radiocarbon dates could be as early as 370 cal. BC. As well as the metalworking debris, consisting of slag, vitrified hearth lining, crucible and mould fragments, forge waste and offcuts and some identifiable iron and bronze objects were also found. Of the 30 fragments of crucible, twelve are rim sherds, representing up to seven complete crucibles. The fragments are too small for reconstruction but they appear to have come from crucibles of triangular shape and probably measure about 55mm across. In Britain the triangular crucible was dominant for much of the Iron Age. At Danebury it lasted into the first century BC, but generally by the first century AD it had been replaced by other types (Northover in Cunliffe and Poole 1991, 411–12). An examination of the fabric prompted Crew and Rehren (Appendix 1) to suggest that the Tara crucibles fall in between the period of open, top-fired vessels of the type used during the Bronze Age and beyond, and the Roman and later crucibles which were fired from the outside. Thin-section analysis established that they are associated with the working of high-tin bronze. An interesting element is the presence of high-iron-content slag or dross adhering to the internal surface of the crucibles (see Appendix

1 for detailed analysis and discussion of crucibles).

Fifty-four small mould fragments were also present in this assemblage, but are unfortunately too small and indistinct to allow identification of the type of object being cast (see Appendix 1).

The finding of blue glass splinters is important. While the larger splinters may have come from either a bracelet or very large beads, it is also possible that they came from a block of imported raw glass. Analysis carried out to determine their chemical composition established that they consisted of soda-lime silica-base glass; although it was not detected by energy-dispersive spectroscopy analysis, it is more likely that the colour was derived from cobalt oxide rather than copper. Their composition is similar to the range typically found with Iron Age and Roman soda-lime silica glass (see Appendix 1). Although these splinters could represent raw material for the production of glass objects, no evidence for glass residues was found associated with the crucibles and therefore this suggestion must remain speculative.

Although many of the iron and bronze fragments which consisted of rods and lumps appear to be offcuts or waste, a small group of identifiable tools and objects were present. The most impressive object was a socketed iron axehead (**31**:20), complete except for the absence of a small portion of the cutting edge of the blade. This type of axe could have been used for tree-felling or in more detailed woodworking. Toolmarks found on Iron Age timbers from the Corlea and Derraghan trackways indicate the use of flat, narrow, relatively straight-sided blades (O'Sullivan 1996, 330, fig. 435), of a type that would have been similar to the Tara axe. Except for a general similarity to the axehead from Feerwore, Co. Galway (J. Raftery 1944, fig. 4:38; B. Raftery 1994, 149), parallels within Ireland for this tool are, to date, unknown. This, of course, is not surprising, as few Iron Age tools are known from Ireland. The earliest form of iron axe in Ireland was the socketed looped axe, of which only a few are recorded. This was followed by the unlooped, socketed Tara type, which was later superseded by shafthole axes (Raftery 1984, 238–41; 1994, 118). Exact parallels are also absent from Britain and the Continent, the closest example coming from the excavations at Beeston Castle, Cheshire. However, that tool is smaller and has a curved blade slightly expanding from the socket. It is also described as being a 'somewhat delicate adze' rather than an axehead (Stead in Ellis 1993, 53, fig. 36:3). Slightly broader examples were also found at Manching and Dünsberg in Germany (Jacobi 1974, Taf. 13:260, 16:287; 1977, Taf. 15:5–10).

Timber construction material is present in the form of nails, a bracket and a joiner's dog, found during the 1997 and also the 1950s excavations. The nails from both excavations are similar, with flat heads and square-sectioned stems (**31**:100, **35**:2, E615:246b, E615:226). The bracket (**31**:8) and joiner's dog (E615:246a) also suggest construction and would have been used to secure wooden boards or planks. Except for similar objects found during the excavation of Ráith na Senad (Grogan et al., forthcoming), other Irish parallels from secure Iron Age contexts are not known. Parallels have been found at Manching, where thousands of examples of nails and identical joiner's dogs occurred in third-century to first-century BC contexts (Jacobi 1974, Taf. 73:1379, 1380–1; Taf. 70:1304–10).

Other iron objects include a possible awl (**31**:70), probably for boring small holes in leather, or a gouge for woodworking (**75a**:1c) and fragments from a knife blade (**31**:80a–c). One length of square-sectioned rod (**31**:2) is of particular interest, as it is hollow. It is not possible to say whether it is fragmentary or is a complete object. However, it certainly demonstrates the skill of the Tara blacksmith in forging such a fine length of iron.

Most of the bronze recovered, the rod fragments, droplets and lumps probably also represent waste or offcuts. Similar pieces were found associated with the metalworking area at Gussage All Saints in Dorset (Wainwright 1979, 125). A small fragment of sheet bronze with small perforations (**34**:2) may have been a decorative strip that was probably attached to a wooden or leather object. The only other identifiable piece was a small nail-like object (**31**:5). This had obviously been hammered flat at one end but was too small to have been load-bearing. It may have been used to attach something relatively light, such as leather, to a wooden background.

Phase 3: the construction of the bank and ditch of Ráith na Ríg

The bank (Figs 3 and 8)

The bank material lay directly on the grey sod layer (F30). The surviving remains were surprisingly shallow, only reaching a maximum height of 0.52m.

Stratigraphically, the earliest deposit was F29, the first upcast layer from the digging of the ditch. It consisted of light brown/orange silt clay, containing charcoal flecks and grey clay inclusions. The layer extended across most of the excavated area, up to 0.5m in length, but varied in depth. Along the eastern

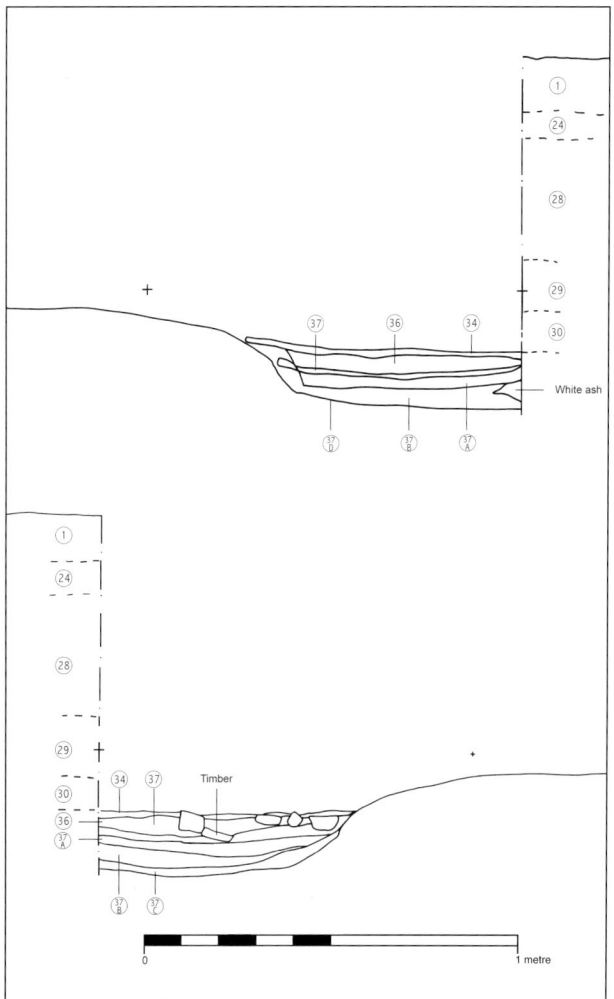

Fig. 10—Cutting 1. Top: section through metalworking hearth (F38) from north. Bottom: section through metalworking hearth (F38) from south.

limit of the area it was quite shallow, at most 0.01m deep, while along the western limit of the excavation it reached a depth of 0.1m; it became extremely inconsistent on the northern end of the cutting. A small bronze droplet, vitrified clay fragments and fifteen lumps of slag were found within the layer. In addition, while examining the slag samples, Crew (this volume) identified a further fourteen iron fragments. These objects were obviously derived from the portion of the charcoal-rich metalworking area that was cut through during the digging of the ditch.

Part of the northern area of F29 was sealed by a layer of shale (F27), within which flat shale blocks ranging in size from 0.01–0.02m up to 0.2m by 0.1m by 0.02m were found. The deposit measured 2.4m in length (north–south), 1.43m in width and 0.2m in maximum depth, and was not visible in the section faces. Eight fragments of slag were found within this layer.

Above this, and at its deepest in the western area of excavation, was a layer of redeposited boulder clay (F28) containing occasional small stones and charcoal flecks. It measured 4.6m north–south and 2m east–west, with a maximum depth of 0.3m. Three pieces of slag were found near the base of this layer.

Concentrated on the northern side of the bank and stratigraphically above F28 was a layer consisting mainly of shale blocks (F22). The blocks ranged in size from 0.02m by 0.04m up to 0.4m by 0.2m by 0.02m. This deposit was present for a distance of 2.5m (north–south) and was approximately 0.3m deep at its northern limit; it faded out at its southern limit. The material was derived from bedrock removed during the digging of the ditch. Two lumps of slag were found within the layer.

Beneath the 1997 sod level, and covering the entire area of excavation, was a layer of cultivation soil (F21). This consisted of dark brown clay silt containing fragmented shale, reaching 0.2m in maximum depth. Nine lumps of slag were found within this layer. Towards the base of the layer two linear features were found (F25 and F26), which represent modern, probably nineteenth-century, cultivation trenches (see below, p. 71). F1 represents the modern sod level, within which an iron key, a sherd of post-medieval pottery and vitrified clay fragments were found.

Finds from the bank (Figs 24 and 27)

BRONZE
29:16. Small, roughly circular solid object. D. 7.6mm. T. 5.5mm.

IRON
1:32. Modern door key. L. 99.8mm. T. stem 7.9mm.
1:23. Modern key.

POTTERY
1:34. Body sherd fragment. Hard, good-quality fabric with a moderate content of what appears to be decayed grey grits (≤ 2mm). The exterior surface appears to be decorated with a broad shallow groove and an oblique incised impression. Dark orange throughout. T. 13mm. Possibly post-medieval or even modern.

CLAY PIPE
1:35. Clay pipe stem.

VITRIFIED CLAY FRAGMENTS
22:20   29:19

29:6	1:22
29:17	1:37
29:18	1:49

IRON SLAG

21:5	22:19–21	29:24
21:9–10	28:1–3	29:1–5
21:12–16	27:3–10	29:7–9
21:18	29:9–13	29:1–5

Discussion

The bank stratigraphy clearly represents, in reverse order, the material that was removed during the digging of the ditch. The bronze droplet, slag and vitrified clay fragments indicate that the layer of industrial activity extended for some distance across the area where the ditch was later dug. This represented the southern limit of this spread as no evidence for it was found on the interior of the ditch. In the area of the ditch excavated it was calculated that the volume of stone quarried was 8.2m^3. Therefore it is reasonable to suggest that when the bank was first constructed the upper layers consisted of shale blocks. However, taking into account a certain amount of slippage back into the ditch and denudation as a result of later agricultural activity, the remaining evidence does not explain the absence of shale blocks either within the make-up of the bank or, as will be seen later, from the fill of the ditch. The volume of stone in the bank material and the fill of the ditch is only a mere 1.2m^3, which leaves 7m^3 of stone to be accounted for. There is no obvious explanation as to where the stone was taken or, indeed, for what it was used. The only suggestions that can be made are that the stone was deliberately removed from the bank before slippage occurred, or that most of the stone was removed from the site during the initial construction of the bank and ditch.

Ditch stratigraphy: Extension 2 (Figs 3, 7 C–C, E–E, F–F, 11–13)

This refers to the excavation of ditch fill west of Ó Ríordáin's section face (Fig. 3). The basal layer (F110), which was present across the entire area of excavation, was composed of shale fragments, very wet in consistency, and reached a maximum depth of 0.27m. It represents naturally eroded shale from the bedrock steps that formed the edge of the ditch. Above this was a fairly thin layer, 0.08m deep, of light brown/yellow clay (F109). It contained small stones and was sticky in consistency. The only finds recovered were two lumps of slag. The next layer, consisting predominantly of shale with clay and finer shale layers (F108), measured up to 0.38m in maximum depth, with the lower 0.19m having a greater stone content. Again this layer is the result of natural erosion. A quantity of bone representing cattle and horse was found throughout the layer, and samples produced a date of 193–95 cal. BC (UB-4479; 2105 ± 21 BP).

Above this was a very thin layer (F107) of decomposing shale fragments, 0.04m deep, which was present only in the western area of the cutting. Fourteen fragments of human bone, mainly skull and facial bones from an adolescent or younger adult (see Appendix 4), as well as cattle and sheep/goat bones (see Appendix 2) were found on the surface of the shale. This layer was probably deliberately deposited. The next layer (F106) was a deposit of light brown clay (Figs 11, 12 and 13). Above this was F103, a stony clay layer with a high proportion of decomposing shale, which extended across the entire cutting. On the surface of this layer, and situated towards its north-eastern limits, was the largely articulated skeleton of a six-month-old child (Fig. 14; Pl. 11; see Appendix 4). A small number of dog bones were also present and appear to have been deliberately deposited with the child. The burial was sealed with sod-like material (F104). This feature was not visible in section. Also within the fill of F103 was a human mandible, which belonged to the same individual as the portion of mandible found in a later layer, F15 (see p. 47). Bones representing cattle, sheep/goat, pig and dog were found, as well as two lumps of slag. Above this, and again extending across the entire cutting, was a thick layer of sticky stony clay (F102), 0.41m deep, which contained fine veins of charcoal. A small group of finds was found within this layer — a portion of a purple glass bangle of suggested Iron Age date (102:1), two pieces of iron and a lump of slag. Fragments of burnt and unburnt bone were present, representing cattle, horse, sheep/goat and dog (see Appendix 2). Bone samples produced a date of 68–138 cal. AD (UB-4480; 1890 ± 20 BP), and a date of 67–289 cal. AD (UCD-9821; 1875 ± 50 BP) was obtained from charred wood.

In the eastern part of the cutting, and overlying F102, a limited deposit consisting of charcoal with inclusions of ash was found (F101), 0.05cm in maximum thickness. The surrounding stones appeared to have been scorched, perhaps as a result of the dumping of hot ash and charcoal on them, or the stones and charcoal/ash material may represent a hearth that was thrown into the ditch. Fragments of burnt and unburnt bone, too small to be identifiable,

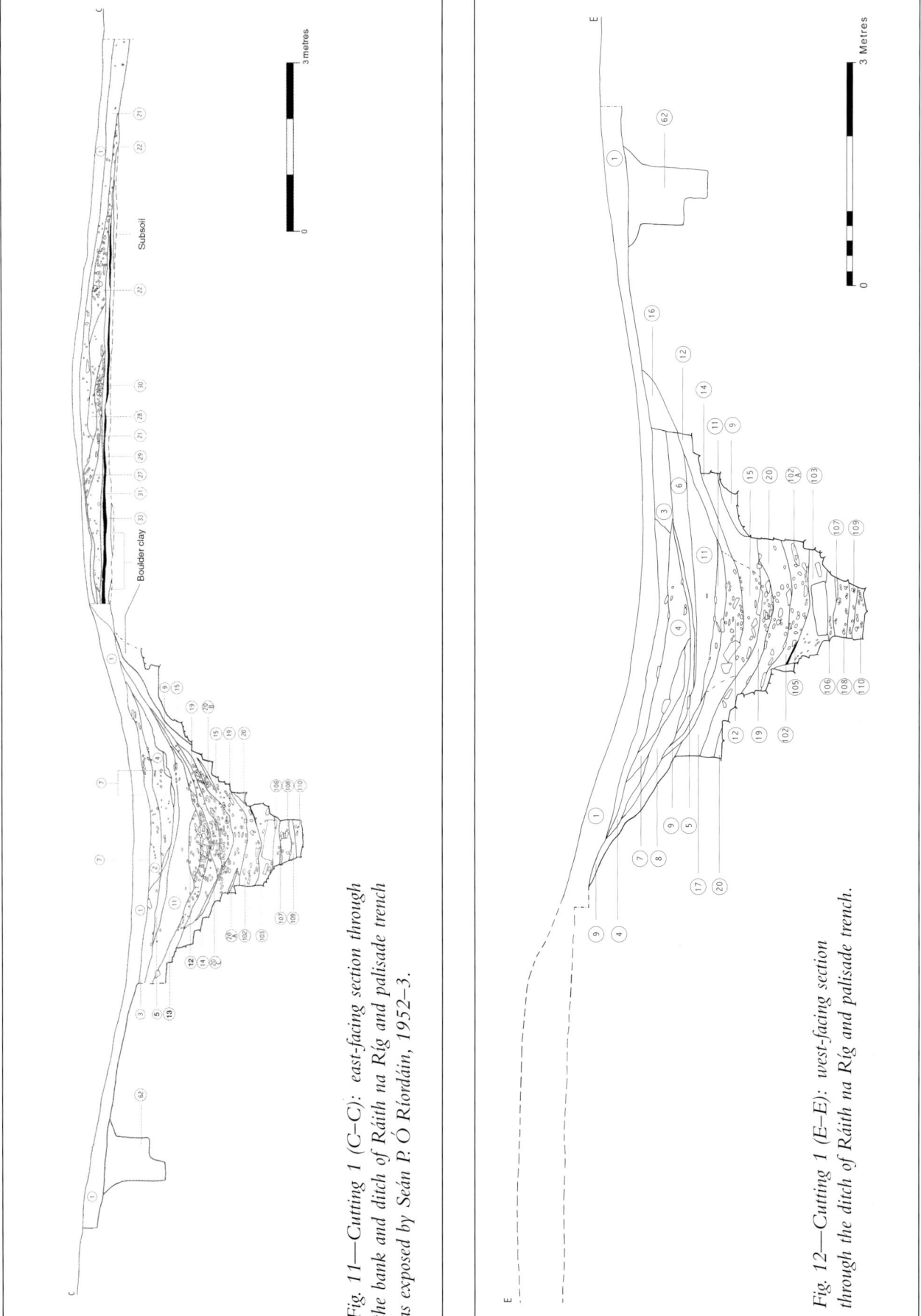

Fig. 11—Cutting 1 (C–C): east-facing section through the bank and ditch of Ráith na Ríg and palisade trench as exposed by Seán P. Ó Ríordáin, 1952–3.

Fig. 12—Cutting 1 (E–E): west-facing section through the ditch of Ráith na Ríg and palisade trench.

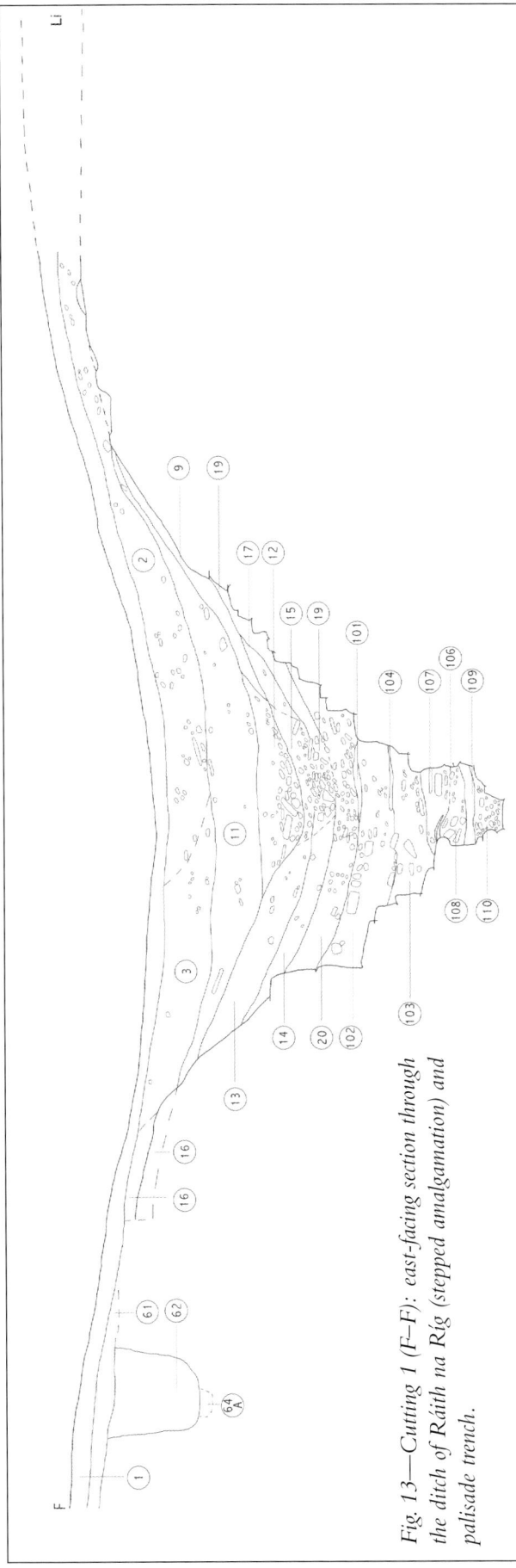

Fig. 13—Cutting 1 (F–F): east-facing section through the ditch of Ráith na Ríg (stepped amalgamation) and palisade trench.

were present within this deposit. Above this, and extending across the entire cutting, was a layer of sticky clay (F20), 0.23m in maximum thickness, with a high content of stones, especially on the northern side of the ditch fill. The fill on the southern side was paler in colour and contained less stones, but it appeared to merge with the fill to the north rather than constituting a separate layer. A small circular iron object was found within the fill, as well as bone representing cattle, horse, sheep/goat, pig and dog. Above this, and again extending across the entire northern area of the cutting, was a stony layer (F19) which reached a maximum depth of 0.18m. The soil surrounding the stones consisted of brown silty clay. A large amount of animal bone representing cattle, horse, pig and dog was found within this layer, and one piece of slag. Above this, a spill of essentially shaly material (F17), 0.21m in maximum thickness, was present on the northern slope of the ditch. This was made up of shale and brown stony clay and was very similar in composition to F9. Two lumps of slag were found within the layer.

The next layer (F15) was concentrated in the centre of the cutting and consisted of dark brown, stony material, 0.28m in maximum thickness. A small quantity of human bone was found, consisting of fragments of the hip-bone of an adult and part of an adult mandible, which joins with that found in F103 (see Appendix 4). This layer also contained a large number of bones, representing cattle, horse, pig and a red deer antler (see Appendix 2), and two lumps of slag. Above this was F14, which occurred on the southern slope of the ditch, abutting F15. It measured 0.21m in maximum depth and consisted of light brown-yellowish clay that contained some stones. F13, 0.33m in maximum thickness, was located on the southern slope of the western area of the cutting. It consisted of mid-brown silty clay with an admixture of small stones. The soil was moderately compact but very sticky in texture. Dark moist heavy clay (F12) with large stones was then revealed, extending over F13 and F9. It measured 0.44m in maximum thickness and contained two quartz fragments, two lumps of slag and a large quantity of bones, representing cattle, horse, sheep/goat, pig and dog, that were present from the surface of the layer to its base (Fig. 15; Pl. 12; Appendix 2). Bone samples produced a date of 261–406 cal. AD (UB-4476; 1689 ± 16 BP). Above this was a substantial layer (F11) which extended right across the upper fill of the ditch and was 0.47m thick. It consisted of light brown silty clay with very few stones. A sherd of post-medieval pottery was found within the layer, as well as two horseshoe nails, flint, composition very similar to F6, was a fairly thin layer (0.1m in maximum depth) of stone-free silty clay (F5). It was orange in colour, becoming light brown towards the northern slope. This was only visible on Cutting C–C (Fig. 11). A piece of flint and a fragment of quartz were the only finds recovered. Above this was a layer of loosely compacted grey/brown stony silt (F4), which was only present in the western area of the cutting. It measured 0.34m in maximum depth and contained flint, three fragments of quartz and two lumps of slag. F3 was present across the southern side of the ditch and consisted of loosely compacted, light brown/orange clay-like material containing small stones. It measured up to 0.26m in maximum thickness. The only objects found within this layer were a hollow scraper and quartz fragments. F3 merged with but was slightly overlain by F2, which was present on the northern side of the slope and consisted of a mixture of clay, stone and gravel. A bronze spearbutt fragment (2:11), part of a joiner's dog, flint, quartz fragments, six lumps of slag and fragments of unidentifiable cremated bone were found within this layer. F2 was quite similar in composition to F4, the main difference being that F4 contained larger stones. This was sealed by the modern sod layer (F1), within which iron objects, modern crockery, a fragment of quartz and slag were found.

Finds from Cutting 1 ditch (Figs 26 and 27; Pls 21 and 22)

BRONZE

2:11. The basal knob and fragments of the socket of a spearbutt. It is broken at the junction between the knob and the possibly openwork socket. This is hollow and bowl-shaped with an expanded lip, probably part of a cylindrical socket. The object has a thin wall and the exterior is decorated with three plain bands in semi-relief that wind in a loosely curved swirl across and down the body of the bowl, blending into the wall. The base has a slightly flattened, almost biconical, cross-section. Part of a raised band survives around the lip. Two small fragments appears to be from the socket. One has a moulding of two raised bands around the mouth and the second has part of a circular perforation, probably a rivet-hole. Basal dimensions 27.6mm by 27.7mm. Surviving height 14.7mm.

IRON

102:2. Small irregular-shaped lump. L. 12.3mm. D. 9.1mm.

102:3. Small corroded lump, 24.5mm by 24mm.

20:1. Small circular solid object, possible

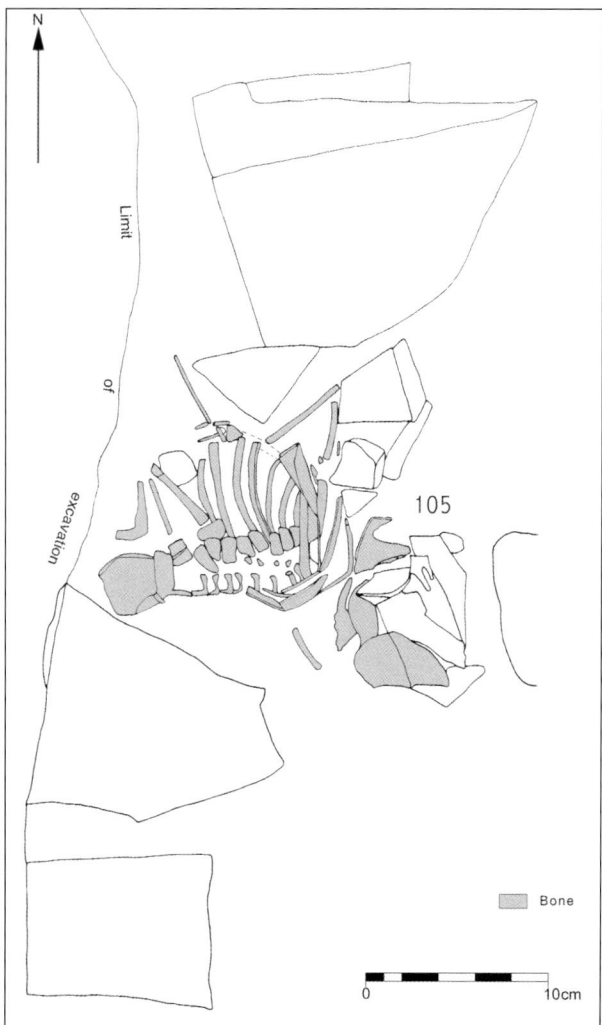

Fig. 14—Cutting 1: burial of child F105, 0.96m above the base of the ditch fill.

two pieces of quartz and a lump of slag. Above this was F9, which was situated on the northern side of the slope. It consisted of stony, shaly material, 0.12m in depth, which resembled slippage from the bank material of Ráith na Ríg. Three fragments of quartz and a lump of slag were found within this layer.

Concentrated mainly on the eastern part of the cutting and extending down from the southern side of the ditch was F8. It consisted of a dark brown silty soil with shale fragments throughout, measuring 0.23m in maximum thickness. It was relatively stone-free and may represent natural silting in the ditch rather than deliberate backfilling. The next layer (F7) was only present in the western area of the cutting and consisted of yellow clay and clay layers. Above this and extending from the southern slope was a layer of compact sandy earth (F6) containing stones and charcoal flecks. Sherds of post-medieval pottery, flint, fragments of quartz, a lump of slag and a fragment of unidentifiable cremated bone were found within the layer. Above this, but in incomplete perforation at one end; 7.1mm by 5.7mm, T. 5.3mm.

11:5. Horseshoe nail with flattened head and square-sectioned stem.

11:6. Horseshoe nail; one end is rounded, the other end appears to be a rectangular-sectioned stem. L. 32mm. D. head 12.2mm. D. stem 7.1mm.

2:2. Part of a staple with one of the tangs(?) missing. Used to hold two pieces of timber together. L. 84.5mm. D. 16.6mm.

1:24 Portion of round-sectioned iron object, both ends are missing. A seam is visible along its length, showing the junction of the two edges of where the iron is folded. Possibly part of a handle. L. 55.1mm. D. 3.1mm.

1:56 Probable nail with extensive corrosion around the area of the head. The stem is round in section, the lower portion is missing. L. 47.1mm. D. stem 8.6mm.

1:58 Horseshoe nail with rectangular-sectioned stem, the lower portion is missing. L. 28.9mm. D. head 11.2mm. D. stem 6.1mm.

1:60a–b 60a is a portion of a corroded round-sectioned thin shank, both ends are missing. Possibly part of a needle. L. 36.8mm. D. shank 1.7mm

GLASS

102:1. Portion of a violet glass bangle. Striations are present on the flat inner surface. Roughly oval in section. L. 41.6mm. W. 6.2mm.

POTTERY

11:2. Body sherd fragment; hard, compact, slightly chalky orange fabric with a low content of very fine grits. Brown glaze on the interior surface. T. 4.8mm. Post-medieval Brown Ware, seventeenth-eighteenth century.

6:1. Base sherd; hard, compact fabric with a low content of very fine grits. Brown mottled glaze on exterior and interior surfaces, buff core. T. 5mm. Post-medieval Mottled Ware, late seventeenth century.

6:2. Three body sherds; hard, compact, slightly chalky orange fabric with a low content of very fine grits. Brown glaze on the interior surface. T. 6–7.4mm. Post-medieval Brown Ware, seventeenth–eighteenth century.

1:33. Modern willow pattern body sherd.

FLINT

11:3. Unmodified flint flake, 39mm by 21.6mm.
11:1. Utilised flint flake, 26.1mm by 19.2mm.
11:4. Flint scrap, 9.3mm by 4.7mm.
6:5. Flint fragment, 10.2mm by 7.5mm.
5:1. Flint core, 27.4mm by 27mm.
4:3. Flint fragment, 21.3mm by 6.6mm.
4:5. Worked flint flake, 26.5mm by 18.1mm.
3:10. Hollow scraper, secondary flint flake, 35.9mm by 25.9mm.
2:6. Small unutilised flint flake, 13.3mm by 6.8mm.

CHERT

109:1. Unworked chert.
10:4. Unworked chert.

UNWORKED QUARTZ

12:2	6:4	3:6–8
12:4	6:6a–b	3:11
11:7	6:7–8	3:1–4
11:8	6:9–10	2:4
9:1–3	5:2	2:7–10
4:4a–c	1:21	

IRON SLAG'";;;

109:2–3	12:1	2:3
103:1	12:3	2:5
103:3	11:9	2:13–14
102:4	9:4	1:2
19:1	6:13	1:15
17:1–2	4:1–2	
15:1–2	2:1	

MODERN FINDS:

3:5. Clay pipe stem.
1:1. Coin of George V (1915).
1:4. Clay pipe bowl fragment.
1:19. Modern glass fragment.

From Extension 1a

77:1. Knife, of which the blade and part of the tang survive. L. 42mm. T. 5.9mm. L. blade 28.9mm. L. tang 6.2mm.

A discussion of the ditch fill and the finds is presented after the stratigraphic details of the ditch fill in Cutting 2 (see pp 57–63).

Cutting 2 (Fig. 6)

The backfill was removed from the area across the bank and ditch and the sections were recorded and drawn.

Finds recovered from Cutting 2 backfill, ditch area (Fig. 27)

POTTERY

B:77. Body sherd; hard brittle fabric with a high content of large grits (≤ 5.3mm). Decoration in the form of fingernail impressions is present on the exterior surface. Exterior surface and core: orange. Interior surface: black. T. 18.2mm. Neolithic Carrowkeel or Broad-rimmed Ware.

B:84. Body sherd, modern crockery.

QUARTZ

B:16–23	B:86
B:67–70	B:91
B:76	B:95
B:78	

FLINT:

B:1. Worked flake, a possible hollow scraper, 25.9mm by 13mm.

B:3. Flint fragment, 12.7mm by 11.7mm.

B:4. Small modified flake, 13.7mm by 6.3mm.

B:63. Small unmodified tertiary flake, 16.6mm by 11.1mm.

B:89. Utilised flake, 31.7mm by 25.9mm.

B:90. Flint fragment, 16.5mm by 7.5mm.

B:96. Large secondary worked flake, 60.7mm by 34.5mm.

IRON SLAG

B:24
B:25b

MODERN FINDS

B:83. Clay pipe stem.
B:84. Twentieth-century china.
B:85. Twentieth-century glass.

Time only allowed for an extension, which will be referred to as Extension 3, to be excavated across the ditch. On re-examining the sections it was clear that the stratigraphy was broadly comparable with that in Cutting 1, and the same four phases of activity were identified.

Phase 1: pre-bank activity (Figs 16, 17 and 7 I-I, H–H)

The layer interpreted as the old ground surface (F33) was present in the form of a yellow/brown sticky clay layer, which was only visible in the east-facing section. The trench or pit referred to by Ó Ríordáin was still visible in both sections and ran in an east–west direction, 1.1m wide and 0.82m deep; it is possible that it curves slightly to the north. This trench/pit (F69) was cut from F33 and the fill consisted of initial slip from the northern and southern sides, which was made up of grey-brown gritty clay/silt (F69a and F69b). The main bulk of the fill consisted of a sticky grey clay with occasional charcoal flecks (F69c), and a lump of iron slag was visible in section. The upper level of the fill consisted of orange/grey silty clay (F69d), which extended over the southern edge of the trench. This feature was obviously contemporary with the phase of industrial activity found in Cutting 1. Traces of the black charcoal layer (F31) were visible in the southern limits of the east-facing section above F33.

Phase 2: grey sod layer F30 (Figs 16, 17 and 7 I–I, H–H)

A grey, sticky sod layer (F30), similar in stratigraphic position and consistency to that found in Cutting 1, sealed the black charcoal-rich layer and the trench.

Phase 3: the construction of the bank and ditch of Ráith na Ríg

The bank material lay directly on the grey sod layer (F30). The first layer to be deposited was F29, a light brown/orange silty clay containing charcoal flecks and grey clay inclusions, which was similar to the basal layer of the bank found in Cutting 1, but not as extensive. In the west-facing section a thin layer of orange clay (F112) was found beneath F29. The bulk of the surviving bank consisted of F28a and F28b, both composed of redeposited boulder clay, with F28b containing more stones than F28a. A layer consisting mainly of shale (F22) was present on the northern side of the west-facing section. Beneath the modern sod level was the layer of cultivated soil (F21) that was also present in Cutting 1. In the east-facing section this layer completely sealed the bank and continued over the ditch fill. However, it was only present in the northern limits of the west-facing section.

Ditch stratigraphy: Extension 3 (Figs 4 and 16-19; Pl. 13)

This refers to the area of the ditch excavated to the east of Ó Ríordáin's excavation. A very thin layer (F70), 0.1m in maximum thickness, formed the base of the eastern area of the cutting. It consisted of light brown waterlogged clay with decomposing shale fragments throughout and was distinguished by the number of small, water-worn pebbles that it contained. Above this, and present across the entire cutting, was F60, a light brown shaly clay, 0.35m in maximum thickness, containing numerous medium to

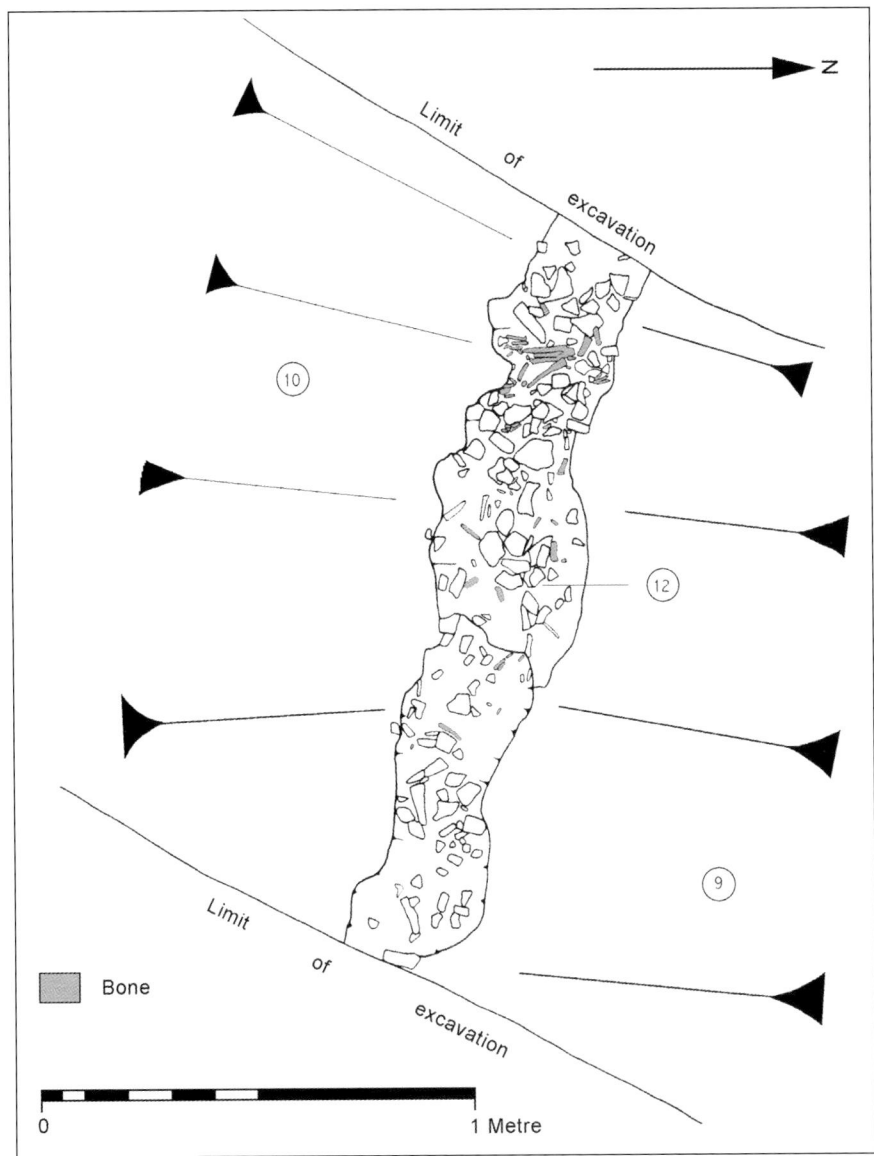

Fig. 15—Cutting 1: animal bone scatter on surface of F12, 1.97m above the base of the ditch fill.

large stones, ranging in size from 0.03m to 0.22m. Embedded in the surface of this layer were two large bones representing cattle and pig. Above this, and again found across the entire cutting, was F59, 0.33m in maximum thickness, which consisted of mainly decomposing shale, containing some large stones and pockets of light brown clay/silt. The surfaces of F59 and F60 were remarkably compact, suggesting that at some stage they marked a distinct horizon within the ditch fill, possibly the surface of a stream bed or the top of the natural water-table. The continuous flow of clear and very cold water, apparently a natural spring, into the bottom of the stone-cut ditch during the excavation strengthens this argument. The next layer, F58, was thin and compact; it was grey-brown in colour with occasional yellow/orange mottling and contained small stones. It measured 0.08m in maximum thickness.

Above this was F57, a light brown sandy clay, 0.23m in maximum thickness, with small and medium-sized stones (5-10cm). Above this was F56a, a layer of stony ditch fill, 0.2m thick. This sandy clay was light brown/grey in colour and friable in consistency. Bones representing cattle, sheep/goat and dog were present (Fig. 20; Pl. 14), and a single fragment of unidentifiable cremated bone. A number of stones, measuring from 0.06m to 0.2m in diameter, were also present. To either side of this deposit the nature of the soil was sufficiently different and distinctive to merit two separate feature numbers, F56b and F56c. F56b was concentrated on the northern slope of the ditch and consisted of gritty, sandy, light grey clay containing small stones 0.02-0.08m in diameter. This layer was 0.1m thick and contained horse bones. Concentrated on the southern slope was F56c, a gritty sandy clay, light brown-grey and practically stone-free, 0.12m thick. Above this was F55, a compact light brown clay

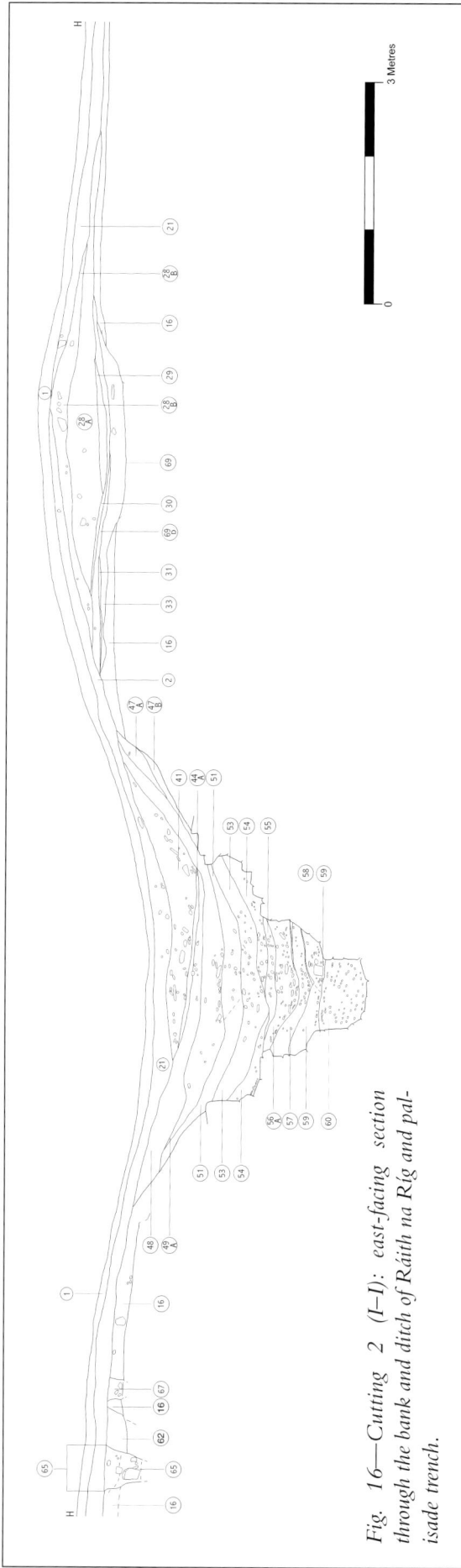

Fig. 16—Cutting 2 (I–I): east-facing section through the bank and ditch of Ráith na Ríg and palisade trench.

containing stones, 0.2m in maximum thickness and concentrated in the centre of the fill. Like the preceding layers, it was shaly on the north side and more clay-rich on the southern side. A small deposit of dog mandibles was found in the upper levels of this layer. Below this a fragment of a bronze fibula (55:1) and a concentration of sheep/goat mandibles and cattle, horse, pig and dog bones were found. The latter produced a radiocarbon date of 118–225 cal. AD (UB-4475; 1842 ± 16 BP).

Above this a limited spread (F50), confined to the eastern area of the cutting, was found. It represented primary slip from the southern side of the ditch and consisted of sticky mid-grey compact clay with partly rotted shale fragments, small stones and pebbles, and was 0.08m in maximum thickness. Finds consisted of a single iron nail. Above this was F54, a grey-brown silty clay layer, sticky in consistency and 0.27m in maximum thickness. The material on the southern side of the ditch was more compact and dense in consistency. It had a high stone content, mainly concentrated in the centre. A marked absence of stones was observed on the northern side of the ditch. A corroded iron nail was found in this layer, and fragments that appear to be from an iron blade or even a binding strip turned up near the base. This object had clearly been damaged in antiquity as other fragments were subsequently found approximately 0.2m to the south. Cattle, horse, sheep/goat, pig and dog bones were also found. On the northern side of the ditch, but confined to the eastern area of the cutting, was a spread of light grey-brown clay/sand with several small and medium stones ranging in diameter from 0.01m to 0.06m, representing primary slip (F46b). This layer was 0.08m thick. The next layer (F46a) consisted of a limited spread, 1.12m by 0.64m, of orange-brown redeposited boulder clay. It appears to represent primary slip over the original cut on the northern side of the ditch. Above this was F53, a layer composed mainly of clay silt, for the most part mid-brown in colour but darker on the northern side of the ditch, and 0.25m–0.3m in maximum thickness. Unidentifiable pottery crumbs and bone representing cattle, horse, sheep/goat and pig, as well as a fragment of red deer antler, and charcoal flecks were found throughout the deposit, particularly concentrated in the centre, where there was also some bright red/orange burnt clay. However, this appears to represent dumped material rather than *in situ* burning. The stones were again concentrated in the centre of the ditch. Above this was F52, a distinct dark grey/brown shaly/stone deposit 0.12m thick, concentrated in the centre of the ditch. This layer was

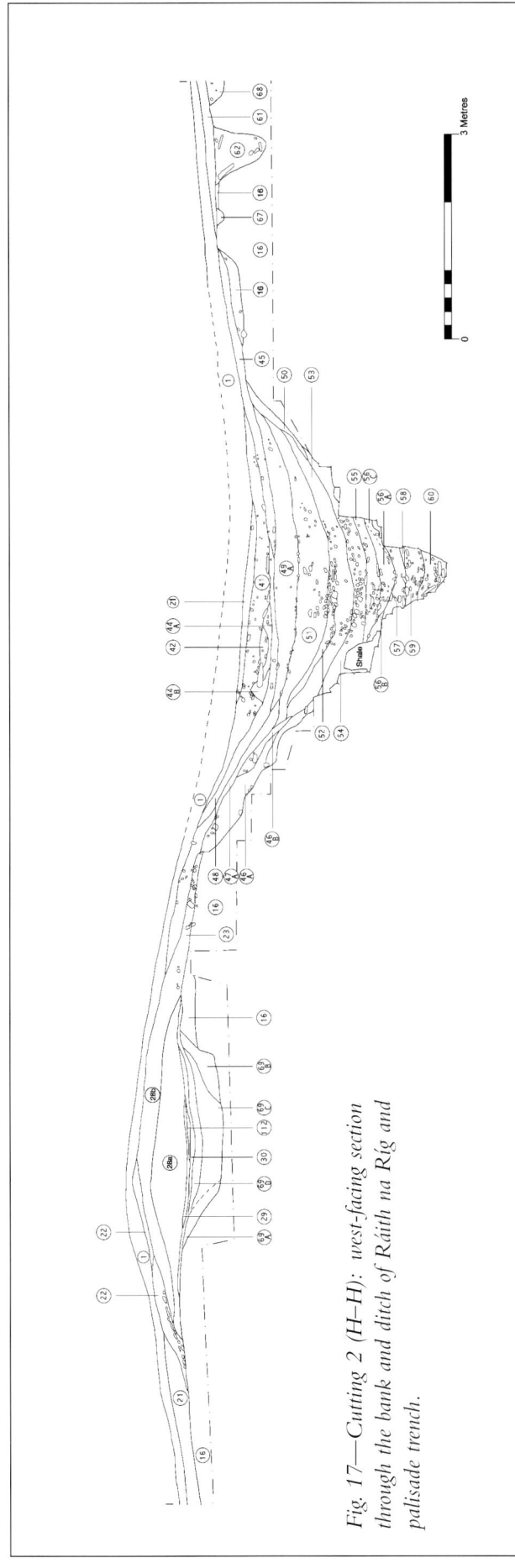

Fig. 17—Cutting 2 (H–H): west-facing section through the bank and ditch of Ráith na Ríg and palisade trench.

mostly composed of stones ranging in diameter from 0.04m to 0.2m, while the northern slope was stone-free. Cattle, sheep/goat and pig bones were found throughout, as well as a small quantity of cremated bone that could be human or animal. Above this was F51, a mid-grey-brown sandy clay deposit with a marked concentration of small stones in its centre. As was the case in the other layers, it was darker in colour and contained more shale on the northern slope, and lighter brown with a higher clay content on the southern side. One iron object, a piece of flint and a significant quantity of bone representing cattle, horse, sheep/goat, pig and a skull fragment from a fox were found in this layer, mainly concentrated on the western side of the ditch. The layer measured 0.3m in maximum thickness.

The next layer (F47b), a stony gravelly deposit 0.1m thick, was only present in the eastern area of the cutting. It represents slip from the bank down the northern side of the ditch. Sherds of post-medieval pottery were found within this layer. Another slip (F47a) was found above F47b, consisting of a very distinct clay distinguished by its dark grey-brown colour and numerous fine shale pieces. It measured 0.6–0.14m in thickness. Above this were layers F49a and F49b, which probably represent the same layer but differ slightly in colour. F49b was a distinct, very well-sorted gravel deposit, sloping off the southern edge of the ditch and confined to the eastern end of the cutting. It measured 0.12m in maximum thickness and yielded five iron objects, sherds of post-medieval pottery, a piece of chert, a quartz fragment and iron slag. F49a was a light brown clay deposit, 0.33m in maximum thickness, composed of friable clay with very small stones, extending over most of the ditch. It appears to have entered the ditch from the southern side, and was common to all sections. It contained sherds of Early Neolithic pottery. F45 was found across the entire cutting on the southern side of the ditch. It consisted of a distinct yellow-orange gravelly deposit, 0.1–0.12m thick, and contained small stones. Two iron objects, sherds of Early Neolithic and post-medieval pottery and a fragment of quartz were found within the layer. The next layer (F48) was also found across the entire cutting. It consisted almost completely of friable light brown clay, almost sod-like in texture, with a few stones, and was 0.05–0.15m thick. It is possible that this layer accumulated when the ditch was open for a considerable time. Two iron objects, a sherd of Early Neolithic pottery and a flint were found within this layer. Above this was F44a, a friable, mainly clay layer with stones scattered throughout it, varying from light brown to mid-grey

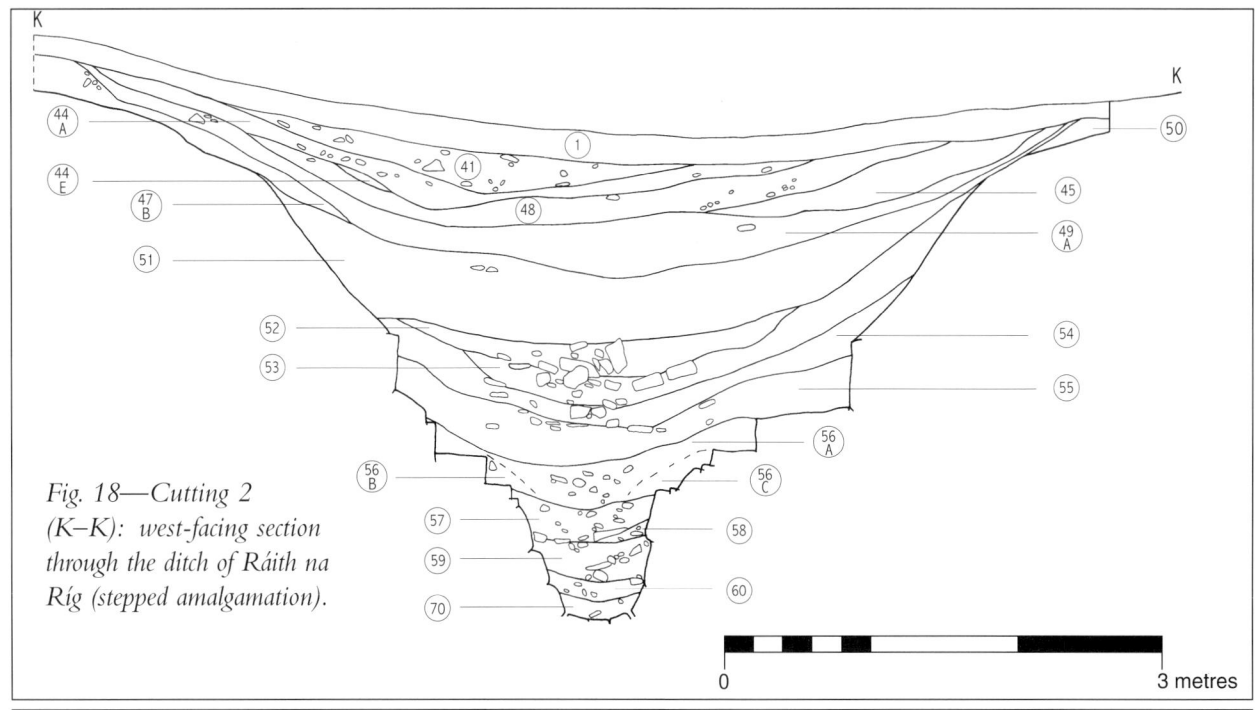

Fig. 18—Cutting 2 (K–K): west-facing section through the ditch of Ráith na Ríg (stepped amalgamation).

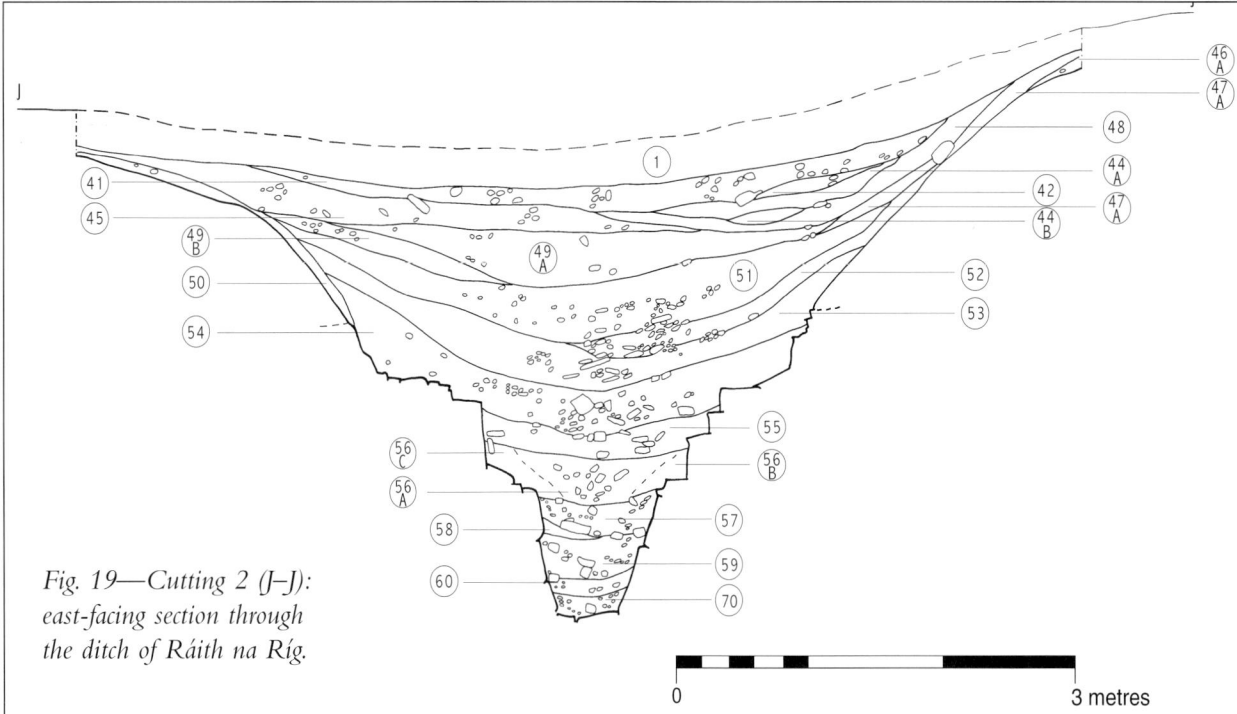

Fig. 19—Cutting 2 (J–J): east-facing section through the ditch of Ráith na Ríg.

in colour and ranging in thickness from 0.4m to 0.22m. It yielded four iron objects, a sherd of post-medieval pottery, flint and iron slag. Four small deposits were found within this layer (F44b-e), consisting of clay, boulder clay and gravel. Unidentifiable fragments of cremated bone were found within F44d. Above this, but confined to the eastern area of the cutting, was F42, a small clay-like deposit with an element of sand, 0.08–0.1m thick. It was dark grey-brown in colour and practically stone-free.

The uppermost layer was F41, which was the first layer of ditch fill under the modern cultivated soil (F21) and the humus layer (F1). It extended over the entire area of the cutting and was composed of grey-brown clay containing small and medium stones. It was mainly concentrated towards the northern end of the cutting, and was 0.1–0.15m thick. Sherds of Early Neolithic and post-medieval pottery, a fragment of window glass, a George V coin, flint, chert, quartz, iron slag and cattle bones were found within this layer. F21, a dark brown clay, represented modern cultivated soil that extended across the ditch. Because of the difficulty in identifying Ó Ríordáin's cutting, it was unavoidably removed from cuttings K–K, J–J and largely from H–H. Sixty-three fragments of cremated bone were found within. Some appear to be human but most are unidentifiable (see Appendix 4). F1 consisted of modern sod, within which three iron objects, a serpentine bead, flint and quartz fragments and a clay pipe stem were found.

Finds from ditch (Figs 26 and 27; Pl. 24)

BRONZE

55:1. Portion of a fibula; only the pin and one coil of the spring survives. L. 25.6mm. D. pin 2.7mm.

IRON

54:1. Fifteen corroded fragments from a blade-like object, possibly a knife or dagger.

54:2. Flat-headed nail with a square-sectioned stem. The stem is in two parts. L. 62.5mm. D. head 20.3mm.

51:1. Curved object, possibly part of a gouge. L. 26.6mm. W. 17.4mm. T. 3.5mm.

50:1. A flat-headed nail with rectangular-sectioned stem; lower portion of stem missing. L. 26.5mm. D. head 12.6mm. D. stem 6.9mm.

49b:4. Horseshoe nail. L. 31.5mm. Max. T. 14.9mm.

49b:2. Horseshoe nail. Lower part of shank missing. L. 24mm. D. head 11.2mm. D. shank 7.2mm.

49b:3. Horseshoe nail. L. 32.6mm. D. 12.3mm.

49b:6. Fragment of a rectangular-sectioned rod. L. 20mm. D. 6.2mm.

49b:8. Short length of iron rod with a rectangular-sectioned stem. L. 17.4mm. D. head 11mm. D. stem 7.1mm.

48:2. Small, round-sectioned solid object, possibly the lower end of the stem of a nail. L. 14.2mm. D. 4.7mm.

48:3. Small irregular-shaped flat object, 13mm by 5.8mm.

45:3. Horseshoe nail; the stem is rectangular in section. The point appears to be missing. L. 31.3mm. D. head 12.9mm. D. shank 5.2mm.

45:4. Thin fragment which curves on one side of its long axis and also bends at its narrow end. Possibly part of a bracket or staple. L. 45.6mm. D. head 15.1mm. D. stem 4.9mm.

44a:4. Portion of square-sectioned rod which either represents a binding strip which actually held something together or two pieces which have fused together. L. 37.8mm. D. 11mm.

44a:5. Horseshoe nail, rectangular-sectioned, lower portion of stem missing. L. 35.5mm. D. head 14.1mm. D. shank 5.4mm.

44a:3. Flat-headed nail or tack with only a fragment of the stem surviving, possibly from a shoe. D. head 11.3mm.

44a:2. Fragment of working end of a fairly modern key, 12.2mm by 8.3mm.

1:6. Rod; one end is round-sectioned, the other tapers to a flattened end. Possibly a chisel. L. 62.1mm. D. 8.9mm.

1:7. Rod with rectangular cross-section with an expansion at one end; the stem bends 36.8mm below the head. Probably a nail. L. 62.5mm. D. head 7.8mm. D. stem tapers from 5.7mm to 3.5mm.

1:28. Large, round-sectioned pointed object, probably a punch. It tapers from 24.7mm in diameter to 8.4mm. L. 150mm.

GLASS

41:3. Fragment of clear green window glass, possibly post-medieval, 30.5mm by 14.7mm.

POTTERY

53:2. Tiny orange crumb. Unidentifiable.

49b:3. Body sherd; hard, rough-textured fabric with a moderate to high grit content (≤ 4.4mm). Grits and mica visible on interior surface. Black carbonised matter covers the exterior surface. Interior surface is orange while the core is grey/brown. T. 6.1mm. Probably post-medieval.

49b:4. Body sherd fragment; hard, rough-textured fabric with a moderate to high grit content (≤ 0.8mm). Grits and mica visible on interior surface. Black carbonised matter covers the exterior surface. Interior surface is orange while the core is grey/brown. T. 5.8mm. Probably post-medieval.

49a:1–3. Three body sherd fragments, probably from the same vessel. Hard micaceous fabric with a high grit content (≤ 1.3mm). Grits and mica visible on both surfaces. Black carbonised matter is present on the interior surface of nos 1 and 2. Exterior surface orange; grey core; interior surface orange. T. 4.5–5.4mm. Probably from an Early Neolithic carinated bowl. From same vessel as B:66, **45**:3, **48**:1 and **41**:8.

48:1. Possible shoulder sherd; hard micaceous fabric with a high grit content (≤ 1.6mm). Grits and mica visible on both surfaces. Exterior surface orange; grey core; interior surface orange. T. 8.3mm. Probably from an Early Neolithic carinated bowl. From same vessel as B:66, **45**:3, **49a**:1–3 and **41**:8.

47b:1. Body sherd; hard, compact, slightly chalky fabric with a low grit content (≤ 3.4mm). Orange, with black glaze on the interior surface. T. 7.6mm. Post-medieval Black Ware. Probably same vessel as **47b**:2.

47b:2. Body sherd; hard, compact, slightly chalky fabric with a low grit content (≤ 5.1mm). Orange, with black glaze on the interior surface. T. 9.1mm. Post-medieval Black Ware. Probably same vessel as **47b**:1.

45:1. Body sherd fragment; hard compact fabric with a low content of very fine grits. Brown mottled glaze on exterior and interior surfaces, buff core. T. 5.7mm. Post-medieval Mottled Ware, late seventeenth century.

45:2. Body sherd fragment; hard compact fabric with a low content of very fine grits. Brown mottled glaze on exterior and interior surfaces, buff core. T. 3.2mm. Post-medieval Mottled Ware, late seventeenth century.

45:5. Body sherd fragment; very hard micaceous fabric with a high grit content (≤ 1.3mm). Grits and mica visible on both surfaces. Exterior surface orange; grey core; interior surface orange. T. 5mm. Probably from an Early Neolithic carinated bowl. From same vessel as **49a**:1–3, **B**:66, **48**:1 and **41**:8.

44a:4. Pottery crumbs. Unidentifiable.

44a:6. Handle; hard compact fabric with a low content of fine grits. Orange, with brown glaze on the exterior surfaces. T. 10.2mm. Post-medieval Brown Ware tankard, seventeenth-eighteenth century.

41:1. Body sherd fragment; hard, compact, slightly chalky-textured fabric with a low visible grit content (≤ 1.4mm). Orange fabric with green glaze on the interior surface. T. 3.7mm. Post-medieval.

41:4. Body sherd fragment; hard, compact, slightly chalky fabric with a low content of very fine grits. Orange, with brown glaze on the interior surface. T. 5.1mm. Post-medieval Brown Ware, seventeenth–eighteenth century.

41:5. Two body sherd fragments; hard, compact, slightly chalky fabric with a low content of very fine grits. Orange, with brown glaze on the interior surface. T. 4.8–4.9mm. Post-medieval Brown Ware, seventeenth–eighteenth century.

41:8. Shoulder sherd; very hard micaceous fabric with a high grit content (≤ 2.2mm). Grits and mica visible on both surfaces. Exterior surface orange; grey core; interior surface orange. T. 7mm. Probably from an Early Neolithic carinated bowl. From same vessel as **49a**:1–3, **45**:3, **48**:1 and **B**:66.

ANTLER
53:1. Portion of cut antler.

LITHICS
51:2. Worked flint flake, 33.8mm by 16.7mm.
48:4. Utilised flint flake, 25.8mm by 16.4mm.
44a:1. Flint scrap, 9.5mm by 8.2mm.
44a:3. Worked flint flake, 28.6mm by 20.5mm.
44a:7. Tiny flint scrap, 6.2mm by 5.9mm.
44a:8. Utilised flint flake, burnt, 24.5mm by 25.2mm.
41:4. Burnt flint scrap, 12.6mm by 10.7.
41:1. Utilised flint flake, 35.1mm by 37.2mm.
1:3. Small utilised primary flint flake, 16.5mm by 14.7mm.
1:1. Neolithic flat serpentine bead of irregular outline with an off-centre hourglass perforation, with the boring concentrated more on one side. Small V-shaped notch carved at the top of the perforation. The surface is smooth, 18.2mm by 13.1mm, T. 4.1mm.

UNWORKED CHERT
49b:1
41:7
41:12–13

QUARTZ FRAGMENTS
49b:5	1:17
45:6	1:72–6
41:10	1:87
1:5	1:94
1:8–14	

IRON SLAG
55:2	44a:1
49b:1	41:2
47a:1	41:2–3
47b:3	

MODERN FINDS
41:11. Coin of George V.
1:36. Clay pipe stem.

Discussion of ditch stratigraphy — Cuttings 1 and 2

The stratigraphy within both areas of ditch excavated was broadly similar (see Table 2, p. 58,. for concordance of features). The lower 2m of fill was the result of slippage from the bank and erosion of the sides of the ditch and consisted mainly of decomposing shale and shale blocks. However, the presence of human burials, animal bones, ash and scorched stones shows that material was also deliberately placed or dumped into the ditch. This level of the fill represents a sequence of Iron Age activity on the site, beginning with the bank and ditch which could have been constructed as early as *c.* 193

Table 1—Radiocarbon dates from 1997 excavations at Tara.

Lab. no.	Context	Feature	Material	BP	Calibrated date (2SD)
OxA-8824	Pre-bank	F31	Animal bone	217 ± 40	370–60 cal. BC
UCD-9822	Pre-bank	F36	Charred wood	2090 ± 60	200 cal. BC–16 cal. AD
UB-4478	Pre-bank	F30	Animal bone	2065 ± 16	153–41 cal. BC
UB-4479	Cutting 1 ditch	F108	Animal bone	2105 ± 21	193–95 cal. BC
UB-4480	Cutting 1 ditch	F102	Animal bone	1890 ± 20	68–138 cal. AD
UCD-9821	Cutting 1 ditch	F102	Charred wood	1875 ± 50	67–289 cal. AD
UB-4476	Cutting 1 ditch	F12	Animal bone	1689 ± 16	261–406 cal. AD
UB-4475	Cutting 2 ditch	F55	Animal bone	1842 ± 16	118–225 cal. AD
UB-4477	Palisade trench	F62	Animal bone	2019 ± 17	95 cal. BC–15 cal. AD

cal. BC, with the final layers being deposited into the ditch as late as 406 cal. AD (see Table 1). The upper fill is derived from material from both north and south of the ditch and would appear mainly to represent deliberate backfilling carried out in the post-medieval period.

Iron Age levels within the ditch

It was observed during the excavation of both areas of the ditch that the nature of the fill changed significantly on reaching the Iron Age level, F12 in Cutting 1 and F51 in Cutting 2. The fill became very stony, had a far greater content of decomposing shale and was damp in consistency. This was also the level at which quantities of animal bone first began to appear, and continued to be present almost to the base of the ditch.

Finds

Few finds were recovered from the Iron Age levels of the ditch, but those that were identifiable were diagnostic of the period. Part of a purple glass bangle was found in the fill of Cutting 1 (**102:1**). Its chemical composition was found to be a typical Iron Age/Roman soda-lime silica-base glass. Analysis also revealed flakes of iron oxide fused onto the inner surface, which have been interpreted as representing scales from the iron tool used to form the bangle while hot. This bangle has a lower iron content than the blue glass splinters, which is an indication of the use of cleaner raw material for the manufacture of the bangle (see Appendix 1 for details).

Portions of two bangles were also found during the excavation of Ráith na Senad (Grogan *et al.*, forthcoming). One was D-sectioned and light blue in colour (E615:168), and came from the habitation layer associated with the earthworks. The other example was also light blue and D-sectioned but it was decorated with lines of white glass. This was found in the spoil on the northern side of the interior of the earthworks. A fragment of blue glass waste (E615:214), with marks on both faces that may have been caused by tweezers while the glass was in a molten state, is another possible indication of glass-working at Tara. It is difficult to suggest an exact date for these bangles as finds dating from the first to the fourth centuries AD were identified from this habitation horizon at Ráith na Senad. However, the plain example, which is similar in form to the purple bangle from Ráith na Ríg, resembles bangles found in first-century BC contexts on European *oppida* (Wailes 1991, 614).

Other glass bangles found in Irish Iron Age contexts include portions of ten bangles from Dún Ailinne, Co. Kildare, as well as a thin glass rod and waste pieces (Wailes 1990, 18). These slender D-sectioned bangles were not unlike the Tara example. It was argued by the excavator that they conformed to Haevernick's (1960) Class 3a La Tène C and D on the Continent, most of which come from *oppida* and date from the earlier first century BC. The Tara bangle could well date from the same period. A light blue bangle found beneath the burial mound at Furness, Co. Kildare (Grogan 1983–4, 305–6), appears to be later in date than the Tara example, as a radiocarbon determination of 425–599 cal. AD (GrN-10472; 1540 ± 30 BP) was derived from a stake-hole within the mound.

Two complete examples were found at 'Loughey', Co. Down, from a probable burial deposit (Raftery 1983, 175). One in particular resembles the example from Ráith na Ríg. It is also deep purple or violet in colour and oval to D-shaped in cross-section, and striations were present on the flat inner surface. The other bangle is deep blue. This glass has been dated to the late first century BC – early first century AD by Henderson (1991, 132). He also argues that one of the beads from the assemblage, which is spirally decorated

Table 2 — Concordance of ditch features — Cutting 1 and Cutting 2.

Cutting 1 features	Cutting 2 features
110	70
109	60
108	59
107	58
106	57
103	56A
104	
102	55
101	
20	54
	46B
	46A
19	53
17	
15	52
14	
13	
12	51
9	47B
	47A
11	49A/49B
8	45
	48
	44A–E
7	42
6	
5	
4	
3/2	41

with tin-rich yellow glass, is a type not found in European *oppida*, strongly suggesting that the beads as well as the bangles were manufactured in Ireland using imported glass (1991, 132).

Another fragment of a bangle that was supposed to have come from a burial mound at Dunadry, Co. Antrim, was of clear glass and D-shaped in section (Raftery 1984, 461). A fragment of a D-sectioned greenish-blue bracelet was found at the occupation site of Feerwore, Co. Galway, but its context is unclear (*ibid.*, 464). Another example, blue in colour and D-shaped in section, came from occupation material within the hillfort of Freestone Hill, Co. Kilkenny (*ibid.*, 465). It was argued by the excavator that this fragment probably dates from the third or fourth century AD because of associated Roman material (*ibid.*, 196).

The pin and one coil of a bronze fibula were found in the Iron Age fill of Cutting 2. Two main types occur in Ireland, those with rod-bows and those with leaf-bows; unfortunately the bow does not survive on the example from Tara so it is not possible to identify its type. It may be that the single coil represents the entire spring mechanism of the fibula. According to Hawkes (1982, 52), it was not uncommon, certainly in Britain, to find brooches with a 'mock spring', where 'resilience was given by as little as a single coil only, separate from the rest, with which its junction was artfully disguised'. Middle European smiths had for long been masters of wirework, but in Britain they often avoided making springs with continuous coils, and subsequently there were often only two coils (Hawkes 1982, 52).

There are not a great number of Iron Age fibulae from Ireland. Raftery (1984, 144) quotes about 26 examples of La Tène type (a number augmented by more recent discoveries), and the preceding Hallstatt period is represented by about six, most of which, he states, 'could be recent imports to the country'. According to Raftery (1994, 144), almost all fibulae from Ireland are of local origin. He suggests a south-west English influence for the development of the Irish fibulae (1984, 149), and points out that close dating of Irish fibulae is difficult but that they are essentially late La Tène in character, dating from around, or shortly after, the birth of Christ (Raftery 1994, 128).

A fibula was also found at Navan Fort, which Raftery (1984, 145–52) suggests belongs to the last century BC–first century AD in that 'it is the only Irish example displaying true Middle La Tène construction with foot wrapped around the bow'. Two fibulae of possible Nauheim-derivative form were found at Dún Ailinne (Wailes 1990, 17–18). The iron fibula from Feerwore, Co. Galway, came from an occupation level that also contained an iron axehead with rectangular-sectioned socket. A date in the first century BC was suggested for this example and this does not conflict with the likely dating of the axehead (Raftery 1984, 151). A fibula of Nauheim-derivative type was also found in association with the glass bangles at 'Loughey', Co. Down. Jope and Wilson (1957) argued in favour of a southern English origin for this assemblage and suggested a first-century AD date. However, this date has since been reviewed and the first century BC is more likely (Henderson 1997, 98; Raftery 1984, 151).

Human remains

During the 1950s excavation two human burials—which, as already mentioned, may have actually represented just one burial (Grogan *et al.*, forthcoming) — were recorded from the basal layers of the ditch in Cutting 1. It was also recorded that fragments of a possible human skull were found near the base of Cutting 2. Just a few metres to the west of the Cutting 1 burials, human remains were also found during the 1997 excavations. At a slightly lower level in F107, fourteen fragments of human bone were found, mainly from the skull and facial area, but in F103 the articulated skeleton of a child could have been part of the same burial uncovered by Ó Ríordáin. Fragments of dog bone were found scattered around the remains of the child, and it is interesting to note that Ó Ríordáin recorded that an animal skull (unidentified) was found close to his burials J and K. Animal bones were also found around and under a crouched inhumation burial found in a secondary position in the barrow at Ráith na Senad (Grogan *et al.*, forthcoming). It is not uncommon to find human and animal remains in the same context on British Iron Age sites, and it has been suggested that they may belong to similar ritual practices of feasting and even sacrifice (Carr and Knüsel 1997, 167). The only other human remains found during the recent excavations were a portion of a mandible, again from F103, and part of a mandible and a hip-bone from a much higher level, F15. However, both mandible fragments were from the same individual, which suggests that these fragments probably represent the disturbed remains from a burial elsewhere rather than a formal deposit.

The finding of human remains from such Iron Age contexts is not unusual. A cemetery containing both cremations and inhumations was found during the 1950s excavation of the adjacent site, Ráith na Senad. Because of this mixture of burial rites it has been argued that the cemetery dates from the first century AD and probably continued into the second century AD (Grogan *et al.*, forthcoming; O'Brien 1990, 38; 1992, 131). With the supporting evidence from the radiocarbon dates (Table 1), there is every reason to suggest that the burials found in the ditch of Ráith na Ríg are outliers of the same cemetery.

Placing fragments of human remains in the enclosure ditches of Iron Age sites was also common in Britain (Fitzpatrick 1997, 82). At Gussage All Saints, two infant burials and scattered fragments of skeletons were found in the enclosure ditches (Wainwright 1979, 191). Isolated skull fragments and frontal bones were also found deposited in pits in Danebury (Cunliffe 1983, 162). As pointed out by Cunliffe (1983, 164), the deliberate deposition of human skulls or fragments is an understandable practice in Iron Age times. It is recorded that the head was looked upon as the centre of a person's power, and in some cases the heads of the ancestors were revered and were kept within the house as a mark of respect. It has also been suggested that the burial of ancestors within, or in close proximity to, areas of habitation ensured continuity of tradition (Fitzpatrick 1997, 83).

Animal bones

Animal bones were found in almost every layer of the Iron Age fill. Cattle were the dominant species, followed by pig, sheep, dog and horse, and all clearly represented food refuse (see Appendix 2). Evidence suggests that all these animals were mature or old at the time of death. Large quantities of pig bones on prehistoric sites are often considered to represent ritual feasting on high-prestige sites, for example Navan Fort (McCormick 1997, 118). However, the higher percentages of cattle bone at Tara and Dún Ailinne lend little support to this theory. Indeed, McCormick (Appendix 2) suggests that regional differences in diet may be a more practical explanation.

Although horse bones comprise only 6.2% of the overall frequency, this represents the highest incidence of this animal from an Irish prehistoric site. Examination shows that these animals were about fourteen hands in height, about the size of a modern Connemara pony. Bones had been shattered for the extraction of marrow, and evidence of burning suggests that the joint was roasted. Tooth-wear from the remains of an old animal in F54 indicates that it was used for riding or traction before being killed and used as food. However, there were also young animals present.

Dogs were also unusually common, representing 9.4% of the overall frequency. Like the horse remains, many of the bones were broken and bore knife-marks, indicating that dogs were eaten. They also represented almost exclusively old animals. The fact that both horse and dog were eaten is interesting as such practices are often regarded as unusual. Raftery (1994, 126) made the point that the scarcity of horse bone at excavated sites is not surprising, since they would have been looked upon as valuable animals and would rarely be eaten except in exceptional circumstances. It is tempting to suggest ceremonial feasting to explain the eating of the two species, and of course this could well have been the case; yet it is also necessary to be cautious when dealing with such a small sample of

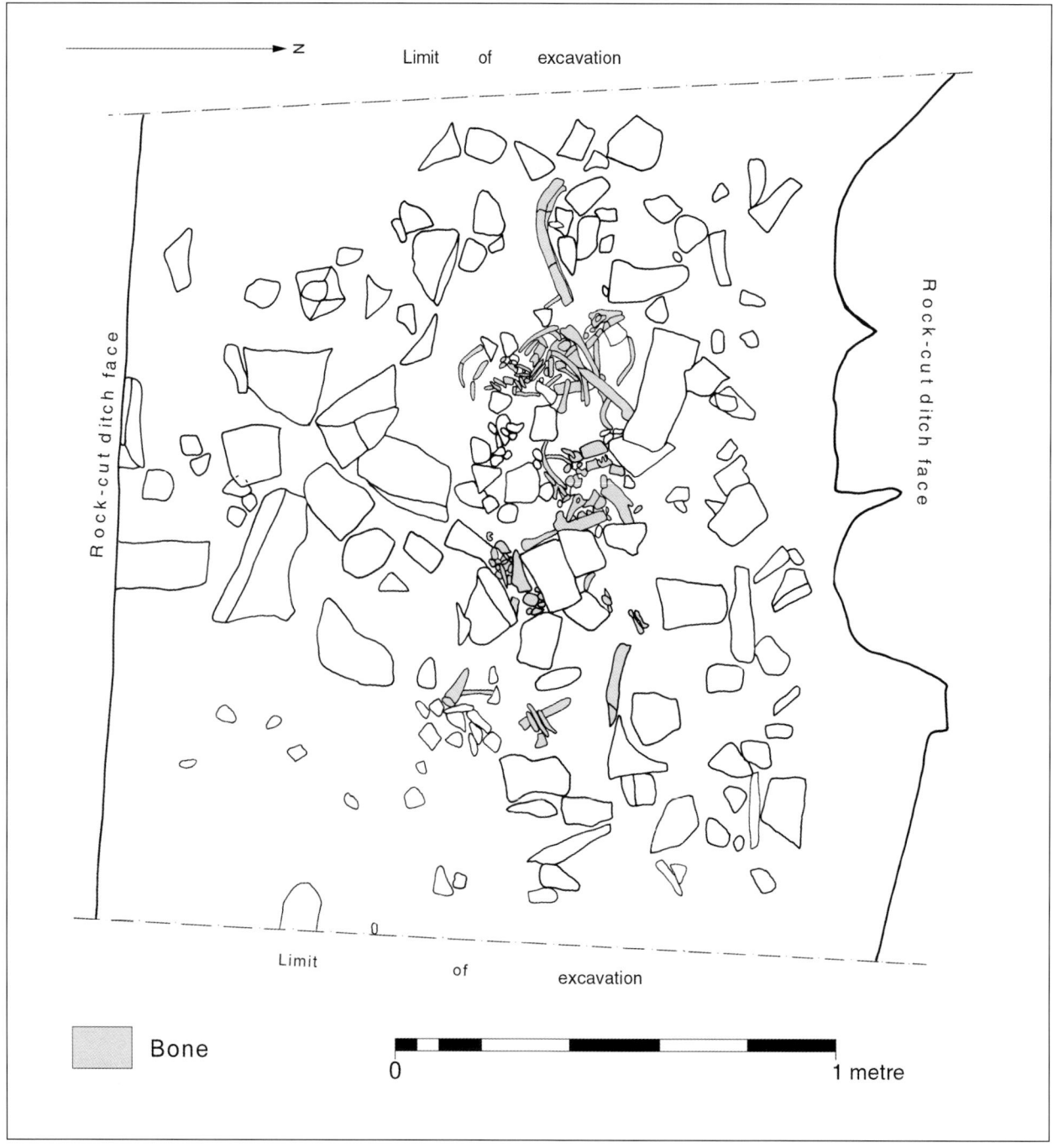

Fig. 20—Cutting 2: animal bone scatter on surface of F56a, 1.25m above the base of the ditch fill.

bone, which might overrepresent the importance of the two animals. Bhreathnach points out (see Appendix 3) that there is certainly evidence to suggest that horseflesh was consumed in Ireland and Britain and on the Continent when the animals were mature or surplus to requirements (Green 1992, 35–43).

The range of animals identified from Ráith na Ríg is identical to those recorded by Ó Ríordáin from Ráith na Senad (Grogan *et al.*, forthcoming). Other Irish Iron Age sites that produced examples of horse and dog include Dún Ailinne, where small quantities of each were found, and Feerwore, Co. Galway, where a dog of sheepdog size was identified (Stelfox in J. Raftery 1944, 50). Butchered horse bones were also found at Navan Fort (McCormick in Lynn 1997, 120).

In Britain an unusually high number of dog and horse remains were also noted at Danebury, and it has been suggested that a special ritual significance may have been attached to these specific animals (Cunliffe 1983, 158; Fitzpatrick 1997, 82). At Highfield in Wiltshire the remains of about twenty dogs were

Pl. 13—Cutting 2 (K–K), east-facing section through ditch of Ráith na Ríg (C. Brogan, Dúchas).

Pl. 14—Cutting 2: Extension 3. Animal bone scatter on surface of Iron Age stony fill (F56a) within ditch of Ráith na Ríg (H. Roche).

found. Some of the bones bore knife-cuts, possibly resulting from the collection of sinews (Cunliffe 1991, 382).

The meagre evidence for the presence of wild animals at Tara is not surprising. A similar pattern has been noted on British Iron Age sites, where their occurrence is often interpreted as representing special deposits (Fitzpatrick 1997, 82).

Post-medieval levels within the ditch, Cuttings 1 and 2

The upper metre or so of the ditch fill is composed of material deposited during the post-medieval period, probably to facilitate agricultural activity. This is suggested because post-medieval pottery sherds were found throughout these layers in both Cuttings 1 and 2. There is also a conspicuous lack of animal bone within these upper layers, in contrast to the underlying Iron Age layers. A puzzling aspect of this transition from Iron Age to post-medieval levels is that there is no evidence for a break to represent this long period of inactivity; neither is there evidence for a later recut into the ditch fill. The evidence therefore suggests a period of inactivity at this stage at Tara, at least in this specific area. It also implies that the depression of the partially filled ditch of Ráith na Ríg was visible until it was backfilled in the seventeenth century. This interpretation is supported by information that Edel Bhreathnach has kindly provided regarding the condition of the ditch of Ráith na Ríg in the first millennium AD. This comes from a short prose tract and poem on the origins of Tara that was edited from a sixteenth-century manuscript by O Daly (1960). The poem, which may pre-date AD 900, is somewhat obscure but appears to incorporate a description of some of the monuments on the summit of the hill. Stanza 1 mentions *cathir Themra*, a similar usage to the seventh-century reference by Tirechán to Tara as a *civitas*. This is followed by a seer's vision of Tara:

> 4. At-chonterc in [n-]aurthuili
> iadais frisin(d) [n-]ard,
> pa maa pa n(d)-adbal in borg
> asais dun imchelt hall.

> He saw the space/outer trench/hollowness
> which closed against the height
> greater still, vaster was the encircling rampart/stronghold
> ??? a hidden/surrounding fort grew yonder.

The words *aurthuili* and *borg*, though difficult to interpret, seem to describe Ráith na Ríg as viewed before AD 900. O Daly suggested reading *aurthuili* as a compound of *tuille* 'hollowness', perhaps meaning 'outer trench', or (as suggested by Myles Dillon) perhaps a compound based on *tul* 'bare, naked' and possibly referring to the bare space surrounding the outer rampart. Although accepting that caution is necessary when using early references to explain archaeological episodes, it can at least be acknowledged that sometime around or before AD 900 a hollow area was still visible within the ditch.

Another feature that is difficult to explain is that much of the upper fill is derived from the southern side of the ditch, which mainly consisted of stoneless, yellow, gritty material with a low shale content. The origin of this material is more difficult to explain than in the case of that derived from the northern side which came from the bank, as is obvious from its darker colour and its shale and stone content.

F11 in Cutting 1 and the equivalent layer (F49A) in Cutting 2 are of particular interest. This deposit — a fine stoneless material consisting mainly of boulder clay — is common to all areas excavated. There is no visible source for this material on the southern side of the ditch, and it is certainly too substantial to represent surplus material from the digging of the palisade trench. Neither is there evidence to suggest that it was slippage from Duma na nGíall, as photographs of that site prior to excavation show that slippage was concentrated on the eastern side. The presence of Neolithic artefacts, quartz and chert within these upper layers, however, may provide a clue to its origin. It can be postulated, although no evidence survives, that a bank was constructed during the Iron Age on the southern side of Ráith na Ríg, most likely at the time the palisade was erected. It is possible that this low bank was revetted by the palisade and would have functioned as an additional defence as well as an observation platform. The material used to construct the bank could have been collected from the immediate area, thus explaining the incorporation of finds from earlier Neolithic activity. This bank was subsequently deliberately levelled into the visible ditch depression of Ráith na Ríg during the post-medieval period. This argument is supported by the results from the soil micromorphological analysis (see Appendix 6). Ellis suggests that the material would originally have been in an exposed position, subjected to rain, and that although there is no evidence for a bank, 'such a bank appears to be the only feasible source as there are no other known high and exposed areas in the immediate vicinity'.

Finds from the post-medieval layers within the ditch, Cuttings 1 and 2

The range and position of the finds recovered within the upper layers of the ditch fill suggest that the material, certainly on the southern slope, was derived from an accumulated source. It would also appear that the upper fill was dumped into the ditch over a relatively short period of time: post-medieval and Neolithic pottery, as well as flint, quartz and chert, were found within the same layers in the upper fill (Cutting 2, F49A/F49B, F45, F41), and the sherds of Neolithic pottery for the most part appear to represent a single pot. Much of the Neolithic assemblage was obviously derived from pre-passage tomb (Duma na nGíall) contexts, apart from the quartz, which is more likely to have been associated with the tomb. When the postulated bank was levelled into the ditch, the early material was incorporated in it, or had already been incorporated into the bank at the time of construction.

Other identifiable finds within the upper layers consist mainly of post-medieval horseshoe nails (**11**:5–6, **49B**:4, 2, **45**:3, **44A**:5). There are a small number of round- and rectangular-sectioned iron rods (**49B**:6, 8, **48**:2) and a possible bracket or staple (**45**:4) which could be earlier in date, though this cannot be demonstrated.

Two interesting Iron Age finds were recovered from the uppermost layer of Cutting 1 (F2), a portion of a probable bronze knobbed spearbutt (**2**:11) and an iron joiner's dog (**2**:2). The exact context for the spearbutt is somewhat uncertain; it was found at the junction between the edge of the ditch and the pre-bank layers, and therefore it is impossible to be certain whether it was actually *in situ* or in a residual position. Nonetheless, this Type 1a spearbutt (Fig. 26; Pl. 21) is an important find and could date from as early as the first century BC (Raftery 1984, 111; 1998, 97). It is also probably the most closely stratified spearbutt yet found in Ireland, as most are found in isolated contexts (Raftery 1984, 120). The semi-relief decoration on the Tara example can be compared with a spearbutt from Lisnacrogher, Co. Antrim (*ibid.*, fig. 60:2). Raftery (1984, 125) suggests that this cast relief is in keeping with the styles of the early centuries AD, which might indicate that the Tara spearbutt does not belong to pre-bank contexts but to later Iron Age activity on the site. Although little of the Tara socket survives, the surviving portion suggests that it was openwork — a feature that, to date, is unique.

Neolithic artefacts were also found in the modern sod layer (F1) of Cutting 2. These consisted of a serpentine bead (**1**:1), a piece of flint (**1**:3) and lumps of quartz, which were obviously displaced from the area of Duma na nGíall as a result of ploughing. Three iron objects were found which could possibly be Iron Age in date. These consist of a possible chisel (**1**:6), a rectangular-sectioned nail (**1**:7) and a smith's punch (**1**:28). Similar punches were found in Roman and Romano-British contexts at Dragonby in north Lincolnshire (May 1996, 293–4).

Palisade trench (F62)

The short stretches of the palisade trench that Ó Ríordáin excavated at the southern limits of Cuttings 1 and 2 were reopened and recorded (Pl. 16). In Cutting 1 it was revealed that the area of the trench had not been completely excavated but that Ó Ríordáin had dug his characteristic trial trench flush with the eastern side of the cutting until he reached bedrock, which in this area was just over 1m below sod. He also extended a narrow trench along the run of the palisade trench itself, but did not attempt to follow its original edges. The fill of the trench was similar to the surrounding boulder clay and was only visible in section when wet (Pl. 18). It measured 0.76m across the mouth and was 1.2m deep. No finds or features were recorded from this area from the 1950s excavations, and the only new feature which was uncovered in 1997 was the base of a post-pipe (F64A).

In Cutting 2 Ó Ríordáin had once again dug a narrow trial trench along the east side. In this area the shale bedrock dips to a much deeper level, ranging from 1.65m on the northern side of the trial trench to 1.84m on the southern side. The profile of the palisade trench was visible on the west-facing section; again the fill was not very different from the surrounding natural boulder clay. In this area the palisade trench measured 0.9m across the mouth and 0.96m in depth. Examination of the fill of the trench in section revealed charcoal flecks, bone fragments and possibly slag fragments. A large block of shale was present within the trench, set at an angle on the northern edge. As the shale bedrock was not penetrated in this area during the construction of the palisade trench, it is likely that it came from the ditch of Ráith na Ríg, indicating that the ditch was dug before the palisade trench. Upon removal of the backfill in this area it became apparent that Ó Ríordáin had failed to recognise the original cut for the trench, which was visible in section 0.27m below the grass level. During the 1950s excavation, 0.51m of soil was removed before the palisade trench was recognised. The seven post-holes recorded by Ó Ríordáin were uncovered

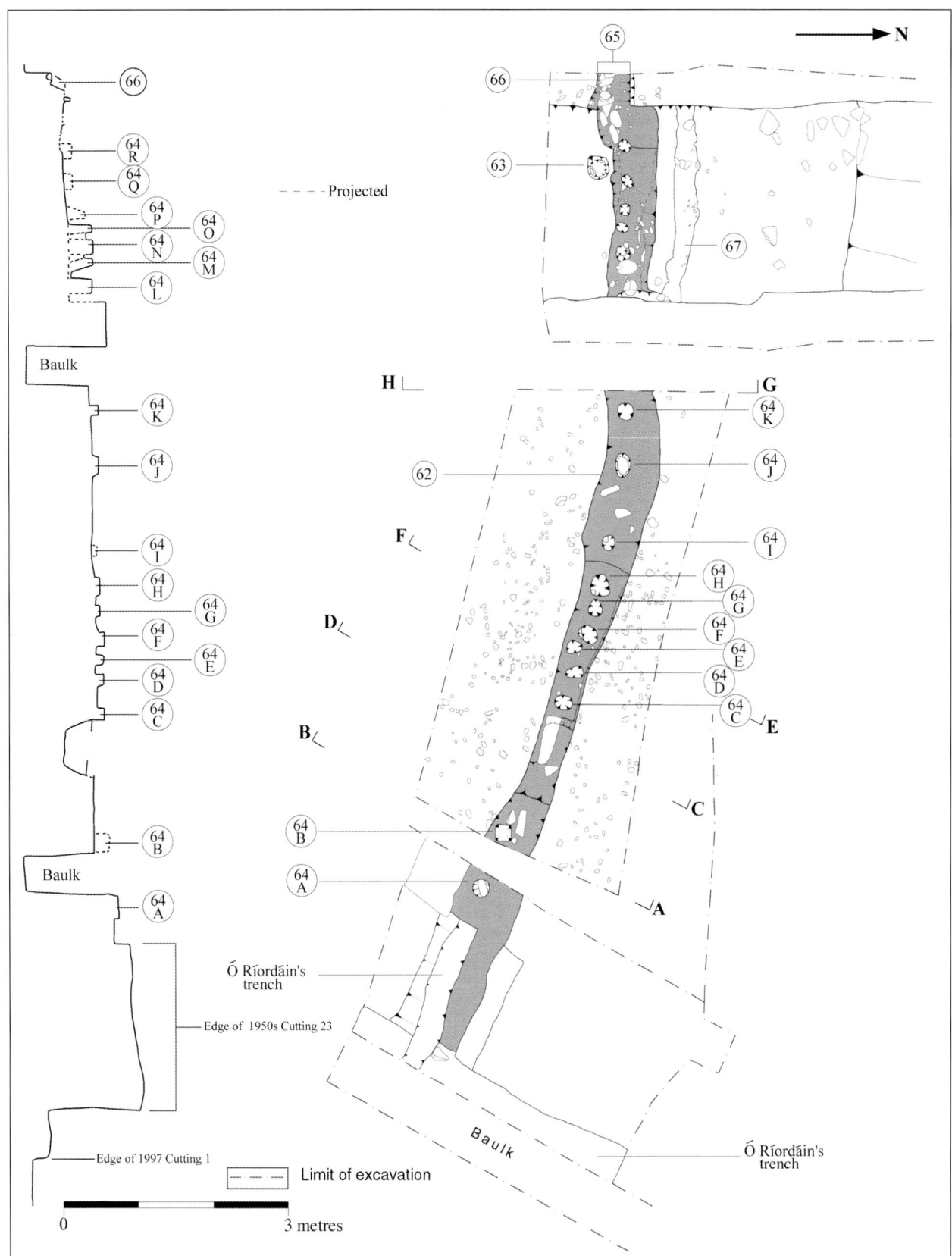

Fig. 21—Palisade trench, ground-plan and long section (running east–west).

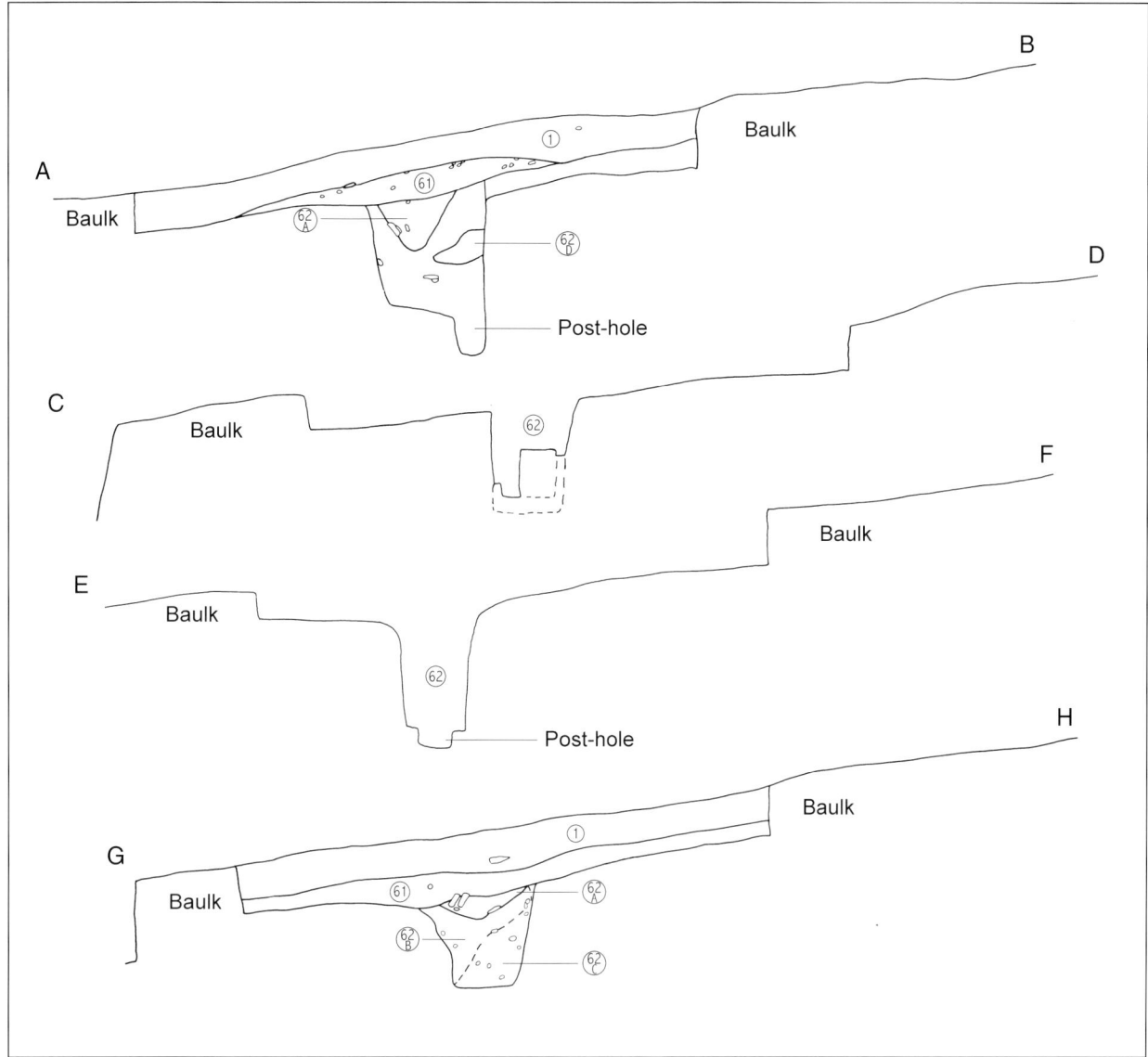

Fig. 22—Sections (north–south) through palisade trench.

(F64L–R). They were very shallow, averaging 0.15–0.2m in depth. Further investigation revealed that Ó Ríordáin had not excavated the post-holes completely, but that they in fact continued down to the base of the trench. There was a change in the direction and make-up of the trench on the exposed western limit. In section a secondary cut (F65) was visible 0.35m south of the original northern edge of the palisade trench, which succeeded in turning the trench fairly sharply southwards. Closely packed stones (F66) were also visible in the fill of this secondary cut. Although time did not allow for this anomaly to be investigated fully, a small cut, 0.3m long, was excavated in the hope of throwing some light on the situation. Only the upper 0.5m of this limited cut was excavated, but it showed that the secondary cut extended into the western baulk and that the fill continued to be tightly packed with stones (Fig. 21; Pl. 17). Finds were not recovered in this area of the trench during the recent excavations although Ó Ríordáin recorded that bronze, iron and crucible fragments had been found during his excavations. Again, it was not possible to locate these objects.

Two previously unrecorded features were uncovered during the 1997 season. The first was a shallow trench (F67) on the northern side of the palisade trench, running parallel to it (Fig. 21). It measured 0.32m in maximum width and 0.13m in depth. The second was a pit (F68), immediately south of the palisade trench, which was only visible in the west-facing section (Fig. 17). Because of the limited amount of work carried out in this area it is not possible to suggest a function for these features.

Pl. 15—*View of excavated portion of palisade trench, from west (C. Brogan, Dúchas).*

Pl. 16—*View of excavated portion of palisade trench, from east (C. Brogan, Dúchas).*

Pl. 17—Cutting 2. View of palisade trench from east, showing secondary cut at western limit of excavation and the shallow trench (F67) immediately to the north (H. Roche).

Pl. 18—Cutting 1. West-facing profile of palisade trench, as exposed by Ó Ríordáin.

Excavation of new portion of palisade trench (Figs 6, 21, 22; Pls 15 and 16)

During the 1997 season 6m of the trench was excavated between the areas exposed by Ó Ríordáin. This line of the trench was located with extreme difficulty as the fill, when dry, was very similar in colour and texture to the surrounding natural boulder clay. The trench, positioned 2.3m from the inner (southern) edge of the ditch of Ráith na Ríg, averaged 0.76m in width and varied in depth from 1.2m at the eastern limit to 1.09m at the western end of the excavation (Figs 3 and 16). The overlying modern sod layer (F1) was quite thick, measuring 0.17m in maximum depth. Immediately below this was a layer of yellow, sandy material (F61), 0.15m deep, which decreased in depth towards the northern side of the cutting. It appeared to represent cultivation soil and sealed the cut of the palisade trench. Sherds dating from the Early Neolithic period, nineteen pieces of unworked chert, a quartz crystal and six quartz fragments were found within this layer.

The cut for the trench (F62) only became visible when the natural boulder clay level (F16) was reached. The fill consisted of a fairly homogeneous mixture of redeposited boulder clay and brown earth (F62), with some large stones that presumably acted as packing stones to support the upright posts. Patches of burnt clay were occasionally present (F62A–C), and F62D was darker in colour and damper in consistency than the rest of the fill. Traces of ten post-pipes (F64B–K) were revealed at a very low level within the trench. They only became visible at a depth of 0.51m below the lip of the trench: basically only the bottom 0.1m or so survived. Few finds were recovered from the fill; these consisted of a portion of a bangle made from opaque red glass (**62:1**), a lump of iron slag and a single cattle bone, which produced a date of 95 cal. BC–15 cal. AD (UB-4477; 2019 ± 17 BP).

Finds from palisade trench (Figs 26 and 27; Pl. 23)

BRONZE
62:2. Circular lump, 18.9mm by 19.1mm, T. 13.1mm.

GLASS
62:1. Portion of a D-sectioned bangle made from opaque red glass. L. 24.7mm. D. 6.6mm.

POTTERY
61:6. Possible shoulder sherd. Hard, rough-textured fabric with a high grit content (≤ 1.5mm). Uneven surfaces; grits visible on both surfaces. Black throughout. T. 6.1mm. Probably from an Early Neolithic carinated bowl.

1:18. Body sherd; very hard micaceous fabric with a high grit content (≤ 1.6mm). Grits and mica visible on both surfaces. Exterior surface orange. Core grey. Interior surface orange. T. 5.8mm. Probably from an Early Neolithic carinated bowl. From same vessel as 49a:1–3, **45**:3, **48**:1, **41**:8 and B:66.

CHERT FLAKES
61:4. Sixteen flakes.
61:5a, b
61:11

QUARTZ FRAGMENTS
61:1. Crystal fragment.
61:2–3
61:7a–c
61:8

Discussion of palisade trench

The re-examination of the palisade trench and the excavation of a new portion clarified certain issues about its nature but also raised interesting questions. The stratigraphic sequence did not satisfactorily reconcile its relationship with the ditch of Ráith na Ríg. The cut for both features only became visible at the level of the natural boulder clay, which suggests contemporaneity, but it is also possible that the original cuts are no longer visible in the cultivation soil because of later farming activity. However, the large blocks of shale found within the palisade trench obviously came from the ditch of Ráith na Ríg, indicating that the construction of the bank and ditch occurred before the palisade enclosure. This, in conjunction with a date of 95 cal. BC–15 cal. AD from the trench, indicates that the palisade was erected not too long after the construction of Ráith na Ríg. Although this date was obtained from a single cattle bone, the fresh condition of the bone suggests that it was incorporated within the fill shortly after disposal and was not a residual bone incorporated into the fill of the trench at a later date.

From the results of the geophysical survey carried out at Tara, Newman (1997, 230) argues that the construction of the palisade trench was part of the final structural phase at Tara, which transformed Ráith na Ríg from a ritual into a defensive enclosure, 'perhaps with the arrival of Christianity and the decline of paganism'. This interpretation is based largely on what appeared to be a 3m-wide gap in the palisade trench in the area of the southern entrance, which was interpreted as representing an entrance (*ibid.*, 174). Results from the survey suggest that the ditch of Ráith na Ríg passed uninterrupted across this gap, thus implying that the large ditch and the palisade were not contemporary. However, it is impossible to arrive at definite conclusions on such limited information and, as Newman suggests, it is possible that a wooden bridge of some sort crossed the ditch at this point. Further excavation is necessary if the relationship between the palisade trench and Ráith na Ríg is to be fully resolved.

The western exposed limit of the trench is tantalising, in that the trench was recut and veers off in a more southerly direction. This part of the trench also contains more stones than were found in the other exposed areas. Only a stretch of 0.5m of this recut section was excavated, but it can be tentatively suggested that it represents either repair work or a possible entrance feature.

There is a brief mention in the 1950s archive of the presence of a bank between two lines of palisades in this area. Although no plans exist to corroborate this comment, it again raises the possibility of the existence of a bank to the rear of the palisade trench. This is extremely interesting and, as previously stated, might explain the origin of the material on the southern side of the ditch of Ráith na Ríg. This material was generally yellow and relatively stone-free and was certainly too dense in quantity to be explained away as surplus material from the palisade trench or slip from the mound of Duma na nGíall. If an earthen bank, perhaps revetted on the northern and southern sides by timber, had originally been present, this would not only be an extremely important feature but would also account for the fill on the southern side of the ditch. In addition, is it possible that the yellow sandy layer (F61) that sealed the palisade trench was the only surviving remains of such a bank?

Finds from the palisade trench

Ó Ríordáin recorded finding fragments of bronze and iron as well as crucible fragments and lumps of slag during the 1950s excavation of the palisade trench. Apart from a lump of slag and an animal bone, the recent excavation uncovered only a single, but very unusual and important, artefact — a portion of an opaque red glass bangle (**62:1**). Red glass or enamel was used during the La Tène period in Europe for the decoration of beads or as a coloured ornament for metalwork (Haseloff 1991, 639). It was not normally used for the manufacture of complete objects, the Tara bangle being the first example found in Europe.

Analysis has shown (see Appendix 1) that the glass used was rich in lead and copper, a type that predominated in the Iron Age. Similar glass from the Meare lake village, Somerset, has been dated to sometime after 200 BC (Henderson 1991, 124). Analysis has also shown that the chemical composition of the Tara bangle is very similar, if not identical, to a lump of red glass/enamel which has been associated with Tara. Ó Floinn (in Youngs 1989, 201) has argued that this lump of enamel dates from the early medieval period, based on the fact that an examination of the lump suggested that the material was very hard and could not be easily fused. This implied that the enamel was not used in a molten state but instead that chips were removed from the lump to be used as decorative pieces. Ó Floinn concluded that enamel found on objects prior to the late seventh century was applied in a molten condition and not in the form of chips.

However, Raftery (1983, 146, 156; 1994, 157–8, fig. 99) identified decorative enamel studs or chips on two ring-headed pins from Lisnacrogher, Co. Antrim, on an example from County Westmeath, and on a Navan-type brooch that was supposed to have been found at Navan Fort, Co. Armagh. He argued for a date somewhere between the last few centuries BC and the first century AD for these objects (Raftery 1984, 154, 173). If these examples are considered, as well as the recent finding of the bangle at Tara and a dumb-bell bead made from opaque red glass found in Iron Age contexts at Dún Ailinne (Wailes 1990, 18), there is no reason why the enamel lump could not date from the Iron Age period. In addition, there is the implication that the manufacture of glass objects could well have been carried out at Tara. It once again raises the question of the provenance of the lump of red glass/enamel. It had originally been thought to have come from Tara, but it was later argued that it had been found in the nearby village of Kilmessan (Newman 1997, 211). Because of the similarity of the chemical composition of the bangle and the lump, a similar context for both must now be considered.

The Neolithic pottery and the chert fragments found in F61 obviously belong to an earlier phase of activity in the area, while the crystal and the quartz may well be derived from the passage tomb (Duma na nGíall).

Phase 4: modern activity (Fig. 23)

This phase deals with later truncations due to agricultural activity in recent centuries. A layer of cultivation soil, consisting of medium brown clay/silt with quite a lot of small, fragmented shale (F21), was

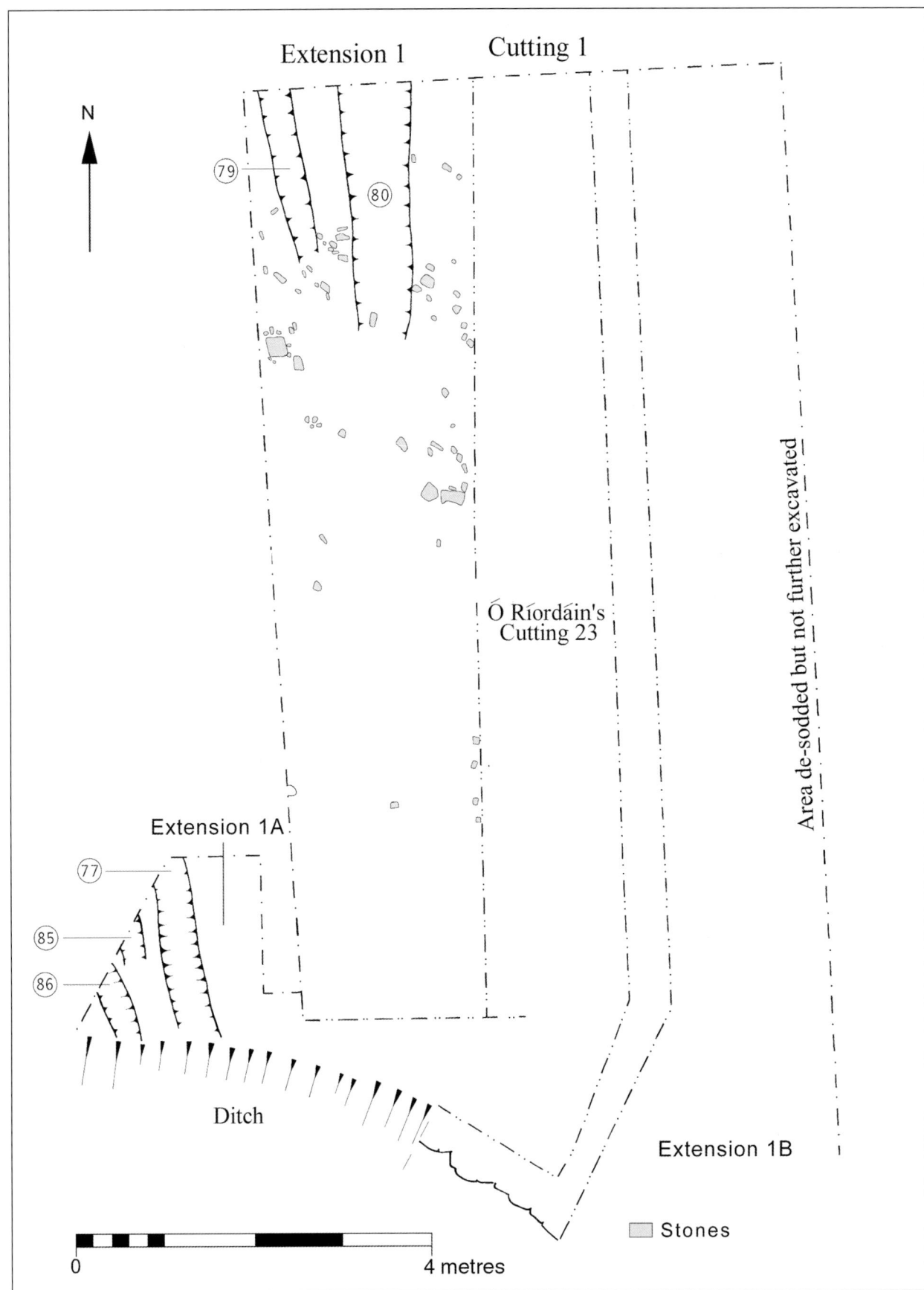

Fig. 23—Cutting 1: ground-plan of features associated with later activity (Phase 4) beneath the bank of Ráith na Ríg.

directly below the 1997 sod-line, and overlay the bank layers of Cutting 1 to a depth of between 0.1m and 0.18m. Within this layer clay pipe fragments (1:4, 35, 36), a sherd of willow pattern china (1:33) and iron slag (1:1, 15) were found. During its removal seven linear features representing cultivation trenches were found (F25, F26, F77, F79, F80, F85 and F86). These probably date from the nineteenth century. They extended across the bank layers parallel to each other on a roughly north–south orientation.

At the base of the uppermost layer across the bank (F21) two linear trenches were found (F25 and F26). F25 was 6m long, 0.5m wide and 0.1m deep. It was flat-based with vertical sides. The fill, in which a single fragment of bronze (25:1) and a lump of slag (25:23) were found, consisted of brown stony material consistent with cultivation soil (F21). The second trench (F26) was located east of and parallel to F25. It was also flat-based and was 6.4m long, 0.6m wide and 0.1m deep. The fill, similar to that found within F25, contained a fragment of vitrified clay (26:6) and two lumps of slag (26:6, 24). Both trenches were at their deepest on the crest of the bank but were quite shallow (0.01–0.02m) at their southern limits.

Approximately 0.4m below the 1997 grass-line two further shallow trenches (F79 and F80) were found in the northern area of the cutting, extending into the northern baulk. Because they were filled with the same material as F21 they were not visible until subsoil or bank layers became visible, and even at that stage they were difficult to identify, especially in dry conditions. F79 rose up across the upper level of the bank material and measured 1.84m in length and 0.33m in width. F80, which ran parallel to F79, cut through the upper fill of the outer ditch of Ráith na Senad (F81) and was 2.76m long and 0.45m wide.

The other three cultivation trenches (F77, F85 and F86) were found in Extension 1A. F77 consisted of a U-shaped trench, 1.9m long, 0.4m wide and 0.06–0.08m deep. The fill consisted of a dark brown clay/silt loam containing small stones. An iron knife blade with part of the tank (77:1) was found within the layer. This type of fill is similar to the overlying cultivation soil F21, which lay directly on the boulder clay in this area.

F85 was located 0.42m west of F77, and the surviving portion was 0.4m long, 0.26m wide and 0.02–0.04m deep. The fill, brown clay/silt, was consistent with the cultivation soil F21.

F86, about 0.15m west of F85, was 1m long, 0.3m wide and 0.03–0.04m deep. The fill was similar to F85 and contained no finds.

In Cutting 2, two cultivation trenches (F10a and F10b) were uncovered on the crest of the bank of Ráith na Ríg (Fig. 6), about 0.26m below the sod during the 1950s campaign. Both ran parallel to each other in a north–south direction. F10a measured 1.11m in length and 0.37m in width, and F10b measured 1.21m in length and 0.32m in width. The backfill was not removed from these features during the recent excavations.

General discussion

The excavations carried out in 1997 were enormously successful in clarifying many of the questions posed. The identification and position of the black layer were clarified, demonstrating that metalworking activity dating from the Iron Age pre-dated the construction of Ráith na Ríg. This information, in addition to the recovery of Iron Age artefacts from the lower fill of the ditch, proved that Ráith na Ríg was indeed a monument dating from the Iron Age and not, as was sometimes speculated, a reused Late Neolithic/Early Bronze Age henge monument (Simpson 1989; Weir 1989). In addition, the evidence obtained from the limited areas of the palisade trench excavated strongly suggests that it was broadly contemporary with the construction of Ráith na Ríg.

On a wider scale, the wealth of information acquired from this relatively limited excavation emphasises the importance of Tara in illuminating one of the least-understood periods of Irish prehistory. The evidence from the excavation of Ráith na Ríg, in combination with that from Ráith na Senad (Grogan et al., forthcoming) and the supporting results from radiocarbon dating, has now produced a chronological sequence extending from c. 370 cal. BC to c. AD 406. This sequence of Iron Age activity, which includes both ritual and domestic structures, industrial activity, burial evidence and artefacts, all found in sealed contexts, is, so far, unique in Irish Iron Age studies.

The earliest Iron Age activity identified was the industrial horizon beneath the bank of Ráith na Ríg. This evidence, in the form of iron- and bronze-smithing and the possible manufacture of glass objects, is without parallel in Ireland. The importance of its contribution to Irish Iron Age studies is underlined by the fact that as recently as 1994 Raftery stated that an Iron Age bronze-smith's workshop had yet to be found in Ireland (1994, 151). The recent work at Tara has changed this perception, with the finding of crucibles bearing bronze residue, moulds, waste bronze and finished objects. Although indirect evidence for such work is known from Ireland, for example the hoard found at Somerset, Co. Galway

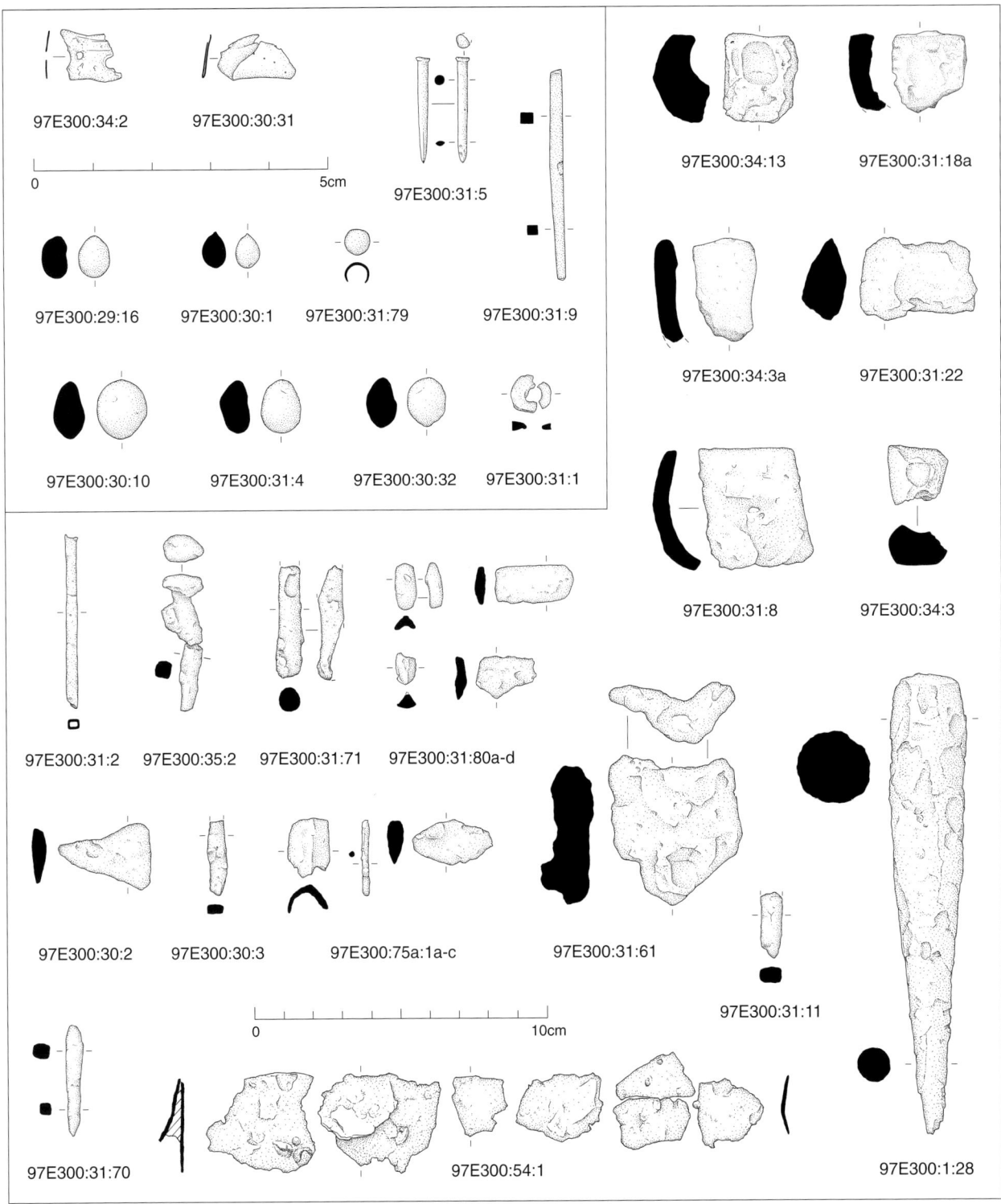

Fig. 24—Iron, bronze and ceramic artefacts from pre-bank layers, bank and ditch fill.

(Raftery 1994, 151), the evidence from Tara is the only assemblage associated with a metalworking hearth found in a sealed context. It shows that Irish smiths were not only acquainted with sophisticated methods of metalworking but were also aware of, and most likely in contact with, Iron Age Britain and continental Europe. This is especially evident in the presence of the iron socketed axe; in its basic form this is similar to the Feerwore axe, which, as Scott pointed out (1990, 66), was a form well known from La Tène contexts across Europe. He also emphasised that the Feerwore axe shows that the smith had mastered the technique of forging a right angle, something that requires confidence and expertise (*ibid.*, 95).

As already mentioned, parallels can also be cited from Iron Age contexts at Beeston Castle in Britain (Ellis 1993, 53, fig. 36:3), from the great *oppidum* site of Manching (Jacobi 1974, Taf. 13:260, 16:287) and from Dünsberg in Germany (Jacobi 1977, Taf. 15:5–10). The large post-holes, stake-holes and trenches found in association with the industrial level indicate that shelters and structures were present. Structural features including pits and post-holes were also found associated with the furnaces at Ballydavis, Co. Laois (Keeley 1999, 29), which appear to be contemporary with the evidence from Tara. Structural evidence was also found at the hillfort of Llwyn Bryn-dinas, Wales, where a smithing and bronze-working area may have been contained within a small circular building (Hingley 1997, 11). The flat-headed, square-sectioned iron nails and joiner's dogs recovered at Tara were obviously used in these constructions. Similar implements were found in later Iron Age contexts in Ráith na Ríg, but there are few from the rest of Ireland. Parallels are, however, known from Britain and continental Europe. The site of Manching, which dates from the middle of the third century BC to the middle of the first century BC, produced thousands of such nails (Jacobi 1974, Taf. 73:1379, 1380–1) and there were also identical joiner's dogs (*ibid.*, Taf. 70:1304–10). The presence of glass splinters in the vicinity of the metalworking hearth, as well as the bangle fragments found in later contexts, strongly implies that glass objects were actually manufactured at Tara. However, it is more likely that the raw glass was imported from continental Europe (Henderson 1997, 100).

The finding of an industrial horizon associated with a probable domestic settlement (see p. 29) in a complex dominated by burial mounds or mounds that appear to be ritual or ceremonial in function is an additional dimension to the archaeological history of Tara. It should be noted that an apparent non-ritual occupation site was also identified at Ráith na Senad dating from between the second and fourth centuries AD (Grogan *et al.*, forthcoming). However, its proximity to Ráith na Ríg and the assemblage of what would be considered high-status finds certainly suggest that it was no ordinary occupation site. This wealthy and prestigious group of people chose to construct their settlement at Tara, with an obvious understanding of its importance in Irish Iron Age society.

In the same way, the industrial activity with probable associated domestic settlement may not only represent ordinary non-ritual activity. In early Irish literature the craft of smithing and metalworking generally appear to have sacred or magico-religious status (Scott 1987, 154). An example of this is illustrated in the *Cath Maigh Tuired*, where a warrior wishing to enter Tara is asked by the doorkeeper to declare a craft not already possessed by one of the court. He is only allowed to enter when he claims to have skill in several crafts, including blacksmithing and non-ferrous metalworking (*ibid.*, 153). Another example is found in the theoretical protocol specified in *Tech Midchuarta*, where the master smith entertained royalty and was seated well above the salt (*ibid.*, 154). There is even a reference to 'Tara's mighty anvil in the east' in the poem *Echtra Mac Echdach Mugmedóin*, which discusses the required tasks that had to be carried out to prove fitness for kingship. These include the rescue of the anvil and block from a burning forge (*ibid.*, 155). In the prose version of this poem there is also a reference to a druid who asks Sitchenn, the smith from Tara, for advice. The special position of the metalworker has also been noted in Britain, where ethnographic and historic accounts suggest that ironworking was considered a mystical process during which rocks were converted into powerful cultural artefacts (Hingley 1997, 9). Although it is understandable that metalworking would have been regarded as an important, if not sacred, craft in prehistoric Ireland and beyond, the place of the metalworker or smith is not fully understood. The literature indicates that they were revered, but it is not known whether they were independent itinerant or permanently settled craftsmen, or whether they were controlled by the chief or king (Henderson 1991, 118).

It is possible that this horizon did not represent isolated activity at Tara. Contemporary activity on the other relevant 'royal' sites consisted of the Phase 3 ring-slots and figure-of-eight structure at Navan Fort and similar structures from the 'Rose phase' at Dún Ailinne, which have been dated to around 300 BC up to 100 BC (Lynn 1997, 211). Identical features were uncovered in pre-ringfort contexts at Ráith na Senad

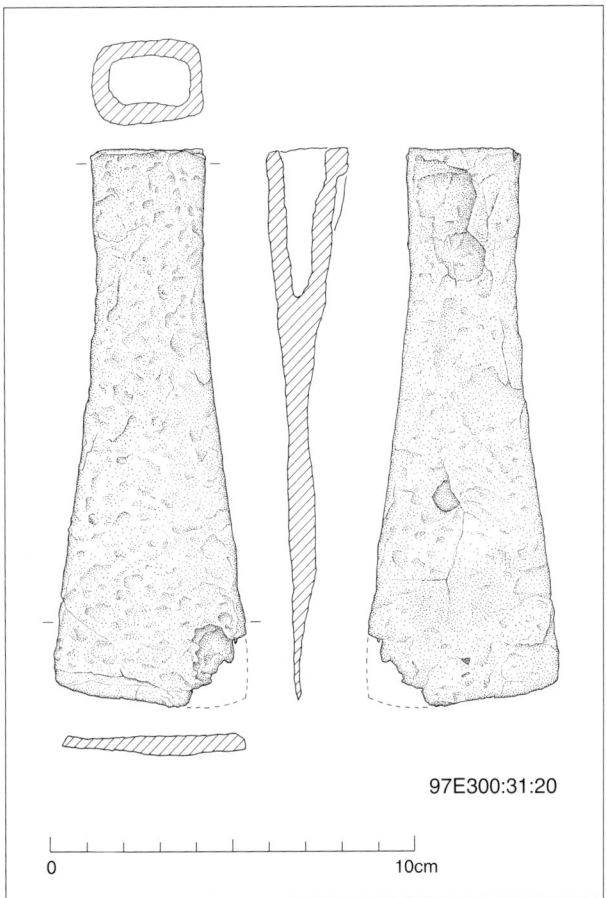

Fig. 25—Socketed iron axehead from pre-bank industrial layer.

(Grogan *et al.*, forthcoming; Cooney and Grogan 1994, 182, fig. 10.2). Although no definite dating evidence is available for these features it is likely that they were contemporary with the Navan Fort and Dún Ailinne structures. It is also possible that this structural phase at Ráith na Senad could have been contemporary with, or at least overlapped with, the industrial activity beneath the bank of Ráith na Ríg.

The archaeological evidence obtained and the supporting radiocarbon results (Table 1) demonstrate that Ráith na Ríg was constructed at the same time as, or indeed sometime earlier than, the Navan Fort enclosure and the multi-ring timber structure, both of which date from *c.* 95 BC (information from Chris Lynn; Baillie 1988). This is also corroborated by the presence of human bone fragments and burials in the lower portion of the Ráith na Ríg ditch, which were found in both the 1950s and 1997 excavations. As already discussed (p. 59), it seems that some of the fragments represented the disturbed remains from burials elsewhere. However, the fragments near the base of the ditch and the child burial obviously represent formal deposits. It is most likely that these deposits are contemporary with the cemetery horizon at Ráith na Senad, for which a date in the first century BC has been suggested, perhaps continuing into the first century AD (Grogan *et al.*, forthcoming).

An amount of animal bone was found within the Iron Age layers of the ditch fill, decreasing in quantity towards the base. As at Dún Ailinne cattle were the dominant species, unlike Navan Fort, where pig was more popular. Pig was the second favourite at Tara, followed by sheep, dog and horse, and the evidence from the bones suggests that all represented food refuse. It has also been noted on British hillforts that cattle and sheep were present in large numbers while pigs played a subsidiary role (Cunliffe 1991, 379). This range of animals identified from Ráith na Ríg is identical to those listed by Ó Ríordáin from the excavations at Ráith na Senad. It is not inconceivable to suggest that the animal bone within the ditch represented dumped food refuse from activity concentrated at Ráith na Senad. It has been suggested that the occupation horizon at Ráith na Senad dates from the second and third centuries AD, and this could account for the greater number of animal bones found in the upper Iron Age layers within the fill of the ditch.

It might be considered unusual that dog and horse meat was consumed at Tara, as such animals are generally regarded as being close to man and therefore a forbidden meat source. However, similar practices have been identified at other Iron Age sites in both Ireland and Britain. Butchered horse bones were found at Navan Fort (McCormick in Lynn 1997, 120), and at Highfield, Wiltshire, the remains of about twenty dogs were found and some of the bones showed knife-cuts. It was suggested that this resulted from the collection of sinews (Cunliffe 1991, 382). Bhreathnach (Appendix 3) also illustrates from anthropological, historical and mythological sources that at certain times such practices were acceptable. For example, it might have been thought that benefits could be gained from the consumption of such meat in the promotion of healing, fertility or prosperity. Although the higher-than-normal percentage of dog bone present might be regarded as a more convincing argument for some form of ritual feasting, there was no evidence for the careful or deliberate deposition of the bones. Both dog and horse remains were discarded into the ditch in the same manner as the cattle, pig and sheep, and there was certainly no evidence for formal ritualistic deposits similar to those found at Danebury (Cunliffe 1983, 155–71), or for the ritual feasting on dogs at the sanctuary of Gournay (Oise) (Green 1992,

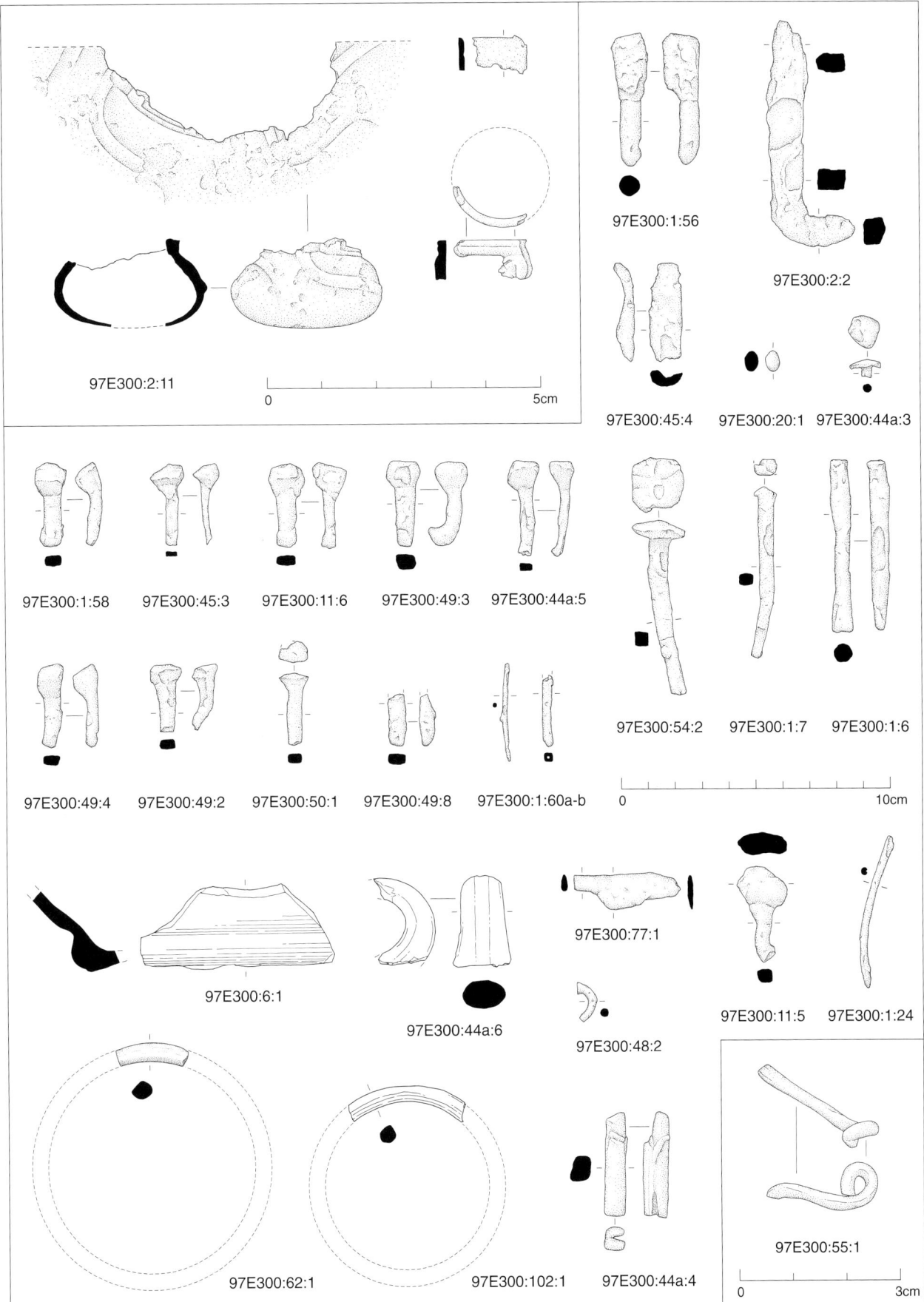

Fig. 26—Iron, bronze, glass and ceramic objects from ditch fill, palisade trench and humus.

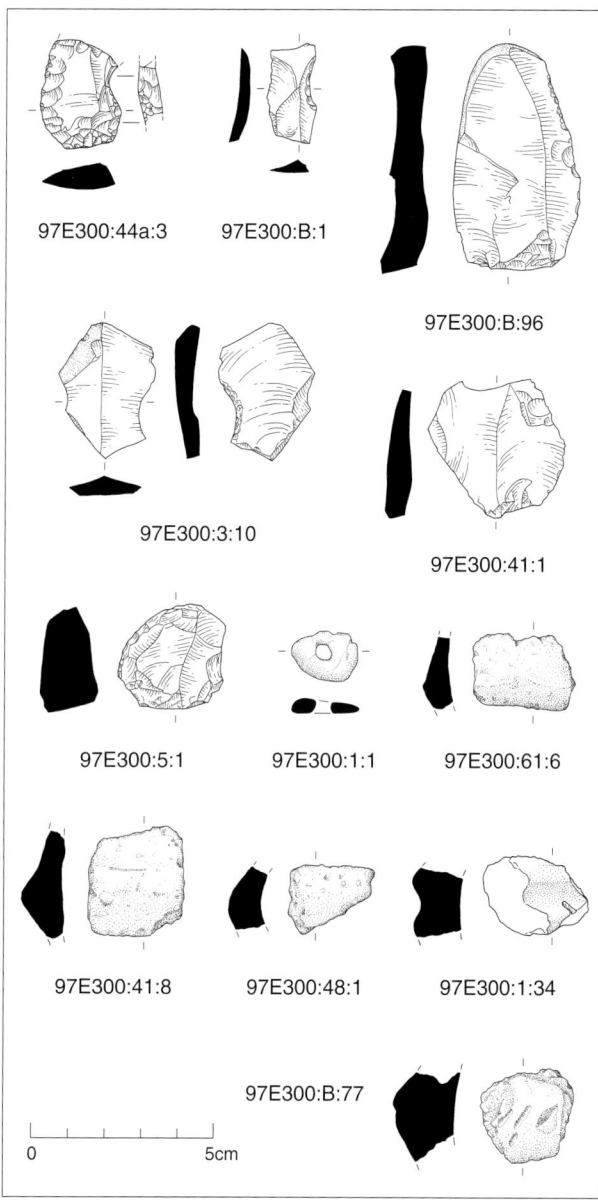

Fig. 27—*Neolithic artefacts from disturbed contexts.*

97). It is difficult to form definite conclusions from such a small sample, but the fact that most of the bone represented old or mature animals, in conjunction with evidence for traction on one of the horse bones, might suggest that these animals were no longer useful and therefore there was no conceived taboo about eating the flesh.

Regarding the palisade enclosure, the balance of archaeological and radiocarbon evidence favours contemporaneity with the construction of Ráith na Ríg. The surviving evidence showed that both features were cut from boulder clay, and large shale blocks originating from the digging of the ditch of Ráith na Ríg were found within the fill of the trench, suggesting that they were broadly contemporary, with the bank and ditch constructed sometime before the palisade trench. The finding of the opaque red glass bangle within the fill of the trench is of no real assistance. This bangle could date from as early as the second or first century BC, and therefore is more likely to be residual and probably contemporary with the industrial horizon beneath the bank. This is supported by the fact that crucible fragments and slag were found within the fill of the palisade trench during the 1950s excavations. The possibility that a bank may have existed to the rear of the palisade trench is an intriguing concept (see p. 69). This would have a significant influence on the perceived view of the function of enclosures, where the bank is external to the ditch. This type of arrangement is regarded as being non-defensive, with the function of the enclosure being more of symbolic than of practical significance (Carr and Knüsel 1997, 168). However, if the enclosure of Ráith na Ríg and the palisade trench were contemporary and a bank was part of the palisade defences, it would obviously introduce a significant defensive element to the enclosure.

The fact that much of the upper metre of the ditch fill originated from the southern side of the ditch, the combination of Neolithic, Iron Age and post-medieval artefacts found throughout the layers and the results of the soil analysis (see Appendix 6) strengthen the argument for the existence of a bank on the southern side of the ditch. The ditch stratigraphy is obviously perplexing in that the recognisable Iron Age layers are followed immediately by post-medieval activity. As already discussed, there is no evidence for a later recut into the ditch fill which would explain this phenomenon. However, if the interpretation that the upper layers of the Iron Age fill represent refuse from the occupation horizon at Ráith na Senad is correct, it seems that this was the last intensive activity on the site until that associated with cultivation in the post-medieval period. This would suggest that from sometime in the fourth century AD this area of Tara, at least, was abandoned, and the ditch of Ráith na Ríg was allowed to grass over until it was deliberately backfilled in post-medieval times.

The excavations carried out at Tara in 1997 were extremely successful and rewarding. Rare and important evidence for bronze- and iron-smithing and possible glass-working was uncovered, dating from as early as 370 cal. BC, and the dating of the enclosure of Ráith na Ríg to the first century BC was confirmed. This is similar to the recent dating of Navan Fort and implies that the Dún Ailinne enclosure is of the same date. In recent years both excavation and geophysical survey have increased our knowledge and understanding of the archaeological history of the so-called 'royal sites'. This is evident from the 1997 excavations and in the ongoing geophysical survey at Tara, which has even over the last few years identified a previously unknown circular enclosure that encompassed Ráith na Senad (Fenwick and Newman, this volume). New and exciting information has also been uncovered as a result of geophysical survey at Rathcroghan, Co. Roscommon, where a large enclosure possibly similar to Ráith na Ríg has been identified (Fenwick et al., 1999).

Despite the importance of the new evidence obtained from the recent excavations at Tara, our understanding of the function of Ráith na Ríg and what was happening within the enclosure is limited. Without further excavation of different areas of the ditch, and areas within the enclosure, much remains unanswered and an enormous amount of the complicated nature of the site remains to be unravelled. What has already been achieved is undoubtedly rewarding, but it is also tantalising when the potential of the site and how further excavation could produce a real understanding of its archaeological history are realised.

Pl. 19—Finely executed bronze nail from pre-bank industrial layer 31:5 (D. Jennings, University College Dublin).

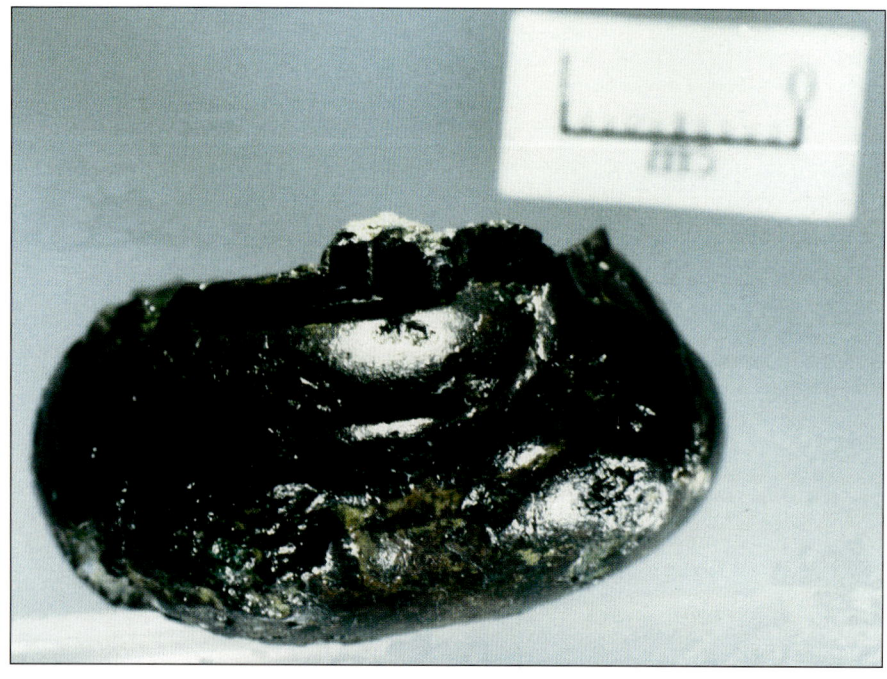

Pl. 20—Socketed iron axehead from pre-bank industrial layer 31:20 (D. Jennings, University College Dublin).

Pl. 21—Portion of a bronze spearbutt from upper level of Cutting 1 ditch fill 2:11 (D. Jennings, University College Dublin).

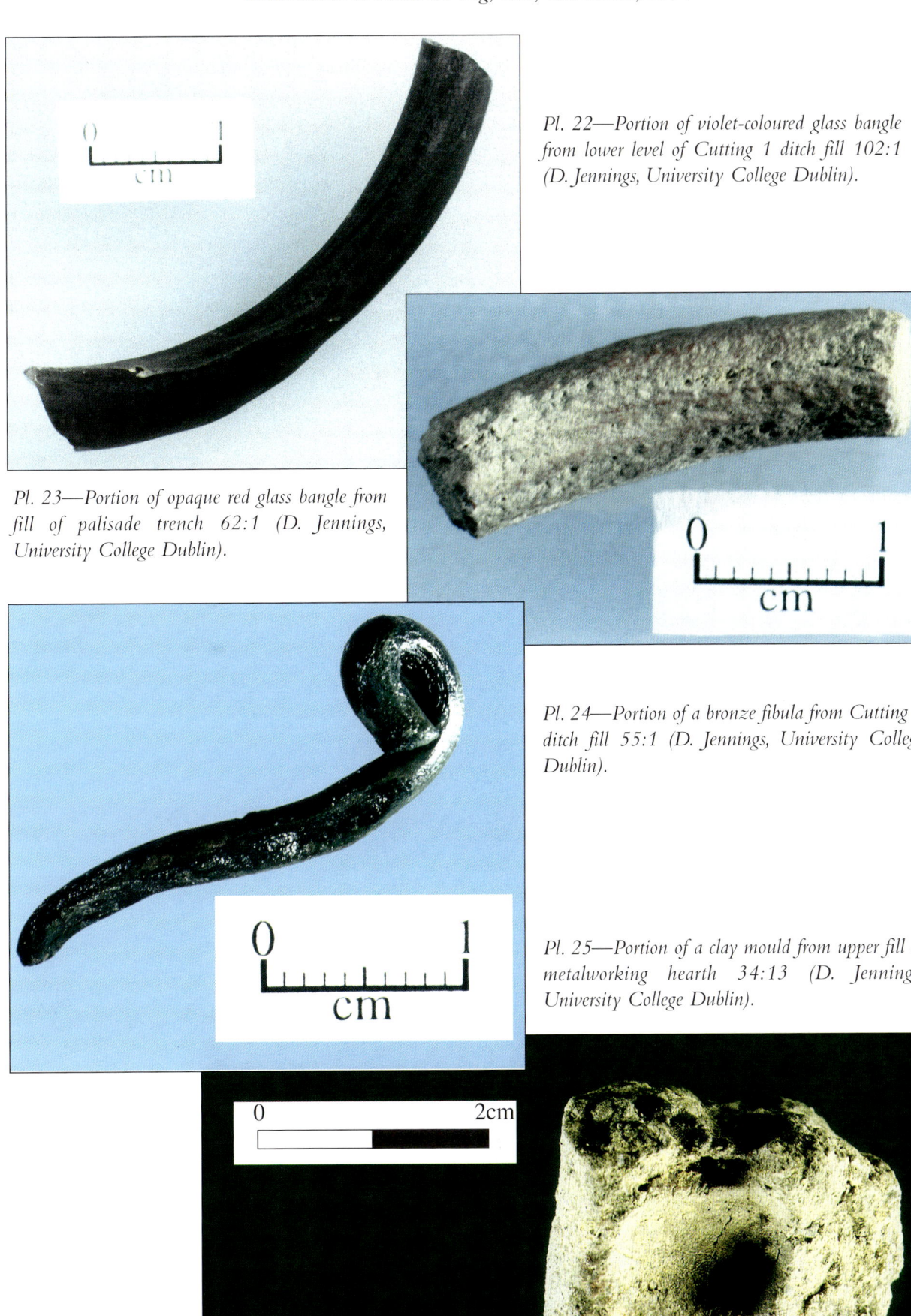

Pl. 22—Portion of violet-coloured glass bangle from lower level of Cutting 1 ditch fill 102:1 (D. Jennings, University College Dublin).

Pl. 23—Portion of opaque red glass bangle from fill of palisade trench 62:1 (D. Jennings, University College Dublin).

Pl. 24—Portion of a bronze fibula from Cutting 2 ditch fill 55:1 (D. Jennings, University College Dublin).

Pl. 25—Portion of a clay mould from upper fill of metalworking hearth 34:13 (D. Jennings, University College Dublin).

Acknowledgements

Firstly, I am enormously grateful to those who assisted me during the excavation of the site: Mr Karl Brady, Mr Emmet Byrne, Mr Kevin Byrne, Ms Sinead Cafferkey, Ms Mary Deevy, Mr Karl Mitchell, Mr Gerald Murran, Mr Niall Murran, Mr David O'Connor, Mr Liam O'Connor (who brought with him his extensive excavation experience from Knowth), Mr Brian Shanahan, and last—but most definitely not least—Mr Kevin Weldon, who shared his remarkable excavation skills with us. I would like to record my thanks to the McGuire family at Tara for their friendship and hospitality and to the local people who showed such interest and enthusiasm during our work. I would also like to extend a special thank-you to Mr Fíonnbar Ó Ríordáin, who shared his memories of his father's work at Tara with me. Much-needed practical advice from Mr William Cumming, Dúchas and Mr Malachy Jenkins, Meath County Council, was very much appreciated.

An integral part of this work are the specialist reports by Dr Peter Crew, Professor Thilo Rehren, Dr Finbar McCormick, Dr Edel Bhreathnach, Mr Barra Ó Donnabháin, Ms Brenda Collins and Dr Clare Ellis, to all of whom I extend my appreciation. I would like to express my gratitude to Ms Gráinne Kelly and Mr Kevin Weldon for preparing the illustrations, Ms Niamh O'Broin for the artefact drawings, Ms Susannah Kelly for the metal conservation, and Ms Caroline Sandes for identifying the post-medieval pottery. I also wish to thank Mr Con Brogan and Mr David Jennings for their photographic work.

I am indebted to those who generously gave their time in discussing the excavation with me and in offering their advice. In particular, Professor Barry Raftery not only shared his knowledge of the Iron Age period but also read the report on more than one occasion, and I thank him for his patience. I am grateful to Dr Eoin Grogan for his consistent help and encouragement, and especially for discussing his work on Ráith na Senad with me and allowing me to refer to the report prior to its publication. Professor George Eogan, as always, was generous in his help and advice. Sincere gratitude is also due to Mr John Bradley, Mr Edward Bourke, Dr Edel Bhreathnach, Mr Tom Condit, Professor Barry Cunliffe, Dr Chris Lynn, Dr Muiris O'Sullivan, Mr Richard Warner, and my colleagues in the Discovery Programme.

References

Baillie, M. G. L. 1988 The dating of the timbers from Navan Fort and the Dorsey, Co. Armagh. *Emania* 4, 37–40.

Bhreathnach, E. 1995 *Tara: a select bibliography*. Discovery Programme Monographs 1. Dublin.

Carew, M. (forthcoming) *The British Israelite explorations at Tara, 1898–1903*. Discovery Programme Monographs.

Carr, G. and Knüsel, C. 1997 The ritual framework of excarnation by exposure as the mortuary practice of the early and middle Iron Ages of central southern Britain. In A. Gwilt and C. Haselgrove (eds), *Reconstructing Iron Age societies*, 167–73. Oxbow Monograph 71. Oxford.

Cooney, G. and Grogan, E. 1994 *Irish prehistory: a social perspective*. Bray.

Cunliffe, B. 1983 *Danebury: anatomy of an Iron Age hillfort*. London.

Cunliffe, B. 1991 *Iron Age communities in Britain* (3rd edn). London and New York.

Cunliffe, B. and Poole, C. 1991 *Danebury: an Iron Age hillfort in Hampshire, vol. 5. The excavations 1979–1988: the finds*. CBA Research Report No. 73. London.

Ellis, P. 1993 *Beeston Castle, Cheshire: a report on the excavations 1968–85 by Laurence Keen and Peter Hough*. Archaeological Report 23. Historic Buildings and Monuments Commission for England. London.

Fenwick, J. 1997 A panoramic view from the Hill of Tara. *Ríocht na Midhe* 9 (3), 1–11.

Fenwick, J., Brennan, Y., Barton, K. and Waddell, J. 1999 The magnetic presence of Queen Medb: magnetic gradiometry at Rathcroghan, Co. Roscommon. *Archaeology Ireland* 13 (1), 8–11.

Fitzpatrick, A.P. 1997 Everyday life in Iron Age Wessex. In A. Gwilt and C. Haselgrove (eds), *Reconstructing Iron Age societies*, 73–86. Oxbow Monograph 71. Oxford.

Green, M. 1992 *Animals in Celtic life and myth*. London.

Grogan, E. 1983–4 Excavation of an Iron Age burial mound at Furness. *Journal of the Kildare Archaeological Society* 16, 298–316.

Grogan, E., Donaghy, C. and Caulfield, S. (forthcoming) *Tara, Co. Meath. Excavations by Seán P. Ó Ríordáin: the Rath of the Synods*. Seandálíocht. Department of Archaeology, University College Dublin, Monograph Series.

Haevernick, T.E. 1960 *Die Glasarmringe und Ringperlen der Mittel- und Spätlatènezeit auf dem Europäischen Festland*. Bonn.

Haseloff, G. 1991 Celtic enamel. In O.H. Frey, V. Kruta, B. Raftery and M. Szabó (eds), *The Celts*, 639–42. Milan.

Hawkes, C. F. C. 1982 The wearing of the brooch: Early Iron Age dress among the Irish. In B. G. Scott (ed.), *Studies on early Ireland*, 51–73. Belfast.

Henderson, J. 1991 Industrial specialization in late Iron Age Britain and Europe. *Archaeological Journal* 148, 104–48.

Henderson, J. 1997 The glass objects from Navan Site B, composition and archaeological implications. In C. J. Lynn (ed.), *Excavations at Navan Fort 1961–71 by D. M. Waterman*, 95–100. Northern Ireland Archaeological Monographs 3. Belfast.

Hingley, R. 1997 Iron, ironworking and regeneration: a study of the symbolic meaning of metalworking in Iron Age Britain. In A. Gwilt and C. Haselgrove (eds), *Reconstructing Iron Age societies*, 9–18. Oxbow Monograph 71. Oxford.

Jacobi, G. 1974 *Werkzeug und Gerät aus dem Oppidum von Manching*. Die Ausgrabungen in Manching, Band 5: Römisch-Germanische Kommission des Deutschen Archäologischen Instituts zu Frankfurt-am-Main. Wiesbaden.

Jacobi, G. 1977 *Die Metallfunde vom Dünsberg*. Wiesbaden.

Jope, E. M. and Wilson, B. C. S. 1957 A burial group of the first century A.D. from 'Loughey' near Donaghadee. *Ulster Journal of Archaeology* 20, 73–94.

Keeley, V. 1999 Iron Age discoveries at Ballydavis. In P.G. Lane and W. Nolan (eds), *Laois: history and society*, 25–34. Dublin.

Lynn, C. J. (ed.) 1997 *Excavations at Navan Fort 1961–71 by D. M. Waterman*. Northern Ireland Archaeological Monographs 3. Belfast.

Macalister, R.A.S. 1919 Temair Breg: a study of the remains and traditions of Tara. *Proceedings of the Royal Irish Academy* 34C, 231–404.

Macalister, R.A.S. 1931 *Tara: a pagan sanctuary of ancient Ireland*. London.

Macalister, R.A.S. 1938–56 *Lebor Gabála Érenn* (5 vols). Dublin.

McCormick, F. 1997 The animal bones from site B. In C. J. Lynn (ed.), *Excavations at Navan Fort 1961–71 by D. M. Waterman*, 117–20. Northern Ireland Archaeological Monographs 3. Belfast.

May, J. 1996 *Dragonby: report on excavations at an Iron Age and Romano-British settlement in north Lincolnshire*. Oxbow Monograph 61. Oxford.

Murphy, D. and Westropp, T.J. 1894 Notes on the antiquities of Tara. *Journal of the Royal Society of Antiquaries of Ireland* 24, 232–42.

Newman, C. 1992 The Tara Survey: interim report. *Discovery Programme Reports* 1, 70–87.

Newman, C. 1997 *Tara: an archaeological survey*. Discovery Programme Monographs 2. Dublin.

O'Brien, E. 1990 Iron Age burial practices in Leinster: continuity and change, 37–42. *Emania* 7, 37–42.

O'Brien, E. 1992 Pagan and Christian burial in Ireland during the first millennium AD: continuity and change. In N. Edwards and A. Lane (eds), *The early Church in Wales and the West*, 130–7. Oxford Monograph 16. Oxford.

O Daly, M. 1960 On the origins of Tara. *Celtica* 5, 186–91.

Ó Ríordáin, S. P. 1955 A burial with faience beads at Tara. *Proceedings of the Prehistoric Society* 21, 163–73.

O'Sullivan, A. 1996 Neolithic, Bronze Age and Iron Age woodworking techniques. In B. Raftery, *Trackway excavations in the Mountdillon Bogs, Co. Longford, 1985–1991*, 291–342. Irish Archaeological Wetland Unit. Transactions: Vol. 3. Dublin.

Petrie, G. 1839 On the history and antiquities of Tara Hill. *Transactions of the Royal Irish Academy* 18, 25–232.

Raftery, B. 1983 *A catalogue of Irish Iron Age antiquities*. Veröffentlichung des Vorgeschichtlichen Seminars Marburg. Sonderband 1. Marburg.

Raftery, B. 1984 *La Tène in Ireland: problems of origins and chronology*. Veröffentlichung des Vorgeschichtlichen Seminars Marburg. Sonderband 2. Marburg.

Raftery, B. 1994 *Pagan Celtic Ireland: the enigma of the Irish Iron Age*. London.

Raftery, B. 1998 Knobbed spearbutts revisited. In M. Ryan (ed.), *Irish antiquities: essays in memory of Joseph Raftery*, 97–109. Bray.

Raftery, J. 1944 The Turoe Stone and the Rath of Feerwore. *Journal of the Royal Society of Antiquaries of Ireland* 74, 23–52.

Roche, H. 1999 Late Iron Age activity at Tara, Co. Meath. *Ríocht na Midhe* 10, 18–30.

Scott, B. G. 1987 The status of the blacksmith in early Ireland. In B. G. Scott and H. Cleer (eds), *The crafts of the ancient blacksmith*, 153–6. Belfast.

Scott, B. G. 1990 *Early Irish ironworking*. Belfast.

Sharples, N. 1991 *Maiden Castle: excavations and field survey 1985–6*. English Heritage Archaeological Report 19. London.

Simpson, D. D. A. 1989 Neolithic Navan? *Emania* 6, 31–3.

Swan, D. L. 1978 The Hill of Tara, Co. Meath: the evidence of aerial photography. *Journal of the Royal Society of Antiquaries of Ireland* 108, 51–66.

Waddell, J. 1998 *The prehistoric archaeology of Ireland*. Galway.

Wailes, B. 1990 Dún Ailinne: a summary excavation report. *Emania* 7, 10–21.

Wailes, B. 1991 Dún Ailinne. In O.H. Frey, V. Kruta, B. Raftery and M. Szabó (eds), *The Celts*, 614–15. Milan.

Wainwright, G. J. 1979 *Gussage All Saints: an Iron Age settlement in Dorset*. Department of the Environment, Archaeological Reports No. 10. London.

Weir, D.A. 1989 A radiocarbon date from the Navan Fort ditch. *Emania* 6, 34–5.

Youngs, S. (ed.) 1989 *'The Work of Angels': masterpieces of Celtic metalwork, 6th–9th centuries AD*. London.

Notes

[1] M. O'Sullivan, *The Mound of the Hostages, Tara, Co. Meath, excavations by Seán P. Ó Ríordáin* (Department of Archaeology, University College Dublin, Seandálíocht, monograph series, forthcoming). E. Grogan, C. Donaghy, and S. Caulfield, *Tara, Co. Meath, excavations by Seán P. Ó Ríordáin: the Rath of the Synods* (Department of Archaeology, University College Dublin, Seandálíocht, monograph series, forthcoming).

[2] The number E615 refers to the 1950s excavation.

[3] Abbreviations for finds: L.=length; D.=diameter; T.=thickness; W.=width.

[4] Cuttings 23 and 24 will be referred to as Cuttings 1 and 2 respectively when discussing the 1997 excavations.

[5] The letter B before the find number refers to backfill.

[6] The 1997 excavation number (97E300) will be omitted throughout the text; only the feature number (in bold) followed by the find number will be included.

APPENDIX 1
High-temperature workshop residues from Tara: iron, bronze and glass

PETER CREW[1] AND THILO REHREN[2]

Introduction

The occurrence of technical debris and related installations, together with finished objects which may or may not relate to each other, is always a tempting setting for investigation. As well as the allocation of otherwise hard-to-identify pieces to specific classes of materials, such as ferrous or non-ferrous metallurgy or glassworking, it is in particular the reconstruction of a chain of operations which brings life to an archaeologically documented workshop area. At Tara, it was the putative furnace structure, ash layers with slag and crucible sherds, a few fragments of glass, bronze and iron, all found in close proximity during the 1997 excavation (Roche 1999), which stimulated this study of the material.

Visual inspection of the workshop residues from Tara gave rise to a number of thoughts and ideas which could be tested scientifically. Firstly, there was the obvious occurrence of crucible fragments, often featuring bright red internal slag films and, in at least one instance, a blue-coloured droplet on the outer surface. Secondly, there were fragments of coloured glass bangles, of a bright opaque red and of transparent purple, together with numerous tiny splinters of transparent blue glass. Is this enough to establish the presence of a glass workshop? On the other hand, there were fragments of moulds and heavily corroded specks of copper-bearing material trapped in some of the crucible slags, both usually associated with bronzeworking rather than glassworking. Finally there were large quantities of dark-coloured dense slags, mostly smithing hearth bottoms of rather unusual character, indicating that iron had also been forged in the same workshop.

In total about 17kg of high-temperature debris was recovered from the excavations at Tara. This includes some material diagnostic of both iron-smithing and non-ferrous metalworking, but a large proportion of the debris requires further detailed classification to allocate it to a specific process. Although this is not an especially large amount of material, it is of significance because of its discovery in a well-stratified prehistoric level and it is of particular interest as it was found in a workshop context, together with a possible metalworking hearth and other associated structures. The value of this material is enhanced because of the careful excavation and recording of the debris and the retention of the full assemblage for further study.

After initial washing, the material was examined visually and a detailed catalogue of the individual pieces and their weights was prepared. The crucibles and a few of the other unusual slag types were then selected for scientific examination by a variety of techniques, to try and allocate various finds to specific groups of materials and to reconstruct the activities which took place in the workshop. In addition to close macroscopic inspection, aided by a binocular magnifying lens, the analytical techniques used were non-sampling qualitative surface microanalysis by means of a secondary electron microscope with energy-dispersive spectrometry (SEM-EDS) and the fully fledged investigation of polished thin sections by light microscopy, SEM-EDS and quantitative microanalysis, using wavelength-dispersive techniques (SEM-WDS).

For curatorial reasons, sampling for thin sectioning had to be restricted to an absolute minimum, despite the fact that this technique leads to the most conclusive results. As an outcome of this study it has been possible to assign most of the finds to more specific classes of material, to put them in relation to each other and to link them to the outside world. In doing so, some peculiarities could be identified in regard to the slags, and the crucibles as well. Although the picture produced appears conclusive, there may still be the odd piece which has been overlooked or misinterpreted. In particular, some of the less

---

[1] Plas Tan Y Bwlch, Snowdonia National Park Study Centre, Wales.
[2] Chair of Archaeological Materials and Technologies, Institute of Archaeology, University College London.

diagnostic samples were difficult to approach without excessive sampling and thus had to be ignored except for visual examination. It is hoped, however, that no significant information was missed owing to this limitation in sampling.

Had the collection of materials been more comprehensive, for instance by the discovery of iron stock or non-ferrous raw materials, more definitive pieces of mould, a wider range of the diagnostic smithing debris or even fragments of glassworking debris, then this report could have been much more specific in defining the details of each process. But this is the nature of archaeological material and in this instance only the broad outlines can be recovered.

Material types

The majority of the metallurgical debris identified was attributed to six broad classes—vitrified hearth lining, low-density fluxed lining slags (FLS), dense slags (DS), amorphous slags (AS), crucibles and moulds. Both the dense slags and the amorphous slags include a small number of smithing hearth cakes or fragments thereof. A brief description, discussion and interpretation of each of these types of material is given below, together with the details of the scientific investigation where appropriate.

In addition to these six classes of material there is other related metallurgical debris. A small quantity of hammer scale, mostly fragmented to magnetic dust, was recognised during the washing of the slags prior to identification, but this is certainly not representative of the amount and distribution of hammer scale and other small debris which would normally occur on an iron-smithing site. Fragments of bronze, apparently casting debris, and iron were also recovered from the excavations, as described in the finds catalogue. It is unfortunate that these semi-finished products were not available for study as part of this investigation. Various other fragments of iron, including forge waste and lumps of amorphous shape, were recognised amongst the slags. Finally, there are the fragments of glass bangle, which suggested that some of the crucibles and slags may indeed have been related to glassworking.

As with most slag assemblages, all of these classes include material which is intermediate in character, and this continuum of material makes the allocation of individual pieces to specific types and processes rather difficult. This continuum is particularly noteworthy between the amorphous and dense slags, and between the vitrified hearth lining and the fluxed lining slags respectively. In reality, much of the smaller and less dense material is not diagnostic of, or attributable to, a particular process, and it is not possible from visual examination alone to allocate every piece of slag to a precise category. A great deal of detailed work would be required to produce a more considered typology and characterisation of the debris. However, the residues which are diagnostic of a particular process, such as the smithing hearth cakes and hammer scale, and the crucible and mould fragments allow recognition of the primary activities which were carried out, to which the less diagnostic pieces can then be assigned with, more or less, a degree of confidence.

Quantification of the metalworking debris

Over 900 pieces of metalworking debris have been identified. A breakdown of the different classes, by number of pieces and total weight, is given in Table 1. From this it can be seen that the low-density FLS and the amorphous slags account for the major proportion of the pieces of slag, but as these slags generally occur as very small fragments they account for only about one third of the total weight. In contrast, the dense slags constitute only about 12% of the number of pieces but nearly 60% of the total weight, most of

Table 1—Tara metalworking debris: numbers of pieces and total weights, by type.

Slag type	No. of pieces	%	Weight range (g)	Total weight (g)	%
Vitr. lining	111	12%	0.3 – 45	693	4%
FLS slags	309	33%	0.5 – 54	1443	8%
AS slags	287	31%	0.5 –290	4571	26%
DS slags	108	12%	9.5 –531	10,201	58%
Crucibles	22	2%	0.5 – 13	84	0.5%
Moulds	54	6%	0.3 – 10	71	0.4%
Forge waste	41	4%	2.5 – 55	662	4%
Totals	932			17,725	

which is accounted for by the smithing hearth cakes. There is a large number of pieces of vitrified lining, but these are mostly very small fragments, which comprise only 4% of the total weight.

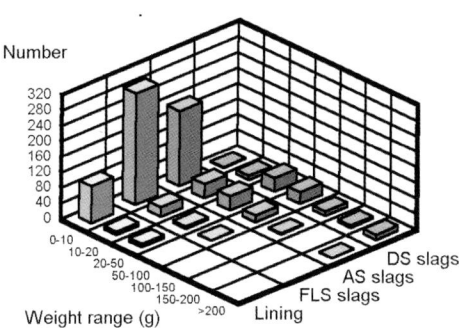

Fig. 1—Slag types, by weight range, by number.

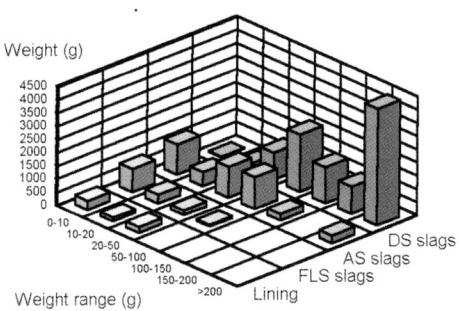

Fig. 2—Slag types, by weight range, by weight.

These statistics are more meaningful if they are broken down into a number of nominal weight ranges. Figure 1 emphasises the large number of very small pieces of lining and FLS slags, indicating the fragility of this material and its tendency to break into small fragments. The large number of small pieces of AS slags is partly a reflection of the difficulty of allocating small and unspecific pieces to a particular category. In contrast, Fig. 2 shows the significance of the heavier cakes of dense slag, which form the bulk of the weight of this collection. Few detailed quantifications of this type have been carried out, but this method of representing the data appears to have some potential for defining the essential characteristics of a slag assemblage. The size distribution of the Tara slags is typical of small-scale secondary metalworking and the large number of low-density slag fragments seems to be a particular characteristic of non-ferrous metalworking.

Vitrified lining

This material consists of clay which has been vitrified on one face in the high-temperature zone of a hearth. There are two principle types of lining. The majority of the pieces have a rather fine, light grey, sandy fabric. This is normally oxidised to an orange-red colour, but occasionally there is a thin inner zone of grey colour, indicating locally reducing conditions (Fig. 3). The highly fired clay is rarely more than a few millimetres thick, but this is simply because less-fired material, further from the hotter zone of the hearth, has degraded since it was deposited. The overall thickness of the lining is likely to have been several centimetres. The second type of lining, occurring in smaller quantities, has a rather coarser fabric, with small angular stone inclusions, fired to a brown-black colour. In some cases the coarser fabric has been applied over the finer fabric, suggesting that the former was used to prepare or repair the lining in the high-temperature zone (Fig. 4).

The inner face of all of the fragments has been vitrified to a vesicular vitreous material. The vitrification varies considerably in character and thickness, partly depending on its position in the hearth and its proximity to the higher-temperature zones. The thinnest fragments have only a thin veneer of vitrification, whereas the thickest fragments can have a vitrified zone up to 25mm thick, probably representing an accumulation of material through the repair of the high-temperature zone. It is usually these thicker fragments which have the intermediate zones of grey reduced clay, and this invariably merges with a highly vesicular zone of vitreous slag.

The vitrified surface of the lining varies considerably in colour. It is predominantly pale buff to yellow, but a proportion is a distinctive pale olive green and occasional fragments are a dark brown-black. These colour changes are not particularly significant, being dependent on both temperature and redox conditions within the hearth and the chemical composition of the clay.

Rare fragments have a muddy orange-red colouration, but this is due to oxides of iron rather than copper. Despite the clear evidence for non-ferrous metalworking, there are only a very small number of fragments with traces of the distinctive red copper oxide glaze or specks of secondary copper corrosion products. In the majority of cases the surface of the vitrification has been heavily corroded by the aggressive soil conditions, which has revealed the internal vesicular structure, and this post-deposition corrosion could also have removed any traces of the characteristic copper products which normally can be a good visual indication of the process for which the lining was used. The crucible fragments, though, still show some clear signs of green copper stains, indicating that the almost complete absence of such stains from the vitrified lining reflects the use environment rather than post-depositional corrosion.

Vitrified lining of this type is generally not diagnostic either of the type of feature or of the type of metalworking. In this case, however, it can be argued that the lining comes from a metallurgical hearth, which could have been used both for iron-smithing and non-ferrous metalworking. Most of the fragments recovered are too small to estimate the diameter of the hearth, and the few relatively large pieces show little or no curvature. There are no tuyère fragments, and there are no indications of any shaped fragments of lining which might indicate the diameter of a blowing-hole through which the air from the bellows would be directed into the hearth.

Low-density fluxed lining slags (FLS)

This class of material contains a series of subtypes but all are characterised by their vitreous and vesicular nature, pale colour and generally low density. This type of slag is often described as fuel ash slag, which is slightly misleading as it is mostly formed by the fusion of the hearth lining under high-temperature conditions, fluxed by the ash content of the charcoal fuel used in the hearth. Most of these slags have the form either of small irregular prills or of larger concretions with smooth cooling surfaces, sometimes with the characteristic impressions caused by the slags accumulating and cooling in the charcoal bed of the hearth (Fig. 5).

These slags are mostly rather friable and they tend to fragment easily into smaller pieces, thus accounting for the large number of fragments of relatively small overall weight (Fig. 6). A few of the more complete concretions weigh up to 50g and indicate that the hearth was being blown hard enough for significant quantities of the lining to become molten and to flow into the hearth. At one extreme, these slags are little different in character to the vitrified lining from which, indeed, they gradually develop. At the other extreme they become more amorphous in character and are generally denser, probably from the assimilation of iron-rich metallurgical slag.

As with the vitrified lining material, these low-density slags are not diagnostic of any particular process, unless they incorporate characteristic copper corrosion products, and they can form under high-temperature conditions in a variety of metallurgical operations. Slags of this type are formed in iron-smithing hearths, but in this case the bulk of the fluxed lining material would become incorporated into the smithing hearth slags or slag cake, mixed with denser slag and iron oxides from the material being worked. Usually only a small proportion of FLS slags are recognisable as such from an iron-smithing site. In a crucible hearth the main source of the slag would be the hearth lining being fluxed by the fuel ash and so the large number of fragments of FLS slag from Tara are probably from this process.

Dense slags

A significant proportion of the Tara slags are dense, relatively homogeneous and crystalline in fracture, with few vesicles. There are a few small examples of individual flows of slag, with clean smooth surfaces, typical of cooling in a bed of charcoal. Flows of this type are commonly found in abundance on smelting sites, but small quantities can also form in a smithing hearth, where the slag becomes liquid enough to flow into the charcoal bed and does not become incorporated into the hearth bottom.

The majority of the dense slags from Tara, however, are in the form of roughly circular cakes, usually with a convex lower surface which has the small-scale contortions typical of cooling on a bed of charcoal (Fig. 7). These are often fragmented into smaller pieces, usually with a characteristic blocky fracture, but their shape is still recognisable. They sometimes contain small amounts of metallic iron, which causes the slag cakes to break up when the iron corrodes and expands (Fig. 10). Slag cakes of this kind accumulate in an iron-smithing hearth just below the blowing-hole.

The upper surfaces are usually rather irregular and vesicular, owing to the slag not having fully consolidated at the end of the smithing process before the cake was removed from the hearth. Some of the cakes have typical flat fracture lines, indicating that they were removed from the hearth when they had cooled down. Some of the cakes have clay and stones incorporated into the lower surface, which are a result of the slag forming on the bottom of the hearth and picking up basal debris. Two of the cakes have distinct layers and would have formed when separate episodes of smithing had been carried out without the hearth being cleaned in between (Figs 8 and 9). In both cases, the second layer is a smaller cake of slag welded to the top surface of a larger cake. In practice, depending on the type and quality of the work being carried out, the blacksmith tries to keep the hearth clean of slag and so the cakes would be removed fairly frequently. If welding is being carried out a clean hearth is essential, and such a high-temperature operation will also increase the rate at which the hearth cake is made.

Only nineteen of the Tara cakes survive in a form which is complete enough for the weight to be meaningful (Table 2). There is a small number of rather large cakes, up to 8cm in diameter and 3cm thick, typically weighing 300–400g. These tend to be the densest of the cakes and have the most well-defined shape, which is indicative of the hearth being held at a relatively high temperature for a long enough period of time for the shape of the cake to fully develop. Hearth bottoms of this type and size would usually result from the forging of either blooms or partially refined bulk stock which still contained a large proportion of slag. One of these larger cakes is strongly magnetic and is corroding badly because it contains a relatively large piece of iron, which could have been lost in the refining of rather poor-quality stock. One example of a fractured cake has a number of unreacted stone inclusions, which probably derive from the stone grog of some of the lining material.

More than half of the cakes are rather small, with diameters around 5cm and a thickness of 2–3cm, weighing less than 150g. Most examples have a well-defined shape, but some are slightly different in character and are more vesicular or more amorphous in shape. These would be a product of a short episode of smithing during which several smaller objects or one larger object could have been made. The consistent size and character of these small cakes may indicate that a specific type of smithing was being carried out.

Small, dense smithing hearth cakes of this type are not entirely typical and an example was examined in more detail. In contrast to more typical smithing hearth cakes, some of the Tara cakes are much less porous and in fracture exhibit a coarse crystalline texture of mostly fayalite. This is probably due to slow cooling within the hearth of a slag that was more liquid than normal. Consequently, these cakes expose fewer iron metal particles to the environment and are less prone to corrosion and cracking. Chemical analysis showed only iron oxide and silica in any significant quantity, with alumina and lime at just above 1wt% each. Copper oxide is present at only about 500ppm (i.e. 0.05wt%) and tin oxide was below the detection limit of 0.001wt%, thus a relation to non-ferrous metallurgy can be excluded. In addition, there are small inclusions of metallic iron which would seem to confirm the visual identification that these cakes are indeed from smithing. A similar type of small and particularly dense cakes is known from the iron-smelting and smithing site of Meroe in the Sudan, dating from the very early first millennium AD (Rehren 1995).

Table 2—Tara slag cakes: number of pieces and total weight.

Weight range (g)	No.	Total weight	Mean weight
50–100	10	735	74
100–150	8	1110	139
150–200	2	349	175
200–250	1	224	225
250–300	2	565	283
300–350	2	670	335
350–400	3	1117	372
>400	1	531	531
Totals	29	5301	

Amorphous slags

As in most slag collections, a significant proportion of the material cannot be classified easily. Within this general class is a variety of material of indeterminate character. These slags are generally amorphous in shape and are often coated in secondary iron-rich corrosion products, which distinguishes them from the dense slags. The density of these slags is variable and some have large vesicles. A few examples are partially magnetic. Many of these slags are fragments which are too small to have any distinctive characteristics. In the case of the Tara material, some of the amorphous slags appear to be a non-diagnostic fraction of the dense slag, and the bulk of them probably formed during iron-smithing.

Hammer scale

Refining and smithing usually produce a variety of very small residues which can be diagnostic of the stage of ironworking being carried out. Material of this type is usually recovered from the systematic sampling of deposits and can indicate the layout of a workshop floor and the location of anvils. Unfortunately very little of this debris was recovered, and the small quantity of hammer scale and magnetic dust, all found at various levels within F38, simply confirms that iron-smithing was carried out.

Iron fragments

In addition to the iron listed in the finds catalogue, 41 pieces were recognised amongst the slag collection. Some of these are small fragments of mineralised bar or rod and there are several irregular flakes of iron. All of these are typical of forge waste, being fragments of iron breaking off during forging and being discarded because they are too small to be recovered. The majority of the iron fragments are of amorphous shape and are typical of small pieces breaking off bulk stock during refining. Some of these iron lumps are rather slaggy, suggesting that some of the stock may not have been of especially high quality.

The iron pieces listed in the finds catalogue are mostly small fragments of bar or rod, which seem to be typical forge waste or offcuts which were discarded because they were too small to be worth working.

The crucibles

Twenty-two fragments of crucible were found, most of which are rim sherds (Fig. 11). Only one of the body sherds may be from the base of a crucible. All are heavily vitrified and seem to be of a generally similar fabric, but there is some variation in the colour of the sherds. The majority of the pieces have splashes of the distinctive reddish-purple copper oxide glaze, and some have small fragments of copper corrosion products. There is one fragment of crucible which has a distinctive spot of pale blue glassy material on the vitrified surface, which was initially thought to be an indication of glassworking.

The rim sherds are mostly 7–8mm thick and have either rounded or rather sharp edges. The body sherds are mostly of the same thickness as the rims, but one fragment is 18mm thick, perhaps indicating that it had an extra layer of clay for additional stability. The typically small size of the sherds and the limited number of matching pieces precludes any reconstruction of the shape or profile of the crucibles, except for the general impression that the majority may have been triangular in shape and probably no bigger than 5cm across. A few fragments only could originate from round, thumb-sized crucibles, about 3cm deep and wide (e.g. F30:30). With almost exclusively rim sherds being preserved it is impossible to estimate the original depth of the vessels. Not more than about six or seven complete crucibles are represented by this collection, and the uneven thickness of some of the samples suggests that they were formed individually and not to a particularly high standard.

Macroscopically, the fabrics fall into two broad groups. One is dark-coloured throughout most of the body of the sherd ('black' group) but grey nearer to the surfaces (e.g. F34:05, Figs 12 and 13), while the other has a much lighter appearance, up to a full grey in some instances ('grey' group, Fig. 14). Often, sherds of both groups have surface layers rich in silica grains, resulting in an almost white outer surface, sometimes extending over the rim into the upper parts of the inside. Most sherds are heavily vitrified both externally and internally, with a thin colourless glassy film barely covering the outside, and a much thicker and typically black slag layer inside. This slag layer often contains tiny metallic prills, just visible with the binocular lens.

Thin section analyses were carried out on four sherds (two 'black' and two 'grey' ones) to identify the structure and composition of the ceramic, of the metal prills, and of the slag, with its relation to the ceramic body. Non-destructive analyses were carried out on other samples to check the homogeneity of evidence for the prills and to characterise the blue glass droplet on the outside of one of the sherds.

Microscopically, the divide between the inner, black, body and the outer, grey, skin of the 'black' vessels simply reflects a different content of organic temper. The inner parts show abundant charcoal remains, while the outer parts are virtually free of these particles. The mineral content of the ceramic is composed of a fair amount of quartz temper in a fine-grained matrix. The quartz grains are mostly angular, suggesting the use of crushed quartz or short-distance sediments rather than well-rounded sand. The porosity in the central part is elongated, while the outer parts typically have a well-rounded porosity, indicating a higher degree of vitrification and some initial bloating of the ceramic. A distinctive feature of the black core region is its high degree of organic matter, mostly crushed charcoal rather than decomposed fibres. The charcoal spans a wide range of grain sizes, from relatively coarse particles down to fine dust intimately mixed into the clay matrix. Its absence from the outer grey skin is paralleled by an absence of iron phases, either finely dispersed oxide particles or tiny metal prills, as compared to the core region of the ceramic. The EDX results, however, reflect this difference in the mineralogy only to a limited extent, suggesting the dissolution and incorporation of the iron-rich particles into the glass which formed when the matrix vitrified. The homogeneously grey crucibles, in contrast, show no signs of organic carbon temper, and no layered or banded structure other than the use-

Appendix 1

related inner slag layer. Their body is composed of a clay matrix with the same type of angular quartz temper as the other crucibles.

Chemically, the ceramic of the black vessels is a rather unspecific (not to say boring) composition, with about 70wt% silica (depending on the amount of quartz temper in the area analysed), somewhat less than 20wt% alumina, 4wt% iron oxide and 2wt% potash as the main constituents. Lime is relatively low with 1–2wt% only, while phosphorus oxide is present at about 2wt%. The latter, however, is probably not a primary ingredient of the ceramic body but due to uptake from the soil, a common feature with ceramics (Freestone *et al.* 1985). In summary, the level of iron oxide and potash present, both fluxing components, and the relatively limited amount of alumina make it a not particularly refractory ceramic. The lack of significant quantities of lime most probably reflects the local geology of the clay source area.

The grey vessels are more silica-rich, reflecting a higher amount of quartz temper, while the clay-derived matrix is of a composition similar to the black parts of the vessels. The slightly lower content of alumina and iron oxide probably reflects the dilution of the ceramic body by the use of more quartz temper rather than the use of a different clay type.

The more or less thin slag films present on the inside of the crucibles are much less homogeneous, both in the quantity present and in their mineralogical and chemical composition, than the ceramic body. A coarse separation may be made between the glassy slag matrix, formed from a reaction of fused ceramic material, fluxing components and metal oxides from the charge, and material which could be called dross, i.e. agglomerates of metal oxides, as the result of oxidation of the metal charge in the heat. There is, however, a gradual continuum from more glassy slag, which develops from the ceramic, to the dross which typically prevails at the outermost surface area. While this dross component, i.e. mixed copper and tin oxides, is easily explained as burnt bronze, the extremely high iron content of the slags is noteworthy.

The metal prills trapped in the slag span a wide range from technically pure copper up to high-tin bronze (α–δ eutectic, about 10wt% Sn, 90wt% Cu). Typically they are rather small, less than a millimetre and often only a few tens of microns in diameter. Of particular interest are frequent occurrences of high-tin phases (δ, ε and η with 33wt%, 37wt% and 60wt% Sn respectively) which go well beyond the average tin content in bronze (Fig. 15). The presence of these phases, together with the overwhelming dominance of tin oxide over copper oxide in most of the dross-rich slag areas, indicates that a tin or tin–copper master alloy was melted in some of the crucibles at one stage at least. One sample (F30:35) contained a bronze droplet about 5mm in diameter adhering to its inner surface (Figs 16 and 17). This prill consists of areas in various degrees of oxidation, from bronze with about 10wt% tin to low-tin bronze charged with tin oxide needles to copper intergrown with both tin oxide and copper oxide particles. This sequence, and the pattern in which the oxide phases are formed and intergrown with the metal, is characteristic of bronze being oxidised at a high temperature, i.e. being burnt rather than corroded (Northover and Rehren 1992).

Further research is necessary to explain the surprisingly high iron oxide content of the slag. This cannot be due to the simple remelting of pre-existing bronze alloys which typically contain much less than one per cent iron. Nor can it be explained from the underlying ceramic, which contains only about one fifth of the slag's iron oxide. Neither alkali nor earth alkaline oxides are significantly enriched in these slags, precluding a significant contribution of fuel ash to their formation. Thus the high concentration of iron

Table 3—Semi-quantitative SEM-EDX analyses of crucible and mould fragments, measured over small areas in thin section. All data in wt% and normalised to 100%. Mean of three or four areas per sample. Top two rows are from black cores, while the next three rows represent grey areas. The final two analyses are of the crucible slags.

Sample	SiO_2	TiO_2	Al_2O_3	FeO	MnO	CaO	MgO	K_2O	P_2O_5	Cu_2O	SnO_2
F34:35 Core (bl)	74	0.6	16	3.5	0.0	1.3	0.3	2.1	2.0	0.2	0.0
F34:05 Core (bl)	71	0.6	18	4.0	0.0	1.5	0.7	2.2	2.3	0.0	0.0
F34:05 Rim (gr)	70	0.7	18	2.8	0.0	1.2	0.3	3.4	2.4	0.0	0.0
F34:09 Body (gr)	83	0.6	10	2.0	0.1	0.6	0.5	1.8	1.2	0.0	0.0
F34:06 Body (gr)	80	0.6	12	3.4	0.1	0.7	0.8	1.8	0.5	0.2	0.7
F34:03 Mould	80	0.5	11	2.6	0.0	1.2	0.4	1.1	3.3	0.1	0.0
F34:09 Slag	41	0.2	5.4	25.0	0.1	3.0	1.2	1.7	1.1	11.1	10.1
F34:06 Slag	72	0.3	7.2	13.4	0.1	1.0	0.5	1.3	0.7	3.0	0.7

in the slags has to be explained by the metal charge treated in these vessels.

Interpretation of crucible findings

The crucible fragments from Tara represent a small number of vessels of no particular quality or standard, and clearly relate to the working of high-tin bronze. Two aspects are particularly worth noting, namely the making of the fabric and the high tin content of the charge remains. Chronologically, the crucibles fall in between the period of open, top-fired vessels which dominated crucible metallurgy well beyond the Bronze Age, and the Roman and later crucibles which were fired from the outside (Freestone 1989; Rehren 1997). The major differences between the two firing modes is in the design of the vessels and the ceramic used. Top-fired crucibles are typically of an open form, to expose as large a surface to the fuel as possible, while outside-fired vessels typically have a smaller opening to reduce heat loss. Furthermore, the ceramic of the older crucibles has to be a good insulator to keep the heat inside the vessel. The outer layers of the ceramic were thus kept relatively cool, maintaining a high enough mechanical stability of the fabric to handle the vessels while hot. Therefore no specific refractory clay was needed, and mostly organic temper was used to increase the porosity, and thus the insulating properties, of the body. Thick walls were also helpful. Externally fired vessels, in contrast, had to conduct the heat through the fabric into the interior of the vessel. Thus the ceramic material used had to be sufficiently refractory, and thin walls were preferred. Temper was now mostly quartz to enhance the refractoriness of the material, although this resulted in increased problems with cracking owing to temperature-related stress.

The Tara vessels appear intermediate between the two variants, with significant heat transfer through the body of the vessels but still also with a considerable heating component from the top. The 'black' cores of some vessels offer charcoal as an interesting temper, being sufficiently heat-resistant under reducing conditions while at the same time ensuring these same conditions by partially reacting with any excess oxygen and carbon dioxide. Thus the outer skin of these vessels turned white from the burning of the charcoal, while the core region still contained sufficient temper to remain rigid. The extra layer of crushed quartz applied to the outer surface of these vessels is found also in some European Iron Age (Rehren 1997, 15) and Early Christian crucibles (Tylecote 1987, 191), which is understood as a means of enhancing the surface refractoriness of the ceramic.

The metal melted in these vessels very obviously was bronze. Neither lead nor zinc could be identified at any significant level in the alloy. The working conditions of the crucibles, as evident from the phase assemblage preserved in the inner slag film, was rather oxidising throughout most areas, as one would expect from a melting process being carried out with an insufficient cover of charcoal. Remarkable, however, is the frequent occurrence of high-tin phases, which do not occur in normal bronze with around ten per cent by weight of tin. There seem to be two different possible interpretations for this. The first assumes that the charge being melted in these vessels contained significantly more tin than the actual bronze which eventually was cast into objects, indicating the preparation of average-tin-level bronze from alloying copper with either tin or a high-tin master alloy. Another interpretation could be based on a scenario where average-tin bronze is being melted under oxidising conditions, leading to the preferential burning of tin into tin oxide, as often seen in the archaeological record and in experiments (Northover and Rehren 1992). This is then followed by more reducing conditions, at least locally, in some areas rich in tin oxide, resulting in them being reduced back to tin metal or, together with copper oxide, into high-tin bronze. While the latter sounds more complicated in terms of variable redox conditions in the crucibles, the former implies use of an ingredient for which we have no archaeological evidence yet from Tara: tin metal or a high-tin master alloy.

The other highly interesting aspect is the slag and dross adhering internally, and in particular the high iron content of this (see Table 3, above). Possible interpretations include the addition of tin metal high in iron to the charge, or the smelting of tin ore. Iron–tin intermetallic phases ('hard head') form easily in tin-smelting and contaminate the resulting tin metal if it is not sufficiently refined. Upon remelting and alloying with copper, which is a much less reducing operation than the initial smelting, this iron component can be slagged off. Alternatively, smelting tin ore which typically contains variable, often considerable, amounts of iron oxide results in an iron-rich slag. Thus the identification of a heavily iron-enriched crucible slag, together with the frequent occurrence of high-tin copper phases, demands further attention. Research is continuing on this aspect, for which the closest parallel probably stems from the Middle Bronze Age excavation at Cham, Switzerland (Rehren 2001).

Appendix 1

Table 4—Tara metallurgical debris, numbers of pieces, by context.

Context	Lining	FLS	AS	DS	Crucible	Mould	Iron	Total
Humus			1					1
Backfill	17	6	30	14			1	68
Bank	7	41	61	23			14	146
Grey sod layer	22	1	23	20	4		2	72
Industrial level F31	33	93	113	44	10	1	19	309
Hearth F38	7	23	21	1	3	8	3	71
Hearth SS64, F34	8	132		1	14	44		186
Features	17	13	38	5	3	1	2	79
Totals	*111*	*309*	*287*	*108*	*30*	*54*	*41*	*932*

Moulds

There are 54 fragments of mould, but most of them are very small and abraded, with the result that any shaped surfaces or surface deposits have not survived. A few of the larger pieces do have part of a shaped surface surviving, but none of them have any indication of the type of object being cast (Fig. 18). The moulds have a distinctive very fine sandy fabric. Some of the fragments have a characteristic sandwich colouration, with reddish-brown oxidised zones on both the inside and outside surfaces, with the interior of the sherds being usually a grey-black colour, indicating more reducing conditions.

One example was thin-sectioned and analysed (Table 3; Fig. 19). The ceramic shows little, if any, heat impact beyond low-temperature baking of the primary clay. Some quartz and small rock temper is present. No traces of bronze or glass were detected in the thin section. The chemical composition differs from the average crucible ceramic only in so far as the potash content of the mould material is lower, while the phosphorus content is higher than in the crucibles. Whether this is indicative of a different, specific, clay being used for mould-making or is simply a reflection of the overall scatter in clay compositions and post-deposition alterations is hard to decide owing to the need to keep the number of samples for analysis to a minimum.

Bronze

All of the bronze fragments are catalogued in the finds report. From the descriptions given there, some of them may be casting waste rather than objects, supporting the impression that part of the high-temperature debris from Tara stems from a bronze-casting workshop. Unfortunately they were not available for analysis and thus nothing can be said about their composition and how it relates to the findings from the crucibles.

The metallurgical debris by context

In Tables 4 and 5 the types of metallurgical debris are classified by the broad contexts in which they were found. The majority come from well-stratified contexts sealed by the bank and grey sod layer. All of the classes of debris were found in all of the stratified contexts, and no clear features or areas of activity

Table 5—Tara metallurgical debris, weight, by context.

Context	Lining	FLS	AS	DS	Crucible	Mould	Iron	Total
Humus				25				25
Backfill	194	53	415	1495			6	2163
Bank	59	369	1730	3670			168	5996
Grey sod layer	101	16	402	1274	15		34	842
Industrial level F31	181	645	1535	2970	12	2	432	5777
Hearth F38	68	101	236	94	5	32	9	575
Hearth SS64, F34	6	95		16	13	35		165
Features	84	164	228	682	9	2	13	1182
Totals	*693*	*1443*	*4571*	*10,201*	*84*	*71*	*662*	*17,725*

relating to a specific process can be identified. The general impression is that both the iron-smithing and non-ferrous metalworking were being carried out in the same workshop, perhaps using the same hearth, and that the resulting debris has become thoroughly mixed. It should be noted that the quantification of the iron fragments in these tables is only of those pieces which were recognised amongst the slag assemblage and does not include the items listed in the finds catalogue.

Broadly the same types of debris occur also in the grey sod layer, the overlying bank and the backfill of Ó Ríordáin's excavations, though fewer of the FLS slags, crucible or mould fragments were recognised. All of the material from these contexts is clearly secondary and probably derives from the prehistoric phase of metalworking activity.

Although these excavations have identified a focus of metalworking, it seems very likely that this activity extended beyond the area excavated, especially in the area between Cutting 1 and Cutting 2, and that part of the workshop area would have been within Ó Ríordáin's 1950s trench. It is clear, therefore, that the quantities and proportions of the types of debris recovered are not necessarily fully representative of what would have been produced.

Feature 38, a possible metalworking hearth

This is the only feature found within the excavation area which may have been used for high-temperature metalworking. It was originally identified as a possible furnace, but as there is no evidence for the smelting of either iron or copper this possibility can be discounted. It is an unusually large feature to have been used for metalworking, being about 1m in diameter and some 30cm deep. It consists of a shallow bowl-shaped feature, the base and sides of which were burnt to a generally consistent orange-red oxidised colour. However, the photographs give the impression that the burning does not penetrate the subsoil to any significant depth, which might argue against it having been used for high-temperature working for any length of time. A number of stake-holes were found, some cutting into the base of the hearth and some around the south edge. The internal stakes are unlikely to be directly associated with the operation of the hearth, but the double row of stakes on the south edge may have been to support a low clay superstructure, as has been recognised at a number of metalworking sites.

Deposits within F38

The fill of this feature consisted of a series of well-defined layers, some of which incorporated both non-ferrous and ironworking debris. Although the basal layer may have formed *in situ*, the upper layers showed clear stratification of the charcoal-rich and clay-rich layers which seems more likely to have resulted from the systematic dumping into a redundant feature of material from metallurgical and other activity being carried out nearby. This is partly confirmed by the occurrence of unburnt material in the fill, including a piece of bone, a tiny piece of flint and frequent fragments of clay.

A bulk sample (No. 64) was kept from F34, one of the upper layers filling F38, from which fragments of bronze, crucible and slag had been recovered during the excavation. The sample was greasy and black, comprising degraded clay discoloured by charcoal. After drying the sample weighed about 2kg, and it was then carefully examined for metalworking debris. This included one of the larger fragments of crucible, 44 tiny and abraded fragments of mould, a small quantity of lining and a large number of small fragments of the low-density FLS slags (see Tables 4 and 5; Fig. 6). Similar tiny pieces of metallurgical residues would have been difficult to recognise and collect during the excavation of the rest of the feature, or indeed during the excavation of the F31 layer. This suggests that the quantities of mould and of FLS slags in particular may be significantly underrepresented in the overall collection of slags.

In addition, the fine black matrix of the dried sample was tested with a magnet. Between 5% and 10% of this material is magnetic dust, which is degraded hammer scale, but only a few small fragments were recognisable as such with a x10 hand lens. Small quantities of hammer scale were fortuitously preserved along with two bags of unwashed slag, which came from F37b at the base of the feature and from the F34 layer itself. As well as indicating that significant quantities of hammer scale could have been present, the mixture of materials in the F34 layer tends to confirm the hypothesis that these layers were secondary dumps of material.

A notable feature of this sample was the frequent occurrence of small clusters and flakes of iron pyrites or chalcopyrite. This is most probably a secondary formation of this material, from the iron and copper available in the hearth, under the wet and strongly reducing deposition conditions.

Interpretation of F38

The question of whether or not F38 had originally been a metalworking hearth cannot now be fully resolved. This is a great pity, as surviving hearths from secondary metalworking, especially from the prehistoric period, are not common. None of the fragments of vitrified lining found in the hearth was *in situ*, though none of them showed any signs of curvature, implying that they could have derived from a large-diameter feature such as this hearth. A hearth requires some form of low clay superstructure, which need only be around part of the feature, which would have helped both to contain the bed of charcoal and to protect the bellows and its nozzle from the heat. Only a small hot zone would have been needed within the hearth and only the lining above the blowing-hole zone would have become vitrified.

However, for iron-smithing, even the refining of relatively large pieces of bulk stock, a hearth of this size seems unnecessarily large, and it is unlikely that a smithing hearth of this size and depth would not have retained some of its vitrified lining *in situ*. Exactly the same argument could be used for a hearth for non-ferrous metalworking, where close control of the hot zone is equally important. It is possible, however, to suggest a model for the use of a large-diameter hearth for the melting and casting of non-ferrous alloys. In this case, the crucibles could have been placed immediately in front of the blowing-hole (or blowing-holes) to melt their contents in the hottest zone, and additional space at the rear of the hearth, full of hot charcoal, could have been used for drying and preheating the moulds, ready for casting, thus allowing rapid transfer of the hot metal from the crucible to the mould. If this had been the case with F38, it might suggest that relatively large or long objects were being cast, though there are no surviving mould fragments of sufficient size to support this contention. Experiments have been carried out in France in a hearth of this kind which is only slightly smaller then F38, based partly on archaeological evidence from Fort Harrouard, showing the practicality of such an arrangement (Andrieux 1991).

On balance the size of F38 would seem to argue against its having been used as a metallurgical hearth, though unfortunately there is at present no satisfactory alternative interpretation which can be offered. It should be stressed, however, that there must have been a hearth somewhere in the near vicinity, and that the close admixture of the residues from both processes suggests that the same feature may have been used both for the iron-smithing and for the non-ferrous metalworking.

Glass finds

The selection of glass finds from the 1997 excavations at Tara is limited in number, comprising two fragments of bangles, one transparent purple and one opaque red, and several splinters of transparent blue glass which were found immediately in front of the supposed furnace excavated in 1997 (Roche 1999). Investigation of the bangle fragments was carried out by low-power optical microscopy and secondary electron microscopy (SEM) to study the workmanship, and by energy-dispersive spectroscopy (EDX) for all samples to determine the chemical composition (Table 6). The aim of this work was — besides the necessary chemical characterisation of these finds — to establish a reference base against which the analyses of coloured slags and glazes from the crucible finds could be compared.

The bangles

The red bangle is made of an opaque red glass with a density of about 3.5–4g/cc (Fig. 20). This and the typical red colour are in good accord with the chemical composition as determined by EDX. It is lead-rich soda-lime silica glass with high amounts of copper oxide. Figures found are 45wt% SiO_2, 30wt% PbO, about 8wt% Na_2O, about 7wt% CuO, about 4wt% CaO, 2–3wt% Al_2O_3, and close to 1wt% Cl. Other oxides measured were all found below 1wt%, in decreasing order MgO, FeO, K_2O and MnO. Likely errors for these figures are about 5% relative for silica and lead oxide and 10–20% relative for all other oxides. Qualitative wavelength-dispersive spectroscopy (WDS) proved the presence of small quantities (fraction of a per cent) of antimony, but no tin was detected. On the bangle's inner side a tiny metal prill is trapped in the glass (Fig. 21). This droplet consists of metallic lead, indicating that the making and/or working of the glass occurred under more reducing than oxidising conditions.

The purple bangle consists of a glass with a density of about 2.5g/cc (Fig. 22). The chemical composition was found to be a typical Iron Age/Roman soda-lime silica base, with 70wt% SiO_2, 15wt% Na_2O, 8wt% CaO, 2–3wt% Al_2O_3, close to 2wt% MnO and 1wt% Cl. The other oxides measured are all below 1wt%, in decreasing order MgO, K_2O, FeO and CuO. Analytical errors are as above. A particularly interesting feature of this bangle fragment is the many flakes of iron oxide fused onto the inner surface. The position of these and the flow pattern visible on the glass, nicely enhanced by corrosion effects, strongly suggest that they are scales from the iron tools used to work

Table 6—Semi-quantitative SEM-EDX analyses of glass samples, measured over small areas. All data in wt% and normalised to 100%. Mean of two or three areas per sample. The presence of Co in the first three and its absence in the last two were confirmed by qualitative WDS scans. By the same method, antimony was found in the opaque red sample, but no tin.

Sample	Colour	SiO_2	Al_2O_3	FeO	MnO	CaO	MgO	Na_2O	K_2O	Cu_2O	PbO	Cl
F31:58	Co blue	69	2.9	0.7	1.3	8.5	0.6	16	0.4	0.0	0.0	0.8
F31:57	Co blue	68	3.0	0.7	1.3	8.2	0.8	16	0.5	0.0	0.0	0.8
F31:60	Co blue	68	3.1	0.8	1.1	8.1	0.7	17	0.4	0.2	0.0	0.9
F102:1	Mn purple	70	2.7	0.3	1.8	8.0	0.8	15	0.6	0.0	0.0	1.0
F62:1	Cuprite red	45	2.3	0.3	0.2	4.2	0.6	8.5	0.3	7.5	30	0.7

the bangles while hot (Figs 23 and 24). This is a characteristic feature of most glass bangles, and ethnographic evidence from India indicates that the bangles would have been worked by slowly turning a gather of glass around a tapered iron rod, in the mouth of a furnace, to enlarge the diameter of the bangle. The iron scales forming on the surface of the hot tool would have been picked up by the soft glass.

The glass splinters

Several transparent blue glass splinters were also analysed for their chemical composition (Fig. 25). They consist again of a soda-lime silica-base glass with about 70wt% SiO_2, 15wt% Na_2O, 8wt% CaO, about 3wt% Al_2O_3, slightly above 1wt% MnO, close to 1wt% each MgO and Cl, and below 1wt% FeO and K_2O. From the light blue colour it is either a copper or a cobalt-blue glass; neither element was found in the EDS analyses, however. Cobalt oxide has a much higher colouring capacity than copper oxide. Less than a tenth of a per cent of the former suffices to impart a good colour, while the latter usually needs one per cent at least to colour a glass. In view of the detection limit of the technique used here, being about half a per cent for both copper and cobalt, it is concluded that the glass splinters are coloured by cobalt. A qualitative scan using the WDS proved the presence of cobalt, though at a significantly lower level than the manganese present. The ratio of manganese to iron is higher here than in the purple glass, with absolute lower iron and higher manganese concentrations in the purple bangle. No compositional differences were found among the various splinters analysed.

Interpretation of glass findings

The composition of the transparent blue and purple glass fragments analysed lies well within the range typically found with Iron Age and Roman soda-lime silica glasses. The systematically lower soda value found here is most likely due to analytical problems of the EDS system, underestimating the low energy lines. The low values for MgO and K_2O are characteristic of glasses whose alkali compound is derived from mineral natron rather than plant ash. The colouration is also in good accordance with known glass technology, with a pinch of cobalt being used to impart a blue colour and some manganese for a purple. The lower iron content in the purple glass as compared with the blue splinters is noteworthy, indicating the use of a 'cleaner' raw material for the making of the bangle. While the manganese in the purple glass obviously acts as a colourant, its function in the blue glass is probably to counteract the colouring effect from the iron content, i.e. to suppress a green hue. Whether the manganese and iron found in the cobalt-blue glasses are contaminants from the colourant or from the base glass is impossible to decide from the data available.

The red bangle is of particular interest for its lead glass composition in comparison with the well-known lump of opaque red enamel from Tara Hill (Ball and Stokes 1893). According to a recent publication (Stapleton *et al.* 1999), this lump of red glass is also essentially of a 'Roman' composition, and differs significantly from early medieval enamels from Britain and Ireland. Considering the limitations of our own analyses, being restricted to the immediate surface area, the glass bangle is chemically very similar, if not identical, to the lump of glass from Tara as analysed by Stapleton *et al.* This could hint at the working of such glass at Tara, but no proof in the form of real glassworking debris exists for this hypothesis.

Although further research is necessary, it appears at present that the red glass clearly belongs to the high-lead high-copper subvariant of this glass type as defined by Freestone (1987), which predominates in the Iron Age (in contrast to copper-red glasses of the second millennium BC, which are typically lead-free), but differs from British and Irish medieval enamels. The use of a certain type of bright red, lead-rich metallurgical slag from Roman silver-refining (Rehren and Kraus 1999), as recently identified for early medieval enamel in Britain (Stapleton *et al.* 1999), can be excluded here. The red slag adhering to some of the Tara crucible fragments is of a composition quite different from the glass bangle, precluding any relationship between the crucibles and possible glassworking.

A set of similar analyses has also been published by Brun and Pernot (1992) for Celtic enamels from continental Europe. Although these red opaque glasses occur widely throughout Europe, their origins, technologically and geographically, are poorly known and it is felt that they need more scientific attention, including lead isotope and phase analysis characterisation, before we can get a clearer picture of the pattern of their making, working and trade. The presence of metallic lead as noted above emphasises the necessity to work these glasses under reducing conditions, which is a long-known fact (e.g. Ahmed and Ashour 1981; Freestone 1987).

Discussion

The high-temperature debris from Tara, along with fragmentary objects of iron, bronze and glass, allows us to distinguish three different crafts: iron-smithing, bronze-casting and, possibly, glassworking. The nature of the evidence available for each of these crafts is rather different and this affects the interpretations which can be offered. For iron and bronze there is clear evidence for the working of these metals, but only indirect indications of the raw materials used and nothing to show the type or quality of the objects being made. For glass there is some raw material and the finished objects, but only circumstantial evidence for their manufacture at Tara.

The archaeological context of the high-temperature debris indicates that these crafts were closely related. Much of the material comes from one particular charcoal-rich layer, F31, and from the fill of F38, though comparable debris is found in a wide range of secondary contexts. It thus appears that there was a high-temperature activity centre which served several crafts at the same time, or at least in close succession. This is considered a common feature in urban settings, responding to varied needs rather than focusing on the mass production of a single, often specialised, commodity. It also seems to be a recurring feature at a number of later prehistoric Irish sites, some of which may have had multifunctional high-temperature workshops similar to that at Tara. Although the type of evidence from these sites is variable in character and usually occurs in small quantities, owing to both the scale and the location of the excavations, a thorough review of the available material would be rewarding. For example, at Clogher all three crafts are well represented, though not necessarily from the same period of occupation (Scott 1991, 100, 160); from Freestone Hill there are indications of glassworking and of iron production, from ironstone nodules and slags (Raftery 1969); and from Dún Ailinne there is some evidence for both glassworking and non-ferrous metalworking (Wailes 1990), but the lack of slags indicates that any workshop would be beyond the excavated area.

Although the total weight of material recovered from Tara is not large and represents only a few cycles of smithing and casting, from a prehistoric site this is a significant amount and is of particular interest since it was found in a workshop context. Compared with the rather limited evidence from other sites in Britain and Ireland, the metallurgical debris from Tara would seem to be fairly typical of the non-intensive, but perhaps high-quality, metalworking which was carried out at defended sites in the later prehistoric period. The question of whether this high-temperature workshop was that of resident metalworkers and glassworkers or of peripatetic specialists must await further excavations and analytical data, both from Tara and from other comparable sites.

Workshop structures

It needs to be stressed that high-temperature crafts of the kind which would have been undertaken at Tara would certainly have been carried out within a roofed structure of some sort. Reconstruction drawings of metalworking usually show it being carried out in the open air, ostensibly because of the supposed danger from noxious fumes, but this is a misconception. Shelter would have been necessary, to keep both the metallurgical structures and the raw materials as dry as possible. A large number of experimental reproductions, both of ironworking and non-ferrous metalworking, have been carried out all over Europe in the past thirty years or so, demonstrating the practicality and necessity of working under cover. Unfortunately it is only rarely that firm archaeological evidence has been recovered for the form of prehistoric workshop structures.

At Tara there is sufficient evidence from both stake-holes and post-holes to suggest that the high-temperature activity was carried out in some kind of structure, but its precise form and layout are far from clear. The significant concentration of stakes in the south-eastern zone of the cutting and the alignment of the two post-holes F71 and F76 hint at a square or rectangular structure aligned south-west to north-east. Assuming that the F38 feature was central to this structure, it could have been at least 4m in each direction, but it would probably have been larger than this.

Iron-smithing

The evidence for iron-smithing accounts for the majority of the debris from Tara. Of the 17kg of slag recovered, about 90% by weight derives from iron-smithing. This seems to have involved the refining either of blooms or perhaps partially refined bulk iron, but the hammer scale in F38 and the fragments of forge waste both indicate that the refined iron was also smithed into objects. The raw material would probably have been produced elsewhere and traded to Tara. However, there are few prehistoric primary iron production sites yet known from Ireland and so the source of this raw material must remain speculative.

A number of raw blooms and partly refined blooms have been found in Ireland, but these are almost wholly without context (Tylecote 1986, 191; Scott 1991, 162). The myth of Irish iron-smelting in the so-called bowl furnace still persists (Scott 1991, 158–63; Raftery 1994, 148), and the bowl furnaces and 'furnace bottoms' reported from a number of prehistoric and Early Christian sites are better regarded as the remains of smithing hearths and smithing hearth slags. Early small-diameter furnaces, of the kind likely to have been used to smelt Irish bog ores, would indeed leave bowl-shaped hollows in the ground, but the superstructure of the furnaces would have been low cylindrical shafts, perhaps 70cm or 80cm high (Crew 1990). Experimental reproduction of smelting bog ores in a prehistoric technological context has demonstrated that the iron would have been a valuable commodity, which perhaps explains the paucity of iron objects found in early settlement contexts and emphasises the value of objects found in ritual contexts (Crew 1991; 1999).

The smithing hearth cakes from Tara are a useful index of the level of activity carried out there. This was not especially intensive and perhaps only between 25 and 35 episodes of smithing are represented by these slag cakes, which could have been carried out in a few weeks. However, it is likely that the debris recovered is only a fraction of the total quantity produced and much more work than this may have been carried out.

Only a few prehistoric sites have so far produced evidence for the smelting of iron, but small quantities of smithing slag are relatively common. For comparison, the intensive excavation at Danebury hillfort, Hampshire, has produced about the same quantity of iron-smithing slag, despite the finds there of a hoard of currency bars, large numbers of iron objects and significant quantities of forge waste (Crew 1995). There would probably have been a difference in the scale and quality of the smithing work being carried out at high-status sites like Tara in comparison with more normal settlements, but the evidence to support this is difficult to recognise and has rarely been found. Special attention needs to be paid to the rather small and dense smithing slag cakes, which appear unusual when compared with other assemblages of smithing debris and which may eventually tell us more about the kind of smithing activity which was being carried out at Tara.

Bronze-casting

The melting and casting of bronze was clearly another regular activity, though the number of crucible and mould fragments is much smaller than one would expect if it were a large-scale and continuous operation. There is no evidence for the size or type of objects which may have been made, and it is unclear in what form the raw material may have been brought to the site. The presence of high-tin phases is noteworthy, indicating the use of technically pure tin, probably containing some 'hard head', or a high-tin master alloy, both of which should be considered as precious metals. This is not a common feature and probably relates to the importance of Tara.

There are surprisingly few direct indications of non-ferrous residues having been incorporated into the lining and slag debris. It may be that they have mostly been removed by post-depositional corrosion of the slags, but it could indicate that the raw materials used were relatively clean, that the processes were well controlled and that there were few losses of raw material. The small number of crucible fragments and the low weight of the mould fragments imply that only a relatively small number of casting episodes were carried out. However, few systematic experimental reproductions have been made and they have usually concentrated on the manufacture of the objects themselves, so there are few data available to quantify the losses and to assess the significance of metallurgical residues of the kind found at Tara.

It is not unusual for settlement sites, both defended

Appendix 1

and undefended, to produce small quantities of non-ferrous metalworking debris and this seems invariably to be found with debris from iron-smithing. For comparison, only about 3kg of metalworking debris, broadly of the same character as the Tara assemblage, were recovered from extensive excavations at a group of defended enclosures in Pembrokeshire, south-west Wales (Williams and Mytum 1998). From Llwyn Bryn Dinas, in the Welsh borders, a limited area of rescue excavation of part of a workshop just inside the rampart of the hillfort produced only 4.2kg of both iron-smithing and non-ferrous metalworking debris (Musson *et al.* 1992).

Glassworking

The working of glass is the least well documented of the high-temperature activities at Tara. It was initially speculated that the fragments of glass found within the workshop area, together with a crucible sherd with what might have been a blue glass droplet and several others with bright red slags adhering, were indications that glassworking may have been carried out. However, none of the technical debris could be related to glass-melting or glassworking and it remains for this activity to be proved conclusively.

The presence of glass bangles on metalworking sites is not unknown. The finds of unusual glass bangles at the primary iron production sites of Bryn y Castell and Crawcwellt, in north-west Wales (Crew 1989), were also initially thought to indicate the presence of a multifunctional high-temperature workshop, but it is now thought that the bangles were imported to these sites as part of a reciprocal trade arrangement. Nevertheless, the bangles do seem to be an indication of the relatively high status of the sites, and there are also ethnographic parallels which suggest that the bangles may have been worn by the metalworkers themselves.

From Tara, however, the fragment of an opaque red bangle, which has a very similar composition to the rough lump of glass excavated some 150 years earlier, provides strong circumstantial evidence for the making of glass objects. The use of red glass of this type is usually restricted to the decoration of beads or the enamelling of bronze objects, and its use for complete objects is rare. Indeed, the opaque red bangle from Tara is without parallel anywhere in Europe, perhaps indicating the relative value of this material and the additional difficulty of working it under more strictly controlled and more reducing conditions than normal.

This combination of raw glass and unusual bangles may be compared with the finds from Hengistbury Head, Dorset, which include several fragments of purple glass together with both decorated and plain bangles of Continental type (Henderson 1987). However, as at Tara, there was no conclusive evidence for the actual working of glass.

The bangles from the 1997 excavations at Tara find ready parallels in the plain examples from Hengistbury, as well as the two complete bangles from Loughey (Jope and Wilson 1957, 82–4), ten examples from the Dún Ailinne excavations (Wailes 1990) and individual finds from Ballybarrack, Co. Louth, Freestone Hill, the Rath of Furness and Rathtinaun. These are all of a type frequently found in later La Tène contexts on the Continent, which may indicate that the bangles were imported from a Continental workshop. However, the presence of raw glass at both Hengistbury and Tara might indicate the further intriguing possibility that this glass was part of the stock of a peripatetic specialist who may actually have made the bangles at these sites.

There are other unpublished glass objects from earlier excavations at Tara, including two bangles (NMI Dublin, 136, 168) and a small distorted fragment of waste glass, with suggestions of toolmarks, which hints strongly at glassworking at Tara itself. One of the bangles is exactly similar to those found in 1997, but the other example, with a light blue body and thin opaque white trails, like the opaque red bangle, is so far without parallel. This has been stated to be unquestionably of 'foreign' origin (Hughes 1980, 55), though there are no Continental examples with decoration of this kind and the few British examples are both different in detail and probably later in date. In contrast to the interpretation of the beads from Tara, which have been dismissed as 'small and miserable specimens, acquired in all probability from some area (Wales perhaps) under Roman influence' (Guido 1978, 40), the cumulative evidence from the bangles and the raw glass lump is probably best seen as an indication that some high-quality glass objects were being made at Tara. Only further excavations and post-excavation studies can demonstrate this beyond question.

References

Ahmed, A. and Ashour, G. 1981 Effect of heat treatment on the crystallisation of cuprous oxide in glass. *Glass Technology* **22**, 24–33.

Andrieux, P. 1991 La reconstitution des comportments technique et thérmique de foyer pour la technologie du Bronze. In *Archéologie*

Fig. 3—Vitrified lining with fine sandy fabric. Left-hand examples: vitrified surfaces with post-depositional corrosion. Top right: side view with sequence of vitrified clay, grey reduced clay and oxidised clay. Bottom right: rear view with thin veneer of red-orange oxidised clay. Scale 10cm.

Fig. 6—Low-density fluxed lining slags (FLS type), small fractured pieces from the SS64 sample. Fragments of this size are difficult to recover under excavation conditions and would normally be recovered from the post-excavation processing of bulk samples. Scale 10cm.

Fig. 4—Vitrified lining with coarse stone-grogged fabric. Upper pair: vitrified surfaces with typical colour variation. Lower pair: rear view showing coarse clay fabric. Scale 10cm.

Fig. 7—Smithing hearth slag cakes, upper surfaces. Top row: larger cakes. Bottom row: small dense cakes. Scale 20cm.

Fig. 5—Low-density fluxed lining slags (FLS type), showing the highly vesicular fabric in a range of sizes from small fractured pieces to larger intact flows. Scale 10cm.

Fig. 8—Double smithing hearth cake: side view of fractured surface showing dense internal structure. The vesicular zone is the upper surface of the lower cake. Scale 10cm.

Fig. 9—Double smithing hearth cake: front view. The lower cake has a fractured surface, probably caused on its removal when cold from the hearth. Scale 10cm.

Fig. 12—Section of crucible sherd from F34:05, showing the dark core and a bronze prill trapped in the surface slag layer. Scale 10cm.

Fig. 10—Smithing hearth cake with heavy corrosion products, within which was a large piece of iron. The characteristic cracking has probably developed in post-excavation storage. Scale 10cm.

Fig. 13—Thin section through crucible sherd from F34:05. The dark, carbon-rich core is surrounded by a lighter layer of clay. Length of sample 2.5cm. Sample prepared by A. Ludwig, Bochum.

Fig. 11—Crucible rim sherds, internal faces, showing red cuprite slags, black crucible slags and copper corrosion products from metallic prills trapped in the slag layer. Scale 10cm.

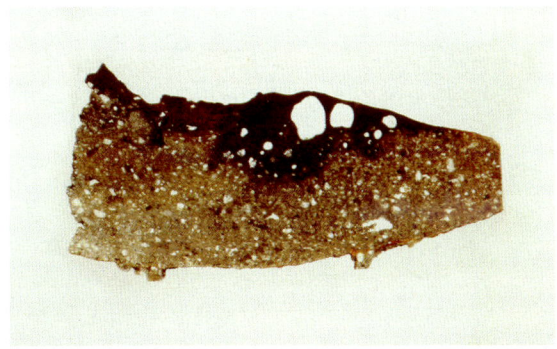

Fig. 14—Thin section through crucible fragment from F34:09. The dark slag is much more iron-rich than can be explained by the underlying light-coloured ceramic. Length of sample 2.5cm. Sample prepared by A. Ludwig, Bochum.

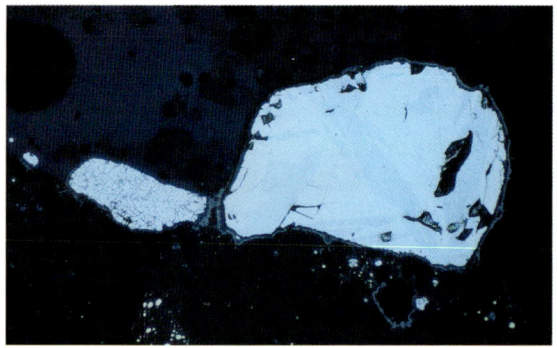

Fig. 15—Reflected-light image of a high-tin phase in a crucible fragment from F34:09. Width of image about 1mm. Sample prepared by A. Ludwig, Bochum.

Fig. 18—Mould sherds, larger examples showing traces of surface shaping. Scale 10cm.

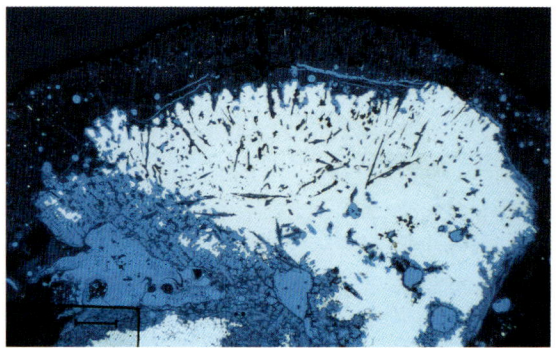

Fig. 16—Reflected-light image of highly oxidised bronze prill on crucible fragment from F30:35. The bronze (yellowish) has turned into almost pure copper intergrown with tin oxide needles (dark), and is surrounded by a layer of copper oxide and mixed oxide phases. Width of image about 2mm.

Fig. 19—Thin section through mould fragment from F34:03. The difference in colour probably reflects different degrees of oxidation of the iron component in the clay. Note the coarse mineral temper fragments visible. Diameter of sample 1.5cm. Sample prepared by A. Ludwig, Bochum.

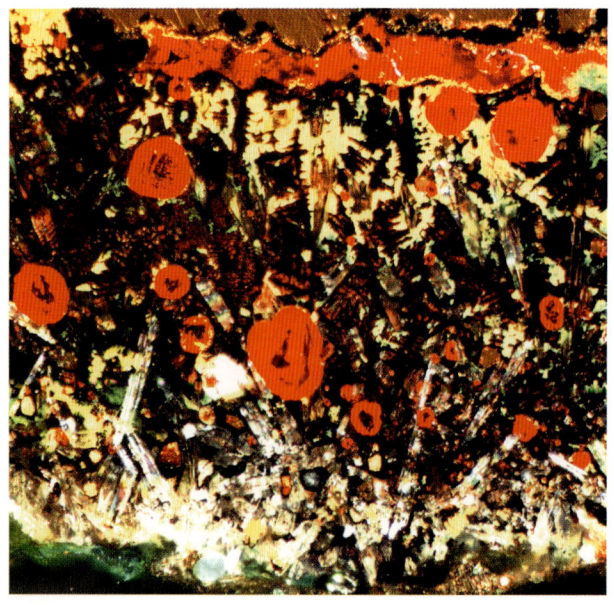

Fig. 17—Internal reflection image of the mixed oxide seam around the oxidised bronze prill from F30:35. The tin oxide needles appear white, cuprite crystals dark red. Yellow are extremely fine-grained dendrites of cuprite in glass, and green are various copper corrosion products. Width of image about 0.2mm. Sample prepared by A. Ludwig, Bochum.

Fig. 20—Outer face of fragment of red opaque bangle from F62:1. Scale in cm.

Fig. 23—Inside face of purple bangle from F102:1, showing iron oxide scale. Scale in cm.

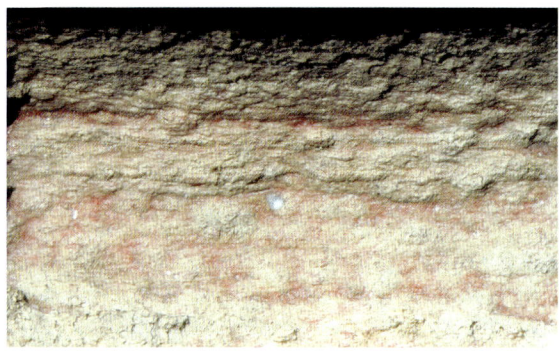

Fig. 21—Detail of inner face of red opaque bangle from F62:1 with the lead droplet.

Fig. 24—Detail of inner face of purple bangle from F102:1, showing iron oxide scale.

Fig. 22—Side view of fragment of purple bangle from F102:1. Scale in cm.

Fig. 25—Fragment of transparent blue glass from F31:58. Scale in cm.

Expérimentale I, Le Feu: le métal, la céramique, 118–22. Actes du Colloque Internationale, Expérimentation en Archéologie: Bilan et Perspectives, Beaune 1988. Paris.

Ball, C. B. and Stokes, M. 1893 On a block of red glass enamel said to have been found at Tara Hill. *Transactions of the Royal Irish Academy* **30** (5), 277–93.

Brun, N. and Pernot, M. 1992 The opaque red glass of Celtic enamels from continental Europe. *Archaeometry* **34**, 235–52.

Crew, P. 1989 Excavations at Crawcwellt West, Merioneth, 1986–1989: a late prehistoric upland ironworking settlement. *Archaeology in Wales* **29**, 11–16.

Crew, P. 1990 Late Iron Age and Roman iron production in north-west Wales. In B. C. Burnham and J. L. Davies (eds), *Conquest, co-existence and change; recent work in Roman Wales*, 150–60. Trivium 25. Lampeter.

Crew, P. 1991 The experimental production of prehistoric bar iron. *Historical Metallurgy* **25** (1), 21–36.

Crew, P. 1995 Aspects of the iron supply. In B. Cunliffe, *Danebury, Volume 6: A hillfort community in perspective*, 276–84. CBA Research Report 102. London.

Crew, P. 1999 Excavations at Crawcwellt West, Merioneth, 1990–1998: a late prehistoric upland iron-working settlement. *Archaeology in Wales* **38**, 22–35.

Freestone, I. 1987 Composition and microstructure of early opaque red glass. In M. Bimson and I. Freestone (eds), *Early vitreous materials*, 173–91. British Museum Occasional Paper 56.

Freestone, I. 1989 Refractory materials and their procurement. In A. Hauptmann *et al.* (eds), *Old World Archaeometallurgy*, 155–62. Der Anschnitt, Beiheft 7. Bochum.

Freestone, I., Meeks, N. and Middleton, A. 1985 Retention of phosphate in buried ceramic: an electron microbeam approach. *Archaeometry* **27**, 161–77.

Guido, M. 1978 *The glass beads of the prehistoric and Roman periods in Britain and Ireland*. London Society of Antiquaries, Research Report No. 35. London.

Henderson, J. 1987 Glass working. In B. Cunliffe, *Hengistbury Head, Dorset. Volume 1: The prehistoric and Roman settlement, 3500 BC–AD 500*, 180–5. Oxford University Committee for Archaeology, Monograph No. 13. Oxford.

Hughes, M.M. 1980 The earliest glass in Ireland. Unpublished MA thesis, Department of Archaeology, University College, Cork.

Jope, E.M. and Wilson, B.C.S. 1957 A burial group from the first century AD from Loughey, near Donaghadee, Co. Down. *Ulster Journal of Archaeology* **20**, 73–95.

Musson, C.R., Britnell, W.J., Northover, J.P. and Salter, C.J. 1992 Excavations and metalworking at Llwyn Bryn Dinas hillfort, Llandegwyn, Clwyd. *Proceedings of the Prehistoric Society* **58**, 265–89.

Northover, J.P. and Rehren, T. 1992 The oxidation of bronze. Abstract 75, 28th International Symposium on Archaeometry, Los Angeles.

Raftery, B. 1969 Freestone Hill, Co. Kilkenny. An Iron Age hillfort and Bronze Age cairn. *Proceedings of the Royal Irish Academy* **68**C, 1–108.

Raftery, B. 1994 *Pagan Celtic Ireland*. London.

Rehren, T. 1995 Meroe, Eisen und Afrika. *Mitteilungen der Sudanarchaeologischen Gesellschaft zu Berlin* **3**, 20–5.

Rehren, T. 1997 *Tiegelmetallurgie. Tiegelprozesse und ihre Stellung in der Archaeometallurgie*. Bochum/Freiberg.

Rehren, T. 2001 Die Schmelzgefässe aus Cham-Oberwil. In U. Ginepf Horisberger and S. Hämmerle (eds), *Cham-Oberwil, Hof (Kantonsarchaeologie Zug)*, 118–31. Antiqua 33. Basel.

Rehren, T. and Kraus, K. 1999 Cupel and crucible: the refining of debased silver in the Colonia Ulpia Traiana, Xanten. *Journal of Roman Archaeology* **12**, 263–72.

Roche, H. 1999 Late Iron Age activity at Tara, Co. Meath. *Ríocht na Midhe* **10**, 18–30.

Scott, B.G. 1991 *Early Irish ironworking*. Belfast.

Stapleton, C., Freestone, I. and Bowman, S. 1999 Composition and origin of early medieval opaque red enamel from Britain and Ireland. *Journal of Archaeological Science* **26**, 913–21.

Tylecote, R.F. 1986 *The prehistory of metallurgy in the British Isles*. London.

Tylecote, R.F. 1987 *The early history of metallurgy in Europe*. London.

Wailes, B. 1990 Dún Ailinne: a summary excavation report. *Emania* **7**, 10–21.

Williams, G. and Mytum, H. 1998 *Llawhaden, Dyfed: excavations on a group of small defended enclosures, 1980–1984*. British Archaeological Reports, British Series 27. Oxford.

APPENDIX 2
The animal bones from Tara

FINBAR McCORMICK[1]

Introduction

The animal bones from Tara came mainly from two ditch cuttings (Cuttings 1 and 2) at the northern end of the Ráith na Ríg enclosure, with two small samples from beneath the bank of the enclosure (F30 and F31). The bones came from a large number of separate contexts within the ditches and the individual samples are rather small. The material from the individual contexts is recorded in Tables 6–21.

Methodology

The minimum numbers of individuals (MNI) were calculated on the basis of the most frequent skeletal element present, taking left and right sides into consideration. No attempt, however, was made to increase MNI on the basis of bone size or state of epiphyseal fusion and tooth eruption, as this method is only valid for very small samples. The fusion data are based on Silver 1969, while the age of the state of tooth eruption is based on Higham 1967. The abbreviations used for cattle bone measurements are those of von den Driesch 1976.

General results

The material from the different samples is summarised in Tables 1–3 and in general shows that cattle were the dominant species present in terms of fragment totals. The use of MNI data for such small contexts is rather unreliable, as it tends to overemphasise the importance of animals that are represented by a small number of bones. Thus if there was one sheep tooth representing one MNI value and twenty cattle bones representing one MNI value it is likely that cattle were more numerous in the diet and livestock economy despite the two species having equal MNI values. Adding together MNI values from different small samples is also a questionable practice. In Cutting 1 the aggregate MNI data suggest that cattle were the dominant species. In Cutting 2 there seems to be a more even balance between the three main species, i.e. cattle, pig and sheep/goat, but this is in fact due to an unusually high incidence of sheep/goat and pig in two individual contexts. Considering the fragments and MNI data it would seem reasonable to conclude that cattle were the dominant species present. Dog bones were present and wild species were represented by a few incidences of fox and red deer.

Table 1—Fragments and MNI distribution (values in brackets) from Cutting 1 contexts.

Feature	Cattle	Horse	Sheep/goat	Pig	Dog	Red deer
F12	28 (3)	1 (1)	2 (1)	7 (1)	11 (2)	—
F15	29 (3)	2 (1)	—	21 (3)	—	1 (1)
F19	5 (1)	1 (1)	—	1 (1)	3 (1)	—
F20	20 (2)	1 (1)	16 (2)	9 (1)	5 (1)	—
F102	3 (1)	2 (1)	1 (1)	—	3 (1)	—
F107	1 (1)	—	2 (1)	—	—	—
F108	1 (1)	2 (1)	—	—	—	—
Total fragments	87	9	21	38	22	1
Total aggregate MNI	12	6	5	6	5	1

[1] School of Archaeology and Palaeoecology, Queen's University, Belfast.

Table 2—Fragments and MNI distribution (values in brackets) from Cutting 2 contexts.

Feature	Cattle	Horse	Sheep/goat	Pig	Dog	Red deer	Fox
F41	1 (1)	—	—	—	—	—	—
F51	18 (1)	1 (1)	11 (1)	3 (1)	—	—	2 (1)
F52	20 (1)	—	2 (1)	3 (1)	—	—	—
F53	22 (2)	5 (1)	2 (1)	31 (4)	—	1 (1)	—
F54	24 (3)	2 (1)	7 (1)	8 (1)	3 (1)	—	—
F55	13 (1)	2 (1)	10 (4)	5 (1)	12 (1)	—	—
F56A	3 (1)	—	2 (1)	—	1 (1)	—	—
F56B	—	3 (1)	—	—	—	—	—
F60	1 (1)	—	—	1 (1)	—	—	—
Total fragments	102	13	34	51	16	1	2
Total MNI	11	5	9	9	3		1

Table 3—Fragments and MNI distribution (values in brackets) from features beneath the bank of Ráith na Ríg.

Feature	Cattle	Horse	Sheep/goat	Pig
F30	5 (1)	1 (1)	—	2 (1)
F31	1 (1)	2 (1)	—	1 (1)

The samples from Tara are too small to allow worthwhile consideration of the MNI data, so comparison with other sites must be made on the basis of the less-reliable fragment values. In Table 4 it can be seen that cattle are the dominant species present, as is also the case at Late Bronze Age Ballyveelish, Mooghaun and Haughey's Fort, and Iron Age Dún Ailinne. The Early Iron Age levels at Navan are dominated by pig, and McCormick (1997, 118) has argued that this must be due to high status or some other social or economic factor as it cannot be explained on the basis of environmental determinism. It would be difficult to deny, however, that Tara and Dún Ailinne were high-status sites so it may be that there were regional differences in diet in Ireland during the Early Iron Age. In all the sites, excepting Navan and Dún Aonghasa, pig are numerically the second most important species, and the data from Tara agree with these results. The extremely high incidence of sheep at Dún Aonghasa can be attributed to environmental factors, as the Aran Islands are more suitable for sheep-rearing than for the rearing of pigs, which are essentially forest animals. The incidence of sheep at Tara is the second-highest noted in the late prehistoric sites, but this still accounts for only 13.8% of the fragment totals.

Ballyveelish and Tara contain the highest instances of horse bones, with 6.0% and 6.2% of the total fragments respectively. In the two main samples from Ballyveelish, however, the great majority (80%) of the horse bones were teeth, which probably represented single skulls (McCormick 1987, fiche table 2:1 and 2:2). At Tara only 35% of the horse remains were teeth. It seems, therefore, that horse was much more important at Tara.

Table 4—Fragment distributions from different late prehistoric Irish sites (after McCormick 1994, 182, and Murray and McCormick, forthcoming).

	Cattle %	Horse %	Sheep %	Pig %	Dog %	Sample size
Tara, Co. Meath	48.1	6.2	13.6	22.7	9.4	405
Haughey's Fort, Co. Armagh	65.7	1.8	2.9	25.0	4.7	1075
Navan, Co. Armagh	30.4	0.8	8.5	60.2	0	4431
Dún Ailinne, Co. Kildare	54.4	2.5	7.4	35.7	0.1	2611
Ballyveelish, Co. Tipperary	65.2	6	12.5	15.4	0.8	827
Dún Aonghasa, Co. Galway	58.7	0.2	39.1	1.9	0.0	7688
Mooghaun, Co. Clare	75.8	0.6	6.6	16.9	0.1	1954

Appendix 2

Table 5—*Cattle epiphyseal fusion data from Tara compared with Dún Aonghasa, Haughey's Fort, Ballyveelish 2 (McCormick 1987) and Newgrange (van Wijngaarden-Bakker 1986) using the data of Silver (1969). The Dún Aonghasa samples used were 2, 3, 9, 12, 15, 16, 19 and 20. The sample size from Newgrange is larger than from any of the other sites. *Excluding Site A, cutting 1–10. The Dún Aonghasa and Navan data are based on unpublished data. D = distal, P = proximal.*

Site	Bone	Approx. age at fusion (in months)	Fused	Unfused
Tara	Pelvis	7–10	3 (100%)	0 (0.0%)
Mooghaun*			1 (33%)	2 (66%)
Dún Aonghasa			14 (61%)	9 (39%)
Haughey's Fort			23 (92%)	2 (8%)
Ballyveelish 2			22 (73%)	8 (27%)
Tara	Humerus D, radius P	10–18	19 (90.%)	2 (10%)
Mooghaun*			86 (98%)	2 (2%)
Dún Aonghasa			43 (71%)	14 (29%)
Haughey's Fort			62 (90%)	7 (10%)
Ballyveelish 2			12 (75%)	4 (25%)
Newgrange			90–96%	4–10%
Tara	Tibia D, metacarpal D, metatarsal P	24–36	13 (65%)	7 (35%)
Mooghaun*			49 (86%)	8 (14%)
Dún Aonghasa			13 (36%)	23 (64%)
Haughey's Fort			35 (78%)	10 (22%)
Ballyveelish 2			14 (70%)	6 (30%)
Newgrange			84–92%	8–16%
Tara	Femur P	36–42	7 (78%)	2 (22%)
Mooghaun*			29 (57%)	22 (43%)
Dún Aonghasa			27 (44%)	35 (56%)
Haughey's Fort			14 (45%)	17 (55%)
Newgrange			49%	51%
Tara	Femur D, tibia P, humerus P, radius D	42–48	13 (81%)	3 (19%)
Mooghaun*			33 (67%)	16 (33%)
Dún Aonghasa			18 (40%)	27 (60%)
Haughey's Fort			13 (38%)	21 (62%)
Ballyveelish 2			8 (57%)	6 (43%)
Newgrange			22%	78%

Cattle

Most of the cattle bones had been deliberately broken and they clearly represented discarded food refuse. The best butchering data came from Cutting 1, F20. Two pieces of tibia which had been broken in antiquity could be fitted together. Chop-marks were noted on some cattle thorasical vertebrae, and the direction of the marks indicated that the carcass was lying on its back, rather than being hung by its legs, when it was chopped. Knife-marks were also noted on the articular ends of the femur and the distal humerus, and these presumably represented the cutting of ligaments in order to separate the main bones from each other. Knife-marks on the blade of the scapula seem to represent boning. A humerus from Cutting 1, F108, displayed cuts at the distal end, indicating the cutting of ligaments, and other knife-marks indicative of boning. Gnawing-marks, presumably made by dogs, were occasionally encountered. In Cutting 2, F53, both a femur and a second phalanx displayed such marks.

Only a small number of metrical data were present (Table 22), and the measurements all fall within the range of later prehistoric cattle in Ireland as indicated at Haughey's Fort and Navan (McCormick 1991, 32; 1997, 120). There were insufficient data to provide evidence concerning the sex distribution of the cattle.

The ageing data are also extremely limited and are presented in Table 27. Only one mandible is present and it comes from a mature/old animal. The epiphyseal fusion data support the impression that the majority of the animals were of this age at time of slaughter. Table 5 compares the Tara data with other Irish Bronze Age and Iron Age sites, and it can be seen that in most cases the majority of the cattle were more than three years old at time of slaughter. This contrasts with the data from early medieval sites, where the peak in slaughter occurs in semi-mature individuals (McCormick 1992), a pattern reflecting a dairying economy.

Pig

The pig bones again clearly represented discarded food refuse. In Cutting 2, F54, a distal radius and its unfused articulation were found together, indicating that the material was in a primary rather than a redeposited context. As is usual, there were fewer chop/knife-marks than on cattle bones. This is presumably because less disarticulation and boning were necessary because it was possible to cook pig in larger segments, if not as a whole carcass. The same applies in the case of sheep. Chop-marks were, however, present on a distal humerus (F15) and gnawing-marks were also occasionally noted, i.e. on a metatarsal from F19.

There were no mandibles present, which precluded sexing data, and the ageing information was limited to the epiphyseal fusion of the bones (Table 29). This indicates that the pigs were mature or old at time of slaughter. There was no evidence for the slaughter of young pigs.

The metrical data from Tara are presented in Table 24. McCormick (1991, 31) noted that the pigs from Later Bronze Age Haughey's Fort were generally larger than those noted during the early medieval period, and the Navan evidence suggested that this decline had already occurred by the Early Iron Age (McCormick 1997, 119). The limited number of Tara data are, however, equivocal. The mean pelvis LAR width from three examples is 31.7mm. The average at Beaker Newgrange is 31.8mm and at Haughey's Fort 31.2mm, suggesting that the Tara pigs are still large.

The two Tara tibia Bd values are, however, 26.5mm and 27.0mm, which fall below the lowest limits of the Newgrange (27.8mm) and Haughey's Fort (30.9mm) examples and are less than the early medieval means from Moynagh crannog, Co. Meath (27.8mm) and Fishamble Street, Dublin (27.9mm). The Tara samples are too small to allow a conclusion to be reached on the matter.

Sheep/goat

No definite goat remains were found, while the few which could positively be attributed to a species were sheep. It is therefore assumed that all the remains are of sheep. The ageing data are extremely limited (Table 28), with the only mandibular evidence coming from Cutting 2, F54 and F55. In that instance there were three mandibles with erupted and worn third molars and one with an erupting third molar. On the basis of Silver's data (provided in Higham 1967, 106) the former would be of adult individuals while the example with the erupting tooth would be in the region of two years of age. A high incidence of old animals is generally taken as indicating that they were reared for their wool (Payne 1973). The metrical data were limited and there are very few later Irish prehistoric data with which to compare them (Table 23).

Horse

Small amounts of horse were present in most contexts, and while the overall frequency was rather low at 6.2% this is nonetheless the highest incidence from an Irish prehistoric site. There were no articulated bones present so it is likely that the bones, like the other faunal material, represent discarded food debris. Many of the bones are broken, deliberately shattered for the extraction of marrow. The conclusion that the horse was eaten would seem to be confirmed by a radius from F108. The articulation of the ulna and the proximal radius display knife-marks indicating separation of the humerus from the lower leg (Fig. 1). In addition, the front face of the radius shaft has burning-marks indicating that the joint has been roasted (Fig. 2). It seems likely that the horse was being consumed nearby, as Cutting 1, F19, contains parts of a radius which had been broken in antiquity yet which fitted together. A small number of horse bones displayed gnawing-marks.

The ageing data were limited. Cutting 2, F54,

contained a complete mandible with all the teeth erupted and worn. This was clearly an old animal, but bit-wear on the second premolar indicated that it had been used for riding or traction before ending up as food. Young horses, however, were also present. Cutting 2 sample 54 contained three loose unworn teeth of a young animal. The small number of fusion data represent mature or old animals (Table 30).

The metrical data are presented in Table 25. They are limited but include a complete radius and tibia. On the basis of the multiplication factors of Kiesewalter (quoted in von den Driesch and Boessneck 1974, 333), this indicated shoulder heights of 130cm and 133cm. These represent horses of 13–14 hands, which is similar to a modern Connemara pony.

The ditch cuttings are located near the Mound of the Hostages, which Warner (1988, 57) regards as a royal inauguration site. It is tempting to equate the horse bones with the inauguration rite described by Geraldus Cambrensis which entailed the killing, butchery and consumption of horseflesh (O'Meara 1982, 109–10). The finding of such horse bones, however, is not unique to Tara. Butchered horse bones were also found at Navan Fort (McCormick 1997, 120), and in Iron Age settlement sites in southern Britain horse bones usually comprise 3–6% of faunal assemblages, with their incidence sometimes attaining 15% (Grant 1984, 113–14).

Dog

Dog was unusually common, comprising 9.4% of the identifiable fragments. In general, dog comprised less than 1% of the fragments on Irish late prehistoric settlement sites, the only exception being Haughey's Fort at 7.4% (Table 4). In Iron Age England dog bones usually comprise between 1% and 4% of the total (Grant 1984, 114), although their incidence can be much higher if individual skeletons are present. The only prehistoric Irish site to have provided high instances of dog is the King's Stables, Co. Armagh. At this site, which can best be described as a Late Bronze Age ritual pool, dog comprised 31% of the total fragments (Penn 1977, 58).

There was no evidence for articulated dog skeletons in the material and many of the bones were broken, suggesting that the dogs were eaten. This is supported by the fact that there are knife-marks on the acetabulum of a pelvis in Cutting 1, F20 (Fig. 3). This is consistent with the dismemberment of the leg from the hip, and is not the type of knife-mark that one would associate with only the skinning of the animal. At Haughey's Fort no chop-marks were noticed on the bones but the remains were again disarticulated and often broken. In southern England butchery marks have been noted on several sites (Grant 1984, 114) so it is difficult to avoid the conclusion that dog was occasionally eaten in Ireland at this time.

In what context was dogflesh eaten at Tara? It may have been consumed in times of starvation. The eating of dogflesh at such times is recorded in the annals (Kelly 1997, 355) and at a later stage it is attested in Ireland at the siege of Derry in 1690. In that instance a quarter of a dog fetched 5s 6d and a dog's head commanded a price of 2s 6d, the dogs being 'fattened by eating the bodies of the slain Irish' (McCrory 1980, 291). Generally there has been a cultural prejudice against the eating of dogflesh in Europe, presumably because as a carnivore it was regarded as unclean. Simoons (1994, 238–40), however, has shown that dogflesh was consumed during Roman religious ceremonies, with puppyflesh being eaten at feasts for the inauguration of priests. He also notes that the culinary consumption continued in some parts of Europe, such as Spain, Switzerland and Germany, until the twentieth century (*ibid.*). In early Ireland there certainly seems to have been a taboo against the eating of dogflesh. In the story of the Death of Cú Chulainn contained in the Book of Leinster (LL 13882–93), the hero was forbidden to eat dogflesh and he died after he transgressed this order. In the tale three crones had 'cooked on spits of rowantree a dog with poisons and spells', and by eating 'his namesake's flesh' he had ensured his own death (Cross and Slover 1969, 334). On the other hand, it seems to have been permissible to eat, or at least chew, dogflesh in certain circumstances. In the tenth-century Cormac's Glossary (Stokes 1862, 25) there is a description of a poet, or perhaps a druid (*filid*), consuming dogflesh as part of a ritual that would produce revelations from the pagan gods. It records that 'The poet chews a piece of the flesh of a red pig, or of a dog or cat, and places it afterwards on the flagstone behind the door, and sings an incantation on it and offers it to the idol-gods and afterwards calls his idols to him … and what he seeks is then revealed to him' (Ó hÓgáin 1999, 79). There are, therefore, several circumstances that could potentially account for the eating of dogflesh at Tara.

The fusion data from the dog bones are presented in Table 31 and clearly indicate that the dogs present were almost exclusively old animals. The metrical data are presented in Table 26. Only one complete long bone was present, a radius, which provided an estimated shoulder height of 57.4cm. This falls within the range of Irish dog sizes known at this time. At the King's Stables dogs had a range of 54–62.6cm (McCormick 1987), while at Haughey's Fort the range was 54–65.1cm (McCormick 1988; 1991).

Wild animals

Very few wild species were present. Red deer were represented only by two pieces of antler. The example from Cutting 1, F15, displayed a few knife-marks, while the example from Cutting 2, F53, was sawn at both ends, indicating that it was used as a raw material for industrial purposes. In sample F51 fox was represented by a mandible, with all the teeth erupted, and a maxilla fragment.

Conclusions

The excavation at Tara produced a small but interesting sample of bone. It indicates that beef from mature cattle was the principal component of the diet. Pork, which was regarded as the appropriate feasting food in early Irish heroic literature, played a much smaller part. There was evidence for the eating of both dogflesh and horseflesh. One can interpret this in many ways. It may simply have been an acceptable, though minor, part of the Irish Iron Age diet. Alternatively, it could be interpreted as a feature of ritual feasts during the inauguration of kings or priests, or as 'magical' food that allowed one to foresee the future. The latter interpretations are more attractive but, on balance, less likely.

Table 6—Feature 12, fragment distribution and minimum numbers of individuals.

	Cattle	Horse	Sheep/goat	Pig	Dog
Skull	—	—	—	1	—
Mandible	3	—	—	—	1
Teeth	3	—	1	2	1
Axis	1	—	—	—	—
Scapula	1	—	—	—	—
Humerus	1	—	—	1	1
Radius	3	—	—	1	—
Ulna	1	—	—	1	1
Metacarpal	2	—	—	—	—
Pelvis	1	—	—	1	1
Femur	5	—	—	—	1
Tibia	4	—	—	—	—
Astralagus	1	—	—	—	—
Calcaneus	1	—	1	—	—
Metatarsal	1	—	—	—	—
Metapodial	—	1	—	—	5
Total	28	1	2	7	11
Total %	57.1	2.0	4.1	14.3	22.4
MNI	3	1	1	1	2

Table 7—Feature 15, fragment distribution and minimum numbers of individuals.

	Cattle	Horse	Pig	Deer
Antler	—	—	—	1
Skull	—	—	6	—
Mandible	5	—	3	—
Teeth	7	—	2	—
Atlas	2	—	2	—
Axis	—	—	1	—
Scapula	1	—	—	—
Humerus	1	—	—	—
Radius	4	—	—	—
Ulna	2	—	—	—
Pelvis	1	—	3	1
Femur	1	—	3	—
Patella	—	—	—	—
Tibia	2	1	1	—
Calcaneus	1	—	—	—
Metatarsal	1	—	—	—
Phalanx 1	1	—	—	—
Phalanx 3	—	1	—	—
Total	29	2	21	1
Total %	54.7	3.8	39.6	1.9
MNI	3	1	3	1

Appendix 2

Table 8—Feature 19, fragment distribution and minimum numbers of individuals.

	Cattle	Horse	Pig	Dog
Skull	—	—	1	—
Mandible	1	—	—	—
Teeth	—	—	1	—
Humerus	1	—	—	—
Radius	1	1	—	1
Ulna	—	—	—	—
Metacarpal	—	—	—	1
Pelvis	—	—	—	1
Metatarsal	2	—	—	—
Total	5	1	2	3
MNI	1	1	1	1

Table 9—Feature 20, fragment distribution and minimum numbers of individuals.

	Cattle	Horse	Sheep/goat	Pig	Dog
Skull	—	—	2	5	—
Mandible	—	—	—	—	—
Teeth	—	1	9	2	—
Atlas	3	—	—	—	—
Axis	1	—	—	—	—
Scapula	2	—	—	—	—
Humerus	1	—	—	1	—
Radius	1	—	1	—	—
Metacarpal	1	—	2	—	1
Pelvis	—	—	—	—	1
Femur	3	—	1	—	1
Tibia	2	—	—	1	—
Astragalus	—	—	1	—	—
Metatarsal	2	—	—	—	—
Metapodial	—	—	—	—	2
Phalanx 1	3	—	—	—	—
Phalanx 3	1	—	—	—	—
Total	20	1	16	9	5
Total %	39.2	2.0	31.4	17.6	9.8
MNI	2	1	1	1	1

Table 10—Feature 30, fragment distribution and minimum numbers of individuals.

	Cattle	Horse
Humerus	1	—
Tibia	—	1

Table 11—Feature 31, fragment distribution and minimum numbers of individuals.

	Cattle	Horse	Pig
Teeth	—	1	—
Scapula	—	1	—
Astralagus	1	—	—
Calcaneus	—	—	1
Total	1	2	1
MNI	1	1	1

Table 12—Feature 51, fragment distribution and minimum numbers of individuals.

	Cattle	Horse	Sheep/goat	Pig	Fox
Skull	—	—	—	—	1
Mandible	—	—	1	—	1
Teeth	4	—	6	—	—
Scapula	1	—	1	1	—
Humerus	2	—	1	—	—
Radius	1	—	—	—	—
Ulna	1	—	—	2	—
Metacarpal	2	—	—	—	—
Pelvis	—	—	2	—	—
Femur	3	—	—	—	—
Tibia	2	—	—	—	—
Metatarsal	1	—	—	—	—
Metapodial	—	1	—	—	—
Carpal/Tarsal	1	—	—	—	—
Total	18	1	11	3	2
Total %	51.4	2.9	31.4	8.6	5.7
MNI	2	1	1	1	1

Table 13—Feature 52, fragment distribution and minimum numbers of individuals.

	Cattle	Sheep/goat	Pig
Horn	—	1	—
Mandible	2	—	—
Teeth	3	—	1
Scapula	1	—	—
Humerus	2	—	1
Radius	3	—	—
Ulna	1	—	—
Metacarpal	1	—	1
Femur	1	—	—
Tibia	4	1	—
Metatarsal	2	—	—
Total	20	2	3
Total %	80	8	12
MNI	1	1	1

Table 14—Feature 53, fragment distribution and minimum numbers of individuals.

	Cattle	Horse	Sheep/goat	Pig	Dog	Red deer
Horn	—	—	1	—	—	1
Skull	—	—	1	3	1	—
Teeth	6	1	—	2	—	—
Atlas	1	—	—	4	—	—
Axis	2	—	—	1	—	—
Humerus	1	—	—	3	—	—
Radius	1	2	—	1	—	—
Ulna	—	1	—	4	—	—
Pelvis	1	—	—	1	—	—
Femur	4	—	—	2	—	—
Patella	1	—	—	—	—	—
Tibia	2	—	—	4	—	—
Astralagus	1	—	—	4	—	—
Metapodial	—	1	—	—	—	—
Phalanx 1	—	—	—	1	—	—
Phalanx 2	2	—	—	1	—	—
Total	22	5	2	31	1	1
Total %	35.5	8.1	3.2	50.0	1.6	1.6
MNI	2	1	1	4	1	1

Table 15—Feature 54, fragment distribution and minimum numbers of individuals.

	Cattle	Horse	Sheep/goat	Pig	Dog
Mandible	—	1	2	—	—
Teeth	1	1	1	1	—
Atlas	1	—	1	—	—
Axis	4	—	—	—	—
Scapula	1	—	—	—	—
Humerus	4	—	—	1	—
Radius	1	—	—	3	—
Metacarpal	2	—	—	—	—
Pelvis	—	—	—	1	—
Femur	2	—	—	1	—
Tibia	1	—	1	—	2
Astralagus	2	—	—	—	—
Metatarsal	2	—	1	—	1
Metapodial	—	—	—	1	—
Carpal/Tarsal	1	—	—	—	—
Phalanx 1	1	—	—	—	—
Phalanx 2	1	—	1	—	—
Total	24	2	7	8	3
Total %	54.5	4.5	15.9	18.2	6.8
MNI	3	1	1	1	1

Table 16—Feature 55, fragment distribution and minimum numbers of individuals.

	Cattle	Horse	Sheep/goat	Pig	Dog
Skull	—	—	—	1	—
Mandible	—	—	5	—	1
Teeth	5	—	2	3	1
Ulna	—	1	1	—	—
Metacarpal	1	—	—	—	—
Pelvis	—	—	—	1	—
Femur	2	—	—	—	3
Patella	1	—	—	—	—
Tibia	2	—	2	—	—
Astralagus	—	1	—	—	1
Calcaneus	1	—	—	—	1
Phalanx 1	1	—	—	—	—
Total	13	2	10	5	12
Total %	31.0	4.8	23.8	11.9	28.6
MNI	1	1	4	1	1

Table 17a—Feature 56A, fragment distribution and minimum numbers of individuals.

	Cattle	Sheep/goat	Dog
Teeth	—	—	1
Axis	1	—	—
Tibia	—	1	—
Astralagus	—	1	—
Calcaneus	2	—	—
Total	3	2	1

Table 17b—Feature 56B, fragment distribution and minimum numbers of individuals.

	Horse
Teeth	3
Total	3

Table 18—Feature 102, fragment distribution and minimum numbers of individuals.

	Cattle	Horse	Sheep/goat	Dog
Teeth	—	1	—	—
Humerus	1	—	—	—
Ulna	—	—	—	1
Metacarpal	1	—	—	—
Femur	1	—	—	1
Tibia	—	—	1	1
Tar/Car	—	1	—	—
Total	3	2	1	3
MNI	1	1	1	1

Appendix 2

Table 19—Feature 103, fragment distribution and minimum numbers of individuals.

	Cattle	Sheep/goat	Pig	Dog
Mandible	3	—	—	—
Teeth	5	—	—	—
Scapula	—	—	—	1
Humerus	—	—	1	1
Radius	1	—	—	1
Ulna	—	—	—	1
Pelvis	1	1	—	—
Phalanx 1	—	—	1	—
Total	10	1	2	4
MNI	1	1	1	1

Table 20—Feature 107, fragment distribution and minimum numbers of individuals.

	Cattle	Sheep/goat
Scapula	—	1
Humerus	—	1
Pelvis	1	—
Total	1	2
MNI	1	1

Table 21—Feature 108, fragment distribution and minimum numbers of individuals.

	Cattle	Horse
Humerus	1	—
Radius	—	1
Ulna	—	1
Metatarsal	1	—
Total	2	2
MNI	1	1

Table 22—Cattle measurements (after von den Driesch 1976).

Feature no.	Bone	Gl	Bp	Bd	Sd	Bt
12	Radius		73.5	66.2		
12	Tibia			56.4		
12	Tibia			59.9		
12	Humerus					45.1
15	Radius	265.5	74.1	63.8	38.1	
15	Radius		86.5			
15	Tibia			54.5		
15	Tibia			56.9		
15	Humerus					81.9
19	Metatarsal		43.1	52.5		
20	Scapula	72.9 (GLP)				
20	Tibia			61.2		
20	Humerus					69.5
51	Scapula	60.0 (GLP)				
52	Radius		71.5			
52	Humerus					70.5
52	Metatarsal			60.1		
52	Tibia			52.1		
53	Astralagus	63.1	42.1			
54	Metacarpal	180.9	56.9		35	
54	Metatarsal	201.2	50	54.8	31	
54	Humerus					78.1
103	Radius	256.1	78.9	68.4	38.5	
108	Humerus					70.2

Table 23—Sheep/goat measurements (after von den Driesch 1976).

Feature no.	Bone	GL	Bp	Bd	SD	
12	Astralagus	27.1 (GLl)	18.1			
52	Tibia			27.0		
54	Metatarsal	132.7	18.8	21.1	10.5	Sheep
55	Radius		26.9			

Table 24—Pig measurements (after von den Driesch 1976).

Feature no.	Bone	GL	BP	Bd	SD	Bt
15	Pelvis	31.9 (LAR)				
19	MT IV	93.3				
20	Tibia		46.9			
30	Tibia			27.5		
31	Calcaneus	69.2				
52	Humerus					27.2
53	Tibia	178.9	43.9	26.5	18.3	
53	Astralagus	43.1 (GLl)	27.5			
53	Astralagus	42.6 (GLl)	26.1			
53	Astralagus	40.2 (GLl)	25.1			
53	Humerus			41		32.5
53	Humerus			45.4	35.2	
53	Humerus			40.6	32.6	
54	Pelvis	30.6 (LAR)				
54	Humerus					31
53	Pelvis	32.5 (LAR)				
103	Humerus			40.6		31.1

Table 25—Horse measurements (after von den Driesch 1976).

Feature no.	Bone	GL	Bp	Bd	SD	GLl
15	Tibia	328	—	61.4	42.2	298±2
19	Radius		62.8			
53	Radius	323	69.9	—	37.9	307.4
30				62		

Table 26—Dog measurements (after von den Driesch 1976), with estimated shoulder heights (ESH) based on the multiplication factors of Harcourt (1974, 154).

Feature no.	Bone	GL	Bp	Bd	SD	Bt	ESH
12	Femur			46.4			
12	Tibia			22.5			
12	Scapula		37.5				
12	Tibia			42.5±			
12	Astragalus	53.9					
20	Femur			32.9			
20	Calcaneus	46.4					
20	Pelvis	26.4					
54	Tibia			24.9			
55	Femur			31.4			
55	Calcaneus	41.2					
103	Radius	189.0	20.1	26.4	18.7		57.4
103	Scapula		33.6	28.5			
103	Humerus			34.6	25.2		

Table 27—Cattle ageing data. Tooth wear stage after Grant 1982.

		Fused	Unfused	Tooth eruption
Scapula	Prox.	2	1	F12 M3 erupted G
Humerus	Prox.	2	0	
Humerus	Dist.	9	2	
Radius	Prox.	10	0	
Radius	Dist.	5	0	
Metacarpal	Dist.	1	2	
Pelvis		3	0	
Femur	Prox.	7	2	
Femur	Dist.	3	2	
Tibia	Prox.	3	1	
Tibia	Dist.	6	5	
Metatarsal	Dist.	6	0	

Table 28—Sheep ageing data. Tooth wear stage after Grant 1982.

		Fused	Unfused		Tooth eruption	
Humerus	Prox.	2	0	F54	M3 erupted G	
Radius	Prox.	1	1	F54	M3 tertiary eruption C	
Radius	Dist.	0	1	F54	M3 G x 2	Loose teeth
Metacarpal	Dist.	0	2	F55	M3 erupted G	
Pelvis		1	0	F55	M3 erupted G	
Femur	Prox.	0	1			
Tibia	Prox.	2	1			
Calcaneus	Prox.	1	0			
Metatarsal	Dist.	1	0			

Appendix 2

Table 29—Pig ageing data (excluding sod layer).

		Fused	Unfused
Humerus	Dist.	8	0
Radius	Prox.	3	0
Radius	Dist.	0	1
Pelvis		5	0
Femur	Prox.	1	1
Femur	Dist.	1	0
Tibia	Prox.	2	0
Tibia	Dist.	3	0

Table 30—Horse ageing data.

		Fused	Unfused
Radius	Prox.	3	0
Radius	Dist.	2	0
Tibia	Prox.	1	0
Tibia	Dist.	1	0

Table 31—Dog ageing data.

		Fused	Unfused
Humerus	Dist.	2	0
Radius	Prox.	3	0
Radius	Dist.	2	0
Ulna	Prox.	1	0
Metacarpal	Dist.	0	1
Pelvis		2	0
Femur	Prox.	2	0
Femur	Dist.	3	0
Tibia	Prox.	3	0
Tibia	Dist.	4	0
Calcaneus	Prox.	2	0

References

Cross, T.P. and Slover, C.H. (eds) 1969 *Ancient Irish tales.* New York.

Grant, A. 1982 The use of tooth wear as a guide to the age of domestic ungulates. In B. Wilson, C. Grigson and S. Payne (eds), *Ageing and sexing animal bones from archaeological sites*, 91–108. British Archaeological Reports, British Series 109. Oxford.

Grant, A. 1984 Animal husbandry in Wessex and the Thames Valley. In B. Cunliffe and D. Miles (eds), *Aspects of the Iron Age in central southern Britain*, 102–19. Oxford.

Harcourt, R. A. 1974 The dog in prehistoric and early historic Britain. *Journal of Archaeological Science* **1**, 151–75.

Higham, C. F. W. 1967 Stock rearing as a cultural factor in prehistoric Europe. *Proceedings of the Prehistoric Society* **33**, 84–106.

Kelly, F. 1997 *Early Irish farming.* Dublin Institute of Advanced Studies.

McCormick, F. 1987 The animal bones from the Late Bronze Age settlement at Ballyveelish 2, Co. Tipperary. In R. M. Cleary *et al.* (eds), *Archaeological excavations on the Cork–Dublin gas pipeline (1981–82)*, 26–9. Cork Archaeological Studies No. 1. Cork.

McCormick, F. 1988 The animal bones from Haughey's Fort. *Emania* **4**, 24–7.

McCormick, F. 1991 The animal bones from Haughey's Fort: second report. *Emania* **8**, 27–33.

McCormick, F. 1992 Early faunal evidence for dairying. *Oxford Journal of Archaeology* **11** (2), 201–9.

McCormick, F. 1994 Faunal remains from Navan and other late prehistoric sites in Ireland. In J.P. Mallory and G. Stockman (eds), *Ulidia: Proceedings of the first International Conference on the Ulster Cycle of Tales*, 181–6. Belfast.

McCormick, F. 1997 The animal bones from Site B. In C.J. Lynn, *Excavations at Navan Fort 1961–71 by D.M. Waterman*, 117–20. Belfast.

McCrory, P. 1980 *The siege of Derry.* London.

Murray, E. and McCormick, F. (forthcoming) The mammal bones from Mooghaun, Co. Clare. In E. Grogan, *The later prehistoric landscape of south-east Clare.* Discovery Programme Monograph.

O'Meara, J.J. (ed.) 1982 *Gerald of Wales: The history and topography of Ireland.* Harmondsworth.

Ó hÓgáin, D. 1999 *The Sacred Isles—belief and religion in pre-Christian Ireland.* Cork.

Payne, S. 1973 Kill off patterns in sheep and goats: the mandibles from Asvan Kalé. *Anatolian Studies* **23**, 281–303.

Penn, C. 1977 An osteological analysis of the animal remains from the King's Stables. In C.J. Lynn, 'Trial excavations at the King's Stables, Tray Townland, Co. Armagh'. *Ulster Journal of Archaeology* **40**, 58–9.

Silver, I.A. 1969 The ageing of domestic animals. In D. Brothwell and E. Higgs (eds), *Science in archaeology* (2nd edition), 283–302. London.

Simoons, F.J. 1994 *Eat not this flesh: food avoidances from prehistory to the present* (second revised edition). Wisconsin.

Stokes, W. 1862 *Three Irish glossaries*. London.

van Wijngaarden-Bakker, L. 1986 The animal bones from the Beaker Settlement at Newgrange, Co. Meath: final report. *Proceedings of the Royal Irish Academy* **86C**, 2–111.

von den Driesch, A. 1976 *A guide to the measurement of animal bones from archaeological sites*. Peabody Museum Bulletin, Harvard.

von den Driesch, A. and Boessneck, J.A. 1974 Kritische Anmerkungen zur Widerristhoherberechnung aus Langermassen vor und frühgeschtlicher Tierknochen, *Saugetierkundliche Mitteilungen* **22**, 325–46.

Warner, R.B. 1988 The archaeology of Early Historic Irish kingship. In S.T. Driscoll and M.R. Nieke (eds), *Power and politics in early medieval Britain and Ireland*, 47–68. Edinburgh.

Appendix 2

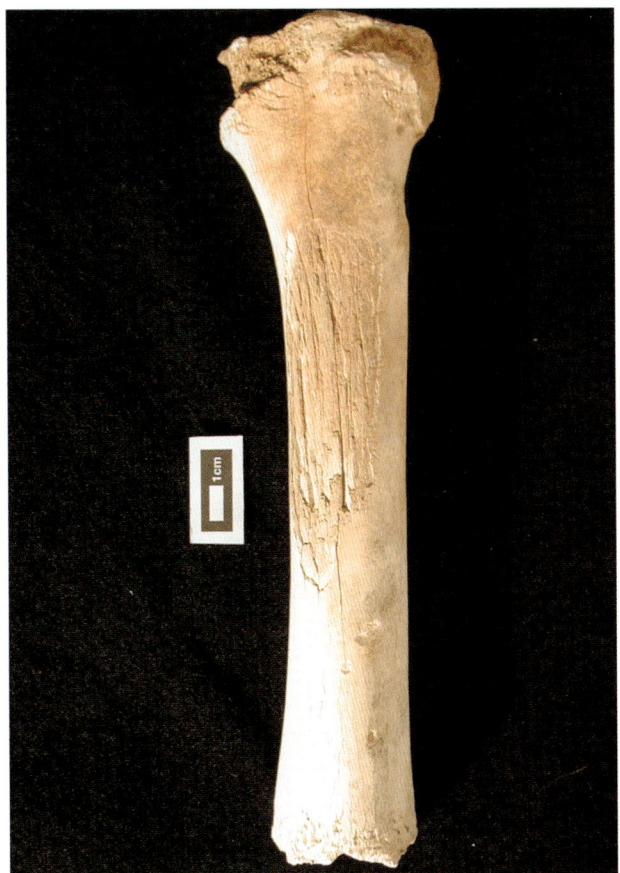

Fig. 1 (top)—Horse radius 9 (F108). Chop-marks on medial face of proximal metaphysis.

Fig. 2 (left)—Horse radius showing roast-marks on the shaft.

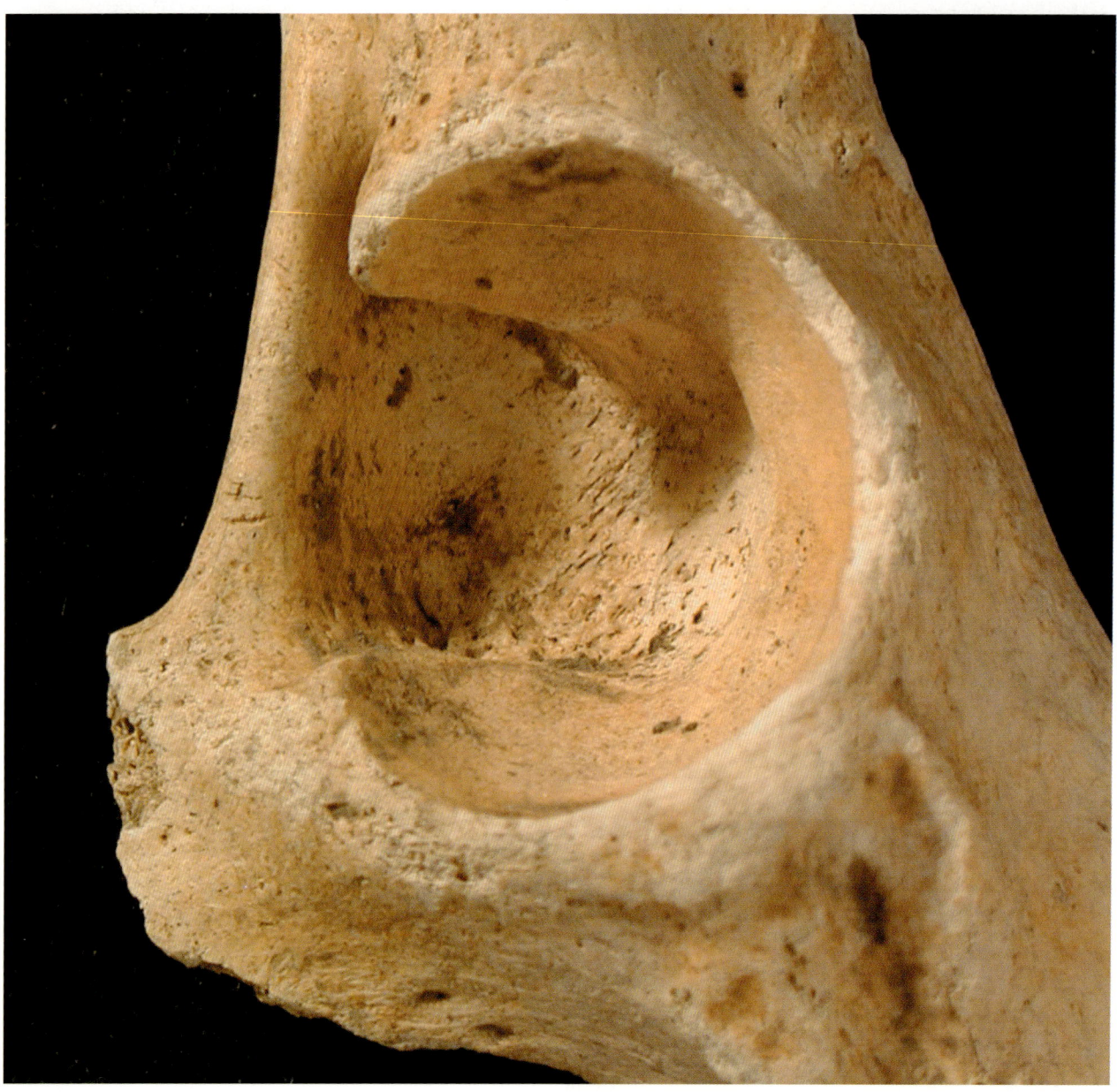

Fig. 3 (above)—Dog pelvis (F20). Cut-marks on medial aspect of acetabulum below pubis.

APPENDIX 3
Observations on the occurrence of dog and horse bones at Tara

EDEL BHREATHNACH[1]

Introduction

Observations on the occurrence of dog and horse bones in the two ditch cuttings at the northern end of the Ráith na Ríg enclosure at Tara require critical consideration from a number of perspectives: anthropological, archaeological, historical and mythological. It must be stated from the outset, however, that these perspectives have to be tempered with a certain amount of caution. McCormick has already alluded to the dangers of relying on meagre evidence which tends to overstate the importance of animals that are represented by a small number of bones (see p. 103). The evidence of the 1997 excavations may be insufficient to offer any conclusive explanations for the occurrence of dog and horse bones at Tara unless corroborated by evidence from elsewhere on the hill (such as from Ráith na Senad) or from other Irish monuments.

Anthropological, historical or mythological material can be used to infer a prehistoric society's attitude to dogs and horses, but subject to various caveats, particularly as regards the lengthy time-span involved. The customs and beliefs of the society which discarded these bones probably underwent significant changes over the course of the period from which the bones date. The conclusions which can be drawn from sources, be they anthropological, onomastic, linguistic or medieval historical, need to be understood primarily in their own specific contexts and should be applied to the archaeological evidence as a range of optional explanations rather than as dogmatic tenets. The hazards of such interdisciplinary work are cogently outlined by Miranda Aldhouse Green in a recent paper on the horse in 'pagan Celtic Europe': 'Because all this evidence [archaeological evidence of the Celtic horse] is indirect and non-explicit and since belief-systems belong to the realm of thought, it is necessary to exercise extreme caution in making inferences about ancient perceptions of the supernatural' (Green 1997, 2). A further difficulty lies in the varying distinctions in the prehistoric, medieval and modern mind between normal and paranormal, ritual or supernatural activity. Eating dog or horseflesh may seem somewhat foul to Anglocentric modern tastes, whereas certain other contemporary societies regard such meat as a delicacy. The presence at Tara of dog and horse bones which show evidence of butchery might immediately conjure up the unusual or ritual because of the nature of the site, but such a conclusion has to be examined in the scientific context of the bones: their maturity, their size, signs of unusual practices, evidence for their occurrence elsewhere on the site, including stratigraphic details which might reveal whether they are simply food debris or deliberate deposits.

McCormick notes the presence of the normal range of domesticated animals from both Cuttings 1 and 2 at Tara, thirteen horse fragments from Cutting 1 and nine from Cutting 2, and 22 dog fragments from Cutting 1 and sixteen from Cutting 2 (McCormick, Tables 1 and 2). In all cases of discarded animal bone, he suggests that they are food debris and that marks indicative of boning are clear on the cattle, pig and horse bones. With regard to the horse in Cutting 1, many of the bones were broken and shattered deliberately for the extraction of marrow, a practice known from elsewhere. McCormick also suggests that this animal was roasted and consumed nearby. The remains of both young and old horses were represented. That horseflesh was eaten at Tara need not be immediately linked to ceremonial feasting. Archaeological evidence from Ireland, Britain and the Continent suggests that horseflesh was a relatively common part of the diet and that, as with cattle and sheep, horses were often consumed when mature or when surplus to requirements (Green 1992, 35–43). In this context, this fits with McCormick's assertion that one of the horses found at Tara showed signs that it had been used for riding or traction before being

---

[1] Research Fellow, Discovery Programme, 34 Fitzwilliam Place, Dublin 2.

consumed, and hence had possibly come to the end of its useful life (p. 107). The higher-than-normal percentage of dog bone (9.4% as opposed to a norm of 1–4% on late prehistoric sites in Britain and Ireland) represented in the cuttings at Tara, however, is more convincing as an indicator of ceremonial activity, if prehistoric society made such a distinction. The dogs at Tara were almost exclusively old and compare well in size with those found at the King's Stables and Haughey's Fort (McCormick, Table 26). McCormick argues that they were eaten, noting in relation to the knife-marks on the pelvis of sample 20 of Cutting 1 that they were consistent with dismemberment of the leg from the hip and were 'not the type of knife-mark that one would associate with only the skinning of the animal' (p.107). It would appear from British and Continental evidence that dogs were both eaten and skinned. The classical pseudo-ethnographer Diodorus Siculus describes how the Continental 'Celts' when dining sat on the earth with the skins of wolves and dogs strewn beneath them (Green 1992, 25).

The dog and horse bones at Tara could be interpreted simply as the food debris of one group who frequented the hill with no intended ritual significance. There is no evidence of deliberate burial patterns associated with the bones that might correspond, for example, to the animal pit-burials at Danebury (Cunliffe 1986, 155–71) or the ritual feasting on dogs at the sanctuary of Gournay (Oise) (Green 1992, 97). Nevertheless, certain determinants compel us to consider the likelihood at least that late prehistoric people frequenting Tara, be they local inhabitants, Romano-Britons or of mixed race, did not partake of dog or horseflesh oblivious of the cultural associations of these particular animals. Primary among these considerations must be Tara's own function as a necropolis containing ancestral burials, a *temenos* or sanctuary/shrine where certain cults were venerated, and possibly the location for some form of royal inauguration rites. The accumulated evidence from other such centres in Britain and on the Continent is conclusive that any activity at similar sites was subject to an all-pervasive belief-system, which also intruded into most daily activities (Woodward 1992).

What might the consumption of dogs and horses at Tara evoke? The guardian or practitioner of the prevailing belief-system was no doubt conversant with the whole gamut of supernatural attributes of both species, which he probably attempted to communicate to the upper echelons of society. That they understood all the intricacies of his message is highly unlikely, given the experience of later Christian missionaries. The general populace probably concentrated on the cultic associations of dogs and horses in the hope that they might bring some benefit to their personal lives —healing, fertility and prosperity being the most obvious benefits. Details of attitudes towards dogs and horses in Britain and Ireland and on the Continent can be adduced from contemporary archaeological, artistic and epigraphic material, from classical and medieval sources, and from linguistic evidence. Anthropological evidence, based on descriptions of contemporary and near-contemporary societies, substantiates to a certain degree the earlier sources. Fundamental to all sources is the belief that both these animals were particularly close to humans, the dog being the guardian of the house and of flocks, and the horse a means of transport and used for farmwork (for a summary of the prehistoric evidence see Green 1992, 35–43, 111–16; for medieval evidence see F. Kelly 1997, 88–101, 114–21).

Dogs

The dog's relationship with humans is described in the fragmentary early Irish law-tract *Conshlechtae* (Breatnach 1996) and in the parallel Hiberno-Latin canon *De canibus sinodus sapientum* 'A synod of wise men: concerning dogs'(Bieler 1975, 174–5). A dog was trained to guard house and animals, one description being *cú chethardoruis, canis quattuor ostiorum* 'a dog of four doors', representing the house, the sheepfold, and the byres of calves and oxen. Similar grades are noted in other medieval sources, as in the laws of the Salian Franks, which distinguish between a trained hunting dog, tracking dogs, watchdogs and herd dogs (Fischer Drew 1991, 70–1, 207). The Irish laws required that the domestic guard-dog, if slain, should be replaced by another fully trained dog, and fines were imposed on the slayer. Breatnach (1996, 19–20) argues that the tale in which Cú Chulainn volunteered to replace Culann's hound, which the boy-hero had slain, until another pup was reared follows the requirements of early Irish legal practice, with the exception of the payment of a fine.

Apart from the dog's essential practical role as guard-dog, some of these legal references, probably unintentionally, offer us an insight into the extension of practical to supernatural: from guardian of the doorway or threshold to a role as guardian against chthonic or Otherworldly forces, often malevolent ones. It has been suggested that the burial of dogs in grain pits (e.g. at Danebury) is an expression of the appeasement of such forces on whose ground a particular settlement was built (Cunliffe 1986, 46). The fragmentary *Conshlechtae* may retain an element of this belief where it refers to the replacement of a lapdog that assumed the role of protecting a pregnant woman or a woman in labour from outside forces (*túaithgeinti*): … *nó fer Dée lee co forgairiu cen chotlud conda tí aithgin a con* 'otherwise a man of God with her watching over (?) without sleep until she gets a replacement for her dog' (Breatnach 1996, 16).

The role of the dog as guardian survives in early Irish and Welsh literature, and also in the common use in Continental, British and Irish personal names of the term CUNA-, -CUNAS (Old Irish nominative singular *cú*, genitive singular *con*) 'dog, hound' (for the etymology of *cú* see Joseph 1990). Ogam inscriptions and medieval genealogies corroborate Continental and British epigraphic evidence. There is a considerable variation of name-formation reflecting the many facets associated with dogs: CVNOCENNI (199) (*Conchenn* 'dog-head'), CVNORIX (Wroxeter ogam-stone) (*Conrí* '?dog-king'), OLACON 147 (*Ol(?l)chú* '?mighty hound'), MAGLOCVNI (Welsh *Maelgwn* 'cropped hound/hound-lord') (McManus 1991, 102, with numeric references to Macalister's *Corpus*); *Cú-Chaisil* 'hound of Caisel', *Cú-chocríche* 'hound of the boundary', *Cú-Nuadat* 'hound of Nuadu', *Cú-Ulad* 'hound of Ulster' (M. O'Brien 1962, 572–5). *Cinmarch* 'dog-horse' was the name of the reputed founder of the dynasty of Reget in north Britain (Koch and Carey 1995, 160).

Noteworthy among these are personal names that associate dogs with the protection of a territory or a boundary. In early Irish literature there are many instances of guardian hounds, both in their human-heroic forms, as with Cú Chulainn, or in their animal form, one of the most notable being Ailbe, a hound of Leinster, around which the early Irish tale *Scéla Mucce Meic Da Thó* (Thurneysen 1935) was formed. While this tale has been viewed traditionally as an expression of the activities of divine or semi-divine beings, including Ailbe and his master Da Thó, recent interpretations would caution against portraying the tale as reflecting the undiluted continuity of a belief-system from a pre-Christian to a Christian, medieval society. The tale is firmly rooted in the latter, and contemporary moralistic, misogynistic and pseudo-political themes heavily mask the residue of any distant pagan past (Poppe 1997). Nonetheless, testimony to Ailbe's importance survives in placename evidence, represented in Brega by Cluain Ailbe (Clonalvey, near Fourknocks) and Mag n-Ailbe, one of the chief fortresses of Mag Breg. Lia Ailbe 'the stone of Ailbe', the chief monument of Brega, a boundary stone with similar attributes to the Lia Fáil at Tara, probably stood at Clonalvey near Fourknocks (Byrne 1994, 112). According to the Annals of Ulster it fell in 999 and was broken into four millstones by Máel Sechnaill II (d. 1022).

The link between dogs, the gods Nodons and Apollo Cunomaglus, and water is well documented. The shrines at Lydney Park (Wheeler and Wheeler 1932; Casey and Hoffmann 1999), Nettleton Scrubb (Wedlake 1982) and Pagan's Hill (Rahtz and Harris 1957; Boon 1989) revealed sculptural representations of dogs associated with healing water cults. Although Ireland is bereft of such sculptural representations, Nodons appears in the Irish and Welsh traditions in various manifestations—Nuadu, Nechtan and Finn in Irish, Lludd and Gwyn in Welsh—and through echoes of his original attributes which survived in literature (Carey 1984, 20–2). Carey attests to the survival, albeit but a shadow of the original cult, of Nuadu's aquatic aspect, represented by the deity Nechtan, who was the husband of Bóinn (the River Boyne's tutelary goddess). Nuadu is a silver-armed king linked with water and dogs, while Finn is a figure of the wilderness, leader of a war-band, linked with water and dogs (*ibid.*, 20). It is probably no coincidence, therefore, that dog bones have been found at watery sites or in sacred ponds dating from the Bronze Age to the Romano-British period, as at Caldicot (Gwent), Flag Fen (Cambridgeshire), Ivy Chimneys (Essex) and Upchurch Marches (Kent) (Green 1992, 111), and the Late Bronze Age ritual pool at the King's Stables, Co. Armagh (Penn 1977).

Though chronologically representing a very long time-span and unlikely to have been sustained as one immutable tradition, basic tenets relating to water and cures (which are universal) were constant. The healing properties of dogs are known from other cultures that offer valuable and reasonable comparisons to popular prehistoric belief-systems. Contemporary or near-contemporary evidence from Nigeria attests to similar customs pertaining to dogs being practised by certain people (e.g. the Yoruba, Zuru and Tokuoje people) (Olowo Ojoade 1990). Dogs are eaten as a delicacy and are regarded as possessing magical properties to protect humans from *juju* ('harmful magic') and as a means to increase sexual potency. Concoctions from dog bone and flesh are prepared to cure eyes and to aid barren women. Most notably, in the context of an Irish prehistoric society, Olowo Ojoade explains that dogs were sacrificed by the Zuru to appease the gods because 'the dog has now taken the place of human beings as a sacrificial victim because he is the next best victim after man. Thus some gods particularly demand dogs for sacrifice' (*ibid.*, 220).

Horses

Horses had an equally close relationship with humans, although their best breeds were more valuable and more useful. Horses were prized by many societies for their power, beauty, swiftness, bravery in warfare and sexual vigour. Their prestige and religious significance are probably best expressed in the widespread custom of horse burials practised in Europe as far north as Iceland from the Roman to the Viking period (Richards 1992, 139; E. O'Brien 1999, 112–13). The earliest words for 'horse' in Irish and Welsh vocabularies distinguish between various grades and types of horse (P. Kelly 1997). The Old Irish *ech* (<**epo-*) would appear to be the highest grade, although the word *marc*, somehow related to Welsh *march* 'a riding horse', is also used, possibly reflecting the existence of different breeds of horse or dialect differences in terms relating to horses (*ibid.*, 46–7). Most interesting in an archaeological context is the etymology of Old Irish *capall*, Welsh *cafall*. Patricia Kelly has postulated that the Latin word *caballus* was borrowed into British and that a diminutive form **cappillos* was borrowed into Irish to give the form *capall* 'a workhorse'. This pattern of borrowings from Latin through British into Irish is corroborated by other terms related to equine equipment (e.g. *abann*, *cabastr*, *srían*, *srathar*). It also fits well with the constant references in early Irish sources to the high value placed on British horses, although it is more likely that these valuable horses were called *eich* rather than the derogatory *capaill*. 'One has to envisage a speech community where British and Irish speakers were in such close contact that the borrowing of every-day, low-register words was possible' (*ibid.*, 49–50). The rarer word *gabor* evokes an array of mythological equine associations. The horse described by the term *gabor* is defined as an *ech gel* or *airegdae* 'bright, white, silver horse' in *Sanas Cormaic*, the glossary ascribed to the king-bishop of Cashel, Cormac mac Cuilennáin (d. 908) (Meyer 1913, no. 675). Kelly (1997, 52) suggests that its origins may lie in a borrowing from Welsh *gawr* 'light-coloured, grey'. Whatever about the etymology of the term, it is primarily a poetic word for a white horse and a mare. It occurs in the placenames Loch Da Gabor (Lagore, Co. Meath) and Sciath Ghabra (Lisnaskea, Co. Fermanagh) (McKay 1999, 97), both sites associated with kings and in the latter case the inauguration site of the Maguires.

Traces of links between the cult of horses, kingship rites and goddesses survive in early Irish literature (Borgeaud 1971; Ní Chatháin 1991), probably faintly retaining elements of widespread 'Celtic' cults such as that of Epona (Green 1997, 11–14) or her Irish reflex, Macha (MacKillop 1998, 281–2). As with *cú*, the word *ech* is prevalent in personal names, as in ogam ECHADI 366 and EQOD[I] 129 (McManus 1991, 108, 122), and Eochu, Eochaid, Echbél, Echraide (MacKillop 1998, 147, 162–6). Though often difficult to interpret, these names may signify the associations between a horse cult, the sun, warfare and horse-riding. In practical terms, horses were an essential element of the legal procedure of establishing a hereditary claim to land, known in early Irish law as *tellach* (Charles-Edwards 1993, 259–73). This legal procedure took the form of two phases, in the first part of which the claimant made three entries, accompanied progressively by two horses in hand, four unyoked horses and finally eight horses (*ibid.*, 260). The early Irish text *De Shíl Chonairi Móir*, which describes the ordeals awaiting the hero-king Conaire Mór prior to his recognition as king of Tara (Gwynn 1912, 134, 138–9), contains elements of the legal procedure *tellach* and its use of horses.

Both dogs and horses were essential for hunting, and it would appear that their relationship to man in this primary activity was acknowledged culturally. It is possible that the Romano-British sunken shrine in Cambridge (Anon. 1978), dated to the second or third century AD, in which a complete horse, bull and hunting dog were carefully interred, was dedicated to Apollo Cunomaglus, the 'Hound-Lord', as seems to have been the case at the temple of Nettleton Scrubb (Green 1992, 199). It has also been suggested that the presence of two large, well-fed dogs deliberately buried in the southern banks at Dinas Powys in Wales may be further indications of hunting (Dark 1994, 208–9). In literature Finn mac Cumaill's image as a hunter with preternatural hounds (his two dogs were his nephews) forms part of the Nodons culture (Carey 1984, 21).

From prehistoric to early medieval

References to the consumption of dogs and horses in early medieval sources—and the theory that these preserve strong elements of an earlier belief-system—need to take account of many factors. Not least among these is the universal difficulty of understanding the process of conversion and the accommodation of two belief-systems in a society. Milis, in an analysis of the 'pagan Middle Ages', attempts to correlate the experience of the Indians of Central and South America (among others) with the likely patterns of conversion in early medieval Europe. He propounds three phases: (i) the imposition of a new social, collective form of behaviour on society by the emerging church with the assistance of a secular authority, which would likely lead to a ban on celebrating pagan festivals; (ii) the regulation of external but individual practice, which might lead to popular Sunday observance; and (iii) the regulation of internal behaviour, which was the most difficult to impose and was based on the understanding of an individual's conscience (Milis 1998, 10–11). Once a new religion becomes official and widespread, the earlier belief-system normally retreats into magic, folk custom or popular superstitions (terms coined for it by the Romantic movement) (Knight 1999, 120–3). It is also worth reiterating the likely gulf between practitioner and populace in their depth of understanding and practice of any religion. Early Irish sources undoubtedly reflect all these conflicts and issues, even in regard to the topic of this paper. Medieval Irish attitudes to consumption of dog and horseflesh suggest that the practice was frowned upon by ecclesiastics and ultimately was only resorted to when food was scarce (F. Kelly 1997, 355). The Irish Canons are unambiguous in their distaste for horseflesh and for anything to do with the lowly dog. A person who consumed horseflesh was subject to a penance of four years on bread and water, while the penance for eating flesh which dogs may have touched was forty days on bread and water (Bieler 1975, 160–1, 216–17). Adomnán in his *Life of Columba* best illustrates this ecclesiastical attitude in an incident when the saint relaxed the rules of diet on the island of Hinba and was disobeyed by one penitent, Neman mac Cathir, who refused the indulgence offered him. Columba berated Neman, foretelling that the time would come when in the company of thieves in the forest he would eat the flesh of a stolen mare. Columba's prophecy was fulfilled. Neman gave up his penitent life and was caught with thieves, eating such flesh from a wooden griddle (Sharpe 1995, 127–8, 282–3 (note 118)).

The early Irish law-tract on sick-maintenance, *Bretha Crólige*, while inferring that horseflesh was consumed, cautioned against feeding it to the sick and suggested that it was not highly regarded: 'does not horse flesh stir up sickness in the stomach of wounded heroes' (Binchy 1938, 20–1 (para. 25)). Alongside such sanctions, which are clearly the expressions of a predominantly Christian society, other sanctions, possibly the remnants of an earlier belief-system, crept into medieval literary texts, such as that found in the early Irish tale *Tochmarc Emire*. Cú Chulainn informs Eimer of taboos (*col* or *geiss*) relating to horses, one of which was the prohibition on anyone who had consumed horseflesh to enter a chariot for three minutes *fo déig is ech foloing in carpat* 'since it is a horse which supports the chariot' (Van Hamel 1933, 35, para 32). For a charioteer to consume horseflesh was presumably regarded as a form of cannibalism, and this taboo amounted to a totemic prohibition. How the medieval redactors or copyists of *Tochmarc Emire* perceived this taboo and its ramifications is at the core of a greater debate about perceptions of the past in early medieval Ireland.

Conclusion

Anthropology, combined with historical and literary sources, offers a series of explanations as to why dogs and horses might have been present at Tara in prehistory. However, one must be constantly mindful of the apparent time-lapse between the use of these animals and their bones and the date of the sources. Definitive conclusions can only be drawn when the date and context of the archaeological evidence are refined and an expansive interpretation of the material from Tara can be exploited.

Acknowledgements

The author wishes to thank Dr John Carey, Mr Charles Doherty and Mr Raghnall Ó Floinn for their advice.

References

Anon. 1978 The Cambridge shrine. *Current Archaeology* **61**, 57–60.
Bieler, L. (ed.) 1975 *The Irish penitentials*. Scriptores Latini Hiberniae V. Dublin.
Binchy, D.A. (ed.) 1938 *Bretha Crólige*. *Ériu* **12**, 1–77.
Boon, G.C. 1989 A Roman sculpture rehabilitated: the Pagan's Hill Dog. *Britannia. A Journal of Romano-British and kindred studies* **20**, 201–17.
Borgeaud, W.A. 1971 Hibernica: Echu–Echoch, Echoid–Echdach, Temair. *Beiträge zur Namenforschung* **6**, 40–4.
Breatnach, L. 1996 On the glossing of early Irish law-texts, fragmentary texts, and some aspects of the laws relating to dogs. In A. Ahlqvist, G.W. Banks,

R. Latvio, H. Nyberg and T. Sjöblom (eds), *Celtica Helsingiensia: proceedings from a symposium on Celtic Studies*, 11–20. Helsinki.

Byrne, F.J. 1994 Two lives of Saint Patrick: Vita Secunda and Vita Quarta. *Journal of the Royal Society of Antiquaries of Ireland* **124**, 5–117.

Carey, J. 1984 Nodons in Britain and Ireland. *Zeitschrift für celtische Philologie* **40**, 1–22.

Casey, P. J. and Hoffmann, B. 1999 Excavations at the Roman temple in Lydney Park, Gloucestershire in 1980 and 1981. *The Antiquaries Journal* **79**, 81–143.

Charles-Edwards, T.M. 1993 *Early Irish and Welsh kinship*. Oxford.

Cunliffe, B. 1986 *Danebury: anatomy of an Iron Age hillfort*. London.

Dark, K.R. 1994 *Civitas to kingdom. British political continuity 300–800*. London and New York.

Fischer Drew, K. 1991 *The laws of the Salian Franks*. Philadelphia.

Green, M. 1992 *Animals in Celtic life and myth*. London.

Green, M.A. 1997 The symbolic horse in pagan Celtic Europe: an archaeological perspective. In S. Davies and N.A. Jones (eds), *The horse in Celtic culture. Medieval Welsh perspectives*, 1–22. Cardiff.

Gwynn, L. 1912 De Shíl Chonairi Móir. *Ériu* **6**, 130–43.

Joseph, L. 1990 Old Irish *Cú*: a naïve reinterpretation. In A.T.E. Matonis and D.F. Melia (eds), *Celtic language, Celtic culture. A festschrift for Eric P. Hamp*, 110–30. California.

Kelly, F. 1997 *Early Irish farming*. Dublin.

Kelly, P. 1997 The earliest words for 'horse' in the Celtic languages. In S. Davies and N.A. Jones (eds), *The horse in Celtic culture. Medieval Welsh perspectives*, 43–6. Cardiff.

Knight, J.K. 1999 *The end of antiquity: archaeology, society and religion AD 235–700*. Stroud.

Koch, J.T. and Carey, J. 1995 *The Celtic heroic age. Literary sources for ancient Celtic Europe and early Ireland and Wales*. Malden Mass.

Macalister, R.A.S. 1945 *Corpus inscriptionum insularum Celticarum i*. Dublin. (Reprinted 1996, Four Courts Press.)

McKay, P. 1999 *A dictionary of Ulster place-names*. Belfast.

MacKillop, J. 1998 *Dictionary of Celtic mythology*. Oxford.

McManus, D. 1991 *A guide to ogam*. Maynooth Monographs 4. Maynooth.

Meyer, K. 1913 *Sanas Cormaic. An Old-Irish glossary*. Dublin and Halle. (Reprinted 1994, Llanerch Publishers.)

Milis, L.J.R. (ed.) 1998 *The pagan Middle Ages*. Woodbridge. (Translated by T. Guest from *De heidense Middeleeuwen* (Brussels and Rome, 1991).)

Ní Chatháin, P. 1991 Traces of the cult of the horse in early Irish sources. *Journal of Indo-European Studies* **19**, 123–31.

O'Brien, E. 1999 *Post-Roman Britain to Anglo-Saxon England: burial practices reviewed*. British Archaeological Reports, British Series 289. Oxford.

O'Brien, M.A. 1962 *Corpus genealogiarum Hiberniae* (reprinted 1976). Dublin.

Olowo Ojoade, J. 1990 Nigerian cultural attitudes to the dog. In R. Willis (ed.), *Signifying animals. Human meaning in the natural world*, 215–21. London.

Penn, C. 1977 An osteological analysis of the animal remains from the King's Stables. In C. J. Lynn, 'Trial excavations at the King's Stables, Tray townland, Co. Armagh'. *Ulster Journal of Archaeology* **40**, 58–9.

Poppe, E. 1997 *Scéla Muicce Meic Da Thó* revisited. *Studia Celtica Japonica* **9**, 1–9.

Rahtz, P.A. and Harris, L.G. 1957 The temple well and other buildings at Pagan's Hill, Chew Stoke, N. Somerset. *Proceedings of the Somerset Archaeological and Natural History Society* **101–2**, 15–51.

Richards, J.D. 1992 Anglo-Saxon symbolism. In M. Carver (ed.), *The age of Sutton Hoo. The seventh century in north-western Europe*, 131–47. Woodbridge.

Sharpe, R. 1995 *Adomnán of Iona. Life of Columba*. London.

Thurneysen, R. (ed.) 1935 *Scéla Mucce Meic Dathó*. Mediaeval and Modern Irish Series vi. Dublin.

Van Hamel, A.G. 1933 *Compert Con Culainn and other stories*. Mediaeval and Modern Irish Series iii. Dublin.

Wedlake, W.J. 1982 *The excavation of the shrine of Apollo at Nettleton, Wiltshire, 1956–71*. Reports of the Research Committee of the Society of Antiquaries of London XL. London.

Wheeler, R.E.M. and Wheeler, T.V. 1932 *Report on the excavation of the prehistoric, Roman, and post-Roman site in Lydney Park, Gloucestershire*. Reports of the Research Committee of the Society of Antiquaries of London IX. Oxford.

Woodward, A. 1992 *English Heritage book of shrines & sacrifice*. London.

APPENDIX 4
Human remains from Tara, Co. Meath

BARRA Ó DONNABHÁIN[1]

Summary

The lower ditch fill in Cutting 1 produced the remains of an infant that was probably aged about six months at the time of its death. This skeleton was mostly complete: the only major elements missing were the bones of the lower legs and feet. All of the other remains were very fragmentary and many had been cremated. Fragments of the unburnt skull of what was tentatively identified as an adolescent or younger adult were also found in the ditch fill. This skull was not complete; only portions of the parietals were recovered. The right half of the mandible of what was identified (with considerable diffidence) as a younger adult male was also recovered from the ditch fill, as was a fragment of the right hip-bone of an adult of unknown sex.

Many fragments of burnt bone were recovered, mostly from disturbed contexts. All of these pieces of burnt bone were relatively small, ranging in maximum length from about 4mm to about 25mm. With the exception of the two fragments in F52 (Cutting 2), all had been completely incinerated and were the chalky white colour of efficiently burnt bone. Only one of the fragments of burnt bone could be positively identified as human. Most of the rest may be portions of cremated human bones but alternative explanations could not be ruled out.

Unburnt remains: Cutting 1 ditch fill

F107—No. 122

The remains from this context consist of fourteen fragments of human bone. It is likely that these all belong to one individual. Twelve of the fragments belong to the left and right parietals of an adolescent or younger adult. Neither of the parietals is complete and the fragments recovered are all from the anterior halves of the bones. Of the remaining two fragments, one is a portion of the nasal bones while the other is a fragment of the orbital surface of the frontal.

F105—No. 124

The remains consist of a virtually complete skeleton of an infant. The bones of the skull, arms and forearms, hands, vertebrae, ribs, pelvis and thighs are present. The only major elements of the skeleton that were not recovered are the tibiae and the bones of the feet. There are also about twenty small fragments of what appear to be animal bones mixed with those of the infant (see Appendix 2).

Portions of both the maxillae and the mandible were recovered. None of the teeth had erupted at the time of death but a number are still present in their crypts in the alveolar bone. The state of development of these teeth suggests that this infant was about six months old ($\pm$ two months) at the time of its death. Of the long bones recovered, two are intact. These are the left and right humeri, and their respective maximum lengths are 74.04mm and 75mm. These measurements are consistent with the age estimate given above. No anomalies or pathological conditions were noted in the remains.

F15—No. 57

The human remains from this context consist of two fragments of bone. One is a portion of a right hip-bone which is probably from an adult. The superior margin of the sciatic notch and much of the auricular surface are present. It is not possible to determine the age or sex of the individual.

The other fragment of bone from this context is the anterior portion of the right side of the mandible of an adult. The following teeth were present in the mandible at the time of this person's death:

$$\overline{7\ 6\ 5\ 4\ 3\ 2\ |}$$

Of these teeth, only the molars were present in the

[1] Department of Archaeology, University College Cork.

fragment at the time of its recovery. The degree of wear on the first molar is moderately severe while that on the second molar is mild. This pattern of attrition might be compatible with the remains of a younger adult individual, though it would be unwise to base an age estimate on this criterion alone. There is a small ridge of calculus on the buccal and lingual surfaces of both teeth. This individual also has a slight mandibular torus. This bone matches with the mandibular ramus (no. 163) found in F103.

F103—No. 163

The human remains recovered from F103 comprise the right ramus of the mandible with the lower right third molar of an adult who may have been male. There is a mild degree of attrition of the occlusal surface of the tooth and a small amount of calculus. This fragment of mandible comes from the same individual as the portion of the same bone recovered from F15. Based on the form of the ramus and the degree of dental attrition, it is possible that these remains belonged to a younger adult male, though this is stated with considerable diffidence.

Burnt bone/cremated remains: Cutting 1 (ditch fill)

F6—No. 59

The remains recovered from F6 consist of a single small fragment of calcined bone. This appears to be a portion of a skull vault. There is no way to determine whether or not the bone is human.

F2—No. 18

The remains recovered from F2 consist of two small fragments of calcined bone. Both may be portions of long bones but the particular bone or the species to which they belong cannot be identified.

Ó Ríordáin's backfill—No. 45

The remains consist of one fragment of unburnt bone that is not human.

Cutting 2—ditch fill

F56a—No. 1

This consists of a single small and unidentifiable fragment of calcined bone.

F52—No. 1

These remains consist of five small fragments of calcined bone. One of these appears to be part of a skull vault, while the remainder appear to be fragments of long bones. Two fragments of the latter, which were originally in one piece, are not fully calcined. The centre of the bone is black rather than the chalky white that is characteristic of fully calcined bone. It is not possible to determine whether or not these bones are human.

F44d—No. 1

Three (probably one originally) tiny and unidentifiable fragments of calcined bone.

F2—No. 14

Twenty-six fragments of uniformly calcined bone and one unburnt human tooth. The latter is a lower left canine that has been subjected to a moderate degree of wear. The calcined bone may be human. The largest fragment has a maximum length of just 25mm. Two fragments are from the skull while the others are either small portions of long bones or unidentifiable.

F2—No. 15

These remains consist of about thirty small fragments of uniformly calcined bone that appear to be human. The largest fragment has a maximum length of just 20mm. All of the identifiable fragments in the collection are portions of long bones.

F2—No. 16

These remains consist of four very small fragments of calcined bone. These are probably all portions of long bones but they cannot be identified to species.

F2—No. 17

These remains consist of three small fragments of calcined bone. Two of these cannot be identified while the third is a portion of a long bone. It is not possible to determine these remains to species.

Ó Ríordáin's backfill: Cutting 2—ditch fill

No. 26

These remains consist of three small fragments of calcined bone. Only the largest of these can be identified. This is a portion of the right frontal bone in the region of the supraorbital notch and ridge. The form of the latter suggests that this piece of bone is probably from the skeleton of an adult male.

No. 28

These remains consist of two small fragments of calcined bone. One is a portion of a rib, possibly human, while the other cannot be identified.

No. 43

These remains consist of four small fragments of calcined bone that cannot be identified.

No. 44

These remains consist of ten small fragments of calcined bone. Six of these are from the skull vault while the other four appear to be fragments of long bones. These remains are probably human.

No. 62

These remains consist of three very small fragments of calcined bone that cannot be identified.

No. 64

These remains consist of four very small fragments of unburnt bone. One fragment appears to be a portion of the pedicle of a vertebra. None of the fragments can be identified to species.

No. 80

These remains consist of three small fragments of unidentifiable calcined bone.

No. 81

These remains consist of eight small fragments of calcined bone. One of these is a portion of the vault of a human skull, while the others appear to be fragments of long bones.

No. 88

These remains consist of a single small fragment of calcined bone. This is a portion of a long bone but cannot be identified to species.

No. 92

These remains consist of eleven small fragments of human bone. Three of these are skull fragments while the rest are portions of long bones.

No. 93

These remains consist of a single calcined fragment of the midshaft region of a long bone. If the bone is human, it is likely to be a portion of either the radius or ulna.

APPENDIX 5
Plant remains from Tara, Co. Meath

BRENDA COLLINS

Samples and method

Forty samples were selected for microscopic examination. A subsample of one litre was initially processed to assess their potential with a view to further examination where appropriate. One litre sub-samples were soaked and gently disaggregated in warm water. They were passed over stacked Endecotts sieves (2mm, 1mm, 0.5mm and 0.3mm), and the residue in each sieve and the heavier mineral deposit retained in the bucket were microscopically examined. Evidence of occulation in the form of charred plant remains would have broadened the archaeological record. The results were disappointing with only small quantities of charcoal present in fourteen samples.

Results

Cutting 1 pre-bank industrial level
   F37 (layer within metalworking hearth): Charcoal, isolated bone and slag.
   F37b (layer within metalworking hearth): Charcoal, isolated bone and slag.
   F75 (L-shaped trench): Charcoal and slag.
   F40a (pit fill): Charcoal; burnt bone with isolated fragments of slag.

Cutting 1 pre-bank sod layer F30
   F30: Charcoal, bone, root fragments and one fragment of slag.

Cutting 1 ditch fill
   F20: Isolated flecks of charcoal.
   F13: Isolated flecks of charcoal.
   F15: Flecks of charcoal.

Cutting 2 ditch fill
   F48: Isolated flecks of charcoal.

Area of palisade trench
   F61 (layer which seals trench): Charcoal and two unidentifiable charred cereal grains were present.
   F62 (fill of trench): Charcoal, burnt bone fragment and a few charred twig fragments.
   F64b (post-hole): A few charred twig fragments, flecks of charcoal and one fragment of charred bone.
   F64c (post-hole): Charcoal flecks.
   F64e (post-hole): Bone fragments and a little charcoal.

APPENDIX 6
Ráith na Ríg, Tara: soil micromorphological and bulk sample analysis

CLARE ELLIS[1]

1. Introduction

AOC Archaeology was commissioned to assess the archaeological and palaeoenvironmental potential of specific soil and sediment units associated with the bank and ditch of Ráith na Ríg, Tara. Initial sedimentological analyses were limited to two methodologies, micromorphology and routine soil analyses, as these techniques provide the most informative archaeological and environmental data and were the most cost-effective for the number of contexts to be examined.

Micromorphology is an analytical technique by which soils and sediments are made into thin, transparent, glass-mounted slices (usually 30mm thick) which can then be examined using a petrographic microscope. The dynamics of sedimentary processes, *in situ* physico-chemical soil processes and processes related to the impact of humans upon soils and sediments can all be studied using micromorphology.

Routine soil analyses comprise pH, loss on ignition, calcium carbonate ($CaCO_3$) content and phosphate content. PH is a measure of soil alkalinity and acidity and can reflect very localised conditions. Loss on ignition is the measurement of organic content (not including carbon derived from calcium carbonate) within a given context; such data can help to identify the agricultural production potential of given soils and characterise the type of soil or sediment. Measurement of the calcium carbonate content aids in the determination of the amount of dissolution/reprecipitation processes in soils originally rich in calcium carbonate. Determination of phosphate will enable an assessment of the natural levels of phosphate compared to that introduced into the soil or sediment through the activities of animals and/or humans. In combination, these soil analyses allow characterisation and comparison of sediments, and aid in the interpretation of their depositional history.

2. Aims and objectives

The three main aims of micromorphological analysis of soils and sediments from Tara are:
- to produce and consolidate evidence for the interpretation of archaeological and pedological site formation and post-depositional processes;
- to verify the nature of specific archaeological contexts;
- to achieve a greater understanding of sedimentary and pedogenic processes.

The three main objectives of micromorphological analysis are:
- to characterise and determine the nature of sampled contexts;
- to ascertain the mode of formation and/or deposition of specific contexts;
- to evaluate the micromorphological evidence for the presence and effects of human activity.

Specific secondary objectives have been proposed for some of the samples and are discussed within the respective contexts given below.

3. Methodology

3.1. Thin sections

Eight thin-section samples were taken during a brief visit to the site and four further samples of sediment, not available for sampling at the time of the visit, were subsequently sent over to Scotland; these samples were taken to address those main aims and objectives stated above. Eleven of the twelve samples were prepared for thin-section analysis using the methods of Murphy (1986) and analysed using the descriptive terminology of Bullock *et al.* (1985) and FitzPatrick (1993). The samples were prepared by Mr McLeod at the University of Stirling, in the Department of Environmental Sciences. The samples are listed above.

[1] AOC Archaeology Group, Edgefield Road, Loanhead, Midlothian, EH20 9SY, Scotland.

Sample no.	Section reference	Context nos
1	Cutting 1 (Bank of Ráith na Ríg, west-facing)	F33, F31, F30, F28
2	Cutting 1 (Bank of Ráith na Ríg, west-facing)	F33, F31, F30, F28
3	Cutting 1 (Bank of Ráith na Ríg, west-facing)	F16, F33
4	Cutting 1 (Bank of Ráith na Ríg, west-facing)	F33, F31, F30, F28
5	Cutting 2 (Bank of Ráith na Ríg, west-facing)	F69D, F30, F28
6	Cutting 2 (Bank of Ráith na Ríg, west-facing)	F69B, F69D, F30
7	Cutting 2 (Bank of Ráith na Ríg, west-facing)	F16A, F16
8	Cutting 1 (Ditch of Ráith na Ríg, east-facing)	F11
10	Cutting 1 (Bank of Ráith na Ríg, east-facing section)	F30, F29
11	Cutting 1 (Bank of Ráith na Ríg, east-facing section)	F16, F84A, F31, F30
12	Cutting 1 (Bank of Ráith na Ríg, east-facing section)	F33, F31, F30
13	Cutting 1 (Bank of Ráith na Ríg, east-facing section)	F16, F33

Detailed descriptions of the thin sections are given in Section 10, and summary descriptions are included with the main body of the text.

3.2. Bulk routine samples

Ten bulk samples were taken, one from each context sampled for micromorphological analysis: F28; F30; F31; F33; F28; F69D; F30; F69C; F69B; and F11. All samples were subjected to four analyses, using soil in a field-moist condition. pH was determined in a 1:2.5 soil to distilled water mixture. Loss on ignition used $c.$ 10g oven-dry soil ignited to $400°C$ for four hours. Determination of phosphate used a spot test for easily available phosphate (Hamond 1983). Samples were rated on a three-point scale using the time taken for a blue colour to develop following the addition of the two reagents to the sample. The scale was high (30 seconds), medium (30–90 seconds) and low (more than 90 seconds). Calcium carbonate content was assessed semi-quantitatively using a simple field test and the samples assigned to the following classes (based on Hodgson 1976, 57):

Test rating	$CaCO_3$ (%)	Description
0	0.1	Non-calcareous
1	0.1–1	Non- to very slightly calcareous
2	1–5	Slightly calcareous
3	5–10	Calcareous
4	10+	Very calcareous

4. Section descriptions

4.1. Cutting 1, bank of Ráith na Ríg

4.1.1. INTRODUCTION

The natural soils at Tara are grey-brown podzolic soils or gleys (F16, F16A). The section cuts, at right angles, the bank and ditch of Ráith na Ríg. Four kubiena tins (aluminium thin-section tins) were taken from the west-facing section below the bank to provide a short continuous sequence of samples through the profile; these were Samples 1, 2, 3 and 4 (Fig. 1). Four kubiena tins were also taken from the east-facing section below the bank; these samples targeted the sequence (excluding negative features) below the bank and were numbered Samples 10–13 (Fig. 2).

4.1.2. PROFILE DESCRIPTION (WEST-FACING SECTION)
(The depths, in cm, are taken from the excavated ground surface.)

0–30 Bank material comprising silt, mixed boulder clay (till) clasts, angular rock clasts and rootlets. (Upcast from ditch.) Poorly sorted. Sharp boundary into:

30–42 Context F28. Pale silty clay. Redeposited boulder clay. (Bank material.)

42–47 Context F30. Dark grey clayey silt with grit and occasional stones. Moderately sorted. Many micropores. Occasional rare iron-staining. (Grey layer, sod.)
Sharp boundary into:

47–48 Context F31. As above, black silty clay but with significant amounts of burnt material

including charcoal fragments. (Black layer.)
Very sharp boundary into:
48–58 Context F33. Silty clay with occasional charcoal and grit.(Old ground surface.)
Sharp boundary into:
58+ Context F16. Till. Silty clay matrix with subangular to angular clasts, poorly sorted. Calcareous. (Natural boulder clay.)

4.2. Cutting 2, main section (facing west)

4.2.1. INTRODUCTION

This section cuts, at right angles, the bank and ditch of Ráith na Ríg. Three kubiena tins, Samples 5, 6 and 7, were taken from this section below the bank to provide a semi-continuous sequence (Fig. 3).

4.2.2. PROFILE DESCRIPTION

(Depth in cm)
0–20 Silty clay loam with many small to medium stones and rootlets. Occasional charcoal. Discrete microlaminations of clay particles. Sharp boundary following the form of the bank into:
20–43 Clayey silt. Mixed silty loam (brown) and redeposited till clasts (buff brown). The deposit is well mixed. Generally horizontally oriented small stones. Rare rootlets. Sharp boundary into:
43–47 Context F30. A very thin (3–4mm wide) discontinuous iron-pan. Below is a grey silt with clay and small stones. Many micropores. Well sorted. Occasional charcoal. Sharp boundary into:
47–55 Context F69D/F69C. Dark brown clayey silt matrix. Many stones. Poorly sorted, especially to southern end of the section. The unit broadens and plunges into the ditch at the northern side. Sharp boundary into:
55–67 Context F69B. Silty sand with stones. Small clasts of slate bedrock. Occasional charcoal flecks. Poorly sorted. Sharp boundary into:
67+ Context F16A. Till.

4.3. Cutting 1, extension 2 (east-facing)

4.3.1. INTRODUCTION

This section is an extension of Cutting 1 and crosses the ditch to the south of the sampled bank. One sample (Sample 8) was taken from an upper sediment fill (post-medieval; H. Roche, pers. comm.) on the southern side of the ditch fill.

4.3.2. PROFILE DESCRIPTION

(Depth in cm)
0–17 Topsoil and turf.
17+ Rich clayey silt. Yellowish-brown. The sediment was extremely wet when sampled but showed prismatic jointing in some locations. Some rootlets. Very few stones and those rare stones are mainly horizontally oriented. Well sorted. No apparent charcoal or other materials, clearly derived from human activity.

5. Summary micromorphological description of the sampled contexts

5.1. Introduction

The summary descriptions are organised according to context, as many of the contexts occur in a number of the samples. The context summary descriptions have been organised according to their broad stratigraphic order, although there is some overlap between Cuttings 1 and 2.

5.2. Context F16A

5.2.1. INTRODUCTION

Context F16A is represented in Sample 7 (Fig. 3). The sediment is described as a natural boulder clay (H. Roche, pers. comm.).

5.2.2. SUMMARY DESCRIPTION

The sediment is poorly sorted with a massive structure with much fine sand-sized material. The porosity is locally variable, measuring between 2% and 5%. The matrix is yellowish-brown to reddish-orange in PPL and reddish-brown to grey in CPL. The matrix shows a weakly speckled b-fabric in CPL.

The coarse mineral component is dominated by fine, sand-sized, well-rounded monocrystalline quartz grains. Potassium- and sodium-rich feldspar mineral grains are also common and many show sericitisation. The mineral grains generally fall into the fine, sand-sized category. The rock fragments are abundant (15–20%) and dominated by well-rounded cherts, with metamorphic, igneous and sedimentary lithologies represented. Many of the rock fragments are chemically weathered.

There are rare oval sclerotia and rare, well-degraded organic matter. There are four different types of clay coatings.

(i) Impure reddish-brown dusty clay coatings of voids; some of the coatings are microlaminated and show compound concentric pattern. The coatings are common and measure up to 1mm in width (Pl. 1).

(ii) Reddish-brown pure clay coatings of voids.

(iii) Yellowish-orange clay coatings of voids especially within chert rock fragments; some are crescentic in form (Pl. 2).

(iv) Brown dusty clay accumulations within the matrix but not necessarily associated with voids.

5.3. Context F16

5.3.1. Introduction

Context F16 is represented in thin sections 4 and 7 and possibly in the lowest portion of Sample 11 (Figs 1, 3 and 2 respectively). This context is described as 'natural boulder clay' (H. Roche, pers. comm.). Field observations recorded a weakly calcareous, poorly sorted silty clay till with angular clasts.

5.3.2. Summary description

The sediment has a complex microstructure, comprising both massive and chambered; there is no ped formation. The porosity varies from 2% to 15%, although the higher porosity of Sample 11 (1–15%) appears to be caused by post-depositional disturbance. The sediment is poorly sorted and shows an open, porphyric-related distribution. The matrix colour is yellowish-brown to reddish-brown in PPL and greyish-brown in CPL. The arrangement of the fine fraction can be defined as a weakly speckled b-fabric, with randomly arranged speckles of clay. The coarse mineral component is dominated by fine, sand-sized, well-rounded monocrystalline quartz grains. Potassium- and sodium-rich feldspar mineral grains are also common. A number of different lithologies of moderately to well-rounded rock fragments are present but these are dominated by chert. Many of the rock fragments have experienced physico-chemical weathering, shown by the presence of much iron oxide.

Dispersed within the matrix are black, isotropic fragments, some of which may be organic in origin. A single sclerotium was observed in Sample 7, as were rare possible pollen grains. Four distinct clay coating morphologies were identified in Sample 7:

(i) reddish-brown dusty clay coatings of voids; some of the coatings are microlaminated and show compound concentric pattern;

(ii) reddish-brown pure clay coatings of voids;

(iii) yellowish-orange clay coatings of voids especially within chert rock fragments; some are crescentic in form;

(iv) brown dusty clay accumulations within the matrix but not necessarily associated with voids.

However, only brown dusty clay coatings and accumulations (iv) were apparent in Sample 4 and no coatings were observed in Sample 11. Small zones of iron or possible amorphous organic matter depletion were also observed. There are also dark reddish mottles within the fine matrix; these are characterised by diffuse edges and partially masked mineral matter.

Dark reddish-brown organo-mineral micro-aggregates measuring 80–600μm in diameter were present in Samples 4 and 11, but extremely rare in Sample 7. Within the upper portion of Sample 4 are a number of vertically oriented biological veriforms.

5.4. Context F69B/F69D

5.4.1. Introduction

Context F69B is described as a silty slip, the fill of the ditch trench, and F69D as a silty clay, the fill of the ditch trench (H. Roche, pers. comm.) (Fig. 3). Field observation revealed F69B to comprise a poorly sorted, dark brown clayey silt with many rock clasts. F69D comprised a poorly sorted, silty sand with stones and small clasts of slate bedrock. There are occasional charcoal flecks. However, these two contexts were not distinguishable in thin section and so are described as one unit.

5.4.2. Summary description

The sediment is poorly sorted and comprises a massive and channelled microstructure. The matrix is yellowish-brown in PPL and dark brownish-grey in CPL. The matrix fabric is mixed, comprising weakly speckled and weakly developed poro/granostriated b-fabrics.

The coarse mineral component comprises very fine, sand-sized monocrystalline quartz grains. Feldspar grains are also frequently observed; many are sericitised. The rock fragments comprise 30% of the context and comprise a mixture of lithologies, but are predominantly well-rounded cherts.

There is a single-cellular charcoal fragment measuring 1mm in diameter. There are single-cellular organic fragments and rare phytolith fragments. Bone fragments are also rare.

The boundary between F30 and F69B/F69D is defined by a layer rich in organic matter and dark reddish-brown microaggregate faecal pellets. Very dark reddish-brown mottling occurs near the base of the slide and is associated with well-decomposed organic matter. There are faunal channels with are partially infilled with semi-fused faecal pellets and mineral concentrations.

Within the matrix are dark brown to pale yellow silty clay accumulations and dusty clay coatings to many of the polyconcave voids. There are rare clay papules. There are rare matrix well-rounded and irregular fabric pedofeatures. The sediment appears relatively undisturbed near the base of the thin-section slide.

5.5. Context F33

5.5.1. Introduction

Context F33 is represented in thin sections 2, 3, 11, 13 and 12 (Figs 1 and 2). The context is described as 'a light brown, pre-bank sod layer' (H. Roche, pers. comm.). Field observations recorded the unit as comprising silty clay with occasional charcoal and grit. It has been postulated that this context may represent a sealed and preserved old ground surface (OGS) and/or buried sod (H. Roche, pers. comm.).

5.5.1. Summary description

The sediment has a massive microstructure with discrete voids and vugs and no ped formation; many of the vugs are polyconcave. The porosity of the sampled context ranges from 2% to 5%. Weak horizontal orientation of some mineral grains and organic matter is evident. Two organic-rich layers are present in Sample 3 (Pl. 3; Fig. 1) and one possible layer in Sample 13 (Fig. 2). These layers share broad characteristics: a high proportion of organic matter; many dark reddish-brown microaggregates (faecal pellets); *in situ* rootlets; and much mite excrement. The sediment is moderately well to poorly sorted. The matrix is dark yellowish-cream to yellowish-brown in colour (PPL) and dark greyish-brown in CPL. The matrix fabric is complex and includes an extremely weakly developed stipple-speckled b-fabric, weakly developed poro/granostriated b-fabric and undifferentiated b-fabric.

The coarse component comprises predominantly fine, sand-sized monocrystalline quartz grains with undulose extinction. Potassium- and sodium-rich feldspar mineral grains are also common. A number of different rock lithologies are present and include chert; the largest rock fragment measures 15mm.

Cellular charcoal clasts range in size from 8mm to *c.* 100µm. Fine disseminated charcoal is scattered throughout the matrix, but in Sample 3 it is particularly found in association with 'ash' material and/or biological activity. Degraded *in situ* rootlets are rare within this context, although ill-defined zones of degraded, amorphous organic matter are more common. Zones of humic acid and/or iron depletion are also associated with areas of higher charcoal concentration and phytolith fragments. There are a number of burnt bone fragments; the largest measures 2mm. Sclerotia are rare. Phytolith fragments are only recorded from Samples 12 and 13.

There are clay silt accumulations which have a slightly convoluted fabric. There are rare dusty clay coatings and accumulations near the base of the unit in Sample 13. Organic-rich mite excrement is particularly common in Sample 3. Reddish-brown microaggregates with abrupt to sharp boundaries (faecal pellets) are present within the matrix; these measure 80–400µm in diameter and depending on the sample analysed comprise roughly 2–5% of the matrix. Rare faunal infilled channels are present. Fabric pedofeatures were noted in some of the samples; these were characterised by the preferred orientation of clay and silt-sized mineral grains. Dark reddish-brown mottles occur in Samples 11 and 12. There are rare iron-rich nodules.

5.6. Context F31

5.6.1. Introduction

Context F31 is represented in thin sections 1, 2, 4, 11 and 12 (Figs 1 and 2). This context is described as a 'dark charcoal-flecked, pre-bank sod layer'. The field description was as for F30 but with additional black silty clay and significant amounts of burnt material, including charcoal fragments. It has been postulated that F31 may represent the *in situ* development of material with manure additions, or perhaps a dumped industrial/midden spread.

5.6.2. Summary description

The sediment has a vuggy to chambered microstructure. The porosity of the sediment is high, 15–20%, and is largely due to the significant charcoal content of the unit. The larger charcoal fragments show weakly developed horizontal orientation. The fine matrix material of the unit varies in colour from yellowish-brown to reddish-brown (PPL) and is greyish-brown in CPL. The fabric of the sediment may be described as a weakly developed stippled b-fabric, although there are significant zones of undifferentiated b-fabric.

The sediment is poorly sorted. The coarse component comprises many well-rounded chert clasts (2–5% of the unit) and fine sand-sized monocrystalline quartz grains. Potassium- and sodium-rich feldspar mineral grains are also common. A number of different rock lithologies are present and include chert; many of these have been subjected to physico-chemical weathering.

Cellular charcoal fragments, many of which are clearly abraded, dominated this context; the largest measures 2cm in diameter. Fine disseminated charcoal occurs throughout the matrix, but is particularly associated with pedofeatures (Pl. 4). *In situ* rootlets are also present. Burnt bone fragments are relatively frequent and measure 100–500µm in diameter (Pl. 5). Fine siliceous material associated with charcoal and phytoliths may be the remnants of ash material. There are possible fragments of sclerotia.

The soil matrix of Sample 3 is redder than that in the other samples and may represent heat-affected soil. Biological activity is indicated by the presence of rounded fabric pedofeatures as well as dark reddish-brown microaggregates (faecal pellets). Mite excrement is also present. Faunal passages are evident and many are infilled with organic- and charcoal-rich matrix.

5.7. Context F30

5.7.1. INTRODUCTION

Context F30 is represented in thin sections 1, 2, 4, 10, 11, 12, 5 and 6 (Figs 1–3). This context is described as a 'grey, charcoal-flecked pre-bank sod' (H. Roche, pers. comm.). Field observations revealed the context to comprise a moderately sorted clayey silt with grit and occasional stones and occasional iron-staining. It has been postulated that this context may represent a sealed and preserved old ground surface (OGS) and/or buried sod (H. Roche, pers. comm.).

5.7.2. SUMMARY DESCRIPTION

The sediment context has a complex microstructure but is dominated by a massive structure. Other microstructure forms include vuggy/alveolar, channel and chamber. There is very limited ped formation (Sample 12 only). The porosity is locally variable and ranges from 2% to 10%. The voids are predominantly vugs with many showing polyconcave form. Channels and fine fissures occur in most of the samples. In some samples there are weakly developed laminations and the preferred orientation of charcoal fragments. The matrix colour is dark yellowish-cream to yellowish-brown in PPL and dark greyish-brown in CPL; it is composed of silt-sized quartz, silt-sized chert rock fragments and unidentified clay minerals. There are rare zones of very pale grey matrix. The matrix generally comprises weakly speckled b-fabric with weak grano/porostriated b-fabric. The sediment is generally poorly sorted with much of the finer material comprising silt and fine sand-sized material. The coarse component is dominated by fine, sand-sized monocrystalline quartz with undulose and occasionally straight extinction. A number of different rock lithologies are present, including chert, micaceous sandstone and shales/slates.

There is 2–5% charcoal in the sampled context. Much of the charcoal is cellular and occurs as abraded clasts ranging in size from 5mm to silt-sized fragments. There is weak horizontal alignment to much of the charcoal and organic matter. Dispersed throughout the matrix and in some infills are fine disseminated charcoal fragments. There are rare sclerotia. Also scattered through the matrix is dark reddish-brown colloidal organic matter. *In situ*, degraded rootlets occur in most of the analysed samples; these are often associated with biological activity (Pl. 6). There is a relatively high proportion of organic matter that occurs in the form of faecal pellets. Well-rounded bone fragments are rare to frequent within the general matrix. Larger irregular burnt bone fragments tend to be associated with charcoal fragments. Fragments of phytoliths occur within the matrix but are especially common in areas depleted in amorphous organic matter and in infills within biological channels.

Fine silt accumulations occur within the matrix, voids and rare channels. Well-rounded, dark reddish-brown, organo-mineral, sharp-edged microaggregates generally measuring 200–640µm are a common feature of this context. There are also smaller, dark reddish-brown, organic-rich well-rounded microaggregates which measure up to 60µm in diameter. Faunal passages are evident and are conspicuous fabric or textural pedofeatures defined by one or some of the following: disturbed matrix material; charcoal clasts; dark reddish-brown amorphous organic matter; rare sclerotia; faecal pellets; bone fragments; and silt-sized mineral grain accumulations (Pl. 7). Other infills are in the form of well-rounded fabric pedofeatures. Dark reddish-brown to black iron-rich nodules are rare.

5.8. Context F28

5.8.1. Introduction

This context only occurs in Sample 2 (Fig. 1). The context is described as a redeposited boulder clay and represents bank material (H. Roche, pers. comm.). Field observations revealed the sediment to comprise a pale silty clay with rock fragments.

5.8.2. Summary description

The sediment has a massive structure with rare polyconcave vugs and fissures. The porosity of the sediment measures between 2% and 5%. The sediment is poorly sorted. The matrix colour is yellowish-brown and dark greyish-brown to dark yellowish-orange in CPL. The matrix has a weakly developed granostriated b-fabric combined with a stipple-speckled b-fabric. The basic mineral component and rock fragments comprise about 20% of the sample. The majority of the quartz is monocrystalline and falls into the fine sand-sized class. A number of different rock lithologies are present, including chert, limestone and shales.

A single sclerotium was observed. Charcoal is predominantly clustered about partially infilled voids and the cellular charcoal measures $c.$ 350µm to 1.5mm in diameter. There are well-decomposed rootlets, and colloidal organic matter occurs throughout the matrix. There are phytolith fragments. One large, 6mm bone fragment was observed.

Iron-rich, dark reddish-brown microaggregates are associated with the organic matter; these tend to measure 60–200µm in diameter. Biological activity is apparent from partially infilled channels comprising disseminated charcoal, faecal microaggregates, bone fragments and amorphous organic matter. There are compound textural pedofeatures and yellowish-orange silty pedofeatures adjacent to rock fragments and within the matrix. Pure, yellowish-orange, clay textural pedofeatures occur as coatings to voids, around and within some rock fragments, especially cherts.

5.9. Context F29

5.9.1. Introduction

This context is present in Sample 10 (Fig. 2). The context was described as brown/orange silty clay and represents bank material (H. Roche, pers. comm.).

5.9.2. Summary description

The sediment has a weakly developed subangular blocky structure with a relatively high porosity ranging between 5% and 15%. The sediment is poorly sorted and yellowish-brown to greyish-cream in colour in PPL and grey-brown in CPL. The coarse mineral component comprises fine silt and fine sand-sized monocrystalline quartz grains. Feldspar grains are also frequently observed. The rock fragments comprise a mixture of lithologies and are dominated by well-rounded cherts.

Rootlets are rare in this context. There are abraded cellular charcoal fragments and other charcoal fragments scattered within the matrix. A layer comprising reddish organic matter occurs 18mm from the top of the slide and marks the base of this unit. The sediment above this layer is yellowish-brown in colour in PPL, and contains more microaggregates and mite excrement and less charcoal but is more organic-rich than that below. There is one well-rounded bone fragment.

There are dark reddish, organic-rich microaggregates measuring 20–240µm in diameter and rare larger microaggregates measuring $c.$ 600µm in diameter. Impure, reddish-orange clay pedofeatures are associated with rootlets. The context also exhibits dusty clay coatings of some voids.

5.10. Context F28 (bank material)

5.10.1. Introduction

This context is represented in Samples 2 and 5 and is described as redeposited boulder clay (H. Roche, pers. comm.). Field description revealed the unit to comprise a clayey silt with silty loam and till clasts with weak horizontal orientation of rock clasts. Rare rootlets were observed.

5.10.2. Summary description

The context is poorly sorted, comprising a massive and a weakly developed vuggy microstructure. The porosity is locally variable and ranges from 0.5% to 20%. The matrix is dominated by silt-sized quartz grains and unidentified clay minerals. The matrix is brownish-yellow in colour in PPL and dark purplish-brown in CPL. The matrix fabric is mixed, comprising weakly speckled and poro/granostriated b-fabric.

The coarse mineral component comprises monocrystalline quartz grains. Feldspar grains are also frequently observed with sericitisation. The rock fragments comprise a mixture of lithologies and are dominated by well-rounded cherts. Rock fragments account for at least 15–20% of the sample.

Organic matter is rare and includes multicellular spores and well-decomposed plant matter. There are a variety of clay coatings ranging from dusty clay to pure clay. There are also within-matrix silty clay intercalations. There are dark reddish-brown microaggregates and rare mite excrement. Rare chambers have partially fused silty microaggregates. There is a possible micrite coating to a single void.

5.11. Context F11

5.11.1. INTRODUCTION

The context is described as a well-sorted light brown clayey silt (H. Roche, pers. comm.). Field observations revealed the sediment to comprise a yellowish-brown, rich clayey silt. Weakly developed prismatic peds were present and rootlets cut through the unit. There were very few stones and those that were present were generally oriented along the vertical.

5.11.2. SUMMARY DESCRIPTION

The sediment is well sorted with a massive structure and rare, weakly developed fissures. The porosity is <2%, with polyconcave voids near the top of the sample. The matrix is yellowish-brown in PPL and dark greyish-brown in CPL. There is a weakly developed speckled b-fabric with rare poro/granostriation.

The coarse mineral component comprises silt-sized subangular monocrystalline quartz. The rock fragments comprise a mixture of lithologies and are dominated by well-rounded cherts. Many of the rock fragments are chemically weathered with iron-staining.

Amorphous organic fragments dominate with rare sclerotia. There is some organic-rich mite excrement and rare *in situ* rootlets. There are possible stomatocysts, and phytolith fragments are common.

There are probable detrital organo-mineral microaggregates and dark reddish-brown mottles; both are associated with organic matter. Weak dusty clay coatings occur on some voids. There is one possible biological veriform.

6. Discussion and interpretation of micromorphological data

6.1. Objectives of thin-section samples

6.1.1. OBJECTIVES OF THIN-SECTION SAMPLES NOS 1, 2, 3, 4, 10, 11, 12 AND 13

The specific objectives have been identified as:

- to characterise and determine the nature of contexts F28, F29, F30, F31, F33 and F16 with specific reference to contexts F30 and F33, which are thought to represent buried soils;
- to evaluate the anthropogenic input and impact upon these contexts;
- to determine the processes of profile formation as observed beneath the bank deposits.

6.1.2. OBJECTIVES OF THIN-SECTION SAMPLES 5, 6 AND 7

The specific objectives have been identified as:

- to characterise and determine the nature of contexts F28, F30, F69D, F69B, F16 and F16A, with specific reference to contexts F69B and F16;
- to evaluate the anthropogenic input and impact upon these contexts;
- to determine the processes of profile formation as observed beneath the bank deposits.

6.1.3. OBJECTIVES OF THIN-SECTION SAMPLE 8

The specific objectives have been identified as:

- to characterise and determine the nature of context F11, the rich clayey silt;
- to determine the source of the sediment and the processes of sediment formation;
- to evaluate potential anthropogenic input and impact upon this context.

6.2. Discussion of contexts from Cutting 1, east- and west-facing sections

6.2.1. INTRODUCTION

The stratigraphic sequence from contexts F16 to F28/F29 is discussed below, commencing with the lowermost context F16.

6.2.2. CONTEXT F16

This context represents a largely undisturbed till. The till is fairly well compacted and comprises a silty clay/fine sand matrix with larger rock clasts, the majority of which are chert or slate. The glacial origin of the sediment is apparent from the eroded and chemically weathered rock fragments and the well-sorted fine sand-sized fraction of the matrix.

Episodic post-depositional pore water movement is indicated by (a) the massive structure, (b) a weak anisotropic fabric, (c) the presence of yellowish-brown dusty clay coatings and matrix accumulations (and three other different types of clay coatings within Sample 7) and (d) iron oxide mottling, also limited to Sample 7. The quantity and range of clay and silty clay coatings indicate that these are the product of translocation (illuviation) rather than pedogenic processes. Limited biological activity is apparent in the form of dark reddish-brown faecal pellets; however, these are extremely rare in Sample 7. Post-depositional biological activity within the upper portion of F16, Sample 4, is apparent in the form of vertical infilled biota channels.

There are no identifiable features to indicate that this unit has been affected by human activity. However, the presence of much amorphous organic matter, especially within Sample 7, the occurrence of rare sclerotia, the presence of biological faecal material and biologically produced channels indicate that this context has been subjected to limited soil ripening, i.e. pedological processes.

6.2.3. BOUNDARY BETWEEN F16 AND F33/F84A

The boundary between F16 and F33 in both Sample 3 and Sample 11 is distinct. In Sample 3 the boundary occurs over *c.* 20mm and is partially defined by the presence of veriforms, as described above. The boundary between F16 and F84A in Sample 11 is defined by an irregular line of rock fragments, planar voids and a change in matrix.

6.2.4. CONTEXT F33

Context F33 occurs in Samples 1, 2, 3, 4, 11, 12 and 13. The basic mineral component and rock fragments are lithologically very similar to those observed within the till samples (F16/F16A) and it is clear that the primary source of this context is the till. The weak horizontal orientation of some mineral grains and organic matter may be indicative of natural soil accumulation, or is perhaps the product of another depositional force, such as surface run-off caused by a sudden downpour upon relatively impervious ground. The two distinct organic-rich layers (Sample 3) are characterised by the presence of rootlets, fragmentary phytoliths, faecal pellets and mite excrement; a similar organic-rich layer is also recorded in Sample 13. These layers are interpreted as remnant turf (or some form of vegetation) surfaces, which were subsequently and relatively rapidly buried by further sediment/soil, or, in the case of the upper layer in Sample 3, by context F31. The upper boundaries of the layers in Sample 3 are sharp, indicative of the relatively rapid cessation of vegetation growth, while the lower are distinct, indicating relatively gradual vegetation colonisation and soil ripening. The rapid but apparently shallow burial of these 'turf' surfaces resulted in their partial, but not complete, biological breakdown.

The presence of cellular charcoal, fine disseminated charcoal and burnt bone fragments associated with the possible siliceous remnants of 'ash' is indicative of human activity. These components are characteristic of low-temperature burning used in cooking or in wood cinder fires for grilling (Courty *et al.* 1989). Because the sediment has experienced some physical post-depositional disturbance the means by which the charcoal, bone and ash entered into the deposit is unclear. However, the limited presence of soil indicators within this context, i.e. rare sclerotia and rare rootlets, may be interpreted as a consequence of rapid profile development owing to the addition of 'ash manure' to a relatively poorly developed soil. The abraded nature of many of the larger charcoal fragments, the dispersed nature of the fine charcoal fragments and the rounded and fragmentary nature of the bone fragments are indicative of biologically reworked, ash midden material. The presence of rare infilled faunal channels and dark reddish-brown microaggregates is indicative of biological activity, although many of these faecal pellets occur within the matrix and may be detrital in origin, perhaps originating from a manure.

The colour of the matrix of Sample 11, context F84A, is reddish-brown and may be interpreted as burnt and oxidised organo-mineral material; the red colour indicates burning under oxidising conditions (Pl. 8). The predominantly reddish hue of the majority of the rock fragments is also indicative of burning, which would have caused the oxidation of iron minerals. The temperature of the fire, probably associated with the metalworking hearth, F38, at the point of sampling was below 800°C, because the quartz grains remain unaltered.

The massive microstructure, the relatively low porosity and the presence of many polyconcave voids are indicative of post-depositional compaction. The anisotropic matrix fabric and the weakly developed grano/porostriation demonstrate that this compaction is partially due to the movement of water through the context. The grey colour of much of the matrix is largely due to the removal of clay minerals and humic acids through the process of leaching. The presence of rare dusty clay coatings at the base of Sample 13 is also indicative of limited silt and clay translocation through the profile. Episodic periods of saturation and dewatering are also evident through the presence of iron oxide mottles. The convoluted silty clay accumulations within the matrix may be interpreted as the product of biological sorting through ingestion, although some of these accumulations are perhaps also a consequence of translocation.

6.2.5. BOUNDARY BETWEEN F33 AND F31

The boundary is generally sharp but often wavy. The change from F33 to F31 is characterised by a sudden increase in charcoal and an increase in faecal pellets. However, the boundary is diffuse in Sample 2 and the two contexts appear to have been mixed through the activity of soil biota.

6.2.6. CONTEXT F31

Context F31 is present in Samples 1, 2, 4, 11 and 12. The basic mineral component and rock fragments are lithologically very similar to those observed within the till samples (F16/F16A), and as with F33 it is clear that the primary source of this context is the glacial till. The context is relatively thin, measuring up to 20mm in thickness, and is characterised by a high charcoal content (Pl. 9). Much of the charcoal is abraded and, coupled with the linear nature of the deposit, it is probable that the unit is a dumped spread of material rather than the remnants of *in situ* burning. The presence of fine siliceous material associated with charcoal and phytoliths suggests that this material is the final 'washed' remnants of organic ash from which all calcareous material has been leached. The occurrence of rounded burnt bone fragments and much colloidal amorphous organic matter suggests that the bulk of the deposit is derived from occupation debris (Pl. 5). Sample 4 contains possible burnt peaty fragments and the matrix is redder than that in the other samples; this may be due to the presence of heat-affected, rubified soil in which geothite has been replaced by haematite (Courty *et al.* 1989). Sample 11 (F84A) also contains a large rock fragment which appears to have been partially vitrified.

The yellowish-brown colour of most of the matrix material is probable due to the presence of secondary crystalline geothite and/or lepidocrocite; the latter is particularly common in soils developed in environments with fluctuating anaerobic and aerobic conditions (FitzPatrick 1993). The high porosity of this unit is largely due to the presence of large charcoal fragments and biological activity.

Post-depositional soil development is indicated by the occurrence of *in situ* rootlets, sclerotia fragments, biologically reworked matrix material, infilled faunal passages and faecal pellets; the latter are derived from worms and mites. In some samples, e.g. Sample 12, biological activity cuts across the boundary between F33 and F31, demonstrating continued post-depositional bioturbation.

6.2.7. THE BOUNDARY BETWEEN F31 AND F30

There is not a distinct boundary between these two contexts. The boundary in Sample 12 is in places diffuse over at least 20mm, although on one side of the slide a sharp boundary between the charcoal and silt can be seen.

6.2.8. CONTEXT F30

Context F30 occurs in Samples 1, 2, 4, 5, 6, 10, 11 and 12.

The basic mineral component and rock fragments are lithologically very similar to those observed within the till samples (F16/F16A) and it is clear that the primary source of this context is the glacial till. However, there are less rock fragments in this context than in those interpreted as natural in origin, e.g. F16/F16A. Abraded cellular charcoal fragments and finely disseminated charcoal are indicative of a detrital, rather than *in situ*, source for this material. As with context F33, there is a weak horizontal alignment of the charcoal and organic fragments, indicating at least limited mechanical deposition. The well-rounded bone fragments can also be interpreted as detrital in origin, but these have also been subjected to biological reworking, namely the ingestion by soil biota. It is probable that much of the charcoal, burnt bone and organic matter is derived from occupational debris purposely added to the deposit (Pl. 10).

Pedogenic processes have affected this deposit. Such processes include biological activity, as indicated by the presence of mite excrement, worm faecal pellets, channels and silt-sized mineral grain concentrations. Biological activity has also resulted in the limited mixing of contexts F31 and F30, with the net upward movement of material. This biological activity has aided the decomposition of organic matter. Soil fungal activity, as indicated by the presence of sclerotia and the mixed nature of the sediment/soil matrix, has also aided the decomposition of organic matter. The growth of *in situ* rootlets is indicative of a vegetated surface and this is confirmed by the presence of phytoliths. The creation of a soil structure is evident in Sample 12 with limited ped formation. An organic-rich, horizontal layer *c.*1mm thick within F30, Sample 10, is interpreted as a relatively rapidly buried vegetation (turf) horizon (Pl. 11).

The yellowish-brown colour of most of the matrix material is probably due to the presence of secondary crystalline geothite and/or lepidocrocite; the latter is particularly common in soils developed in environments with fluctuating anaerobic and aerobic conditions (FitzPatrick 1993). Some of the samples showed zones of greyish matrix, likely to be the result of post-depositional leaching. The presence of polyconcave voids, relatively low porosity, ill-defined crescentic silty clay coatings (Sample 10) and weak granostriation and porostriation is also indicative of post-depositional pore water movement down through the soil profile. However, the occurrence of calcareous rock fragments and calcite grains demonstrates that such movement has been limited.

The noticeable difference in F30 (Sample 6) is that it has a higher percentage of rock fragments, a slightly lower charcoal content, no apparent horizontal orientation of charcoal or mineral grains, and does not appear to have been leached. However, it is important to note that this sample of F30 measures roughly 15mm in width and appears to thin rapidly to the south.

6.2.9. THE BOUNDARY BETWEEN F30 AND F28

The boundary between F30 and F28 is well defined and in some places is marked by planar voids. There is a distinct colour change from dark yellowish-cream (F30) to yellowish-brown (F28). This is indicative of an increase in the amount of clay, demonstrating that F28 has experienced as much leaching as F30. The colour change is also partially caused by a decrease in the quantity of charcoal. The boundary is also marked by a sharp increase in the amount of organic matter, which occurs as an irregular layer about 1mm wide. This layer is characterised by well-decomposed organic matter, rootlets, faecal pellets and a generally well-sorted matrix with some larger organic fragments; it is probable that this layer represents a turf or vegetation horizon upon which F28 was dumped. The dumping of context F28 resulted in the dramatic and sudden decrease in biological activity (see below).

6.2.10. CONTEXT F28

Context F28 occurs in Samples 2 and 5. The basic mineral component and rock fragments are lithologically very similar to those observed within the till samples (F16/F16A) and it is clear that the primary source of this context is the glacial till. The percentage of rock fragments in this context is also similar to that of F16/F16A, confirming the till-like nature of this context.

Limited human input into this context is apparent from the relatively small proportion of charcoal fragments and bone fragments. However, it would appear that post-depositional root development and biological activity are largely responsible for the inclusion of this material from the context below.

The presence of compound textural and yellowish-orange silty pedofeatures are indicative of the episodic and short-lived downward movement of water through the profile, although the effects of this are heightened by the higher clay and silt content of the unit compared to that of F30. The compaction of the unit and the movement of clay minerals are also demonstrated by the presence of a weakly developed granostriated b-fabric.

6.2.11. THE BOUNDARY BETWEEN F30 AND F29

The boundary is visible in the form of a 1mm-thick reddish-brown layer, 18mm below the top of the slide. This layer is interpreted as the remnants of a rapidly buried vegetation surface. The micromorphological evidence indicates that post-depositional bioturbation (which occurred after the initial dumping of bank material) was reduced in quantity but did continue; this indicates that the depth of burial of the biota was such as not to severely inhibit their activity, and hence the depth of the initial bank deposit was not too great.

6.2.12. CONTEXT F29

The basic mineral component and rock fragments are lithologically very similar to those observed within the till samples (F16/F16A) and it is clear that the primary source of this context is redeposited glacial till. The limited charcoal content, the occurrence of bone largely in voids, faecal pellets and rootlets indicate that these indicators of human activity were incorporated into this unit predominantly by turbation and biological activity.

The presence of dusty clay coatings to voids and some clay-depleted zones is evidence of post-depositional, episodic and limited pore water movement downward through the profile.

6.2.13. CONTEXT F16A

The context occurs in Sample 7 and represents a largely undisturbed till. The till is fairly well compacted and comprises a silty clay, fine sand matrix with larger rock clasts, the majority of which are chert or slate. The glacial origin of the sediment is apparent from the eroded and chemically weathered rock fragments and the well-sorted fine sand-sized fraction of the matrix.

Episodic post-depositional pore water movement is indicated by (a) the massive structure, (b) a weak anisotropic fabric, and (c) the presence of four different types of yellowish-brown dusty clay coatings, pure clay coatings and matrix accumulations. The quantity and range of clay and silty clay coatings indicate that these are the product of translocation (illuviation) rather than pedogenic processes (Pls 1 and 2).

There are no identifiable features to indicate that

this unit has been affected by human activity. The limited organic content and lack of biological indicators show that this unit has not undergone pedogenic development.

6.2.14. Context F69D/F69B

The contexts are represented in Sample 6, which was recorded as containing F69D overlying F69B, but the contexts were not distinguishable in thin section. The basic mineral component and rock fragments are lithologically very similar to those observed within the till samples (F16/F16A) and it is clear that the primary source of these contexts is the glacial till. The poorly sorted nature of the sediment demonstrates that any redeposition was not gradual; rather deposition is likely to have been in the form of a slumped mass movement of saturated, poorly sorted clayey till. However, because of the presence of charcoal and rare bone fragments the units may represent the deliberate dumping and infilling of the 'ditch' with previously disturbed till material. Mass movement of the deposit may also be responsible for the presence of clay papules, broken clay coatings, relics of a previous phase of illuviation or pedogenesis. The concentration of mineral grains associated with broken lines of voids and silty intercalations are likely to be products of mass movement (Courty *et al.* 1989).

Charcoal fragments are extremely rare in Sample 6 and the mode of inclusion of charcoal into these contexts is unclear but it may have been incorporated at a later date through post-depositional turbation, as indicated by the presence of degraded *in situ* rootlets. Limited pedogenesis is indicated by the presence of *in situ* rootlets, amorphous organic matter within the matrix, faunal channels and faecal pellets.

Humic acid/iron oxide mottle staining of the matrix and rock fragments is indicative of post-depositional, episodic wetting and drying of the deposit. Compaction of the matrix owing to pore water movement is evident from the presence of polyconcave voids. Within the matrix of Sample 6 are silt clay accumulations and dusty clay coatings to voids; both are likely to be the result of post-depositional illuviation rather than a direct consequence of pedogenesis.

6.2.15. Boundary between F30 and F28

The boundary between these two contexts is sharp and shown by an organic-rich layer which is interpreted as a buried vegetation (turf) horizon.

6.2.16. Context F28

This context occurs in Sample 5 only. The context is described as a redeposited boulder clay. The basic mineral component and rock fragments are lithologically very similar to those observed within the till samples (F16/F16A) and it is clear that the primary source of this context is the glacial till. The redeposited till has undergone limited pedogenesis, evident in the presence of rare organic fragments and faunal excrement. The presence of a variety of clay coatings demonstrates the movement of pore water, although this appears to have been slight. It is also probable that at some point calcium-rich pore water has circulated and reprecipitated out to form the rare micrite coatings of voids.

6.3. Discussion of context F11 from Cutting 1, extension 2 ditch (east-facing)

6.3.1. Context F11

This context occurs in Sample 8. The basic mineral component and rock fragments are lithologically very similar to those observed within the till samples (F16/F16A) and it is clear that the primary source of this context is the glacial till. However, the context is a well-sorted silt and is clearly a reworked sedimentary deposit. The relatively large proportion of phytoliths and the presence of stomatocysts indicate that the source of the sediment is a vegetated (grassed) but possibly damp environment. The well-sorted nature of the sediment and its location within a ditch indicate that this material has been deposited within a still, calm-water environment. The collection of rainwater and silt-laden run-off within the huge ditch of Ráith na Ríg can easily be imagined.

The presence of one charcoal fragment suggests that human input was limited. The unit has been affected by post-depositional turbation and bioturbation and has also experienced some downward pore water movement. The unit was saturated at the time of sampling.

The secondary source of this unit cannot be ascertained, but despite the lack of evidence for a bank on the southern side of the ditch, such a bank would seem to be the most likely source.

7. Results, discussion and interpretations of routine analyses

7.1. Introduction

7.1.1. Phosphate

The major sources of phosphorus in archaeological contexts are domestic refuse, food wastes, plant and animal remains, excreta, bodies and, in early field systems, the deliberate application of manure and other natural fertilisers. Phosphorus occurs naturally in soils in both organic and inorganic forms. Over time some of the organic phosphorus present in the soil will be converted into mineral phosphates. The inorganic phosphorus will be readily leached, or taken up by plants, or fixed into less soluble forms through absorption and adsorption; therefore not all phosphorus added to soil will remain. In particular, in sandy soils and peat phosphorus may be leached rapidly and lost from the profile. It is important to recognise that there is some mobility of phosphorus in the majority of soils.

7.1.2. pH

H^+ is a major source of soil acidity and influences the presence or precipitation of many mobile elements in the soil solution. H^+ is also an important weathering agent and can disrupt crystal structures. A characteristic expression of acid soil processes is the replacement of basic cations at exchange sites by cation exchange with H^+. Even in pure water slight ionisation occurs, but the concentrations of hydronium ion (H_3O^+) and hydroxyl ion (OH^-) are equal. However, increased levels of acidity are reflected in greater hydrogen ion concentrations (H^+), the proton combined with the water molecule. The H^+ concentration increases exponentially and is measured by the logarithm of the reciprocal of active H^+ ions. This unit of measure is called the pH scale:

$$pH = \log(1/H^+)$$

A change of 1.0 in pH corresponds to a tenfold change in the H^+ concentration. At pH 6 there are ten times as many H^+ ions as at pH 7 neutral, and 100 times as many at pH 5. At pH 8 there are ten times the number of OH^- ions compared to neutral and 1000 times at pH 9.

One of the main sources of H^+ is that supplied from CO^2. The decomposition of organic matter also adds hydrogen ions and most organic compounds are acid in nature. pH is not an independent variable but is determined by soil respiration, organic matter decomposition, the nature of clays, parent material, and the rate of leaching.

7.1.3. Loss on ignition

The aim of the assessment was to measure loss on ignition (LOI) and to provide a measure of the volume of organic matter versus mineral matter within a given sample.

7.1.4. Calcium carbonate

The aim of the assessment of calcium carbonate was to determine the amount of dissolution and/or reprecipitation.

7.2. Results

The results of the routine analyses are given below:

Context no.	pH	LOI (%)	Phos	$CaCO_3$ (%)
Cut 1 F30	7.29	3.33	H	0
Cut 1 F31	7.49	9.41	H	1
Cut 1 F33	7.65	1.92	H	0
Cut 1 F205	8.03	1.25	M	0
Cut 1/Ex/F11	7.23	3.80	M	0
Cut 2/ F200	7.30	1.65	M	0
Cut 2/F30	7.62	2.15	M	0
Cut 2/F202	7.63	2.08	M	0
Cut 2/F204/ F205	7.65	1.18	M	1
Cut 2/F206	7.55	1.70	L	0

The pH values from Cutting 1 range between 7.23 and 8.03, with a mean value of 7.54. The mean loss on ignition (LOI%) from Cutting 1 is 3.94% but with a large standard deviation, 3.23, the result of sample Cut 1/F31. The available phosphate from Cutting 1 varies between high and medium and one sample is slightly calcareous.

The pH values from Cutting 2 range between 7.30 and 7.65 with a mean value of 7.55. The mean loss on ignition % is 1.75 and is 0.39. The available phosphate from Cutting 2 is predominantly moderate but there is one low measurement. Only one sample shows a very slight calcareous content.

7.3. Discussion

The natural till in Cutting 2 shows a low phosphate content but that in Cutting 1 shows a moderate content. The remaining samples in Cutting 2 have a moderate phosphate content, which is indicative of the limited addition of phosphate-rich material to these units. The high phosphate content of the contexts from Cutting 1 demonstrates that material rich in phosphate has been added to them. The moderate level in F205 demonstrates that downward leaching of phosphorus has taken place. The moderate phosphate content of F11 is perhaps surprising but may serve to demonstrate that at the source of this sediment the deposit was affected by human activity. It is apparent that human and/or animal activity or manuring was more intense in the location of Cutting 1 than Cutting 2.

The pH values of all the sampled contexts fall into the neutral to weakly alkaline class. The slightly higher pH value of F16 demonstrates that this unit is less leached than those above. The effects of leaching can also be observed in the small but consistent increase in alkalinity of the sampled contexts with depth.

The organic content versus mineral content is relatively low in all the measured samples and demonstrates the generally poor pedological development of these sampled units. The low levels of apparent organic matter in samples F30, F31 and F33 are compounded by their high charcoal content which does not register as organic matter in this test. However, the presence of significant quantities of organic matter is clearly indicated in F31. The organic content of F11 can be attributed to rootlets and amorphous organic matter.

The calcium carbonate content is generally below detectable levels. However, F31 contains a very small amount which may be attributed to either calcareous rock fragments or even the remnants of ash. It is likely that the calcium carbonate detected in F69B is due to rock fragments (see micromorphological description for these units).

8. Summary conclusions of micromorphological and routine soil analyses

8.1. Cutting 1

8.1.1. Context F16

The sedimentary development of the soil/sediment profile of Cutting 1 is initiated with the deposition of glacial till (context F16). Analysis has shown that the basic mineral component and rock fragments of the sampled contexts are derived from the basal till sediment. Following deposition, water moved down through the sediment, carrying silt and clay particles; this clay translocation is characteristic of the basal till deposits. It is probable that with time the surface of the till gradually became colonised by vegetation and associated biota.

8.1.2. Context F33

This context is the result of the gradual accumulation of organo-mineral matter and the *in situ* development of soil. However, it is likely that at least some of the mineral and organic matter was deposited as the result of surface run-off caused by sudden rainstorms upon the relatively impervious clayey till surface. Some of the samples of context F33 show thin organic-rich layers, which have been interpreted as rapidly buried vegetation/turf horizons. It has been suggested that at least some of the soil/sediment accumulation is a result of natural processes, but the remnants of probable ash midden material clearly indicate a human input into this context. It is very probable that this material has been deliberately added to the context to increase soil fertility. The context has been subjected to post-depositional bioturbation and turbation.

This context has been burnt in the vicinity of the location of Sample 11 (F84A). The burning at this location was below 800°C but can readily be equated to burning within the metalworking hearth F38, which may have been of a higher temperature. The presence of fine fissures within F84A, Sample 11, indicates that the soil was burnt *in situ*, rather than representing a dumped layer of burnt sediment from adjacent to the furnace.

Post-depositional compaction and the removal of clay from this context (leaching) have been caused by the movement of water through the profile. The inclusion of charcoal and other artefacts within silty coatings indicates that at least some of this pore water movement took place after the deposition and bioturbation of the majority of the contexts. It is apparent from the presence of iron oxide mottles, the irregularity of the coatings and the leached appearance of this unit that saturation and dewatering cycles were episodic and short-lived.

8.1.3. Context F31

Context F31 appears to have been dumped upon context F30, resulting in a decrease in biological activity. However, the boundary between the two is diffuse in some samples owing to post-depositional bioturbation. Context F31 is interpreted as a primarily dumped spread of low-temperature ash midden, typical of cooking and occupation debris, rather than as the *in situ* burning of organic matter and soil. The high organic content and high phosphate content tend to confirm this interpretation.

This context has been subjected to post-depositional biological activity and turbation. This appears to have been followed by episodic post-depositional movement of pore water which affected the whole of the profile.

8.1.4. Context F30

The precise mode of formation of this context is difficult to ascertain because of the masking effects of post-depositional processes. However, similar processes to those discussed for context F33 are envisaged, with the deliberate deepening, through the addition of manure, of a poorly developed soil. This unit has been subjected to pedological processes such as biological activity, degradation of organic matter, the development of a vegetated surface and the formation of weak peds. The rapid burial of vegetated horizons is clearly demonstrated in Sample 10; such rapid burial may represent specific episodes of manuring.

This context has been subjected to post-depositional biological activity and turbation. This appears to have been followed by episodic post-depositional movement of pore water which affected the whole of the profile.

8.1.5. CONTEXT F28

This context represents till upcast from the digging of the large ditch to the south of the cutting. The presence of an organic layer at the top of context F30 demonstrates the rapid burial of the vegetated land surface immediately prior to the creation of the ditch. During a field visit it was postulated that the turf may have been stripped prior to bank construction but, as demonstrated by micromorphological observation of the boundary between contexts F30 and F28 (Samples 1, 2, 5), remnants of the original vegetated ground surface are clearly present. The unit has been affected by limited post-depositional bioturbation. However, the major post-depositional process that has affected the unit is the episodic movement of water down through the profile resulting in compound textural pedofeatures and microstructural compaction.

8.1.6. CONTEXT F29

The boundary between contexts F30 and F29 is shown by a buried vegetation horizon. The dumped ditch upcast depressed biological activity, although the lower portion of context F29 has been affected by biological processes. In common with context F28, this unit has been affected by post-depositional pore water movement and compaction.

8.2. Cutting 2

8.2.1. CONTEXT F16A

This context occurs below F16, as described for Cutting 1. Context F16A is a relatively undisturbed till. The sediment has been affected by post-depositional pore water movement which has resulted in the formation of impressive clay and silty clay coatings and matrix concentrations. There are no micromorphological artefacts indicative of human activity and the low phosphate content confirms the lack of human and/or animal activity. The evidence for pedological processes is also minimal. The context may be described as an unaltered subsoil.

8.2.2. CONTEXT F69D/69B

These contexts were not distinguishable in thin section. The sediments have been interpreted as the result of the mass movement of water-saturated till into a 'natural' hollow. The minimal charcoal content is likely to have been the result of post-depositional turbation/bioturbation rather than indicative of active human input, although the latter cannot be disproved. The sediment has been affected by post-depositional pore water movement which has resulted in the formation of a compacted unit, impressive clay and silty clay coatings and matrix concentrations. This movement of material has also resulted in the accumulation of leached phosphate.

8.3. Cutting 1, extension 2 (east-facing section)

8.3.1. CONTEXT F11

This context has been interpreted as redeposited, well-sorted till probably derived from the ditch cut. It is probable that the sediment settled out from silt- and clay-laden run-off water which collected in the hollow of the ditch. There are no apparent microlaminations to indicate the direction of the source of this material. However, despite there being no archaeological evidence for a bank on the southern side of the ditch, such a bank appears to be the only feasible source, as there are no other known high and exposed areas in the immediate vicinity.

9. Conclusion

The broad aims and objectives, as listed in Section 2, and those specific objectives listed in Section 6 have been achieved and reported upon in this document.

Micromorphological analysis has demonstrated that contexts F16 and F16A are relatively undisturbed subsoil units. Contexts F69D/69B have been interpreted as 'colluvial' deposits which slumped into the ditch-like feature below the bank exposure in Cutting 2. It is likely that these contexts are natural in origin, although the presence of charcoal and rare bone means that a human influence upon their deposition cannot be ruled out.

The nature of context F11 is consistent with deposition from suspension within still or very calm water. It has been hypothesised that the source of context F11 would have been a high point of exposed silty till from where rainwater (run-off) would have washed silt and clay into the hollow of the ditch; the most likely source would have been a bank on the southern side of the ditch.

From field observations it was originally hypothesised that contexts F30 and F33 represented buried sods, sealed beneath later bank deposits. However, the presence of sharp boundaries between the various contexts and the lack of observable organic-rich layers (which would have indicated buried turves) led to the formation of an alternative hypothesis, namely that these contexts were the product of human dumping of occupational and/or industrial refuse. Using micromorphology it has been shown that both contexts F30 and F33 are weakly developed, *in situ* soils; the presence of relatively sharp boundaries is due to the nature of the subsoil and the weakness of soil pedogenic processes. The addition of charcoal and other organic refuse to the two contexts and their high available phosphate levels have been interpreted as evidence of manuring. However, the presence of preserved vegetated layers, interpreted as old ground surfaces, and the weak horizontal orientation of mineral grains and charcoal indicate that tillage of these soils was kept to a minimum.

It has also been shown that context F30, Sample 11, has been burnt *in situ,* and the source of this burning appears to have been the metalworking hearth (F38) immediately to the south. The temperature of the burning at the sampling location was below 800°C. Sandwiched between contexts F30 and F33 is context F31, a dumped layer rich in charcoal. One possible source of F31 is the metalworking hearth, but the nature of the debris within F31 is more in keeping with a low-temperature, domestic source.

The upcast of the ditch is represented in contexts F28 and F29. Micromorphology has shown that this mixed till material was thrown directly upon the vegetated ground surface, context F30, causing the vegetation to die and biological activity to be severely reduced.

Post-depositional, episodic movement of pore water down through the exposed bank and underlying soil profile has been demonstrated. This has resulted in compaction, translocation of fine material and the leaching of many of the contexts. Perhaps more significantly, the movement of water downward has masked and destroyed evidence of remnant features which may have provided additional information concerning the nature of the human impact upon the Tara soils.

Appendix 6

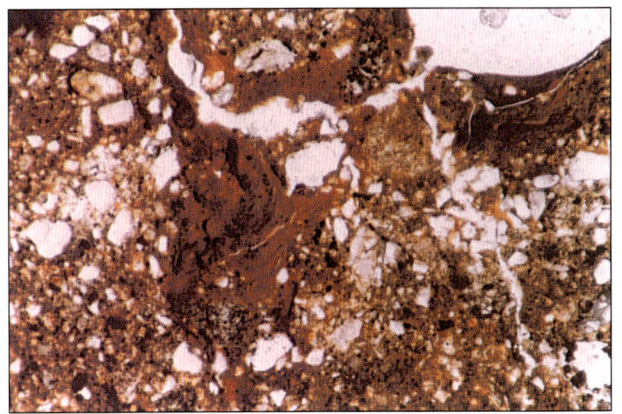

Pl. 1—Sample 7, context F16A, microlaminated dusty clay coatings. Magnification x32.

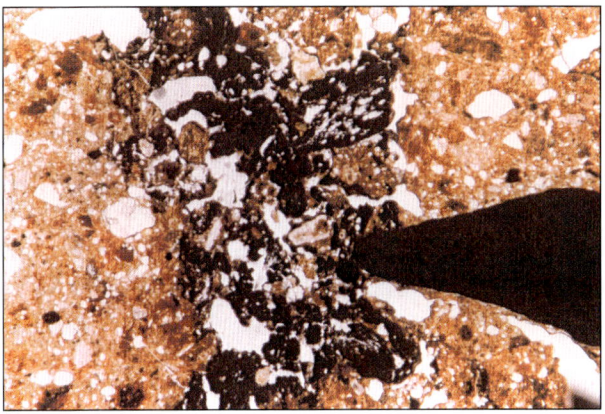

Pl. 4—Sample 12, context F31, charcoal-rich veriform. Magnification x12.5.

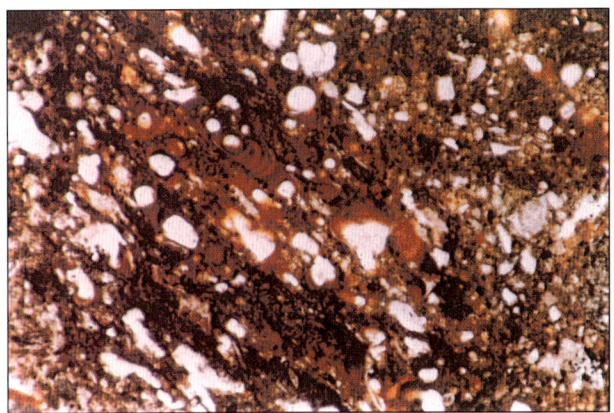

Pl. 2—Sample 7, context F16A, clay coatings within a degraded chert fragment. Magnification x32.

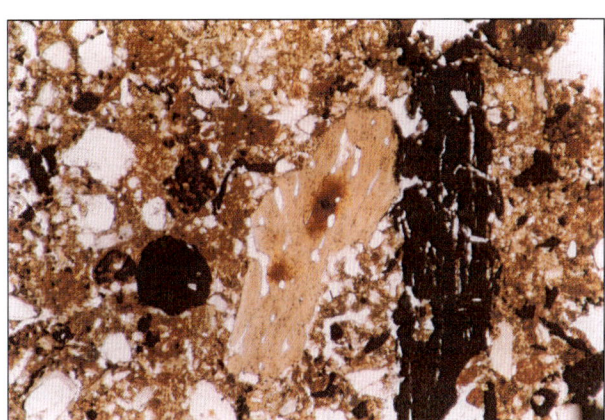

Pl. 5—Sample 11, context F31, burnt bone and charcoal fragments. Magnification x25.

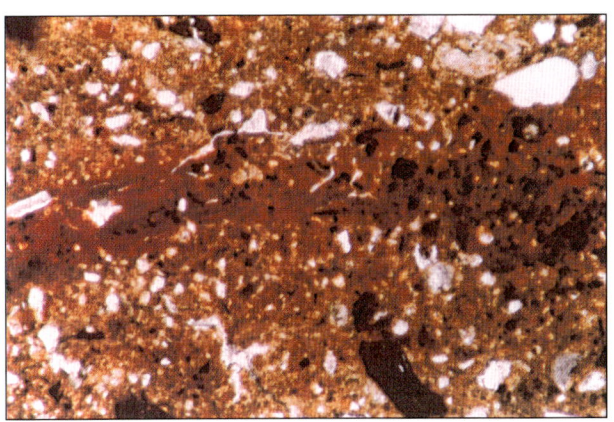

Pl. 3—Sample 3, context F33, organic layer. Magnification x25.

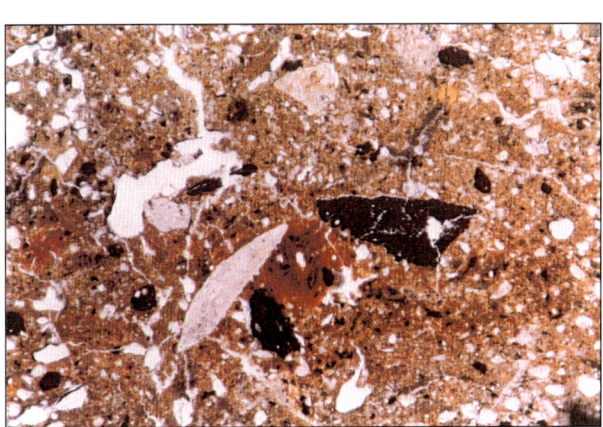

Pl. 6—Sample 2, context F30, in situ rootlet. Magnification x16.

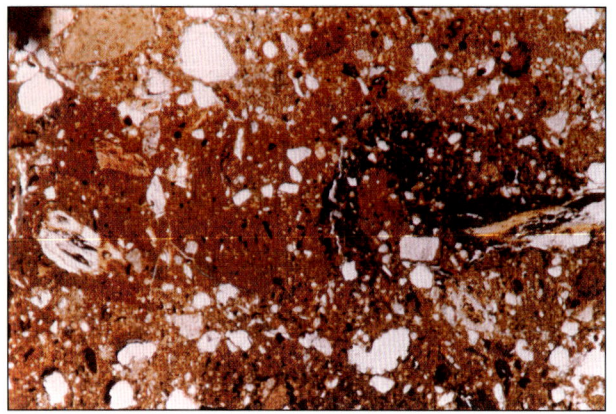

Pl. 7—Sample 11, context F30, charcoal- and silt-rich veriform. Magnification x16.

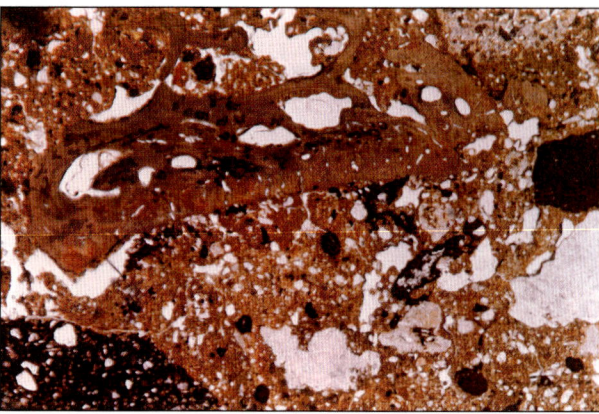

Pl. 10—Sample 2, context F30, burnt bone. Magnification x12.5.

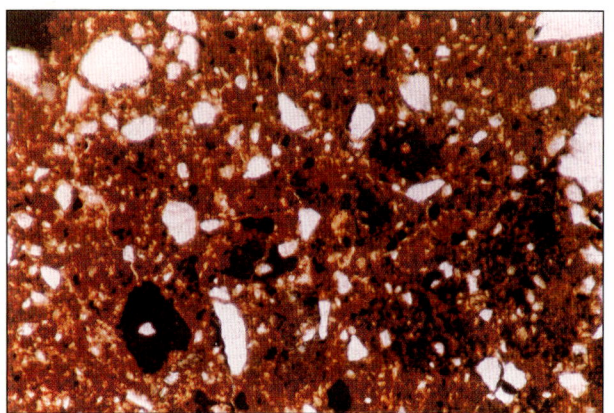

Pl. 8—Sample 11, context F84A, burnt matrix and organic material. Magnification x32.

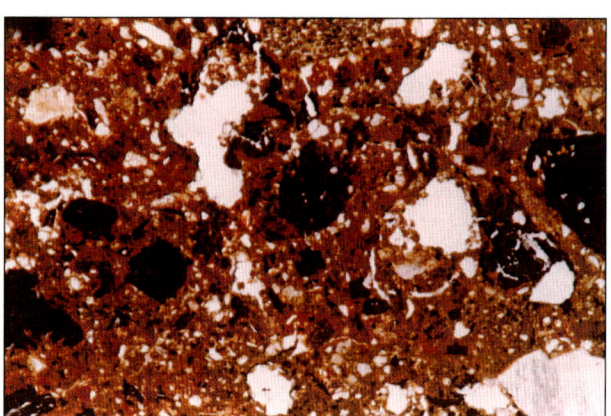

Pl. 11—Sample 10, context F30, buried organic layer. Magnification x16.

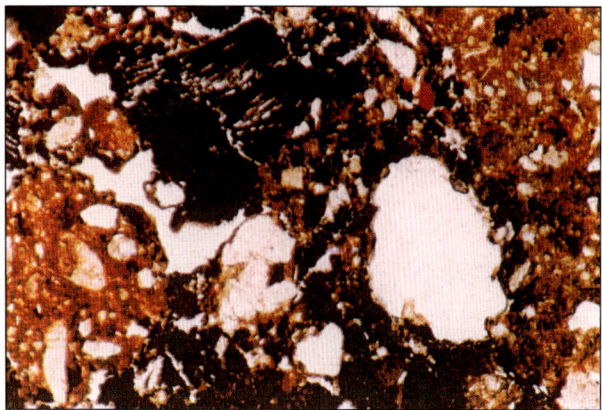

Pl. 9—Sample 12, context F31, charcoal and general 'midden' material. Magnification x32.

Appendix 6

10. Thin sections: descriptive notes

Sample 2, context F28

INTRODUCTION

The sampled context is roughly 3cm wide.

MICROSTRUCTURE

The sediment has a massive structure with occasional discrete vugs and fine fissures. The rare vugs are generally polyconcave. The porosity measures between 2% and 5%.

MATRIX

The context is poorly sorted. The sediment has an open porphyric-related distribution. It is matrix-supported. The matrix is dominated by monocrystalline silt-sized quartz grains and various clay minerals. It is yellowish-brown in PPL and in CPL it varies between dark greyish-brown and dark yellowish-orange clay-rich zones. It comprises weakly developed granostriated b-fabric, and stipple-speckled b-fabric producing a weakly anisotropic matrix.

BASIC MINERAL COMPONENT AND ROCK FRAGMENTS

The basic mineral component and rock fragments make up about 20% of the sample. Quartz is the dominant mineral component and the majority of the quartz is monocrystalline with undulose and occasional straight extinction. There are rare polycrystalline quartz grains with sutured contact. The quartz grains range in size from 500μm to 20μm with the majority falling within the fine sand-sized class. Feldspar grains comprise < 1% of the coarse mineral component; some of the feldspars are sericitised. Rounded black, opaque organic fragments are scattered throughout the matrix and range from *c.* 20μm to 70μm. Rock fragments < 9cm are derived from a variety of metamorphic (schist), sedimentary (shale, cherts and limestone) and igneous lithologies.

BASIC ORGANIC COMPONENTS

A single sclerotium measures 60μm. Other irregular fragments of black, opaque organic matter occur scattered throughout the matrix; it is likely that much of this material represents disseminated charcoal fragments. Charcoal fragments are visible and much of the charcoal is clustered about partially infilled voids. Cellular charcoal fragments measure from 357μm to 1.5mm in diameter.

Moderately humified organic fragments are dark brown to pale reddish-brown in PPL; these fragments represent the well-decomposed remnant of organic material including roots etc. Colloidal organic matter occurs throughout the matrix.

There are extremely rare phytolith fragments. One bone fragment, 6mm in length, has vesicles. The charcoal and mottles are concentrated around rock fragments and bone fragments.

PEDOFEATURES

Fe^{3+} microaggregates are associated with organic matter. The microaggregates are dark reddish-brown and have abrupt to sharp boundaries. They range from 60μm to 200μm in diameter. Compound layered textural pedofeatures are rare (< 2%). Silty pedofeatures occur next to rock fragments and within fissures and the matrix. Clay textural pedofeatures occur as pore coatings and around mineral grains within a chert fragment. Pure yellowish-orange clay coatings are especially common in chert rock fragments. There is a zone of organo-mineral depletion and zones of increased biological activity.

BOUNDARY

The boundary between contexts F30 and F28 is well defined. There is a distinct colour change (visible in PPL) from yellowish-brown to dark yellowish-cream, representing an increase in the amount of moderately decomposed organic matter and a decrease in the proportion of finely disseminated charcoal. The boundary is sharp and in some places defined by straight planar voids.

Sample 2, context F30

MICROSTRUCTURE

The sediment has a massive structure with occasional discrete vugs and fine fissures. The rare vugs are generally polyconcave. There are very weakly developed and poorly defined laminations within this unit, visible through the alignment of colloidal organic matter and charcoal fragments. The porosity measures between 2% and 5%.

MATRIX

The context is poorly sorted. The sediment has an open porphyric-related distribution. It is matrix-supported. The matrix is dominated by monocrystalline silt-sized quartz grains, various chert rock fragments and various clay minerals. It is dark yellowish-cream to yellowish-brown in PPL and dark greyish-brown in CPL. It comprises weakly developed stipple-speckled b-fabric. There are zones of pale matrix which may represent ash or leached matrix.

BASIC MINERAL COMPONENT AND ROCK FRAGMENTS

The coarse mineral component comprises predominantly fine sand-sized monocrystalline quartz grains with undulose extinction. Other coarse mineral grains include plagioclase feldspars, some exhibiting sericitisation and rare pyroxenes. Rock fragments comprise 25% of the context and range in size from *c.* 60μm to 900μm. The majority of rock fragments are cherts, with occasional metamorphic lithologies and one large 4.5cm x 2.5cm calcitic limestone clast.

BASIC ORGANIC COMPONENTS

Large cellular charcoal fragments up to 1400μm make up *c.* 2% of this context. The larger, cellular charcoal fragments are generally well rounded. There is a weak horizontal orientation of these larger charcoal fragments and finer disseminated charcoal fragments are scattered throughout the matrix, but there are areas of greater concentration and very weak horizontal orientation. There are rare, well-rounded bone fragments 240μm and 300μm long. There are rare phytolith fragments. *In situ* roots are frequent and are associated with biological activity.

PEDOFEATURES

Zones of reddish organic staining comprising decomposed organic matter with rare clay textural pedofeatures. Fe^{3+} microaggregates are associated with organic matter. The microaggregates are dark reddish to light reddish-brown. These microaggregates have abrupt to sharp boundaries. The mottles range from 60μm to 400μm in diameter and tend to obscure any mineral material. Rounded colloidal material occurs within the matrix; the colloids are *c.* 12μm in diameter and may represent mite excrement. The preferred orientation of matrix material is associated with some rootlets.

Sample 2, context F31

INTRODUCTION

The unit measures some 10mm in width.

MICROSTRUCTURE

The sediment has a massive structure with discrete and irregular vugs. Many of the vugs are polyconcave. The unit appears to have been compacted around the large calcitic limestone clast of the unit above. The porosity measures 2–5%.

MATRIX

The context is poorly sorted. The sediment has an open porphyric-related distribution. It is matrix-supported. The coarse component of the matrix comprises monocrystalline silt-sized quartz grains (with undulose extinction), rare silt-sized feldspars and chert rock fragments. The fine fraction comprises quartz, various unidentified minerals and amorphous organic matter. The matrix is yellowish-brown in PPL and dark greyish-brown in CPL. It comprises an extremely weakly developed stippled b-fabric with zones of undifferentiated b-fabric.

BASIC MINERAL COMPONENT AND ROCK FRAGMENTS

The coarse component comprises predominantly well-rounded chert and occasional metamorphic rock fragments; these make up 5–10% of the context and range in size from *c.* 60μm to 5000μm. Many of the metamorphic rock fragments show significant iron-staining and other indicators of physical and chemical weathering. The basic mineral component comprises medium and fine sand-sized monocrystalline quartz grains with undulose extinction, rare plagioclase feldspars, some of which are sericitised and extremely rare pyroxenes. Rare micrite and calcite mineral fragments.

BASIC ORGANIC COMPONENT

The context is noteworthy for its high charcoal content. Cellular charcoal fragments are very common; the largest clast measures 7mm in length. The charcoal fragments lie in the horizontal plane (possible burnt phytoliths—grass fragments). All the charcoal fragments show rounded edges (abrasion). The base of the unit is defined by a recently broken but once continuous piece of charcoal measuring 17mm in length. The upper portion of one piece of charcoal (740μm in length) is black and the lower portion reddish-yellow and shows anisotropy pattern similar to clay (possibly ash). Fine disseminated charcoal is scattered throughout this unit.

There are possible sclerotia fragments. Other organic matter includes dark reddish-brown well-decomposed colloid matter. There are phytolith fragments within the matrix. The matrix is jammed with small colloidal well-decomposed organic fragments measuring 4–12μm. *In situ* rootlets are present.

PEDOFEATURES

Silty clay appears to infill some ancient fissures between some of the charcoal fragments. Dark brown silt with very fine charcoal also forms very thin linings (30–7μm) to some of the vugs.

Fe^{3+} microaggregates are associated with organic matter. These are generally well rounded and dark reddish to light reddish-brown. These microaggregates have abrupt to sharp boundaries and range from 80μm to 408μm in diameter; they also tend to obscure any mineral material.

An infilled bio-channel is filled with fine charcoal-rich silt; it is distinguishable in PPL because of the higher disseminated charcoal context as compared to the matrix. The slight convoluted appearance of fine, elongated organic fragments in the matrix show that there has been some post-depositional mixing of the unit.

BOUNDARY

The boundary between F31 and F33 is irregular and particularly indistinct in some areas; there appears to have been some mixing of the two contexts and it is likely that this has been done by soil biota.

Sample 2, context F33

MICROSTRUCTURE

The sediment has a massive structure with discrete vugs. The rare vugs are generally polyconcave. Very weak horizontal orientation of mineral grains and organic matter is evident. The porosity measures 2–5%.

MATRIX

The sediment is moderately well sorted. It has an open porphyric-related distribution. It is matrix-supported. The matrix is dominated by monocrystalline silt-sized quartz grains, with some silt-sized chert rock fragments and rare clay minerals. It is dark yellowish-cream to yellowish-brown in PPL and dark greyish-brown in CPL. It comprises extremely weakly developed stipple-speckled to undifferentiated b-fabric.

BASIC MINERAL COMPONENT AND ROCK FRAGMENTS

The coarse mineral component comprises predominantly fine sand-sized monocrystalline quartz grains with undulose extinction. Other coarse mineral grains include plagioclase feldspars (<2%), some exhibiting sericitisation, and rare chlorite. Rock fragments comprise 2–5% of the context and range in size from *c.* 60μm to 900μm. The rock fragments include chert and metamorphic lithologies (micaceous sandstone and shale or slate).

ORGANIC COMPONENT

Cellular charcoal fragments occur throughout the sediment; the largest is 5mm in length. There is less fine, disseminated charcoal in this unit than in that above. A small sclerotium measures 612μm in diameter and there are possible fungal spores. There are zones of reddish-yellow moderately decomposed organic matter which blend into the matrix. A small bone fragment measures 400μm in length. There are rare phytolith fragments.

PEDOFEATURES

Fabric pedofeatures 400–600μm in diameter comprising matrix material in the form of ill-defined rounded microaggregates. Fe^{3+} microaggregates are associated with organic matter. The microaggregates are generally well rounded and dark reddish to light reddish-brown, with abrupt to sharp boundaries. The pellets range from 80μm to 408μm in diameter and tend to obscure any mineral material. These pellets may represent faecal material; the average size is about 200μm and they comprise <2% of the sample. An infilled veriform extends from the base of the unit above into this unit. The fill is derived from context F31 and is charcoal-rich.

Sample 3, context F33

MICROSTRUCTURE

The sediment has a massive structure with discrete vugs. The voids and vugs are generally polyconcave. The porosity measures 2–5%.

MATRIX

The sediment is moderately sorted. It has an open porphyric-related distribution. It is matrix-supported. The matrix is dominated by monocrystalline silt-sized quartz grains, with some silt-sized chert rock fragments and rare clay minerals. It is dark yellowish-cream to yellowish-brown in PPL and dark greyish-brown in CPL. It comprises extremely weakly developed stipple-speckled to undifferentiated b-fabric.

BASIC MINERAL COMPONENT AND ROCK FRAGMENTS

The coarse mineral component comprises predominantly fine sand-sized monocrystalline quartz grains with undulose extinction. Other coarse mineral grains include plagioclase feldspars (<2%), some exhibiting sericitisation, and rare chlorite. Rock fragments comprise <2% of the context and range in size from *c.* 7mm to 160μm. The rock fragments include chert and metamorphic lithologies (micaceous sandstone and shale or slate).

ORGANIC COMPONENT

Cellular charcoal fragments occur throughout the unit; the largest is 4mm in length. Fine, disseminated charcoal is also present within the matrix. There are zones of reddish-yellow moderately decomposed organic matter which blend into the matrix, and colloidal amorphous organic matter is common. There are small bone fragments and rare phytolith fragments.

PEDOFEATURES

Fabric pedofeatures comprising matrix material are visible in PPL by virtue of the convoluted nature of the matrix and organic matter. Fe^{3+}-rich microaggregates are associated with organic matter. The microaggregates are generally well rounded and dark reddish to light reddish-brown, with abrupt to sharp boundaries. The pellets range from 80μm to 400μm in diameter and tend to obscure any mineral material. These pellets may represent faecal material; the average size is about 200μm and they comprise <1% of the sample. Infilled veriforms extend from this unit into the one below.

BOUNDARY

The boundary between F33 and F205, the natural boulder clay, is distinct, but in thin section can be seen to occur over c. 20mm and is partially defined by the presence of infilled biological channels.

Sample 3, context F16

MICROSTRUCTURE

The sediment is poorly sorted with a massive structure. The porosity is locally variable and measures c. 2%. The pore space comprises irregular and spherical voids; some of these are polyconcave. The till is poorly sorted but contains much fine sand-sized material.

MATRIX

The sediment has an open porphyric-related distribution; it is matrix-supported. The sediment matrix comprises predominantly silt-size monocrystalline, subangular to well-rounded quartz grains, fine irregular chalcedony (derived from cherts) and unidentified clay minerals. The matrix is yellowish-brown in PPL and brownish-grey in CPL. The sediment has a weakly speckled b-fabric.

BASIC MINERAL COMPONENT AND ROCK FRAGMENTS

The coarse mineral component comprises predominantly fine sand-sized, well-rounded monocrystalline quartz grains with undulose extinction. Some of the quartz grains show secondary growth. Other coarse mineral grains include plagioclase feldspars (perthitic), with some exhibiting sericitisation (there is significantly more feldspar than in other contexts). Rock fragments comprise weathered micaceous sandstones and cherts (some only partially decalcified), with the largest measuring 12mm. Many of the rock fragments are weathered, with much iron oxide present.

BASIC ORGANIC COMPONENT

There are common black fragments within the matrix c. 40μm in diameter. These are black in PPL and CPL and may represent a mixture of charcoal fragments or iron minerals. There is some cellular charcoal; this occurs in particular within or associated with biological channels and biological activity. There is one large cellular organic fragment measuring 4mm in diameter; this fragment is detrital.

PEDOFEATURES

There are 2–5% dark reddish-brown organo-mineral microaggregates measuring from c. 80μm to 600 μm in diameter. Iron-rich mottles also occur; these have diffuse edges. The unit is peppered with infilled biological channels (veriforms); these are apparent owing to weak anisotropic fabric and the presence of disseminated charcoal. There are also weak, yellowish-brown, dusty clay coatings to some voids and pores.

Sample 4: general comments

The sample has a large irregular chamber at its centre.

Sample 4, context F30

MICROSTRUCTURE

The sediment has a massive structure with occasional discrete vugs, channels and fine fissures. The rare vugs and channels are generally polyconcave. The porosity is locally variable but is generally between 2% and 5%.

MATRIX

The context is moderately sorted. The sediment has an open porphyric-related distribution. It is matrix-supported. The matrix is dominated by monocrystalline silt-sized quartz grains, various chert rock fragments and various unidentified clay minerals. It is dark yellowish-cream to yellowish-brown in PPL and dark greyish-brown in CPL. It comprises weakly developed stipple-speckled b-fabric.

Basic mineral component and rock fragments

The coarse mineral component comprises predominantly fine sand-sized monocrystalline quartz grains predominantly with undulose extinction; some grains show moderate sphericity and others show smooth sphericity. Other coarse mineral grains include plagioclase feldspars, many exhibiting sericitisation. Rock fragments comprise c. 2% of the context and range in size from c. 80mm to 5mm. The majority of rock fragments are cherts, with occasional acid igneous and metamorphic lithologies. The rock fragments are generally well rounded and many show indications of sustained physico-chemical weathering.

Basic organic components

There is a large, c. 4mm, subrounded, cellular, partially burnt organic fragment with rare reddish-brown tissue remaining in some cells. A second large cellular charcoal fragment appears to have been affected by post-depositional bioturbation. Charcoal fragments range in size from c. 20μm to 4mm and are generally sub- to well rounded. Much of the disseminated charcoal occurs in partially infilled turbation channels.

A degraded *in situ* rootlet measures 600μm in diameter. A single sclerotium occurs, measuring 68μm in diameter. Other poorly defined, thin, degraded rootlets occur within this context.

Organic matter also occurs as well-decomposed subrounded to rounded amorphous clasts c. 45μm in diameter; these are scattered throughout the matrix but are especially common in the form of microaggregates in the large central chamber and in areas of increased biological activity. Reddish-brown amorphous organic matter and staining are associated with turbation pedofeatures.

Phytolith fragments occur scattered throughout the matrix; these are especially common in areas depleted of organic material and biological fills with disseminated charcoal. Burnt bone fragments measuring 350μm and bone fragments 150μm and 800μm occur within the matrix.

Pedofeatures

Fine silt concentrations occur within the matrix and are also associated with some voids and rare channels; these would appear to be the product of biological activity and/or pore water movement. Porostriation and granostriation are frequent, and are formed by dusty silt with clay.

Well-rounded, dark reddish-brown, organo-mineral sharp-edged faecal pellets measuring 200–640μm occur. Some smaller, dark reddish-brown, well-rounded faecal pellets appear to be organic and measure up to 60μm. There are clusters of these associated with infilled biological channels. Infilled faunal passages occur in a variety of forms. One type is readily identifiable by the presence of charcoal-rich matrix, dark reddish-brown amorphous organic matter, rare sclerotia and dark yellowish-brown silt matrix. Other infills are in the form of well-rounded fabric pedofeatures.

Sample 4, context F31

Microstructure

The sediment has a vuggy to chamber structure. The larger charcoal fragments show weak horizontal orientation. The porosity measures 15–20%.

Matrix

The context is poorly sorted. The sediment has an open porphyric-related distribution. It is matrix-supported. The coarse component of the matrix comprises monocrystalline silt-sized quartz grains (with undulose extinction), rare silt-sized feldspars and chert rock fragments. The fine fraction comprises quartz, various unidentified minerals and amorphous organic matter. The matrix is mixed and varies from yellowish-brown to reddish-brown in PPL and dark greyish-brown in CPL. It comprises an extremely weakly developed stippled b-fabric with zones of undifferentiated b-fabric.

Basic mineral component and rock fragments

The coarse component comprises well-rounded chert clasts (these make up 2–5% of the context and range in size from c. 60μm to 5mm) and mineral grains. The basic mineral component comprises well- to subrounded, medium and fine sand-sized monocrystalline quartz grains with undulose extinction and smooth to moderate sphericity and frequent plagioclase feldspars, some of which are sericitised. Some metamorphic rock fragments show significant iron-staining and other classic indicators of physical and chemical weathering.

Basic organic component

Cellular charcoal fragments dominate this context; the largest measures 7mm. Fine disseminated charcoal occurs throughout the matrix, but is particular associated with pedofeatures. Well-decomposed bright orange organic matter is the remnants of rootlets. Bright brown, amorphous organic matter is also scattered throughout the matrix. A single sclerotium occurs and measures 65μm in diameter.

There are seven burnt bone fragments measuring from 100μm to 500μm. A possible coprolite, measuring 5mm in diameter, comprises mineral material and is dark greyish-brown in PPL and isotropic in CPL. There is a possible burnt, organic-rich, peaty soil clast measuring 800μm in length; this clast is well rounded. There is a pale, greyish-white in PPL, fine siliceous material with fragmentary phytoliths and charcoal flecks. This material occurs in irregular but identifiable zones and is also mixed within the general matrix. It is probable that this material is the remnants of ash.

Pedofeatures

There is rare porostriation of dusty clay around some voids. On one side of the slide is an area comprising what appears to be weakly rubified (or burnt) matrix material, lying on mixed charcoal-rich sediment; there is a sharp wavy upper boundary. The slightly redder matrix may be indicative of heated soil. The sediment is also mixed with charcoal, rock fragments and mineral grains and would appear to be dumped and not *in situ*. Biological activity is indicated by rounded fabric pedofeatures. Well-rounded, dark reddish-brown, organo-mineral faecal pellets have sharp edges and measure *c.* 200μm; others are smaller and appear to comprise just organic matter. Partially infilled fauna passages contain dark, charcoal-rich matrix. The juxtaposition of fabric types is indicative of dumping or physical disturbance. There is one calcium oxalate small rootlet measuring *c.* 120μm in diameter.

Sample 4, context F33

Introduction

This context occurs from between 57mm to the base of the slide. The boundary between contexts F31 and F33 is defined by a reddish-yellow organo-mineral layer (layer 1) some 2mm thick. The upper and lower boundaries are sharp to distinct. The layer comprises reddish-yellow, well-decomposed organic matter, moderately degraded cellular organic fragments, fine disseminated charcoal, dark reddish-brown faunal faecal pellets and fragmentary phytoliths.

Microstructure

The sediment has a massive structure with discrete vugs and voids; the porosity is *c.* 2–5%. The voids are generally well rounded and range in size from 80μm to 300μm. Many of the vughs are polyconcave. Very weak horizontal orientation of mineral grains and organic matter is evident. The context becomes more compact and massive with depth.

Organic layer 2 occurs at 9cm below the top of the slide and measures some 1mm in width. The layer extends across the width of the slide. It is dark yellow-red in PPL and largely isotropic in CPL. The layer comprises largely organic matter. There is one possible mixed siliceous/calcite void coating measuring 40μm in width. The upper boundary is sharp and the lower boundary distinct. There are rare dark reddish-brown faecal pellets. The larger organic fragments are unburnt and are well to moderately decomposed. Mite excrement is common on the lower boundary and immediately below the layer. *In situ* vertical rootlets of well-decomposed organic matter are common.

The context shows a slight coarsening upwards and a slight decrease in the amount of amorphous organic material.

Matrix

The sediment is moderately well sorted. It has an open porphyric-related distribution. It is matrix-supported. The matrix is dominated by monocrystalline silt-sized quartz grains, with some silt-sized chert rock fragments and rare clay minerals. It is dark yellowish-cream to yellowish-brown in PPL and dark greyish-brown in CPL; the variety of matrix colour is indicative of its mixed nature. The matrix is complex and comprises extremely weakly developed stipple-speckled, weakly developed poro/granostriated and undifferentiated b-fabric.

Basic mineral component and rock fragments

The coarse mineral component comprises predominantly fine sand-sized monocrystalline quartz grains with undulose extinction. Other coarse mineral grains include plagioclase feldspars (<2%), some exhibiting sericitisation. Rock fragments comprise 2–5% of the context and range in size from *c.* 60μm to 5mm. The rock fragments include chert and metamorphic lithologies. In PPL there are well-rounded clasts of dark brown clay, measuring 30–150μm, which are anisotropic in CPL. These may represent eroded and redeposited clay-rich soil and occur directly above the lowermost organic layer.

Organic component

There are cellular charcoal fragments ranging from 8mm to *c.* 100μm. Small fragments of disseminated charcoal occur throughout the matrix, but with irregular concentration zones associated with siliceous ash material and/or biological activity. There is one large degraded rootlet measuring 5mm in width.

There are irregular zones of reddish matrix; these are areas of higher organic content and indicative of biological activity and rootlets. Some of these reddish organic-rich zones are well defined, and humic acid staining of the matrix is apparent. Zones of iron and humic acid depletion are apparent, although these are associated with a higher concentration of fine charcoal. These zones represent mixed ash deposits and contain rare smooth phytolith fragments. There are less than 1% bone fragments; these are generally well rounded and occur mainly associated with the ash material and zones of concentrated biological activity. One large burnt bone fragment measures 2mm in diameter.

PEDOFEATURES

Organic-rich mite excrement, $c.$ 7μm in diameter, is common at $c.$ 8mm below the top of the slide. Reddish-brown faecal pellets and iron-rich nodules are much more common beneath layer 2 than above it. Clay-rich silt accumulations occur near the base of the slide with a slight convoluted appearance; these are indicative of biological activity.

Sample 5, context F28

MICROSTRUCTURE

The sediment is poorly sorted. The complex structure comprises both massive and weakly developed vugs. The porosity within the vuggy zones measures $c.$ 15–20% and in the massive zones 0.5–2%.

MATRIX

The sediment has an open porphyric-related distribution; it is matrix-supported. The matrix is dominated by silt-sized quartz grains and unidentified clay minerals. It is brownish-yellow in PPL and dark purplish-brown in CPL. The matrix fabric is mixed, comprising weakly speckled and poro/granostriated b-fabric.

BASIC MINERAL COMPONENT AND ROCK FRAGMENTS

The basic mineral component is moderately rounded monocrystalline quartz with smooth sphericity averaging $c.$ 100μm. Plagioclase feldspars are common, many show multiple twinning or sericitisation. There are rare polycrystalline quartz grains. Rock fragments are predominantly well-rounded cherts but igneous, metamorphic and sedimentary lithologies are represented. Rock fragments range in size from approximately 9mm to 100μm. Rock fragments comprise 15–20 % of the sample.

BASIC ORGANIC COMPONENTS

Multicellular spores $c.$ 70μm in diameter occur. There is a mycorrhizal sheath measuring 75μm in diameter and a well-decomposed cellular plant (possibly root) measuring 150μm in diameter.

PEDOFEATURES

There are dusty clay coatings of pores $c.$ 60μm in diameter and dusty clay infillings of pores. Pure and dusty clay coatings occur around many of the rock fragments. There are rare crescentic clay coatings. Much of the matrix has been enriched with clay and dusty clay and may be interpreted as weakly developed intercalations. There are also pure reddish clay infillings of voids and microlaminated clay coatings and a pure pore clay coating (60μm) coated by dusty clay, 10μm in diameter.

There are dark reddish-brown microaggregates 60–600μm in diameter (these may represent localised organic matter/iron-staining or faecal pellets). The microaggregates have sharp edges with smooth and rough sphericity. There is rare organic-rich mite excrement. Black, generally well-rounded isotropic nodules (probably some form of iron mineral) occur from $c.$ 10μm to 100μm. Silt-rich partially fused silty microaggregates $c.$ 100μm in diameter in rare chambers are indicative of biological activity. There is a posssible micritic root replacement measuring 740μm in diameter.

Sample 5, context F30

INTRODUCTION

The boundary between F30 and F28 is sharp and represented by an organic-rich dark reddish-brown layer, $c.$ 4mm in width and associated with vugs and round voids. This layer has many dark reddish-brown (possibly) faecal pellets, intercalcations and clay coatings.

MICROSTRUCTURE

The sediment is poorly sorted. The complex structure comprises both massive and weakly developed channel structure. The porosity measures $c.$ 2–5%.

MATRIX

The sediment has an open porphyric-related distribution; it is matrix-supported. The matrix is dominated by silt-sized quartz grains and unidentified clay minerals. It is pale yellow in PPL and dark grey in CPL. The matrix fabric is mixed, comprising weakly speckled and rare and weakly developed poro/granostriated b-fabric.

BASIC MINERAL COMPONENT AND ROCK FRAGMENTS

The basic mineral component is moderately rounded monocrystalline quartz with smooth sphericity; there are two broad grain sizes, c. 400μm and 80–100μm. Plagioclase feldspars are frequent and many show multiple twinning or sericitisation. There are rare polycrystalline quartz grains. Rock fragments are predominantly well-rounded cherts (some partially micritic), but igneous, metamorphic and sedimentary lithologies are represented. Rock fragments range in size from approximately 5mm to 100μm; many fall between 1mm and 1.5mm. Rock fragments comprise 10–15% of the sample.

BASIC ORGANIC COMPONENTS

Cellular charcoal occurs as well-rounded fragments c. 260μm to 1600mm, and some show heavy 'iron-staining'. Flecks of disseminated charcoal are scattered throughout the matrix, although not densely.

There are rare multicellular spores c. 70μm in diameter. There are in the order of ten *in situ* rootlets associated with amorphous organic matter and humic acid/iron-staining of the matrix. Highly degraded organic matter is associated with the staining and masking of the matrix.

There are rare mite excrement pellets. There is a single well-rounded bone fragment measuring c. 100μm in diameter.

PEDOFEATURES

There are rare pure clay papules. The replacement of an *in situ* root by pure clay 500μm in diameter is evident. There are well-rounded, dark reddish-brown organo-mineral faecal pellets and organic-rich mottling.

BOUNDARY

The boundary between F69D and F30 is marked by a well-defined organic-rich layer some 34mm thick. This layer is characterised by *in situ* roots and faecal material. There are frequent silt coatings to polyconcave voids.

Sample 5, context F69D

MICROSTRUCTURE

The sediment is poorly sorted with a complex structure comprising channels and vesicles. Many of the vesicles are polyconcave. The porosity is locally variable but measures up to 10–15%.

MATRIX

The sediment has an open porphyric-related distribution; it is matrix-supported. The matrix is dominated by silt-sized quartz grains and unidentified clay minerals. It is reddish-yellow in PPL and dark grey in CPL. The matrix fabric is predominantly weakly speckled with rare and weakly developed porostriated b-fabric.

BASIC MINERAL COMPONENT AND ROCK FRAGMENTS

The basic mineral component is dominated by subrounded to rounded monocrystalline quartz with smooth sphericity; there are two broad grain sizes, c. 240μm and 80–100μm, the latter most frequent. Plagioclase feldspars are frequent, many showing multiple twinning or sericitisation. There are very rare polycrystalline quartz grains. Rock fragments are predominantly well-rounded cherts (some partially micritic), but igneous, metamorphic and sedimentary lithologies are represented. Rock fragments range in size from approximately 10mm to 100μm. Rock fragments comprise 10–15% of the sample.

BASIC ORGANIC COMPONENTS

Dark reddish organic matter and associated humic acid-staining occur in a diffuse 34mm layer. Dense charcoal fragments and cellular charcoal fragments also occur and measure from 1mm to 400μm. *In situ* roots are well decomposed and associated with mite excrement. Some of the roots are highly degraded and form organic linings to voids. Amorphous organic matter is scattered throughout the matrix in the form of degrading fragments and associated humic iron-staining ranging in size from 80μm to 360μm (indicative of episodic wetting and drying).

PEDOFEATURES

There are dark reddish-brown organo-mineral clasts (faecal pellets); most have sharp, well-defined edges, although many are of an irregular spherical or oval form. Thin, c. 20μm dusty clay coatings occur on many of the polyconcave voids.

Sample 6, context F30

MICROSTRUCTURE

The sediment is poorly sorted. The complex structure comprises both massive and weakly developed channel structure. The porosity measures c. 5–10%.

MATRIX

The sediment has an open porphyric-related distribution; it is matrix-supported. The matrix is dominated by silt-sized quartz grains and unidentified clay minerals. It is yellowish-brown in PPL and dark brownish-grey in CPL. The matrix fabric is mixed, comprising weakly speckled and rare and weakly developed poro/granostriated b-fabric.

BASIC MINERAL COMPONENT AND ROCK FRAGMENTS

The basic mineral component comprises moderately rounded to subangular monocrystalline quartz with smooth sphericity; there are two broad grain sizes, *c.* 180–200µm and 80–100µm. Plagioclase and some potassium-rich feldspars are frequent, many showing multiple twinning or sericitisation. Rare chlorite. Chalcedony spherules occur within the matrix. Rock fragments are predominantly well-rounded cherts, and igneous, metamorphic and sedimentary lithologies are represented. Rock fragments range in size from approximately 10mm to 100µm; many are about 1mm in diameter. Rock fragments comprise at least 10–15% of the sample. Black isotropic minerals also occur and are some form of magnetite.

BASIC ORGANIC COMPONENTS

There is rare cellular rounded charcoal, 1300µm to 200µm. Fine disseminated charcoal is scattered throughout the matrix. There are rare multicellular spores, measuring 50µm, and rare single-cell spores. *In situ* degraded roots associated with mite excrement are frequent. There are rare well-rounded burnt bone fragments, measuring 1600µm and 200µm. There are rare phytolith fragments.

PEDOFEATURES

There are thin dusty clay coatings to some voids, especially those polyconcave voids; these coatings are *c.* 60µm thick. Partially infilled faunal channels occur with rounded, organo-mineral faecal pellets/microaggregates *c.* 200–600µm in diameter; there is some fusing between the microaggregates. There are other dark reddish-brown microaggregates; these are well-rounded faecal pellets measuring 240µm to 60µm. These occur scattered throughout the matrix, but are particularly common in areas rich in amorphous well-decomposed organic matter. There is one ill-defined veriform extending from the unit below.

BOUNDARY

A thin organic-rich layer occurs at the top of this unit and forms the boundary between contexts F202 and F30. The upper portion of this layer is *c.* 3mm wide and comprises numerous organo-mineral faecal pellets (dark reddish-brown within an organic-enriched matrix) with concentrations of mineral grains. Below this the matrix contains slightly less amorphous organic matter (yellowish-brown) but contains larger and denser dark reddish-brown microaggregates (probable faecal pellets).

Sample 6, contexts F69D/F69B

MICROSTRUCTURE

The sediment is poorly sorted with a complex structure comprising weakly developed channels and massive structure. Many of the vesicles are polyconcave. The porosity is locally variable but measures up to 10–15%.

MATRIX

The sediment has an open porphyric-related distribution; it is matrix-supported. The matrix is dominated by silt-sized quartz grains and unidentified clay minerals. It is reddish-brown to pale yellow in PPL and dark reddish-brown to dark brownish-grey in CPL. The matrix fabric is predominantly weakly speckled with weakly developed porostriated b-fabric. The weakly speckled b-fabric becomes more pronounced with depth. There is a poorly defined coarsening upwards of mineral grains.

BASIC MINERAL COMPONENT AND ROCK FRAGMENTS

The basic mineral component is dominated by subangular to rounded monocrystalline quartz with smooth sphericity; there are two broad grain sizes, the larger averaging 400µm and the smaller 80–100µm, the latter most frequent; there are also rare larger mineral grains ranging between 1mm and 1.5mm. Plagioclase feldspars are frequent, many showing multiple twinning or sericitisation. There are very rare, well-rounded polycrystalline quartz grains *c.* 1400µm. Chalcedony spherules are frequent. Rock fragments are predominantly moderately to well rounded and dominated by cherts with some metamorphic, igneous and sedimentary lithologies. Rock fragments range in size from approximately 15mm to *c.* 100µm. Rock fragments are very abundant and comprise *c.* 30% of the sample.

BASIC ORGANIC COMPONENTS

There is one cellular charcoal fragment, 1mm wide. Dark reddish organic matter and associated humic acid-staining occurs in the diffuse upper layer. Black isotropic fragments (some of which appear to be charcoal) are also common in the uppermost layer. There are rare phytolith fragments and rare single-cellular organic fragments *c.* 100µm in diameter. There are rare bone fragments.

PEDOFEATURES

The boundary between contexts F69D and F30 is defined by a layer rich in organic matter and dark reddish-brown organo-mineral microaggregates (faecal pellets). Most of the pellets have sharp well-defined edges, although many are of an irregular spherical or oval form; these measure 500–20μm. These dark reddish-brown microaggregates are frequent throughout the depth of this unit.

Very dark reddish-brown mottling occurs near the base of the slide and seems associated with well-decomposed organic matter. Faunal channels partially infilled by fused microaggregates and mineral grain concentrations are frequent. There is much humic acid/iron-staining associated with organic matter and weathering rock fragments.

Within the matrix there are zones of silt and dusty clay concentrations within which coarser mineral grains do not occur or are very rare. These zones vary in colour from dark brown to pale yellow. There are thin, $c.$ 20μm, dusty clay coatings to many of the polyconcave voids. Clay coatings also occur within voids of some of the chert rock fragments. A single clay coating to a fissure extends from a void; the coating measures $c.$ 100μm. There are rare clay papules, $c.$ 120μm in diameter.

There are rare matrix, well-rounded fabric pedofeatures $c.$ 300μm in diameter.

There are zones of mineral-grain concentration associated with broken lines of voids and pure clay intercalation/accumulation; this zone occurs near the large mineral-grained rock fragments and demonstrates the *in situ* mechanical and chemical ripening of the sediment/soil.

An area measuring at least 8mm wide is characterised by a dark brown fine silty sand matrix; this area has sharp edges with the surrounding yellowish-brown matrix. The dark brown feature has, in general, a random mineral grain orientation, but the mineral grains appear to be roughly aligned about a curve at the base of the feature. The feature is cut by a vertical, large, infilled (silty clay with some fine sand-sized mineral grains) channel (4mm long) and a further smaller vertical one. The fill of these infilled channels fines downwards. Other similar differential matrix zones occur and are associated with clusters of polyconcave voids, silty clay coatings to voids (biological activity), and short stretches of weakly oriented mineral grains, faecal pellets etc.

Sample 7, context F16

MICROSTRUCTURE

The sediment is poorly sorted with a complex structure comprising a chambered and massive structure. The porosity is locally variable but measures $c.$ 2–5%.

MATRIX

The sediment has an open porphyric-related distribution; it is matrix-supported. The matrix is dominated by unidentified clay minerals and some silt-sized grains. It is yellowish-brown to reddish-brown in PPL and dark reddish-brown to dark brownish-grey in CPL. The matrix fabric is predominantly weakly speckled b-fabric.

BASIC MINERAL COMPONENT AND ROCK FRAGMENTS

The basic mineral component is dominated by subangular to rounded monocrystalline quartz with smooth sphericity and both undulose and straight extinction. Sodium- and potassium-rich feldspars are frequent, many showing multiple twinning and/or sericitisation. Rock fragments are predominantly moderate to well rounded and dominated by cherts with some metamorphic, igneous and sedimentary lithologies. Many of the rock fragments are chemically weathered with iron-staining. The rock fragments range in size from approximately 8mm to $c.$ 100μm. One large rock fragment separates contexts F16 from F69D. Rock fragments are very abundant and comprise $c.$ 10–15% of the sample.

BASIC ORGANIC COMPONENT

A small sclerotium measures 80μm in diameter. A small, irregular black and isotropic fragment within the matrix may represent organic matter. There are possible pollen grains within empty voids; these measure $c.$ 12μm in diameter. The colour of the matrix appears to be largely due to amorphous organic matter coupled with 'iron'-staining.

PEDOFEATURES

A chalcedony void lining measuring 60μm thick is coated with a thin layer of dusty clay, 10μm thick. Clay coatings comprise:
(1) Dusty clay pore coatings, which are brown and reddish-orange in CPL and up to 240μm thick, and often irregular in thickness within voids. Some of these coatings are microlaminated and show compound concentric pattern.
(2) Reddish-brown clay coatings of voids, which are dark reddish-orange in CPL.

(3) Yellowish-orange clay coatings of voids, which are reddish-yellow in CPL. This clay also infills some voids but is particularly common within chert rock fragments. Some of the coatings are in the form of crescentic coatings of voids.

(4) Brown dusty clay accumulations or concentrations occur within the matrix and are indicative of pore water movement and the fine nature of the till matrix.

Some yellowish-orange clay coatings appear to have been incorporated into the matrix through the overlaying of dusty clay coatings. There are increased dusty clay and clay coatings with depth in this unit.

There are small zones of 'iron' depletion which measure $c.$ 500µm in length. There are dark reddish mottlings of irregular form with a distinct boundary.

Sample 7, context F16A

MICROSTRUCTURE

The sediment is poorly sorted with a massive structure. The porosity is locally variable and measures $c.$ 2–5%. The pore space comprises irregular and spherical planar voids. The till is poorly sorted but contains much fine sand-sized material.

MATRIX

The sediment has an open porphyric-related distribution; it is matrix-supported. The sediment matrix comprises predominantly silt-size monocrystalline, subangular to well-rounded quartz grains, fine irregular chalcedony (derived from cherts) and unidentified clay minerals. The matrix is yellowish-brown to reddish-orange in PPL and reddish-brown to grey in CPL. The sediment has a weakly speckled b-fabric.

BASIC MINERAL COMPONENT AND ROCK FRAGMENTS

The basic mineral component is dominated by subangular to rounded monocrystalline quartz with smooth sphericity and both undulose and straight extinction. Sodium- and potassium-rich feldspars are frequent and most show sericitisation. The mineral grains generally fall into the fine sand-size category. Rock fragments are predominantly moderate to well rounded and dominated by cherts (some with calcite grains), with some metamorphic, igneous and sedimentary lithologies. Many of the rock fragments are chemically weathered and iron-stained. The rock fragments range in size from approximately 7mm to $c.$ 100µm. One large rock fragment separates contexts F16 from F16A. Rock fragments are very abundant and comprise $c.$ 15–20% of the sample.

BASIC ORGANIC COMPONENT

There are rare oval sclerotia $c.$ 75µm in diameter and rare well-degraded organic matter $c.$ 450µm.

PEDOFEATURES

There are a variety of different clay coatings:

(1) Impure clay pore coatings, which are brown and reddish-orange in CPL and up to 240µm thick. These coatings are often irregular in voids. Some of these coatings are microlaminated and show compound concentric pattern. The coatings are common and measure up to 1mm in width.

(2) Reddish-brown clay coatings of voids are dark reddish-orange in CPL.

(3) Yellowish-orange clay coatings of voids, which are reddish-yellow in CPL, occur within voids. Voids are also infilled with this material, but the coatings are particularly common within chert rock fragments. Some of these coatings are in the form of crescentic coatings of voids.

(4) Brown dusty clay accumulations or concentrations occur within the matrix and are indicative of pore water movement and the fine-grained nature of the till matrix.

Illuviation is a distinguishing feature of this unit.

Sample 8, context F11

MICROSTRUCTURE

The sediment is well sorted. The sample shows a massive structure with very weakly developed fissures. The porosity measures < 2% and is dominated by irregular spherical voids and accommodating planar voids. Polyconcave voids are present near the top of the slide.

MATRIX

The sediment has an open porphyric-related distribution; it is matrix-supported. The sediment matrix comprises unidentified clay minerals and silt-sized quartz grains. The matrix is yellowish-brown in PPL and dark greyish-brown in CPL. A weakly developed speckled b-fabric dominates with rare poro/granostriation.

BASIC MINERAL COMPONENT AND ROCK FRAGMENTS

The basic mineral component is dominated by subangular to rounded monocrystalline quartz grains with smooth sphericity and both undulose and straight extinction; these grains are predominantly silt-sized, although there are occasional larger grains. Sodium- and potassium-rich feldspars (silt-sized grains) are rare and most show sericitisation. There are rare chlorite grains and rare chalcedony spherules. Occasional opaque black nodules occur within the matrix and measure up to 300μm in diameter. Rock fragments are predominantly subrounded to well rounded and dominated by chert with some metamorphic lithologies. Many of the rock fragments are chemically weathered with iron-staining. The rock fragments range in size from approximately 5mm to *c.* 80μm.

BASIC ORGANIC CONTENT

There is one possible charcoal fragment measuring 460μm. There are amorphous organic fragments measuring up to 160μm and rare sclerotia *c.* 60–260μm in diameter. Zones of slightly redder matrix are associated with finely disseminated organic matter. Reddish-brown oval mite excrement occurs and there are possible stomatocysts, *c.* 8μm in diameter, within the matrix. There are rare, possibly *in situ* rootlets. Phytolith fragments are common.

PEDOFEATURES

Well-rounded dark reddish-brown in PPL and isotropic in CPL organo-mineral microaggregates with straight edges; these may represent biological activity. However, in this sample these would appear to be detrital and measure 300–20μm. There are dark reddish-brown, in PPL, mottles with sharp to diffuse edges, measuring up to 800μm in diameter; some show concentric staining of the matrix. Both mottle and microaggregate concentrations appear to be associated with amorphous organic matter.

There is a probable clay papule which is reddish-yellow clay 120μm in diameter. Weak dusty clay coatings occur to some voids up to 20μm in width. There are weakly defined fabric pedofeatures; these are defined by a weak alignment of clay grains and the circular form of discontinuous planar voids.

There is a possible veriform visible by Fe^{3+} and/or organic matter; this feature occurs near the top of the slide and measures *c.* 1mm in diameter, and the vertical distance is *c.* 5mm.

Sample 10, context F30

MICROSTRUCTURE

No ped or aggregate formation. Alveolar to massive texture where the pore system contains irregular voids (circular, vugs), many of which are polyconcave. Porosity is *c.* 10–15% but locally variable. At the base of this context the charcoal is much more fragmentary, the fabric is much more massive, there are far less faunal pellets, and there are zones of material clearly derived from further up within the unit. There is weak granostriation around some mineral grains.

MATRIX

The context is moderately to locally poorly sorted. The sediment has an open porphyric-related distribution. It is matrix-supported. The matrix is dominated by monocrystalline silt-sized quartz grain and various clay minerals. It is pale yellowish-brown in PPL and dark greyish-brown in CPL. It comprises weakly developed stipple-speckled b-fabric to undifferentiated b-fabric.

BASIC MINERAL COMPONENTS AND ROCK FRAGMENTS

The coarse mineral component comprises predominantly fine sand-sized, well-rounded monocrystalline quartz grains with undulose extinction, with some medium sand grains. Some of the quartz grains show secondary growth. There are rare polycrystalline quartz grains. Other coarse mineral grains include plagioclase feldspars (multiple twinning, perthitic texture), some exhibiting sericitisation. Rare biotite weathering to chlorite. Rock fragments comprise 2–5% of the context. The rock fragments are derived from sedimentary (clay/siltstone, cherts) micaceous sandstones and igneous sources (nature of the rock not identified); the largest measures 5mm in diameter.

BASIC ORGANIC COMPONENT

There are weathered cellular charcoal fragments with weak horizontal orientation measuring between 10mm and 120μm. Some other cellular organic matter appears to be partially burnt with dark reddish-brown tissue in the centre of the cells. The frequency of charcoal (both cellular and amorphous) increases towards the top of the unit to 15–20%, but at the base it is nearer to 5%.

There are rare bright reddish-brown amorphous organic fragments throughout, but these are more common in the upper portion of the unit. There is very decomposed *in situ* organic matter lining root voids. A large decomposed root fragment is orange-red in PPL, measures 1660μm in diameter and is partially infilled with matrix material. The organic content clearly decreases with depth.

There are also rare well-rounded bone fragments *c.* 160μm, and a large elongated burnt bone fragment measuring 2200μm in length. There are rare phytolith fragments. An organic-rich layer occurs at 5mm below the top of the slide.

Appendix 6

PEDOFEATURES

The base of the sampled unit (lowermost 1cm) appears lighter in colour, indicating some leaching of clay material. Well-decomposed organic matter is more clearly visible in this lower zone. There are rare and ill-defined silty clay crescentic and other irregular pore coatings. A large well-rounded dark reddish-brown microaggregate comprising organo-mineral material measures *c.* 2mm. There are dark brown microaggregates, with sharp boundaries; these are especially common in the upper portion of the unit and measure *c.* 40–300μm. Concentrations of reddish organic matter probably represent the residue of biological activity; these generally measure up to 80μm.

There are a couple of partially infilled, poorly defined faunal channels. The fill comprises matrix material, faecal pellets and larger, medium sand-sized mineral grains. These channels are vertically oriented. Near to the top of the unit a planar void (biological channel) is partially infilled with well-rounded faecal pellets measuring *c.* 140μm. Two large iron nodules, 3mm and 5mm in width, are dark reddish-brown with rare mineral material and with thin iron aureole staining the surrounding matrix.

BOUNDARY

The boundary between F30 and F29, at 18mm below the top of the slide, is visible as a 1mm-thick reddish-brown layer which, when observed under the microscope, comprises convoluted orange/red organic matter; dark reddish-brown organo-mineral microaggregates; faunal passages; textured fabric due to ingestion and reworking by biota; partially fused excrement pellets (one including a well-rounded bone fragment) which partially infill some of the larger chambers; and charcoal.

Sample 10, context F29

MICROSTRUCTURE

Weakly developed subangular blocky structure with most of the planar voids accommodating. The porosity is locally variable but ranges between *c.* 5% and 15%.

MATRIX

The sediment is poorly sorted, although there are zones (possibly the result of biological activity) that are well sorted. It has an open porphyric-related distribution. The matrix is yellowish-brown to greyish-cream in PPL (indicative of clay depletion) and grey to brown-grey in CPL. It comprises predominantly quartz grains and unidentified clay minerals.

BASIC MINERAL COMPONENTS AND ROCK FRAGMENTS

The coarse mineral component comprises predominantly silt and fine sand-sized, well-rounded monocrystalline quartz grains with undulose extinction. Some of the quartz grains show secondary growth. Other coarse mineral grains include *c.* 1% plagioclase feldspars (some perthitic), some exhibiting sericitisation (gibbsite). Rock fragments, *c.* 10% of the sample, comprise well-rounded, fine sand-sized chert fragments, weathered mudstones, micaceous sandstone, quartzite (15mm) and a possible basalt.

BASIC ORGANIC COMPONENT

There are rounded cellular charcoal fragments, *c.* 600μm, and black charcoal fragments from *c.* 5μm upwards scattered within the matrix. There are rare single-cellular structures, 75μm. Mite excrement is present within the matrix. Amorphous organic matter ranging from reddish-brown to dark reddish-brown particularly occurs in association with faecal pellets.

At the base of the unit is a layer of reddish organic matter and associated staining of matrix. This layer is broken by planar voids and dips slightly. The sediment above this layer is yellowish-brown and more organic-rich than that below and contains more microaggregates and less fine charcoal. There is a well-rounded, yellow fragment of bone, *c.* 400μm, and bone fragments occur in planar voids.

PEDOFEATURES

There are organic-rich, dark reddish-brown organo-mineral pellets within the matrix measuring 20–240μm. Larger reddish microaggregates measure 600μm. There are impure clay fabric pedofeatures which are possibly associated with a root and may be a root infill or a worm veriform. The clay is reddish-orange in PPL and in CPL shows a striated b-fabric. There is weak porostriation with dusty clay, and rare examples of thicker coatings, *c.* 100μm in width, within some of the pores.

Sample 11, context F30

MICROSTRUCTURE

The sediment has a complex structure with elements of massive, vuggy, spongy and cracked structure. Many of the vugs and planar voids are polyconcave. The planar voids of the cracks are generally accommodating. Voids account for *c.* 10% of the unit area.

MATRIX

The context is poorly sorted. The sediment has an

open porphyric-related distribution. It is matrix-supported. The matrix is dominated by monocrystalline silt-sized quartz grain and various clay minerals, with common chert clasts. It is pale yellowish-brown in PPL and dark greyish-brown in CPL. It comprises weakly developed stipple-speckled b-fabric.

BASIC MINERAL COMPONENT AND ROCK FRAGMENTS

The coarse mineral component comprises predominantly fine sand-sized, well-rounded monocrystalline quartz grains with undulose extinction. Some of the quartz grains show secondary growth. Other coarse mineral grains include plagioclase feldspars, some exhibiting sericitisation, and rare chlorite. Compound mineral grains comprise consertal textured quartz. Rock fragments comprise 5–10% of the context. The majority of rock fragments are cherts, with occasional metamorphic lithologies. The larger rock fragments include two well-rounded micaceous sandstone clasts 4cm and 13cm in diameter, a well-rounded chert, 2mm, well-rounded shale 18cm in diameter oriented along the horizontal plane, and a partially silicified chert 1400μm in diameter; many of the rock fragments are iron-stained.

BASIC ORGANIC COMPONENT

Between 2% and 5% charcoal. The charcoal is abraded, much of it is cellular, and it ranges in size from 5mm to silt-sized fragments. Black organic matter (presumably charcoal) occurs scattered throughout the matrix. There is a weak horizontal alignment to much of the charcoal and organic matter. There is an increased charcoal content with depth.

Within the matrix is scattered dark reddish-brown colloidal organic matter (which has clearly been broken up by biological activity). *In situ* organic matter (a root) has been partially ingested and broken down into small microaggregates and mite faecal pellets. There is a high proportion of organo-mineral material, much of which occurs in the form of faecal pellets.

Well-rounded fragments of bone (which look as though they have been ingested by worms) measure approximately 200μm in diameter. Another burnt bone fragment measures 1800μm. The rounded burnt bone and bone fragments tend to be found associated with charcoal fragments (middenish).

PEDOFEATURES

A fabric pedofeature comprising very fine quartz and clay minerals measures *c.* 700μm in diameter. This clast contains a series of pure clay coatings of pores.

The clay is orange-red in CPL and pale reddish-brown in PPL. The coatings measure about 60μm in diameter. There is weak porostriation in rare vugs and the coatings comprise dust clay. A fine silt infilled channel measures *c.* 2mm in length. The silt is extremely well sorted and shows no microlaminations.

An infilled veriform occurs, comprising silt with disseminated charcoal fragments, burnt bone and dark reddish-brown organo-mineral faecal pellets *c.* 80μm in diameter. The infill fabric is convoluted and the veriform measures about 1cm. A charcoal-rich channel infill (biological) occurs in the upper portion of the slide and measures *c.* 1cm; the channel is vertically oriented. Well-rounded dark reddish-brown organo-mineral faecal pellets occur, measuring 120–300μm. At the base of this context overlying the charcoal of F31 is a silty clay layer some 1600μm in width. This layer is generally well sorted with only a few larger mineral grains. It has weakly speckled b-fabric which is stopped abruptly by a vertically oriented rock fragment and the edge of slide. It has a weak convoluted appearance and has clearly experienced bioturbation. It has a sharply defined upper and lower boundary (seen through the change in size fraction). The layer is 1cm long and may represent a possibly horizontal veriform.

Sample 11, context F31

INTRODUCTION

This unit measures approximately 2cm in width from top to base.

MICROSTRUCTURE

The sediment has a complex structure comprising both cracked and microaggregate structure. The porosity ranges between 10% and 15%.

MATRIX

The context is poorly sorted. The sediment has an open porphyric-related distribution. It is matrix-supported. The coarse component of the matrix comprises monocrystalline silt-sized quartz grains (with undulose extinction), rare silt-sized feldspars and chert rock fragments. The fine fraction comprises quartz, various unidentified minerals and amorphous organic matter. The matrix is yellowish-brown in PPL and dark greyish-brown in CPL. It comprises an extremely weakly developed stippled b-fabric with zones of undifferentiated b-fabric.

BASIC MINERAL COMPONENT AND ROCK FRAGMENTS

The coarse mineral component comprises

predominantly very fine sand-sized, well-rounded to subrounded monocrystalline quartz grains with undulose extinction. Other coarse mineral grains include rare plagioclase feldspars, some exhibiting sericitisation, very rare biotite and rare pyroxenes. Rock fragments comprise *c.* 2% of the context and range in size from *c.* 60µm to 12mm. There is one large rock fragment, 12mm in diameter, that comprises extremely weathered minerals including mica weathering to chlorite and unidentifiable iron minerals. The remaining rock fragments are derived from a variety of lithologies.

BASIC ORGANIC MATTER

Large fragments of cellular charcoal with subrounded edges; the largest measures 2cm. Well-rounded bone fragments, yellow to pale brown in PPL and isotropic in CPL, 401–400µm in diameter; although rare, a bone clast may be seen with each field of view at x50 magnification. The presence of large pieces of cellular charcoal defines the unit. Occasionally some of the cells contain microfaunal pellets, and the breakdown of much of the charcoal into small crumbs may be due to faunal activity. Disseminated charcoal occurs throughout the matrix but is less common than expected.

PEDOFEATURES

Well-rounded dark reddish-brown organo-mineral pellets *c.* 1mm in width. There are zones of organo-mineral silt concentration and depletion which occur in discrete irregular pockets. Biologically produced pellets, comprising well-rounded organo-mineral material, are pale yellow in PPL. Some voids are infilled with matrix, silica-rich material which is depleted in organic matter; this material may represent ash. There are rare fine silt porostriations in some of the voids. There is some partial infilling of channels with faecal microaggregates. Some bioturbation, post-depositional, faunal passages cut the boundary of contexts F33 and F31; these channels are infilled with F31 matrix.

BOUNDARY

A sharp and undulating/wavy boundary with F33.

Sample 11, context F33

INTRODUCTION

This context measures roughly 3cm in thickness.

MICROSTRUCTURE

The sediment has a massive structure in which many of the vugs are polyconcave. Voids account for at least 15% of the sampled unit. The coarse component of the unit occurs in an ill-defined layer near to the base of the unit (2–2.5cm from the top of the unit), on top of which lies finer material.

MATRIX

The sediment is poorly sorted. It has an open porphyric-related distribution. It is matrix-supported. The coarse component of the matrix comprises monocrystalline silt-sized quartz grains (with undulose extinction), rare silt-sized feldspars and chert rock fragments. The fine fraction comprises quartz, various unidentified clay minerals and amorphous organic matter. The matrix is reddish-brown in PPL and dark brown in CPL. It comprises an extremely weakly developed stippled b-fabric with zones of undifferentiated b-fabric.

BASIC MINERAL COMPONENT AND ROCK FRAGMENTS

The coarse mineral component comprises predominantly fine sand-sized, well-rounded monocrystalline quartz grains with undulose extinction. Some of the quartz grains show secondary growth. Other coarse mineral grains include plagioclase feldspars (perthitic), some exhibiting sericitisation. Rock fragments comprise weathered cherts, schist and shales with the largest measuring 15mm. Many of the rock fragments are reddish in colour in PPL.

BASIC ORGANIC COMPONENT

The dark reddish colour of the matrix appears to be partially the result of amorphous organic matter. Other organic matter comprises rare fragments of charcoal and occasional flecks within the matrix. There are rare multicellular spheres (possible spores) *c.* 40µm in diameter.

PEDOFEATURES

There are dark reddish-brown mottles, fingering outwards to resemble coral and some with iron-staining aureoles. Microaggregates, dark reddish-brown, comprise 5–10% of the sample and range in size from 100µm to 500µm. There are pure dark red rounded nodules of organic material or iron-rich mineral measuring *c.* 100µm.

BOUNDARY

The boundary between F33 and F16 is well defined by an irregular line of rock fragments, planar voids and matrix change.

Sample 11, context F16

MICROSTRUCTURE

The unit has a cracked structure; the cracks are generally elongated along the horizontal and may be a function of sampling and sample preparation. The planar voids are accommodating and comprise *c.* 10–15% of the sample.

MATRIX

The sediment is a poorly sorted till. It has a double-spaced porphyric-related distribution. The matrix comprises quartz and various clay minerals and is yellowish-brown in PPL and greyish-brown in CPL. The sediment has a weakly speckled b-fabric.

BASIC MINERAL COMPONENT AND ROCK FRAGMENTS

The coarse mineral component comprises predominantly fine sand-sized, well-rounded monocrystalline quartz grains with undulose extinction. Some of the quartz grains show secondary growth. Other coarse mineral grains include plagioclase feldspars (perthitic), some exhibiting sericitisation (there is significantly more feldspar than in other contexts). Rock fragments comprise weathered micaceous sandstones and cherts (some only partially decalcified), with the largest measuring 7mm.

BASIC ORGANIC COMPONENT

There are common black fragments within the matrix *c.* 40μm in diameter. These are black in PPL and CPL and may represent a mixture of charcoal fragments or iron minerals.

PEDOFEATURES

Less than 2% dark reddish-brown organo-mineral faecal microaggregates.

Sample 12, context F30

INTRODUCTION

This context from the top of the slide extends for *c.* 25mm without much indication of being mixed, i.e. there is not much charcoal. From *c.* 25mm to *c.* 65mm the context is mixed and much more rich in rock fragments and charcoal than F30 proper.

MICROSTRUCTURE

The sediment has a complex structure comprising weakly developed subangular blocky and chamber structure in which the dominant voids are chambers, but with some polyconcave vugs; voids comprise *c.* 10–15%. About 20–30% of the unit is arranged in very fine, weakly developed subangular blocky peds with smooth surfaces. The subangular blocky peds are partially accommodated with undulating surfaces.

MATRIX

The context is poorly sorted. The sediment has an open porphyric-related distribution. It is matrix-supported. The matrix is dominated by monocrystalline silt-sized quartz grains, various chert rock fragments and various clay minerals. It is dark yellowish-cream to yellowish-brown in PPL and dark greyish-brown in CPL. It comprises weakly developed stipple-speckled b-fabric.

BASIC MINERAL COMPONENT

The coarse component comprises predominantly fine sand-sized, moderate to well-rounded monocrystalline quartz grains with undulose extinction and some with straight extinction. Compound mineral grains comprise polycrystalline quartz. There are rare plagioclase feldspars. Rock fragments are generally angular to subangular with smooth sphericity. The rock fragments range in size from 18mm–2mm and from 2000μm to 100μm. The larger rock fragments are derived from sedimentary (silt stone, calcareous chert and limestone), metamorphic (micaceous schists) and igneous lithologies. The majority of the rock fragments show evidence of chemical weathering. Well-rounded sparitic limestone *c.* 100–300μm and well-rounded micrite limestone *c.* 100–300μm occur scattered throughout the matrix; these comprise *c.* < 2%.

Spherules composed of chalcedony measure *c.* 112–300μm and are scattered within the matrix.

BASIC ORGANIC COMPONENT

Rare cellular charcoal occurs scattered throughout the matrix and measures *c.* 800μm, but is concentrated in the large, partially infilled channel (defined below). One piece of charcoal appears to contain the remnants of ash. The charcoal generally has rounded edges. There is a degrading charcoal fragment from which humic acids have diffused into the matrix, creating an organic aureole. Mite excrement also occurs within some of the fragments. Other rare cellular organic fragments occur, *c.* 700μm.

There are single-cellular structures *c.* 90–120μm in diameter; these are rare and show a hollow centre. There is much fine black, opaque organic material scattered throughout the matrix, although it is concentrated in areas of high biological activity.

Mite excrement comprises dark reddish-brown

organic matter in ovals *c.* 50μm in diameter.

There are possible spores comprising multicellular rounded inclusions of *c.* 60μm.

There is one bone fragment; it is elongated, well rounded, with smooth sphericity and occurs in the infilled channel, and is *c.* 700μm in length. There are very rare fragmentary phytoliths.

Pedofeatures

There is one dark reddish-brown nodule comprising organo-mineral material and measuring 600μm in diameter. A dark reddish-brown microaggregate with sharp edges and *c.* 480μm is also present. There is weak porostriation in the minority of vugs and planar voids; the striation is caused by pale yellow (PPL) impure clay.

There are bright reddish-brown microaggregates, which are well rounded with smooth sphericity and measure from 225μm to 460μm. There is one fabric pedofeature comprising matrix material *c.* 440μm in diameter. Another fabric pedofeature comprises matrix material but is richer in amorphous organic material; this pedofeature has been affected by further biological activity as shown by the presence of voids *c.* 2mm in diameter. The fabric of the poorly defined infilled channel is mixed, indicative of a number of phases of biological activity. There is mixing of contexts F30 and F31. Many of the rock fragments in the centre of the slide are associated with small fragments of charcoal and it would appear that this is a large, partially infilled veriform. The evidence suggests the upward movement of material within this channel and the mixing of deposits.

Boundary

There is not a distinct boundary between F30 and F31. The boundary is diffuse over at least 20mm.

However, there is a sharp boundary between the charcoal layer and the silt above (possibly F30) on one side of the slide but on the other side of the slide there is no sharp boundary, showing that post-depositional biological activity was localised. Where distinct the boundary is extremely wavy.

Sample 12, context F31

Introduction

This context is described from *c.* 5cm down from the top of the slide.

Microstructure

The sediment has a vuggy structure with discrete and irregular vugs. Many of the vugs are polyconcave. In areas of high charcoal concentration the structure may be described as crumb. The porosity measures *c.* 15%.

Matrix

The context is poorly sorted. The sediment has an open porphyric-related distribution. It is matrix-supported. The coarse component of the matrix comprises monocrystalline silt-sized quartz grains (with undulose extinction), rare silt-sized feldspars and chert rock fragments. The fine fraction comprises quartz, various unidentified minerals and amorphous organic matter. The matrix is yellowish-brown in PPL and dark greyish-brown in CPL. It comprises an extremely weakly developed stippled b-fabric with zones of undifferentiated b-fabric.

Basic mineral component and rock fragments

The basic mineral component comprises fine, sand-sized, monocrystalline quartz grains with undulose extinction and rare plagioclase feldspar grains, some of which are sericitised. Rock fragments vary in size from 6mm to 60μm and are derived from a variety of sedimentary and metamorphic lithologies. The rock fragments comprise *c.* 2%. Many of the metamorphic rock fragments show significant iron-staining and other indicators of physical and chemical weathering.

Basic organic component

The context is noteworthy for its high charcoal content which occurs predominantly in an 8mm-wide horizontal band. Cellular charcoal fragments are very common but are clearly disseminated (broken up). All the charcoal fragments show rounded edges (abrasion and bioturbation). Fine disseminated charcoal is scattered throughout this unit, but with definite zones of higher concentration. Other organic matter includes dark reddish-brown well-decomposed colloid matter. There are sclerotia fragments.

A large organic fragment, 18mm in length, is dark red, becoming reddish-yellow at the edges; it is much degraded around the edges and has been degraded by biological activity. The excrement occurs within these outer edges and this fragment appears to be partially comprised of root.

There are rare phytolith fragments. There is a well-rounded burnt bone fragment and other rare well-rounded bone fragments measure *c.* 300μm.

Pedofeatures

Silty clay appears to infill some ancient fissures between some of the charcoal fragments. Dark brown silt with very fine charcoal also forms very thin linings (730μm) to some of the vugs.

The matrix comprises a series of ill-defined fabric pedofeatures which have been produced by biological activity; this has resulted in the production of partially fused microaggregates which have in turn been affected by pore water movement. There are irregular patches of matrix with a low percentage of fine charcoal within this context but which contain a high proportion of amorphous organic material which is well decomposed and red in colour.

Many of the larger vugs and planar voids are partially infilled by faecal microaggregates. Fe^{3+}-rich well-rounded faecal material comprises organo-mineral material. The faecal pellets have abrupt to sharp boundaries and range in size from 50μm to 300μm. The biological channel that cuts F33 has well-defined edges infilled with fabric pedofeatures which are the result of biological activity.

BOUNDARY

The lower boundary between contexts F31 and F33 is sharp but again very wavy and can be seen because of a sudden increase in charcoal in F31 and an increase in the quantity of faecal pellets. The boundary is cut by a large, partially infilled channel which has brought F31 material into F33.

Sample 12, context F33

MICROSTRUCTURE

The sediment has a massive structure with discrete vugs. The vugs are generally polyconcave and account for c. 10% of the sample, although the distribution is locally variable.

MATRIX

The sediment is moderately well sorted. It has an open porphyric-related distribution. It is matrix-supported. The matrix is dominated by monocrystalline silt-sized quartz grains, with some silt-sized chert rock fragments and clay minerals. It is yellowish-brown in PPL and dark greyish-brown in CPL. It comprises extremely weakly developed stipple-speckled to undifferentiated b-fabric.

BASIC MINERAL COMPONENT AND ROCK FRAGMENTS

The coarse mineral component comprises predominantly fine, sand-sized, subangular to moderately well-rounded monocrystalline quartz grains with undulose extinction. Other coarse mineral grains include plagioclase feldspars (<2%), some exhibiting sericitisation, and rare chalcedony spherules. Rock fragments comprise <2% of the context and range in size from c. 60μm to 4mm, with the majority measuring about 200μm (on the upper edge of the fine sand class). The rock fragments are generally well rounded, and include chert and metamorphic lithologies (micaceous sandstone and shale or slate); many of the rock fragments are iron-stained and have been chemically weathered.

ORGANIC COMPONENT

Cellular charcoal fragments are rare (<1%); the largest measures 4mm. A well-rounded charcoal fragment measures c. 400μm. Charcoal fragments are common in the fills of large biological channels, and especially in a poorly defined veriform which cuts the whole width of the context. There is very rare opaque organic material scattered throughout the matrix.

There are zones of reddish-yellow moderately decomposed organic matter which blend into the matrix. Dark reddish amorphous organic matter occurs thinly scattered throughout the matrix. A small sclerotium measures 612μm in diameter.

PEDOFEATURES

There are possible fabric pedofeatures measuring 400–600μm in diameter and comprising matrix material in ill-defined rounded aggregates. Fe^{3+} mottles are associated with organic matter. The mottles are dark reddish to light reddish-brown and of irregular form. These mottles have sharp to diffuse boundaries. They range from 80μm to 700μm in diameter and tend to obscure any mineral material.

There are rounded faecal pellets; these are dark reddish-brown and comprise organo-mineral material. They range in size from c. 260μm to 360μm and comprise 1% of the unit.

One partially infilled veriform extends from the base of F31 into this unit. The fill is derived from context F31 and is charcoal-rich. Another partially infilled channel comprises faecal pellets, matrix microaggregates (another form of pellet) and charcoal.

There are patches of increased clay content; these appear to be associated with the dark reddish-brown faecal pellets and may be a product of biological activity. There are areas of concentration of polyconcave vugs with porostriation; these are thin silt coatings indicative of the movement of water through the profile. There are also thin linear (mostly near-vertical) concentrations of fine sand-sized mineral grains and rock fragments.

Appendix 6

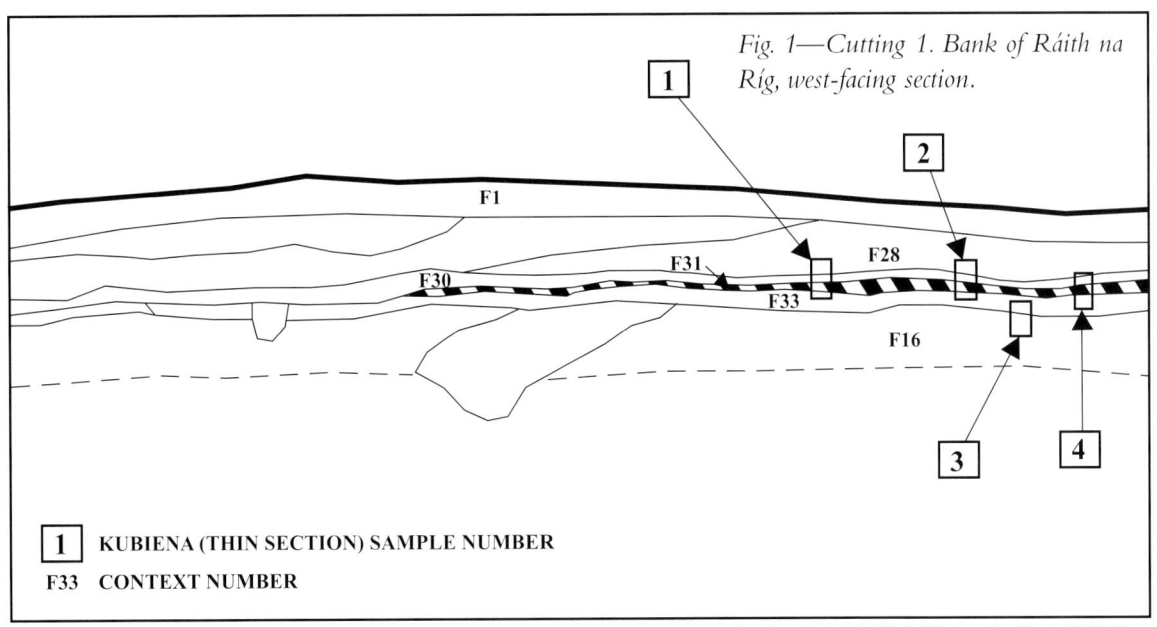

Fig. 1—Cutting 1. Bank of Ráith na Ríg, west-facing section.

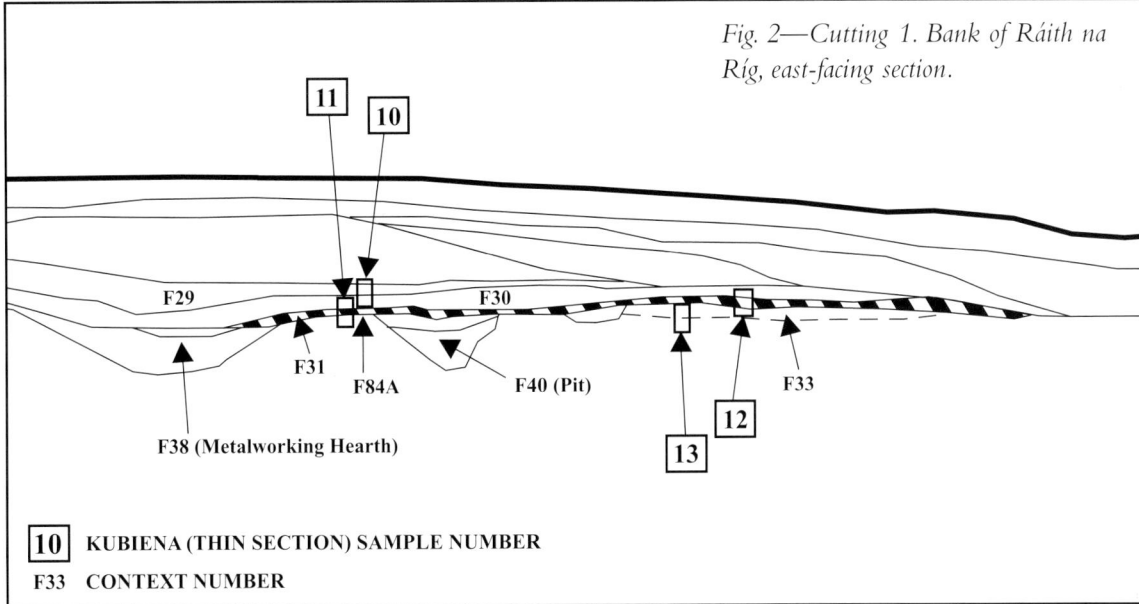

Fig. 2—Cutting 1. Bank of Ráith na Ríg, east-facing section.

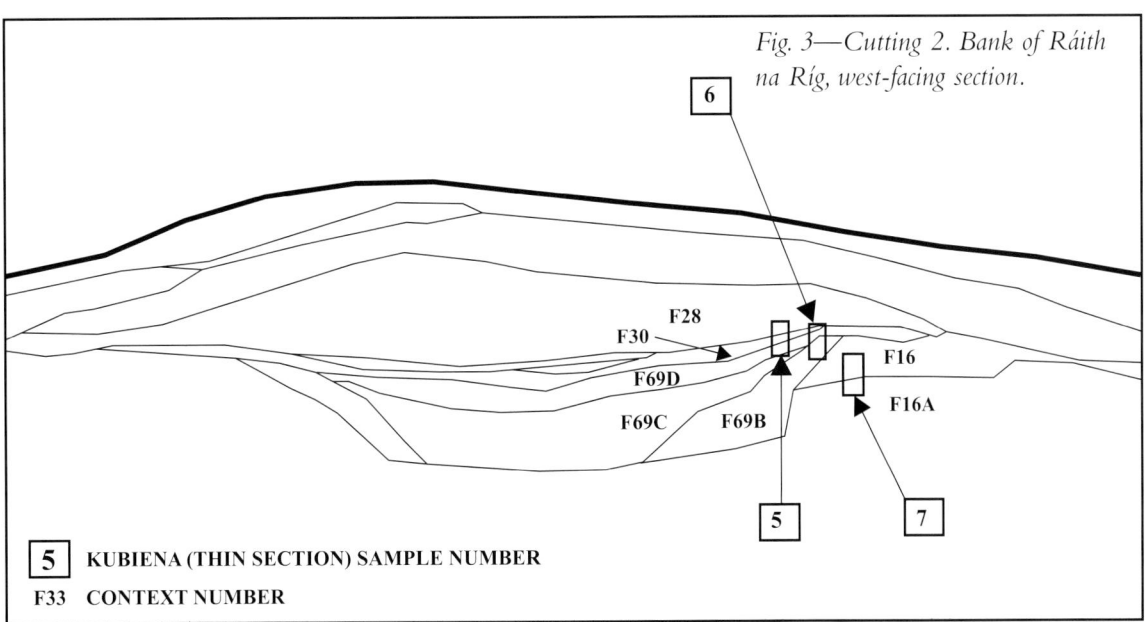

Fig. 3—Cutting 2. Bank of Ráith na Ríg, west-facing section.

Sample 13, context F33

Microstructure

The microstructure of the unit is complex. The upper portion (3.5mm) has an extremely weakly developed subangular blocky structure and a porosity of 2–5%. The central 3cm has an alveolar structure comprising planar voids (faunal chambers) and rare vugs and a porosity of 25%. The lower 3cm comprises a granular structure (although it is possible that this structure was produced during sampling) and a porosity ranging between 10% and 50%.

Matrix

The sediment is moderately sorted. It has an open porphyric-related distribution. It is matrix-supported. The coarse component of the matrix comprises well-rounded to subangular monocrystalline silt-sized quartz grains (with undulose extinction), rare silt-sized feldspars and chert rock fragments. The fine fraction comprises quartz, various unidentified clay minerals and amorphous organic matter. It is yellow-brown in PPL and dark brown-grey in CPL. The matrix comprises undifferentiated b-fabric with zones of an extremely weakly developed stippled b-fabric.

Basic mineral components and rock fragments

The coarse mineral component comprises predominantly fine sand-sized, well-rounded monocrystalline quartz grains with undulose extinction. Some of the quartz grains show secondary growth. Other coarse mineral grains include plagioclase feldspars (perthitic), some exhibiting sericitisation, and compound quartz mineral grains. Rock fragments comprise well-rounded weathered cherts, schist and shales.

Basic organic components

There is <1% cellular charcoal; these fragments are abraded. *In situ* decomposed root material measuring 3mm is associated with organo-mineral humic acid-staining. Decomposed and biodegraded rootlets are associated with dark reddish-brown microaggregates which occur in an ill-defined horizontal band across the slide. There is a cluster of four sclerotia measuring $c.$ 75µm in diameter. Fragmentary phytoliths are common in the upper portion of the slide but occur throughout; the visibility of phytoliths is partially governed by the quantity of organic matter.

Pedofeatures

Well-rounded, dark reddish-brown faecal pellets comprising organo-mineral material are scattered throughout the matrix; they measure 20–280µm, and comprise $c.$ 2% of the unit. There are weak porostriations of dusty clay; these occur in the minority of pores in the upper portions of the slide but are frequent towards the base. An area towards the base has a speckled b-fabric caused by the accumulation of dusty clay within pores and around mineral grains; the majority of the pore coatings occur at the bottom of the pores in the form of crescentic coatings. There is a possible clay papule measuring 50µm in diameter, and another clayey silt papule measuring 300µm.

There are two loosely infilled channels. The infill comprises faecal pellets $c.$ 20–30µm in diameter and clean mineral grains. A large partially infilled channel is defined by an elongated vertically oriented stream of voids, a matrix fill rich in charcoal and a silt-rich matrix; the channel measures $c.$ 3cm. Other similar infilled channels are frequent in the upper portion of the slide.

Sample 13, context F16

Microstructure

The sediment is poorly sorted with a complex structure comprising a chambered and massive structure. The porosity is locally variable but measures $c.$ 2–5%.

Matrix

The sediment has an open porphyric-related distribution; it is matrix-supported. The matrix is dominated by unidentified clay minerals and some silt-sized grains. It is yellowish-brown in PPL and dark brownish-grey in CPL. The matrix fabric is predominantly weakly speckled b-fabric.

Basic mineral component and rock fragments

The basic mineral component is dominated by subangular to rounded monocrystalline quartz with smooth sphericity and both undulose and straight extinction. Sodium- and potassium-rich feldspars are frequent, many showing multiple twinning and/or sericitisation. Rock fragments are predominantly moderate to well rounded and dominated by cherts with some metamorphic, igneous and sedimentary lithologies. Many of the rock fragments are chemically weathered with iron-staining. The rock fragments range in size from approximately 8mm to $c.$ 100µm. One large rock fragment separates contexts F205 and F202. Rock fragments are very abundant and comprise $c.$ 10–15% of the sample.

Appendix 6

BASIC ORGANIC COMPONENT

A small sclerotium measures 80µm in diameter. Small, irregular black and isotropic fragments within the matrix may represent organic matter. There are possible pollen grains within empty voids; these measure *c.* 12µm in diameter. The colour of the matrix appears to be largely due to amorphous organic matter coupled with 'iron'-staining.

PEDOFEATURES

A chalcedony void lining measuring 60µm thick is coated with a thin layer of dusty clay, 10µm thick. Clay coatings comprise:
(1) Dusty clay pore coatings, which are brown and reddish-orange in CPL and up to 240µm thick, and often irregular in thickness within voids. Some of these coatings are microlaminated and show compound concentric pattern.
(2) Reddish-brown clay coatings of voids, which are dark reddish-orange in CPL.
(3) Yellowish-orange clay coatings of voids, which are reddish-yellow in CPL. This clay also infills some voids but is particularly common within chert rock fragments. Some of the coatings are in the form of crescentic coatings of voids.
(4) Brown dusty clay accumulations or concentrations occur within the matrix and are indicative of pore water movement and the fine nature of the till matrix.

Some yellowish-orange clay coatings appear to have been incorporated into the matrix through the overlaying of dusty clay coatings. There are increased dusty clay and clay coatings with depth in this unit.

There are small zones of 'iron' depletion which measure *c.* 500µm in length. There are dark reddish mottlings of irregular form with distinct boundaries.

References

Bullock, P., Fedoroff, N., Jongerius, A., Stoops, G., Tursina, T. and Babel, U. 1985 *Handbook for soil thin-section description*. Wolverhampton.

Courty, M.A., Goldberg, P. and Macphail, R. 1989 *Soil and micromorphology in archaeology*. Cambridge.

FitzPatrick, E.A. 1993 *Soil microscopy and micromorphology*. Chichester.

Hamond, F.W. 1983 Phosphate analysis of archaeological sediments. In T. Reeves-Smyth and F.W. Hamond (eds), *Landscape archaeology in Ireland*, 47–80. British Archaeological Reports, British Series 116. Oxford.

Hodgson, J.M. 1976 *Soil Survey Field Handbook*. Soil Survey Technical Monograph No. 5. Harpenden.

Murphy, C.P. 1986 *Thin section proportion of soils and sediments*. Beskhomstad.